MODERN
STEELHEAD FLIES

Rob Russell and Jay Nicholas
Fly photography by Jon Jensen

STACKPOLE
BOOKS

Guilford, Connecticut

Published by Stackpole Books
An imprint of Globe Pequot
Trade Division of The Rowman & Littlefield Publishing Group, Inc.
4501 Forbes Boulevard, Suite 200, Lanham, Maryland 20706
Distributed by
NATIONAL BOOK NETWORK
800-462-6420

British Library Cataloguing in Publication Information Available

Library of Congress Cataloging-in-Publication Data

Names: Russell, Rob, 1969– author. | Nicholas, Jay W., author.
Title: Modern steelhead flies / Rob Russell and Jay Nicholas ; fly
    photography by Jon Jensen.
Description: Guilford, Connecticut : Stackpole Books, [2017] | Includes
    index.
Identifiers: LCCN 2017028223 (print) | LCCN 2017030558 (ebook) | ISBN
    9780811765961 (e-book) | ISBN 9780811711210 (hardback : alk. paper) | ISBN
    9780811765961 (ebook)
Subjects: LCSH: Steelhead fishing. | Fly fishing.
Classification: LCC SH687.7 (ebook) | LCC SH687.7 .R87 2017 (print) | DDC
    799.17/57—dc23
LC record available at https://lccn.loc.gov/2017028223

Printed in the United States of America

CONTENTS

FOREWORD

As chance would have it, I fell in love with steelhead flies long before I had the patience or skill to actually be a steelheader. In 1974, when I was eight, my father pulled out his lacquered plywood tying box, which he used only on occasion, and showed me the fundamentals of how to tie a Brindle Bug, a basic three-step California steelhead fly. I enjoyed the process and my first primitive product, but the best part was my first glimpse at his box of example flies. It was immediately clear that these flies were sacred and not to be fished or futzed with unnecessarily. There were two flies that were unremarkable and five that were works of art, all tied in nearly monastic seclusion by Ed Hass of Forks of Salmon, California. In terms of simple elegance, Hass's flies will always have a seat with the greats. His custom down-turned-eyed hooks, his consistency of proportion, and the perfection of his small glossy heads still remain beyond me after 40 years of tying. In the box there was a Silver Hilton, a Thor, a Mossback, his minimalist Protein (Hass's self-professed most effective pattern) and a Brindle Bug: a fly that through a self-fulfilling cycle of confidence, application, and results, my father and I came to endow with otherworldly fish-catching abilities.

Since those days, steelhead flies have changed in ways that none of the then-greats could have imagined. The proliferation of synthetic materials, the big fly movement, the advent of shank flies, trailing hooks, tube flies, foam domes, and the remarkable techniques and styles that have accompanied it all have been nothing less than a renaissance that the authors and contributors have had the good fortune to participate in. Equally impressive is what has not changed, namely the dedication and devotion of the true steelhead angler/fly tier to create something uniquely appealing to and respectful of a quarry we will never fully understand. While we could plunge crassly forward with two inches of black bunny strip lashed to a hook and catch our fair share, we instead, out of reverence, create small barbless temples that we hope with all our heart will be seen as unique, worthy, and alluring. Is calling steelhead fishing a religion a stretch? Likely, but for many of the practitioners, it delivers a profound connection to something great and mysterious that few other experiences in the modern world can rival.

I first met Rob Russell in 2003 at a takeout on a well-known northern Oregon winter steelhead river. It had been a long, cold, and utterly fishless day for his boat as well as our own, yet Rob and his clients were upbeat and accepting of what the river had (or in this case, had not) given them. Our paths have crossed many times, both professionally and personally, since then and I feel lucky to consider him a friend. It took longer for me to finally meet Jay Nichols through our mutual friend Chris Daughters. With that said, his reputation as a gifted and wildly committed angler preceded him. When I first heard that they were teaming up to create a book on modern steelhead flies, my interest was piqued and my expectations were high. Now, five years later and with a finished product in hand, I can say that what they have created far exceeded what I thought was possible.

First and foremost, Jay Nicholas and Rob Russell are not academic armchair anglers or the type of tiers who rarely wet their own creations. Quite the contrary, these two are the real deal: guys that by design have created lives for themselves that enable, if not mandate, lots of time on the water and behind the vise. Frankly, I envy this about them both and greatly respect that they have taken considerable time and energy from their drive to fish to assemble and share something of lasting import with the broader community of steelhead anglers. Thanks to Jon Jensen's expertise with a camera, they have added a layer of visual beauty to a book that is instructional, insightful, and brings together poignant lessons gleaned from thousands of hours spent riverside by some of our sport's most dedicated innovators and anglers.

Just glancing through the pages of this book, it is hard not to be impressed by the tying skills of many of the contributors. But what makes this book even more unusual and valuable is the content of the first seven chapters. In them, some strong anglers expound some strong opinions and theories that will engage, if not challenge, the reader. Are some flies more effective than others because they are truly imitative in the eyes of steelhead or alternatively, particularly invasive? Or as Lee Spencer concludes in my favorite chapter, are steelhead simply curious creatures that use their mouths to explore and understand the world around them?

As it is the nature of some steelhead to move to a well-swung fly, so too it is the nature of many steelhead anglers to try to explain why they move. Ultimately though, steelhead fishing and fly tying is not a science, but rather a convergence of many immeasurable elements, including artistry, intuition, technique, and conviction, all of which seem to hold similar weight. In my own little world, steelhead will remain my favorite fish because their very nature, despite all of our advancements and advantages, will remain cloaked in mystery. Because steelhead are so special and at one time or another responsive to virtually every size, shape, and color of fly, they have freed us to become the most unfettered, creative, and artistic tiers the world has known. What we tie to entice a steelhead is a tribute to them, a unique adorned offering steeped in reverence and respect, and this book, above all others, will help us do so like never before.

—Ken Morrish, January 2017

ACKNOWLEDGMENTS

The authors wish to express their deepest gratitude to the many people who generously gave of their time and talents to make this book a reality. First and foremost, to our distinguished fly tiers who contributed their creations, stories, and photographs, asking nothing in return. This is your book, and we hope that rings loud and clear in the decades to come. Big thanks also go out to Marcos Vergara, who helped us source tools and materials and provided insights into the secret underworld of the fly materials market. To the many fly shop owners who connected us with their local, working guides and tiers, several of whom we would otherwise have missed. To our many good friends with whom we have swapped hypotheses and fish stories over campfires and cabin tables. Those were more than just good times we shared.

Our conversations and quarrels, though rarely very serious, were the gristmill that separated kernel from chaff and allowed us to offer such a well-vetted manuscript. To Jay Nichols and the wonderful people at Stackpole Books who never gave up on us, even after we blew past every deadline. And to Lee Spencer, whose devotion to steelhead knows no bounds, and who provides a beautiful example for the generations of steelheaders to come. You are an inspiration to all who know and love you. Finally, we wish to thank the steelhead themselves for putting up with our nearly constant harassment. To you we vow to continue our evolution as anglers so that we may perfect our relationship with steelhead and the rivers in which they swim.

—Rob & Jay, May 2017

INTRODUCTION

uckle up and prepare for a deep dive into the complex and ever-evolving world of the modern steelhead fly. This book serves to document and demystify one of the greatest collections of modern steelhead flies ever assembled. Over the course of five years, we sought out and solicited the most influential steelhead fly tiers on planet Earth for the sole purpose of sharing their flies with you. We cast our net far and wide in order to represent every steelheading region and every modern fly theory we could find. We cashed in all our chips, called in every favor, and occasionally begged

When Justin Miller's flies arrived in the mail, we knew this was going to be a great project.

to get these flies. Even so, there are many conspicuous absences. Some people were too busy, some preferred to stay out of the spotlight, and a couple proved to be unreachable. Sadly, in a couple of cases, we just waited too long and missed our chance. Such was the case with Harry Lemire and Bob Quigley, who both passed away in 2012. These men left indelible impressions on fly fishing, not only in their fly designs. We take some solace in the fact that many of Lemire's flies and philosophies are immortalized in books and articles by Trey Combs and Dec Hogan, and in fly-tying videos from Bennett-Watt Productions. Quigley's legacy has also been partly documented in a video series by Pegasus Productions, as well as in the pages of *Fly Fisherman* and other leading magazines.

But we still managed to end up with a "dream box" of over 400 flies—mostly tied by their original designers—along with stories, photos, recipes, and more than a few detailed specifications. Featured here are many of today's most inspired and successful steelhead patterns, created by men and women whose lives revolve around fly tying and the pursuit of the steelhead trout. They could easily have held back and kept their secrets to themselves. Instead, they gave generously, providing the basis for this long-overdue project. They also took a big chance on us, your writers, to get the facts straight and deliver a genuine article. We took that responsibility seriously, and we have made every effort to fulfill that promise.

The flies and stories that made it into this collection reach back to the early 1990s, picking up threads of the Pacific Northwest fly narrative where Trey Combs left off with the publication of *Steelhead Fly Fishing* (1991). They weave their way through a number of revelations and fads that followed, filling in corners between the later literary works of Dec Hogan (*A Passion for Steelhead*, 2006), John Shewey (*Spey Flies & Dee Flies*, 2002, and *Steelhead Flies*, 2006), Jon Larison (*The Complete Steelheader*, Stackpole, 2008), and Lani Waller (*A Steelheader's Way*, Stackpole, 2008). And they necessarily bring the schools of the Pacific coast and the Great Lakes together under one roof where they belong. As these stories demonstrate, innovation doesn't just flow from west to east. There are important lessons that shine through from every fishery and every school of thought. With that in mind, we tried to be objective and

Steelheading is about a lot more than just the fish, but specimens like this are the magic ingredient. A transparent Olympic Peninsula buck still glowing from the ocean. BEN PAULL, OLYMPIC PENINSULA SKAGIT TACTICS (OPST), PHOTO

open-minded as we collected these flies and recipes. We knew that we might not recognize greatness at first blush. There could be new concepts that would trouble us, even if they were sent from the future to save us. We fought our biases and sought to present an unfiltered history, straight from the tiers themselves. Until, that is, we had to pick the 14 flies featured in the step-by-step portion of the book. At that point we made a huge leap in the direction of our personal preferences. Some of those patterns were chosen for the tying techniques they demonstrate, and some for the specific niche they fill in an angler's fly box. But most were chosen because they spoke to us. They jumped out of the box, just like the right fly beams back at us when we're scanning the bench at game time. We trust that every steelheader has shared that feeling, even if we might never understand the "why" of it. (By the way, we're going to use the term *steelheader* to indicate one of our kind. That's not to trivialize or in any way denigrate our brothers of bait casting; it's just to prevent the noun nightmare that is *steelhead fly fisherman*.) It's not very scientific, we know. But you can trust that the flies presented here are all proven to fish well and catch steelhead.

What emerges from this effort is a spectacular snapshot in time—like a high-speed photo of a passing train.

We know that any attempt at documentation is already old before it can be published. By the time this book hits the shelves, many of our tiers will have moved on to new patterns and may barely recognize the flies they sent us. But this snapshot fills a few gaps in our literature and helps to bring us up to some semblance of the state of our art. As we send this manuscript off to our patient publishers, we are confident that the flies and concepts captured here will have lasting value and relevance for decades to come. May they serve you well!

—Rob Russell & Jay Nicholas, November 2016

Photographer's Note

As a fly fisher, there's probably no greater sense of accomplishment than catching a wild trout or steelhead on a fly I tied myself, or better yet, one I designed myself. It's a dream come true. When I tie a fly I think of where and how I'm going to swing it, and at what depth. I imagine it moving through the current, silhouetted against the light and shadow of the underwater world. I can almost feel the strike. *Fish on!*

Fly tying is a process of passion and practice, a creative mix of art and science. The blending of colors, texture, size, and weight that's all about attraction. Presenting

Jon Jensen's skill in the studio, and his devotion to the project, transformed this book from reportage to high art. *Thank you, Jon!* ROB RUSSELL PHOTO

your well-thought-out best, methodically, over and over again. It's an art, a craft, and a joy.

Photography, too, is a creative process, also bent on capture. I've had as much fun photographing these flies as I have ever had tying and fishing them. There have been a lot of images created that were later deleted from the hard drive—ones that just didn't work, like bad ties that end up in the reject box. We worked to use light that best exhibits the material qualities of the patterns. We chose a classical, formal approach to the color plates that respected each artist and the historical traditions upon which their work is built. I hope you find the photographs beautifully attractive and motivational. I can't thank Rob and Jay enough for affording me the opportunity to work on this book. It's been a joy.

—Jon Jensen, November 2016

THE 21st-CENTURY
STEELHEADER

By Rob Russell

Equipment advances have facilitated the rapid expansion of fly fishing by dramatically improving our effectiveness, especially for winter steelhead.
—Pete Soverel, from Dec Hogan's A Passion for Steelhead *(2006)*

Every generation marvels at the technological advances of its time. So this amazement that many of us feel when we consider the state of our sport is nothing new. Nor is the accompanying fear, the feeling of loss, as quieter times pass away like a clacking train, fading into memory. Today, as I string up my two-handers and casually consult my satellite-enabled smartphone, I am highly conscious of the fact that we are living in an entirely new era for fly fishing. Skagit- and Scandinavian-style tackle are now the norm. They make

Jason Haase surveying his options before heading out for a day of spring steelheading near Terrace, British Columbia. KEN MORRISH, FLY WATER TRAVEL, PHOTO

We've got it easy these days. The fish? Not so much. MARTY SHEPPARD, LITTLE CREEK OUTFITTERS, PHOTO

casting a breeze. I can put my fly just about anywhere I want it with minimal effort. Real-time river levels, tide charts, and weather satellite images are normal parts of the morning routine. Facebook pages and online chat rooms give away information—and misinformation—by the truckload, all in the name of selling trips and tackle. A couple of text messages chime in, and I have yesterday's body count and geo coordinates. A quick chat with my shuttle driver and I know where the boat trailers are parked. Let's face it—the fish are not safe anymore.

Over the last 20 years, the tiny world of steelhead fly fishing has engaged in a chummy sort of arms race, built on a handful of major innovations and driven by the pressures of economics, commerce, and social media. The once-provincial cities of the Pacific Northwest are burgeoning, overflowing with wide-eyed new steelheaders, each wielding terminal gear that is more deadly than ever. The development and marketing of inexpensive fly rods, Skagit-style lines, tungsten-infused sink-tips, welded loops, and fluorocarbon leaders has gone a very long way toward leveling the playing field between fly and conventional tackle. We are "in the zone" a whole

lot more than our predecessors. And every few years a new class of steelhead guides sets up shop, capitalizing on the newfound accessibility of big-water steelheading.

A budding young steelheader shuffling his way into the sport in the 1970s (Jay) or 1980s (me) faced a very different scene. He was both a beneficiary and a victim of incredible timing. On one hand, he had considerably more steelheading opportunities, as there were generally more fish and fewer river closures. And he would eventually benefit from the many innovations to come. But he would also suffer some minor indignities along his path, flogging away a few of his early years—and much of his shoulder and elbow strength—with single-handed rods, doing his best to keep his fly out of the tall grass and trees behind him. Then, if he was an early adopter of two-handed technology, he could look forward to completely reinvesting in tackle two or three times over, to the tune of thousands of dollars. Of course, neither of those qualify as real suffering, just as a bad day of steelheading will always be a hell of a lot better than a good day of just about everything else. But whatever we call it, our old-school steelheader would see his world shift on its axis over the decades to come. The resulting quakes and aftershocks would keep things shaking through the present day.

Trey Combs's masterwork, *Steelhead Fly Fishing*, would give generations of hopefuls a road map to the sport. It would also set a new standard in steelhead fly construction. Dave McNeese, prominent among a stellar cast of tiers for the book, would show the world what a steelhead fly should look like, masterfully blending his personal flair with classic styles and profiles reminiscent of the Old World. John Shewey would take that torch and run with it, eventually providing a small library of intricate, well-researched books on steelhead flies, bringing us into the 21st century.

The early 2000s would see the establishment of the late masters of our time, breaking through many old limitations and raising the entire fly-fishing world to a new level. Dec Hogan would document the lessons learned from a career at the forefront of the Skagit and Deschutes River schools of steelheading. Through magazine articles, videos, and journals, Hogan's uniquely personal style would engage and inspire like none before him. His close friends and fellow guides, Ed Ward and Jerry French, would design flies, fly lines, rods, and casting styles that would revolutionize the sport. Together they would codify a new, modern approach to casting and fishing. On top of those major landmarks would be the unhinged power of the Internet. Boundaries disappeared, and the world shrunk by a couple of sizes.

Today's technologies have woven their way so deep into steelheading culture that it is hard to imagine how things were pre-Skagit. It's easy to take it all for granted. And that's probably okay. This is a recreational pastime, after all, even though many of us have built our entire lives around it. We're allowed to have fun. But with all this power comes responsibility. There are more of us every day, and in many places there are fewer steelhead. And with so many of our old limitations now washed away, our next challenge will be to set our own limits. We owe it to the fish and to future generations of steelheaders.

The man who redefined steelhead fly tying in the late '80s, Dave McNeese is still going strong and sharing his gift with fellow steelheaders at the annual Northwest Fly Tying Expo in Springfield, Oregon. JAY NICHOLAS PHOTO

WHAT MATTERS IN A
STEELHEAD FLY?

By Rob Russell

If one particular style or color or pattern were indeed more effective
than all others, we would all be using that fly by now.
—*John Shewey,* Steelhead Flies, *2006*

Most experienced steelheaders and guides, when pressed, will say that the specific fly we chose to swing is much less important than how—and how confidently—we swing it. Our best-known steelhead writers have echoed those sentiments, boiling fly choice down to a few basic points of profile and functionality. If a fly gives us the confidence to fish with intention and focus, it's bound to be a winner, because the main goal, regardless of fly choice, is to spend as much time as possible "in the zone"—a trajectory that places our fly

There's a certain amount of bugginess that overwhelms a steelhead's better judgment. This is what the fly tier seeks.

Some flies are better than others. It's no accident that black bunny strips and pink marabou are the meat and potatoes of steelhead fly tying. KEN MORRISH, FLY WATER TRAVEL, PHOTO

within striking distance of a steelhead. The more time we spend in there, the more positive feedback we get from fish and the more we learn to recognize the feeling. This progression leads to the experience of anticipating a grab before it happens, further reinforcing our set of beliefs. And since steelhead are capable of almost anything, almost any set of beliefs has the potential to produce at least the illusion of tactical success.

But if the fly doesn't matter as much as the presentation, why are there thousands of different fly patterns and styles, and only a handful of approaches to presentation? And why have so many steelheaders slaved over their vises trying to crack the code if there isn't a code to crack? One reason is the creative enjoyment that fly tying offers. Tying also provides a time to meditate on our quarry and our fishing grounds. As Lani Waller says, we are hunters, flinting away at our arrowheads, reaching out and communing with the spirit of Steelhead. Tying our own flies makes us feel connected with the fish and the whole ecosystem on a deeper level.

But there may actually be a few codes to crack—in fact, they may have already been cracked. After a thorough review of the flies and the literature, it's clear there are certain flies that have proven to be exceptional. Often those flies happen to imitate something in the steelhead's world. Something that steelhead are compelled to grab

ahold of, if only for a quick nibble. The clearest examples are skated caddis patterns, dead-drifted egg patterns and nymphs, and swung "leeches" or sculpins of various sizes and colors. And let's not forget the Desert Island fly, supremely effective for every species of salmonid: the egg-sucking leech. Its power is undeniable, though it probably better imitates an egg-sucking sculpin than a leech in most situations.

So, with apologies to Mr. Shewey, who has more sense and experience in his pinky finger than we have in our whole bodies, we think the evidence goes against his opening quote. There are particular styles, colors, and patterns that are more effective than others. Maybe the reason we're not all using them is the same reason we often refuse to believe facts that are staring us in the face: We're naturally skeptical and stubborn. And we share a varying amount of uncertainty about steelhead behavior. That uncertainty is rekindled every time a steelhead ignores a skating October caddis as it turns to chase a drifting leaf or twig. But when we take the wide view, obvious themes emerge that can direct our fly tying into some very distinct and productive channels.

In the category of "uncertainty," and to acknowledge a viable counter argument, Lee Spencer offers a fascinating analysis of his time watching steelhead at the Big Bend Pool on Steamboat Creek in chapter 7. Lee's

Movement, contrast, prominent eyes, and, of course, the color pink: This has "winter steelhead" written all over it. ROB RUSSELL PHOTO

observations have led him to the conclusion that summer steelhead, when congregated in a cool-water refuge, are more attracted to sticks and leaves than to any potential food item. To that we can only bow and concede to the data. Maybe steelhead change behavioral patterns at that time in their lives. The last 20 years we've spent chasing steelhead has taught us that they put a lot of food in their mouths, whether or not they ever intend to swallow it. So we urge readers to search these chapters for clues and trust your intuition. Through the billowing cloud of anecdotal and sometimes contradictory observations, a few tenets will emerge to direct our fly design and selection:

1. Movement or undulation of a fly's materials is a good thing.
2. Contrast, detail, and prominent eyes seem to be triggers, at least in clear water.
3. Sizing down to a smaller fly is most likely to trigger a strike from a shy or noncommittal steelhead.
4. Color is the least important element, unless it is more important on any specific day.

These rules of thumb are often countered or flatly broken by many steelheaders, and enough steelhead still respond so as to maintain confusion.

Small, dark, and caddis-like: a sure-fire summer steelhead snack.

Fly Size and Weight

By far the biggest downfall in fly selection is a tendency to use flies that are too heavy. Especially in the high, cold flows of winter and spring, our desire to fish deep can work against us. A fly should generally swing all the way through a piece of water without hanging up on the bottom. If it doesn't, we risk swinging our flies under the fish, and we lose valuable fishing time sharpening hooks and changing flies. If we're trying to cover the whole run—especially the soft, inside travel lane—heavy flies usually won't make it. Anglers who are intent on fishing deep must learn to feel their way through the swing and develop tricks for raising the fly when necessary to complete the swing. It's much easier and more dependable to simply lighten up our offering.

Large flies can expand the zone by increasing visibility and vibration. They are not, by definition, heavy flies. In fact, large flies that are not overweighted tend to ride higher in the water than small flies because of their added surface area. That surface area catches moving water like a sail catches wind, generating more movement and pushing the fly upward. Large flies can be extremely effective on steelhead, regardless of the time of year, and for those anglers who have tested the limits, there doesn't appear to be a fly that is too big for hot, grabby steelhead.

That circuitous path brings us back to the concept of being "in the zone." While it's inevitable that the "zone" will mean different things to different people, time and experience tend to lead us toward a shared destination. Evidence of this progression is the relatively recent adoption of small, unweighted tubes like the Reverse Marabou (see page 81) by many leading Pacific steelhead guides. And to further demonstrate that theory, one can compare steelheaders' recent evolution toward small tubes to the much earlier adoption of small, unweighted tubes by many Atlantic salmon anglers a couple of decades earlier. So while the universe of steelhead flies may appear to be expanding, there are forces at work that may eventually narrow our focus down to the things that really matter.

This fly imitates a Popsicle—another point for Lee Spencer's team. KEN MORRISH, FLY WATER TRAVEL, PHOTO

3

THE INTRUDER
REVOLUTION

By Rob Russell

*All the angling experiences produced with the Intruder during that segment in time could,
I think, be easily described as the stuff that angling dreams and stories are made of.*
—Ed Ward, March 2016

To understand this whole Intruder thing, we have to go back to Washington's Skagit Valley in the early 1990s. It was the beating heart of Washington's steelhead country, and one of the few rivers with a winter fly scene. The Skagit and its largest tributary, the Sauk

River, were quickly becoming the mecca du jour for Lower 48 steelheaders, thanks to a steady stream of magazine articles and a booming Seattle metro area. Two-handed rods were still rare, magical beasts. Whenever they made an appearance on the river, people would stop what they

Morning fog lifting on the Skagit River, where the seeds of revolution germinated.
BEN PAULL, OLYMPIC PENINSULA SKAGIT TACTICS (OPST), PHOTO

THE INTRUDER REVOLUTION | 9

were doing and watch in amazement. Sage Manufacturing had just released the 9140—the first decent Spey rod to hit the market. Unfortunately for many early adopters, very few of the lines available at that time were even remotely castable by today's standards. A lot of guys bought them, tried them out a few times, and decided they were some kind of bad Eurotrash joke. Old-timers and curmudgeons clung to their single-handers and laughed at the hipsters and their ridiculous rods.

The few guys who could actually make a Spey rod work stood out from the crowd. And the most visible among them was a bright young steelhead guide named Dec Hogan. Not only could Dec find the fish, but he made casting a two-handed rod look easy. And man could he write. And take great pictures, and keep his dudes smiling no matter what Mother Nature dished out. He was a phenom, and his writing probably inspired more new steelheaders to the sport than anyone before or since.

Meanwhile, a few of Dec's steelheader friends were trying to keep a lower profile and find some water that wasn't being hammered by the masses. There weren't very many places to go, and at that particular time, in that particular place, some of the best available water was downstream of a weeping clay deposit that made the water murky more than 75 percent of the season. Ed Ward and Jerry French, two of Dec's fishier friends, found themselves standing waist-deep in a gray-blue river day after day, dreaming of bigger flies. Since meeting and comparing fly boxes, these two solitary men had found themselves attached at the hip. One of the things that made the friendship click was their shared interest in big flies. Bigger, better, and much more wiggly—what Jerry likes to call "movey." But the complete vision for the Intruder had not yet crystalized. Jerry and Ed fished together most days and traded off at the same tying bench like a couple of mad scientists, producing new, ever-larger prototypes of their experimental monster flies.

"We were *creature constructors*, not fly tiers," Jerry said.

The first proto-Intruders were tied on 8XL streamer hooks of enormous size. No trailing hook, just the factory harpoon. And that created two major issues.

"Three-quarters of the fish we landed were bleeding profusely," Jerry said. "And we lost way more than we landed."

"Yes, that increase in fly size created problems with fish loss and, most importantly, fish injury," Ed said. "And those circumstances started the quest for a large, *large* fly pattern that would give off an alluring impression of life through movement and translucency, provide a high hooking-to-landing ratio, and yield the lowest possible rate of injury to the fish."

So they straightened out their streamer hooks to get the shank length they wanted and cut off the rest of

Ed Ward with a Russian king salmon in 2002. Definitely the stuff that angling dreams and stories are made of. MONTE WARD PHOTO

the point of the hook. They filed the cut end smooth so it couldn't scratch the leader. Then, before tying the actual fly, Jerry lashed down a doubled-over piece of 30-pound Dacron to create a tiny loop at the rear of the shank. The idea was to run the tippet through the eye of the hook, then through the tiny Dacron loop. From there, he tied on a small, fish-friendly hook using Lefty's No-Slip Mono Loop.

"As long as you made your mono loop large enough, it would keep the hook from pulling inside the Dacron loop," Jerry remembered. "But it was far from perfect. Sometimes it was a real pain in the ass."

While imperfect, these modified hook shanks allowed the anglers to rig any size hook necessary. They also provided a perfect base for Creature Construction.

It was about this point in the development of the Intruder that a third and crucial innovator was added to the team.

"While Jerry and I were initially conjuring up the basic Intruder 'platform,' Scott Howell quickly became an integral and valuable part of the Intruder development team," Ed said. "And that 'tripling' of angling experience and perspective made for quite an accelerated and effective evolutionary process."

That summer of 1993, the whole crew went to Alaska to guide for Katmai Lodge on the Alagnak River. Ed, Jerry, and Scott found themselves in the most incredible fly-testing grounds imaginable. They fished for kings and chums in June and early July, coho in August, and big Alagnak rainbows all the time.

"The fact that we guided in Alaska during our 'off-season' for steelhead—summer—proved to be of a significant advantage in the process of the Intruder fly design, and one we put to very good use," Ed said. "The sheer magnitude of possible fly-to-fish encounters in Alaska is about as good as it gets, and one summer of Alaskan angling can produce years-worth of 'Lower 48 rate' hooking data! So, since kings were the first fly quarry of the Alaskan season, they also became the first targeted Intruder test subject. However, a surprising segue of that endeavor was also very noteworthy: the high degree of interest for the Intruder displayed by the Alaskan rainbows. So, the original intent of the Intruder was to be a steelhead fly, but the testing phase on Alaskan salmonids proved that it had a much wider window of application."

The group tied flies whenever they weren't guiding or fishing, and every day they made improvements.

"We would walk down to the river's edge to test each fly as it came off the vise," Jerry said. "That's how the Intruder got its name. Ed was swimming his latest fly, this crazy thing with tentacles going everywhere, and I said 'Intruder alert, Intruder alert.' Like Robby the Robot. Didn't you ever see *Lost in Space*?"

Rethinking Hackle

One of the coolest revelations to come from the Intruder Revolution was the application of large feathers as hackles. First it was turkey feathers, then pheasant tail, ostrich, and rhea. These long, slender fibers created huge flowing shrouds that gave the impression of something large, but were barely there. The technique for hackling such feathers required carefully splitting and detailing feather strips with razor blades. Then the strips were soaked in hot water to make them pliable. As the membranes dried out, the hackles hardened up nicely and could withstand a lot of abuse. It was tedious and time consuming, but it made the stiffest hackles.

Jerry French spinning ostrich herl and other goodies into a dubbing loop to be brushed and hackled. A game changer. BEN PAULL, OPST, PHOTO

A fully fledged Intruder rigged "old school" with speaker-wire insulation. Better than bait.

Spinning the long fibers in a dubbing loop was an easier method, and it allowed almost any material to be hackled. It still took some practice, and a lot of patience, but the results were awesome. Bumps of seal fur and polar bear were added as support behind the hackles. Those materials were also spun in dubbing loops, then brushed out and tightly hackled for maximum flare. This gave the giant hackles a foundation, providing body and shape. It also allowed for a layering of colors that added to the potential for complexity and contrast within the fly. Eventually Jerry would take the dubbing loop hackle concept to yet another level by combining multiple materials of various lengths in a single "compound" dubbing loop.

The Intruder concept involved two of these hackle "stations": one at the front and one at the rear. The shank between the stations was either wrapped with tinsel or palmered with some kind of shorter hackle. Counterwraps of wire were added for durability.

"I was blown away when I realized what those guys were doing," Dec says. "There aren't many real innovations in fly fishing. There's a lot of borrowing and recycling of ideas, but there's very little that's truly new. I have to say, the Intruder was unique."

Those early Intruders caught everything, and the whole gang was eager to try them out on steelhead. So that fall Jerry, Ed, and Scott jumped in Jerry's old Explorer and drove to British Columbia, Scott's drift boat in tow.

"Oh man," Jerry remembers. "Three stinky dudes in my truck. It was bad. But man, the fish destroyed those flies! It seemed like we couldn't tie anything that was too big."

Over the next few seasons, Ed, Scott, and Jerry refined the Intruder and added a couple of tiers to what had become known as the Intruder Clan. First came the final innovation that would complete the Intruder platform— a solution to the less-than-perfect Dacron loop. One night back at his apartment outside of Arlington, Washington, Jerry had a breakthrough. He realized that he needed something that would fit over the rear end of the Intruder shank to hold the tippet tight. He was futzing around with a speaker wire when it hit him, and he ripped the wire out of his stereo. The clear plastic insulation over the copper wires was perfect. He slid a half-inch section of the tubing on a piece of tippet, pushed the insulation onto the butt end of the fly shank, and it fit perfectly. Then he replaced the Dacron loop with one made of 30-pound mono. The shank-style Intruder was born. It fished like an oversized tube, sliding away from the trailing hook and the gnashing jaws of a fish during the fight. And that little piece of just-right tubing accomplished another of the group's engineering goals: It allowed the angler to rig the hook so it would ride point up.

"We used dumbbell eyes of various sizes to 'keel' the fly. Coupling this function with a stinger-hook-point-up positioning, we reduced the occurrence of snagging on the bottom or on river structure."

That was particularly important given the fact that these flies took hours to tie. Losing an Intruder stung badly. But thanks to the new rigging, the flies could generally be fished though a run from top to bottom without hanging up.

"It was at that time that another very talented steelheader was inducted into the group, his name to remain anonymous at this time for the sake of privacy," Ed said. "And finally, for posterity's sake, it is absolutely necessary to declare Raquel Fielder's presence in the group as a part of the original 'Intruder clan.' The angling portfolio accrued by the Intruder clan, both as a group and individually, spanned from Oregon to Alaska, Kamchatka to Chile, and many other places with bright silver fish in flowing waters. All the angling experiences produced with the Intruder during that segment in time could, I think, be easily described as the stuff that angling dreams and stories are made of. We all fished Intruders, but we all also developed our own unique versions of the fly, each seemingly similar in appearance and function to each other. Yet every fly was also remarkably individual enough in character to be identifiable from anyone else's! It turned out that for us, the Intruder was more than just an artificial fishing fly. . . . It was an agent of unification for a small group of very hard-core steelheaders."

Stomping on Tradition

"The creation process of the Intruder was quite different than most other flies in existence in that it was more of a 'mechanical' evolution rather than aesthetic one," Ed said. "Jerry described it best when he said, 'Intruders aren't tied; they are engineered.' Every part of the Intruder platform was instituted into the fly with a *functional purpose* first, and considerations for appearances to the human eye second. I believe this engineered approach to tying is exactly why the Intruder turned out to be so successful."

People seemed to either love the Intruder or hate it. Dec was completely impressed by the ingenuity his friends were bringing to their flies, but he scratched his head over the obsession with going big. These guys were going nuts, pushing the bounds of decency.

"Whether it was true or not, there was a perception that this fly was magic," Dec said. "Some guys lost confidence in everything else. I had a problem with that, I guess. The classic flies still worked fine, and they were a hell of a lot easier to cast."

At some point the Intruder clan picked up another nickname due to their intensity and obsession with big flies: the "Testosterone Gang." They ruffled a lot of

Scott Howell with an Alaska salmon that fell for one of his deadly Intruders. MONTE WARD PHOTO

Ed Ward with a heavy Russian steelhead.
MONTE WARD PHOTO

feathers, camping out on bars to get first water, avoiding conversations on the river, and catching all the fish. Not to mention those crazy flies.

"Intruders were getting bigger and bigger with each new generation," said Scott Howell. "It got pretty ridiculous, but the fish kept on crushing them."

There was a day during the group's second fall in British Columbia when Scott remembers standing on the banks of the Kispiox and having the realization that his Intruders had reached a tipping point. He could no longer cast the really big ones. He says it was then that he thought, "Okay, the fish will eat bigger flies than I can cast." From then on, Scott said, the size wars were over, and each tier stepped down to more castable flies that focused on movement, profile, and sparseness.

"We finally got them up to like 7 or 8 inches, man," Jerry said. "Not only were they a bitch to cast, we were getting a lot of bad hookups."

The longer they made their Intruder shanks, the more they would see fish hooked in bad spots, like the cheek, the isthmus, or the eye. They soon settled on shanks between 1½ and 3 inches, what Jerry calls the "sweet spot."

Ed thought the success of Intruders was at least partly due to the fact that nobody else was using them. The Intruder clan agreed to keep their flies under wraps as much as possible. Those who were brought into the circle were sworn to secrecy. The pact was surprisingly successful, but there were a few leaks in the dam. Intruders had made a few conspicuous cameos in magazines and promotional materials. The first brochures for Kamchatka Fishing Adventures featured spectacular photos of beefy steelhead with strange, gangly flies the size of small birds hanging from their jaws. Dec's articles in *Wild Steelhead and Salmon* magazine occasionally featured teasing photos of Ed holding Skagit steelhead with one of his crazy Intruders hanging below like some alien life-form. By the late '90s the fly had been shared with enough people that every serious steelheader had at least heard of the Intruder, even if they hadn't seen one. It would take another several years before it would go mainstream.

"We had heard about some guy who was trying to take credit for the Intruder, and Ed decided we should set the record straight," Jerry said. And so, after a decade of suppression, the cat was out of the bag. The Intruder went viral, and soon commercial versions were being tied in China and Thailand.

The Sculpin Connection

Jerry French grew up fishing in Washington's Steelhead Country and was fortunate to be mentored by many of the area's legendary anglers. His list of influences is a who's who of the era's greats, but he credits Harry Lemire for teaching him something that helped to drive his fascination with large, lifelike flies. Harry had a thing for sculpin. He was convinced that steelhead had a visceral reaction to sculpin, seeing them as both enemies and prey.

"Sculpin steal eggs from spawning fish," Jerry said. "And if you look behind a group of spawning salmon, you'll usually see some dead sculpins. They kill 'em."

Not only will steelhead attack sculpins that are targeting their eggs, they will eat them. But sculpins are what Jerry calls a "dangerous meal" since they have barbed opercula. If a steelhead or trout miscalculates its attack, it can end up choking on its intended prey.

PERSONAL EXPERIENCE

By Rob Russell

Monte Ward was a later member of the Intruder clan, having been introduced to the fly by Scott Howell on a BC trip in the fall of 1996. Like his compatriots, Monte went all in. He built his entire fishing program around his Intruders, and he spent hundreds of hours perfecting them. In 1999, Monte was recruited as director of marketing for the Wild Salmon Center's Kamchatka Steelhead Project. That fall, instead of their usual trip to British Columbia, Monte and Scott flew to Russia and promptly blew the lid off the place. Traditionalists, of which there were several in the early Kamchatka clique, were mostly put off by the gargantuan flies. Like Dec Hogan before them, these old-school steelheaders saw something almost obscene in the flies—their size, their complicated design, and the almost religious fervor with which devotees obsessed over them. But after a couple of weeks getting their asses kicked, the doubters caved. Intruders were a thing—something big and dramatic, eliciting powerful responses from steelhead.

Back in Northwest Oregon, I took my first job as a steelhead guide in 1999, running trips for the Clackamas River Fly Shop. During the previous year I had bumped into Monte at a couple of trade shows and heard he was booking Kamchatka steelhead trips. I was a conservation writer looking for a ticket to Kamchatka, but I didn't have the résumé or the connections to make it happen. It took

Monte Ward doing his best to handle a hulking Russian steelhead. MONTE WARD PHOTO

a while before it dawned on me that there were people getting paid to go to Russia. The Wild Salmon Center hired fly guides for their Russia program, all of whom were names in the industry and had worked at least a couple of seasons in Alaska. I was a nobody with very little experience, but I set my sites on getting to Russia, even if it took the rest of my life.

My first look at a real, live Intruder finally came in 2003. It was a pitch-perfect April day on the Clackamas River. I was a few months into my fourth season as a steelhead guide, still with a lot to learn. I had arranged a day of fishing with Monte Ward and Jon Jensen on my home waters. Monte was a world-class steelheader, and Jon a world-class photographer. The river had been fishing very well, with a nice mix of winter- and summer-run steelhead. I figured we'd have fun and maybe get some good images in the process. Monte showed up with a small Tupperware container as his fly box. I'd been on the scent of Intruders for a couple of years, but a real specimen had never crossed my path. I guessed what he was hiding in the box. Jon had no idea what he was about to see. At our first stop, just below Fish Wheel, Monte rigged up one of his Burkheimer two-handers and cracked open his box. He lifted a purple Intruder out of the pile, ran his fingers over it, and handed it to me. I must have said "wow" a hundred times.

"Oh my God!" Jon blurted. "What the heck is that thing?"

Monte got a laugh out of our reactions. I think he was used to it. He gave us a brief history of the fly and did his best to explain the principles behind its design. Even with two decades of fly-tying experience behind me, the key elements flew over my head. I knew I was seeing a very important innovation, but I had no idea how it was constructed. Then Monte tied the fly to his tippet and let it swim in the water. Seeing that fly move was a revelation. It was alive.

Monte suggested that Jon swing through the run first with a traditional hair-wing fly. I followed with one of my own mega flies, a Samurai knockoff I called the River Squid. Jon had a tug, but no dice. I had a couple of weak grabs, but again nothing solid. Monte stepped in last, made a couple of casts, and came tight to a fish. He landed a fine wild steelhead, released it, stepped back in the run, and quickly hooked another. Jon and I just stood back and watched. After releasing his second fish, Monte called us around and held the fly in the current so we could see it come alive. Anyone who had a bit of fish sense could see that this fly set a new standard. And as the day went on, Monte continued to hook all the fish. Late in the day he hooked a fish right at my boots as I waded ahead of him. A big, bright hatchery summer steelhead exploded next to me, then sped off across the river. All I could do was laugh as I backed out of the water. He landed the fish as Jon snapped photos. Then Monte clipped the fly off his line and handed it to me.

"Here. You should take this and try it out," Monte said. He showed me how to rig the fly, and I put it to work in the next run, just above the Barton Bridge ramp. Right in the sweet spot my line went tight, and a beautiful hatchery hen started doing backflips. Monte came down and congratulated me, but I couldn't accept any credit.

"Monte, you have landed a half dozen fish today," I said. "Jon and I totally blanked until you gave me this fly. I think your Intruder deserves all the credit." He smiled and patted me on the back.

"It's yours, man. I hope you catch a few more fish on it," he said.

That purple fly went on to catch a number of steelhead over the next year. With each fish, the materials became more and more sparse, until there was almost nothing left. I begged a couple more flies from Monte, but my own attempts at tying Intruders failed miserably. Monte gave me a couple of tying lessons, and I took copious notes. But for some reason his lessons didn't take right away. There were so many tools, materials, and techniques that were new to me. And I could fall back on my standard patterns, even if I suspected they were inferior.

In 2006 Dec Hogan's *A Passion for Steelhead* was published, featuring a brief history of the Intruder, along with a photo and recipe. Some important details were deliberately left out, but the basics were finally in the public sphere. Commercial versions started to show up in the fly-shop bins in 2007 and 2008, most notably Howell's Signature Intruder. An Intruder Revolution swept the industry, though most examples at the time were a far cry from the real thing.

It wasn't until 2009 that I would finally take the deep plunge into Intruder tying, an experience documented in a number of articles published on the Oregon Fly Fishing Blog. From 2009 through 2014, I tied and fished Intruders religiously. I fished with more confidence, and it became fairly common for me to pick up steelhead behind other anglers with my new creatures. ■

Everybody freaks out when they see an Intruder swim for the first time. ROB RUSSELL PHOTO

The sculpin may be the most prevalent and provocative "intruder" in a steelhead's natural universe. KEVIN FEENSTRA PHOTO

For that reason, steelhead attack sculpin headfirst, and they attack hard.

It has often been noted that Intruders have a tendency to elicit savage strikes from steelhead. That reaction starts to make a lot of sense when considered in the sculpin context.

Influences on Skagit-Style Fly Lines and Casting

"It seems like the first custom-spliced fly lines to offer the weight needed to comfortably cast sink-tips and big flies were developed by Al Burr and Harry Lemire in the late 1980s," Hogan said.

It was 1989 when he first replicated one of their short, heavy shooting heads and rigged it on one of his two-handed rods.

"Those first lines were vessels for casting sinking-tip lines," Dec says. "They really had nothing to do with Intruders, as some people think," Dec recalls. "They were more about shortening the casting stroke and providing the grain weight needed to turn over sinking-tip lines. They made Spey casting easy, whether you were a beginner or an expert."

Of course, Dec was not a fan of the mega-fly obsession that was spreading through the steelheading world. For him, Skagit-style lines were about ease of use, plain and simple. But for Ed, Jerry, and Scott, the new heavy lines were a critical tool for launching their Intruders.

"The Intruder definitely drove our line and casting style," Jerry says. "The evolution of the Intruder with its large profile made it pretty tough to cast. With that in mind, the evolution of Skagit-style lines and casting began."

The added weight of a large, wet Intruder required a subtle modification to the casting stroke, leading to another of the Intruder-related innovations.

"When Ed was figuring out his Intruders, one big thing he did was to key in on the sustained-anchor cast," Dec says. "After setting the anchor he gave it an extra second before forming his D loop. The extra tension really loaded the rod."

That is, it allowed the rod to take the full load of a cast before the fly was ripped out of the water. And the insanely heavy new lines that soon would come led many new casters to overpower their forward stroke, blasting their anchor and wearing out their shoulders.

Ed Ward described it this way: "As regards line development, those first lines of Harry's and Al's were, in fact, an attempt to emulate the concepts of Goran Andersson, of underhand casting fame. They were trying to duplicate his crisp style of casting, but using lines more conducive for steelhead-type presentations. Those lines were a 15- or 17-foot section of floating 12-weight fly line, spliced to a 15- or 17-foot section of 9-weight Hi Speed, Hi D sinking fly line. They were more user friendly compared to the other more traditional types of Spey lines available then. However, the casting of big flies was not the

A sustained anchor helped correct the common tendency to overpower the cast with the new shorter heads. Brian Chou demonstrates.
JAIME DELGADO PHOTO

The Intruder Revolution transformed steelheading and helped to bring our sport to its current apex.
MARTY SHEPPARD, LITTLE CREEK OUTFITTERS, PHOTO

intention or forte of those lines. The appearance of the first very-short-and-heavy lines capable of casting truly *big* flies came about years later and can be attributed to Marlow Bumpus's and Bob Strobel's introduction of 30-foot 14- and 15-weight saltwater shooting heads to the Skagit River steelheading scene. Those lines, tipped with sink-tips made from lengths of Teeny 200 or 300, or even Cortland's LC13 lead core line, were *true* big fly casting machines. Once word got out about them, the demand from anglers all over the Pacific Northwest quickly depleted the entire North American supply. At that point in time, a request was made of the Rio fly line company to produce 100-foot lengths of level, floating fly line in 13-, 14-, and 15-weight. Thankfully for us 'Skagiteers,' they obliged us. This circumstance provided many steelheaders the means to construct their own Skagit lines for many years. Then, at some point after those events, Mike McCune and Scott O'Donnell designed the infamous Rio 'beer can' Skagit line, and the Skagit evolution really started to roll! It should be noted here that the entire impetus for 'casting big' can be attributed, in one way or another, to the advent of the Intruder, and, therefore, the Intruder was, in fact, the catalyst for all things 'Skagit.'"

"Contrary to popular belief, we rarely fished super-heavy flies or sinking-tip lines," Jerry said. "We usually stuck with 10 to 12 feet of type VI. If we needed to go heavier, we would make tips out of Teeny 200 or 300. The most important thing was the length of the lines. The heads and tips combined were 2½ to 3 times the length of the rod. This allowed us to fish high banks with very little casting room. It also allowed for creative casting methods, most notably the Perry Poke. 'The Poke' became our bread and butter. Our short, stout line systems allowed for efficient casting, creating higher line speeds and accuracy, and the ability to cast big flies. These improvements opened up many new places to fish that were not possible with longer line systems."

Today, as the steelheading world gleefully retreats to the practicality and comfort of smaller flies, the Intruder Revolution feels like something that has passed. And I get a nagging feeling that it came and went right over most people's heads. Did we ever really get what Ed Ward and Jerry French were doing? Did we ever see what they saw, or feel what they felt? And has there ever been a fly that propelled our entire sport to another technological plane?

One thing is for sure: The only way to really get Intruders is to go all in. You've got to tie hundreds, and you've got to fish them religiously. Intruders are just super-buggy bugs, so in that sense they are fairly simple. But the thought and painstaking construction behind a

Tying and fishing Intruders is a journey—and one that every serious steelheader should take at some point. Prepare for obsession! ROB RUSSELL PHOTO

good Intruder is what makes it a next-level fishing lure. Yeah, it's just a fly, but it's also so much more than just a fly. Remember the 1980s when Lani Waller waxed on about the evocative movement of steelhead flies as we watched a stiff-as-a-board Skunk or Red Wing Blackbird track across the screen like it had rigor mortis?

Today one can find dozens of new fly patterns that are riffs on the Intruder concept, including a growing number of small and even "micro" Intruders. Tiers are getting better and better at engineering their flies to create specific profiles and movements. So besides the massive progression in tackle that came from the Intruder Revolution, it's fair to say we will be seeing the Intruder's influence in new steelhead flies for a very long time.

It's also important to note the parallels between the Intruder story and the following story from the Great Lakes. While the sculpin played a critical role in the early development of the Intruder Revolution, it was also the key to the "Third Coast."

4

THIRD COAST
SWING

By Rob Russell

It took some audacity to swing flies back in the "early days" of Great Lakes steelheading. You were making a statement quartering downstream in the nymphing capital of the world. At the dawn of the 1980s, as the Rust Belt enjoyed a man-made invasion of salmon and steelhead, the collective focus was on productivity and harvest. Snagging was still a condoned and legal method of angling. Spawning fish were openly targeted. Even the dominant "fly" methods were starkly utilitarian.

Fly lines had been widely discarded in favor of straight monofilament. Flies were chucked and bounced along the river bottom with the help of heavy split shot. When worse came to worse, flies were even dosed with salmon egg juice. It was a newly formed sportfishing universe, still raw and in search of its fly-fishing tradition.

In the midst of this free-for-all, a handful of guys were reaching for something more. They couldn't see themselves performing the "chuck-and-duck" or "bobber-dog"

Today it's not unusual to see someone stepping and swinging his way through a Midwestern steelhead run, but it has not always been so. KEVIN FEENSTRA PHOTO

standards around the Great Lakes for decades. Kevin's flies were working-class guide ties, designed to catch fish, not just to catch the attention of anglers searching the fly shop bins, as so many commercial patterns did. Besides sculpin, he imitated Hex and stonefly nymphs, caddis larvae, salmon fry, and an array of bite-sized baitfish, including shiners, darters, chubs, and silversides.

"West Michigan rivers are very fertile, and they are relatively short for a fish that is designed to swim hundreds of miles in some cases," Kevin says. "Steelhead come in and have a lot of time to mill around. There's a lot of food down there, and eventually they just start feeding."

In fact, it seemed that some Muskegon steelhead never stopped feeding. And a new arrival to the Lake Michigan ecosystem was making steelhead more piscivorous than ever. The round goby—an aggressive little sculpin-like predator—had been quietly infiltrating every corner of the watershed since it was first documented by scientists in 1990. Presumed to have been introduced to the Great Lakes from the bilge water of international freighters, round gobies were the latest in a string of invasive species that exploded throughout the system. Gobies were

equally at home in lakes, rivers, and small streams, and they quickly became a favorite food for steelhead.

Dave Pinczkowski explained: "Yeah, at some point I noticed that my flies were looking more and more like sculpin. Then around 2010 gobies came on strong. Or maybe they were there all along and I didn't know it. But our fish *really* hit gobies, man. I'll be watching a steelhead, and then he'll turn real quick, and there'll be this puff of sand. It took me a long time to figure out what I was seeing, but I finally figured out they were slamming gobies."

Both Dave and Kevin, on their opposite sides of Lake Michigan, had come to similar realizations. They also developed a shared belief that an effective sculpin imitation needed to have sufficient size and profile to "move water." They came to believe that steelhead were attuned to the pressure waves created by a forage fish, and that their flies needed to produce a similar signature. And while their beliefs could easily be dismissed as anecdotal, their parallel evolution demanded consideration. Day after day, watching and learning, getting ever closer to their respective fisheries, Dave and Kevin

Mike Decoteau has inspired anglers around the world with his next-level tying and fly design.
JASPER WALSH PHOTO

were adapting to their ecosystems. Then came the next revelation—the power of flash.

"At some point I started adding Flashabou to my baitfish patterns," Feenstra said. "Eventually I came to believe there was no such thing as too much flash. My fly patterns were bulky enough to hold their shape no matter how much Flashabou I added, and the fish loved it."

So did a few other prominent Michigan fly guides of the same time period: Jay Niederstadt, Ray Schmidt, and Matt Zudweg. Each guide experimented with different amounts of flash in different color combinations to see how they affected steelhead. A great story relating these experiences was contributed by Tom Larimer in his chapter titled "Unconventional Wisdom."

Hot on the heels of these Wisconsin and Michigan innovators was an exceptional class of fly tiers from Ohio and Pennsylvania. Thanks to a number of factors—the Clean Water Act of 1972, the filter-feeding zebra mussel, and a number of local efforts to improve water quality—rivers that had once been open sewers of human and industrial waste were clean enough to host runs of steelhead by the 1990s. From Toledo, Ohio, to Buffalo, New York, Lake Erie's new steelheading playground was dubbed "Steelhead Alley." It became a nursery for steelhead fly innovation and evolution, and a number of fly tiers from the region percolated to national prominence. Greg Senyo, Mike Schmidt, and Mike Decoteau (pronounced de-COTE-oh) all stood out for their prodigious skills and creativity.

Today the possibilities for the swung fly in the Great Lakes seem endless. But it will be the success of the fish populations themselves that will dictate the future of angling in the region.

"Right now baitfish are disappearing, and I don't know what the future will bring for fishing," said Pinczkowski. "Steelheading is getting tougher here. More crowded. Seems like guys are having to drive four or five hours to find a quiet place to fish."

Salmon, steelhead, and trout, along with dozens of other nonnative fish species, are still a long way from finding their equilibrium in the Great Lakes. That means they will continue to boom and bust in multiyear cycles until they find their zones. Undoubtedly, there will be more invasive species released into the lakes, each destined to repeat the process and add another variable to the mix. And the only people who will know how those variables affect steelheading are those who are out there on the water, fishing and adapting to what they find.

"The last couple of seasons I've found myself imitating darters more than sculpin or gobies," Feenstra adds. "Even with the explosion of gobies, it's good to see our native rainbow darters are holding their own."

Lessons for Pacific Steelheaders

Kevin Feenstra notes, "The most visible differences between West Coast and Great Lakes steelheading from my perspective are that, first, West Coast steelheaders need to be really good casters because they have to wade big rivers and cast a long way to certain lies. Here we tend to fish a lot from boats on the bigger rivers. And our smaller rivers don't require long casts. Second, Great Lakes rivers have colder water in the winter. That makes the steelhead fishing more technical—you have to get the fly down and stay down. And last, we fish a lot of brush and timber. I'm not sure if that's a big part of West Coast steelheading, but I never hear about it."

Tom Larimer agrees: "Great Lakes tributaries are more technical, at least in the winter. The water's so clear and cold. Guys over there also fish a lot of bass, so they're used to 'patterning' fish, figuring out what they want. I think flies should be designed and tied for specific water, conditions, seasons, performance, and presentation. There are times when it doesn't matter, but there are also a lot of times when the fish are there, and they're not biting. You have to try some things. They've cracked some codes in the Great Lakes. Guys like Feenstra have developed systems for what colors of flash work in certain seasons, light conditions, and water conditions."

A Little Background for the West Coast Folks

Most Pacific steelheaders could benefit from a little background on Great Lakes steelhead fisheries. While many of the West's most accomplished steelheaders were spawned and reared in the Midwest, there are a lot of native Westerners who have never fished east of the Mississippi. As we've tried to demonstrate in this book, the innovations in steelhead fly design don't only flow from west to east. In fact, with each passing year it seems that the Midwestern tiers are the ones pushing our creative boundaries forward.

As we all learned in grade school, the Great Lakes make up the largest group of freshwater lakes on Earth. They are among North America's most defining features, covering 94,250 square miles of surface area and containing 21 percent of the world's surface fresh water by volume. Together their shorelines add up to over 10,900 miles—almost half the Earth's circumference—perforated by thousands of rivers and streams. The Great Lakes Megalopolis—the largest and most populated urban area in North America—surrounds much of the shoreline and is home to an estimated 60 million people and growing. Consequently, the many schools of steelheading encompassed under the "Great Lakes" heading are as

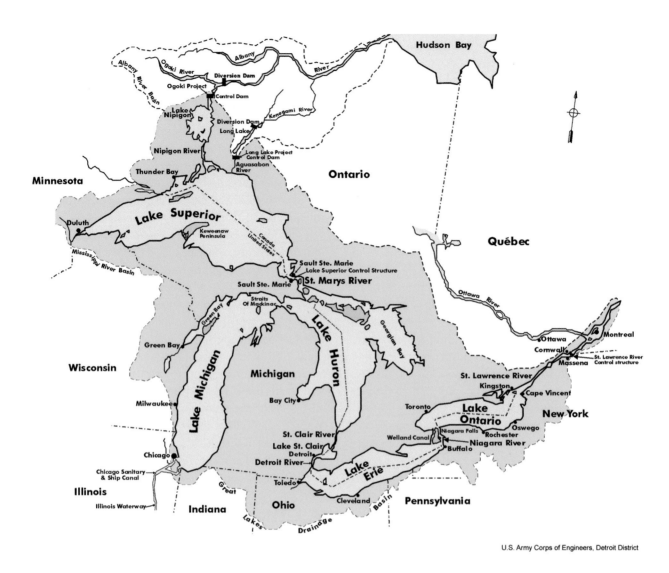

The diverse steelhead fisheries of the Great Lakes have become incubators of new fly designs.
WIKIMEDIA COMMONS PHOTO

diverse as those on the Pacific Coast. Every town with a river and a fly shop has its own steelheading culture. But roughly, the steelheading regions of the Great Lakes can be broken down into four main areas: 1) Northern Wisconsin; 2) Northern Michigan; 3) Steelhead Alley; and 4) Upstate New York.

The lakes are interconnected from the northwestern shore of Lake Superior to the eastern end of Lake Ontario by rivers and navigational canals. The impressive Niagara River connects Lake Erie to Lake Ontario, its world-famous falls creating a natural barrier for the upstream migration of many aquatic organisms. That is, until the 1820s, when shipping canals were painstakingly constructed to bypass the falls. In 1825 the Erie Canal opened, creating a shipping channel from the Hudson River to Lake Erie, and paving the way for nonnative species to infiltrate the entire Great Lakes system. A few years later, the first incarnation of the Welland Canal

was opened, forming the key section of the St. Lawrence Seaway to the Atlantic Ocean. Improvements to Welland Canal in 1919 are most often blamed for giving the sea lamprey access to Lake Erie. The anadromous sea lamprey soon spread to all the other lakes, and by the 1940s was severely impacting native populations of lake trout, lake whitefish, chub, and lake herring, exacerbating the effects of overharvest by commercial fishing fleets. Around the same period, the alewife, a prolific river herring from the Atlantic, also gained access to the lakes. Alewives exploded throughout the system from the 1950s to the 1980s. Their seasonal die-offs resulted in miles of beaches piled with dead fish, stinking out communities and generating public outcry.

By 1964 commercial and sport fisheries in Lake Michigan were officially on the brink. Both billion-dollar industries were considered vital to regional economies, but the native fish those industries had been built upon

ARE GREAT LAKES STEELHEAD REALLY STEELHEAD?

Great Lakes steelhead don't get much respect from the average West Coast angler. They are the unwitting target of a strange sort of fish racism, rationalized by the prevailing definition of steelhead as an "anadromous" rainbow trout. Anadromy refers, of course, to a fish that migrates from salt water to fresh water on its spawning run. And since Great Lakes steelhead never swim in salty water, they must be, by definition, something else. They never undergo full "smoltification" or pay the huge metabolic costs of switching from fresh water to salt water and back again. They eat different things and are subject to smaller predators, on average. In short, they have it way too easy, and we can't go around rewarding slacker lake-run rainbow trout by calling them steelhead, even if they are the same fish, exhibiting their best attempt at a "steelhead" life history. And since we don't have a sexy name for "potadromous" rainbows—those whose migration occurs completely within freshwater systems—the Great Lakes steelhead could have been a fish without a proper name. Thankfully, Great Lakes steelheaders went ahead and decided for themselves what to call their fish: steelhead. In recent years, several state agencies have made the move to expand the working definition of steelhead to include rainbows that migrate to a "sea." In some cases the definition has even been expanded to include any rainbow that is highly migratory.

Recently a friend held court on this subject over beers at Hickman's cabin on the Oregon coast. He demanded that we West Coasters get over ourselves and quit denigrating Midwestern steelhead as inherently lesser. "For Pete's sake, people. Steelhead need friends. The[y're] f**king disappearing, man! We need to stand together, and there are a lot of steelheaders in the Midwest who need to be counted in this conservation movement. Let's not disenfranchise them because of semantics." We couldn't agree more. Besides, what fisherman in history hasn't stretched a few definitions? ■

Lake-run steelhead are a bit "troutier" than most of their West Coast cousins, but they are still the same animal, with the same potential to eat a swung fly. JAY NICHOLS PHOTO

Mia Sheppard contemplates the watery universe on a dreamy summer evening. MARTY SHEPPARD, LITTLE CREEK OUTFITTERS, PHOTO

had crashed. At the same time, salmon hatcheries in California, Oregon, and Washington started reporting surpluses of eggs. Howard Tanner, Michigan's chief of fisheries at the time, thought that coho and chinook salmon might be the radical solution his state needed. If successful, salmon could provide strong commercial and sport fisheries and act as biological controls for the annoying alewife problem. Tanner convinced state officials to get behind the move, and in 1966 Michigan started planting coho. Chinook plantings followed soon after, and both species eventually flourished.

Most early attempts to establish steelhead fisheries in the Great Lakes failed. But the larger, wilder rivers of northern Wisconsin and Michigan were the exceptions. A handful of McCloud River steelhead were first released in Lake Michigan in 1876. Then in 1882, steelhead were widely introduced to most Michigan rivers. By the 1900s, wild-spawned steelhead were returning to Michigan's Muskegon and Pere Marquette Rivers, as well as Wisconsin's Bois Brule.

The older guys—those over 50—can remember the days before steelhead came to Lake Erie. Back then the lowest reaches of most streams had been reduced to open sewers. Toxic algae blooms were commonplace, fouling the surrounding beaches much of the year. Dead zones formed around the mouths of rivers, sometimes extending for miles out into the lakes. Cleveland's Cuyahoga River infamously caught fire at least 13 times between 1868 and 1969. The last documented river fire sparked on June 22, 1969, and while it was barely considered news to Ohioans, *Time* magazine picked up the story. The resulting exposé is widely credited for spurring the US Congress to pass the Clean Water Act in 1972. Soon after, the United States and Canada formed the Great Lakes Water Quality Agreement to aggressively reduce phosphorus levels, and the US Environmental Protection Agency (EPA) was charged with leading the effort. The result has been a rebirth of the region's rivers and a resurgence of fish and wildlife.

By 1980, steelhead fisheries in the Great Lakes were exploding. Every state fisheries agency from Minnesota to New York was operating or developing salmon and steelhead programs, taking advantage of improving water quality, improving aquaculture techniques, and a surplus of eggs from the West. Michigan alone reported the release of 1.8 million smolts, and a reported sport catch of 610,900 steelhead. While the more informed anglers saw the steelhead train coming, many more had

A typical Great Lakes tributary in the "Steelhead Alley" region on the south shore of Lake Erie. Small stream steelheading at its best. JAY NICHOLS PHOTO

the experience of waking up one morning and finding a brand-new steelhead fishery in their backyard.

At first, most Great Lakes steelhead were viewed purely as game to be harvested. They were nonnative hatchery fish, purchased by taxpayers to control another nonnative species. Fisheries managers decided early on to allow snagging as a legal means of harvest, since there was no biological reason to protect spawning steelhead. Little did they know the social and ethical problems that policy would create, or how difficult it would be to undo the damage. Snagging was finally outlawed across the Great Lakes in the early 1990s, though bad practices are still commonly reported.

In 1990 the first round goby was documented by scientists in the St. Clair River near Detroit. Thought to have been introduced in the ballast water of container ships, the goby was the latest—though surely not the last—invasive species to join the Great Lakes melting pot. Today the goby's reach is pervasive, extending from the open lakes all the way to the headwaters of tributary streams and rivers.

As of 2016, fisheries managers say that Asian carp are poised to invade the Great Lakes, most likely through the Illinois River in Chicago or the Maumee River in Indiana. Tens of millions of dollars are being spent to prevent their arrival, but most scientists see it as inevitable.

5

UNCONVENTIONAL WISDOM

By Tom Larimer

When I made the move from guiding Michigan's Big Manistee River to guiding Oregon's Deschutes River in 2002, the overwhelming majority of fly anglers believed that catching a steelhead during the midday sun was akin to discovering a cure for cancer. Conventional wisdom dictated that, because the Deschutes flowed from south to north, the sun "blinded" the fish. It was said that a savvy angler spent his or her time plying the river in the evening and morning when the immense walls of the Deschutes canyon shaded the water. Fishing sink-tips through the middle of the day, while capable of upping the odds slightly, was considered a desperate act.

In 2005 I started guiding the lowest reaches of the Deschutes via jet boat. Unlike the Maupin area where I started my Deschutes career, the lower river had a

Sometimes the best way to wake up sleepy steelhead is to show them something shiny. We can relate to that, can't we? KEN MORRISH, FLY WATER TRAVEL, PHOTO

considerable following of conventional-gear anglers and guides. Watching these anglers hook fish after fish in the midday sun made me realize a very important fact: "Conventional wisdom" was actually a pile of horseshit. Steelhead ate plenty of spinners, spoons, plugs, and jigs with the sun directly in their eyes; they just weren't consistently eating what the fly guys were throwing at them. This epiphany opened up a whole new thought process in my tying and fishing. I started to think about *why* the gear guys were successful. The obvious facts were that almost every lure they fished ran near the bottom, wiggled a lot, and was super flashy—everything my flies didn't do. I started thinking about a fly that would do everything those lures could do.

Around the same time, Spey fishing for Great Lakes steelhead was really ramping up. An old guide friend from Michigan named Jay Niederstadt called me for some advice and encouragement. He was tired of the nymphing game and the corresponding body-count mentality. He was ready to commit to guiding his clients exclusively with two-handers. Considering that dead-drift techniques are the "tradition" in the Midwest and that conventional wisdom (there's that dangerous term again) said Great Lakes steelhead didn't respond well to a swung fly, his was a commitment of monumental proportions. That's not to say that Jay was the first angler to swing flies with a Spey rod in that region. The legendary Dave Pinczkowski from Milwaukee, Wisconsin, started wielding the long rod in the late 1980s. Joe Solockian, Bob Blumreich, Walt Grau, and John Kluesing were also early two-handed pioneers. And by the mid-1990s, a group of punks, including Jason Koertge, Billy Zippel, Scott Clark, and myself, started Spey fishing the Wisconsin tributaries. I was new to the sport but was eager to share my passion and bits of wisdom with clients and friends. That continued when I started working the Manistee in 1996. Around that time, another Michigan guide named Kevin Feenstra was convincing his clients to swing flies on the nearby Muskegon River. I have no doubt that there were many others fishing Spey rods on the countless steelhead tributaries of the Great Lakes at the time. However, there were two elements that made Jay's timing perfect. First, the evolution of Skagit heads and T-14 sink-tips had finally given fly anglers the ability to deliver a swung fly where it had rarely gone before. Secondly, guides like Feenstra and Niederstadt discovered that Great Lakes steelhead loved to crush flies with a ton of flash.

During Jay's first season of dedicated swinging, I would get phone calls on a weekly basis. His demeanor would vary from full-throttle excitement to pure defeat. We were constantly sharing ideas about presentation and flies. I told him about a very simple rabbit-strip tube

Hickman's Flash Taco gives off an explosion of sparkle in the spirit of those early Great Lakes flash flies.

leech that was working for me on the West Coast. The fly consisted of a 2-inch strip of rabbit, a small amount of flash, a collar of schlappen, and dumbbell eyes. Sometimes I would add an egg-colored dubbing ball behind the eyes. The tube fly was rigged stinger-style, using a no-slip-mono-loop knot and a small octopus hook. Jay ran with it. His first flies were simply a long piece of magnum rabbit strip, a heavy wing of Flashabou, and a wad of dubbing for a head. His 4- to 5-inch-long creations had tons of movement. The elementary fly design was a product of his river conditions. The Big Manistee is littered with fly-eating logjams, which the steelhead invariably use as cover. Losing flies was part of the game, so any pattern that took more than a couple of minutes to tie didn't last in the fly-box rotation. Additionally, juggling a family and a full-time guide schedule left little time for the vise. If Jay was running low on a particular color or if he wanted to experiment with different color combinations of rabbit and Flashabou, he would literally lash together flies in hand (no vise) while rigging his client's rod! He got so good at concocting flies without a vise he would use any spare time, including driving to the river, to fill his box. Despite the simplicity of his flies, Manistee River steelhead loved them.

Eventually Jay started to find consistent success swinging flies. Frustration was replaced by anticipation. He found color combinations that worked for specific fishing conditions and hit the water each day with a plan versus a prayer.

Jay's success with super-flashy flies in the Midwest coupled with my observations of the conventional angler's ability to coax Deschutes steelhead during the high sun inspired me at the tying bench. The next time I tied up a few of my purple rabbit-strip tube leeches, I added a ton of "grape" Flashabou. A pink Ice Dub egg on the front completed the fly. The next morning, just before dark, I met my clients at the Heritage Landing boat ramp and ascended the lower Deschutes in the predawn light. After a fantastic morning of fishing floating lines with classic wet flies, we had managed to land two of the three summer steelhead we had hooked. The day was off to a good start, but we were losing our shade quickly. I never like to experiment with new flies unless my clients have landed a fish or two, but given our success in the morning, it was a perfect time to try one of my new Niederstadt-inspired tube leeches.

The grab came in the very first run. What amazed me was how hard the fish slammed the fly. My client almost lost his rod! After an epic battle we landed the beautiful wild buck and proceeded to hook two more fish out of the same pool. It was difficult to act like this was "business as usual" in front of my clients, considering I never told them about my experiment, but three

steelhead from one run with the sun blazing in the fish's face had me jumping out of my waders! As the midday sun rose higher in the sky, we went on to hook five more fish before the afternoon was over. I was beside myself.

One of the greatest elements of fly fishing is our moments of discovery. In my mind, discovery is the fuel for evolution. After that amazing July day, I questioned not only everything I knew about Deschutes River summer steelhead but anything that resembled conventional wisdom. As I drove home that night, my mind was racing with ideas. My first super-flashy leeches were effective but lacked style. They needed to evolve. Though I admired Jay's "utilitarian" approach to fly tying, I wanted to come up with a pattern that didn't require on-the-water assembly and had a little extra something.

As a fishing guide I have a few requirements for what I consider a good "guide fly." First off, it must to be quick to tie. I went through a period of my career where I only wanted to tie elegant flies onto a client's

Larimer's Tube Leech in a few of Tom's favorite color combinations—an example of the growing influence Great Lakes steelheaders are having on the West Coast.

Tom Larimer walking into Salmon Camp on the Kanektok. We spent the day swinging for kings, but we talked mostly about Great Lakes and Deschutes River steelhead. Go figure! ROB RUSSELL PHOTO

line. All of my wet flies were tied with polar bear wings, perfectly shaped bodies, and exactly five turns of ribbing. My Spey flies were meticulously built, sporting faultless feather wings. The heads on my Muddlers were trimmed flawlessly. As far as surface and near-surface flies go, I still appreciate the art and craft of a well-tied wet fly with perfect proportions and super trick materials. I still fish them today. However, I quickly realized this was completely unreasonable when it came to subsurface patterns designed for sink-tip fishing. Nothing is worse than giving a client a beautiful Intruder that took 45 minutes to tie and watching them snag the bottom on their second cast. It's painful for the guide and the client! Consequently, my sink-tip patterns have taken on a more function-versus-fashion design, while still maintaining a bit of aesthetic appeal. A good guide fly also must be easy to cast. Despite the efficiency of modern Skagit heads, many of the subsurface flies steelheaders swing are overly bulky, making them difficult to lift out of the water while setting the anchor of a Spey cast. Moreover, an effective sink-tip fly should *sink* quickly. An overly dressed fly will, for a lack of a better term, "parachute,"

causing it to hover in the water column. I want my fly to dig toward the bottom once I've made my mend. That being said, the fly must also move well. I hate it when a fly looks like a stick in the water. I want my fly to breathe life as it swings across the current. This is achieved by a combination of the right materials and a head design that pushes the water, creating a vortex behind it. Such a head propels movements within the body of the pattern. Of course, there is a balance between building a head that facilitates movement while not hindering the sink-rate of the pattern. And last but not least, the fly obviously must catch fish.

Although my Tube Leech has a little more of a finished look, by sharing our ideas and experiences, Jay and I worked together to come up with a pattern that works for steelhead on the West Coast as well as the "Third Coast." The rabbit-strip tail with a wing of Flashabou provides both seductive movement and flash. I believe this combination is the catalyst for some truly fierce grabs. I added an undercollar of spun rabbit for two reasons. First, it gave the fly a more appealing look by hiding the tube and filling out the underbody. Second, I realized that it helped create the sought-after vortex effect within the fly. Another addition was the barred wood duck collar. I have to thank Michigan steelhead guide Jeff Hubbard for this idea. He incorporated wood duck into some of his leech patterns, and I loved the look of it. Most animals in nature have some type of camouflage. The barring on the feather breaks up the monotone rabbit body and gives the fly a more natural look in the water. Like my first leeches, I used a schlappen collar to give the fly a more finished look and to give the front of the pattern a bit more bulk. The biggest difference in our designs is the head. Jay takes a massive wad of Ice Dub or a similar dubbing and clumps it in. This gives his version of the fly a huge head, creating a sculpin-like profile. Conversely, I dub a small ball of dubbing to create an egg. Finally, my leeches are about 2½ to 3 inches in length, which seamed about right for the 4- to 8-pound steelhead most common in the Deschutes. Jay's original patterns were massive in contrast. However, as time went on, Jay's patterns started getting smaller and more refined. He realized that in many fishing situations, a 3-inch fly was just as effective as a 5-inch fly. In the end, our flies became very close in size and in profile. However, the color of flash and rabbit does seem to vary from river to river. Two versions of my patterns that have found success in both the Great Lakes and the West Coast are the Halloween and Storm color schemes, though I have no doubt that the two purple versions would find Midwest fish in the right water conditions.

I've heard more than one West Coast angler proclaim that Great Lakes fish are simply "lake-run rainbows," usually with a very dismissive tone. Most of the anglers I've met with this negative view on the Great Lakes have never even been there. While it's true that the steelhead of that region don't migrate to the salt, they have lineage to the West Coast stock dating back to the late 1800s. Consequently, Great Lakes steelhead grab, run, and jump just like West Coast fish. They also live in some truly beautiful places and are stunning creatures to behold. More to the point, steelheaders in the Great Lakes swing their flies for all the same reasons West Coast anglers do. They spend countless hours plying cold rivers in hopes of the big grab and the opportunity to connect with one of the most elusive fish pursued with a fly. They also share the love of creating innovative flies that might help catch "lightning in a bottle." As steelheaders, we should embrace our diversity and celebrate our passion for the fish and the flies we tie to chase them. We are all part of the same tribe and can learn a lot from each other. Had it not been for Jay's willingness to share his knowledge and experiences, I'd probably still be wondering how to catch Deschutes steelhead during the midday sun.

6

WILD SUMMER STEELHEAD AND ARTIFICIAL FLIES:
A North Umpqua River Example

By Lee Spencer

My dog—Sis or Maggie—and I sit on a pool on a creek that that has been off-limits for anglers since the 1930s. This pool serves as a cool refuge for wild summer steelhead from the warmer waters of the summer. We sit here because the pool used to be poached many times each season, even to the extent of using dynamite. We are here to deter poachers, but we also watch the hundreds of wild summer steelhead that gather every season for seven or so months. Much of the information contained herein comes from watching these steelhead. My dogs and I have watched the pool now for 13 seasons, and we have cast flies for North Umpqua summer steelhead for 31 seasons.

—Lee Spencer

Are the wild summer steelhead in Steamboat Creek becoming vegetarians? LEE SPENCER PHOTO

A careful look at the life history of the steelhead and other Pacific salmon, paying particular attention to comparisons of the growth possible in freshwater streams compared to the ocean, clearly shows that adult steelhead returning to their home streams not only do not but cannot effectively feed in fresh water. Steelhead and other Pacific salmon continue to grow during their lives to the extent that available food allows. Other than incidentally and idiosyncratically, foraging stops 24 or 48 hours—or some short time—after leaving the ocean.

The abundant productivity of the North Pacific Ocean allows anadromous Pacific salmon to put on an average of 4 to 6 pounds a year. Even the lower weight of 4 pounds is significantly more than a resident rainbow trout weighs at the end of eight years spent in a Northwest Coast river. Adult summer steelhead of 15 to 20 pounds, while uncommon, are found in the North Umpqua River. Here in the Pacific Northwest, by the time a resident—non-anadromous—trout grows to 22 or 23 inches, not only has it absolutely maxed out the growth allowed by the fluvial resources, but it has taken eight or nine years to do so.

The half-pounder life history type sheds some light on how big a large population of feeding rainbow trout can be while subsisting in fresh water. Half-pounders are immature steelhead that leave the ocean during the fall of their first ocean year and forage in their home stream until the following spring, when they migrate to the ocean again, not to return until they are mature and on their spawning run. These steelhead average 12 to 16 inches long.

The only sure way for a resident trout to get larger than, say, 22 inches is by adding other fish to their menu, a thing that our local rainbows do not characteristically do. This option—piscivory—while adopted by some coastal cutthroat, would seem counterproductive considering the large number of wild summer and winter steelhead that used to inhabit the waters of the Pacific Northwest—probably tens of millions. (I am only considering wild fish, native to the Pacific Northwest, in this discussion.) If all those 6- to 10-pound steelhead were regularly feeding on small fish during their freshwater stay, there could not have been enough food available to keep them alive. In these once-pristine rivers flowing into the eastern edge of the North Pacific Ocean, Pacific salmon parr, fry, and smolts were the dominant fishes. Does killing your own offspring make much sense, evolutionarily or otherwise, for a population of fish? I believe that eating or feeding with any regularity in fresh water after a few days away from the ocean would be adaptively suicidal to adult anadromous Pacific salmon—especially so for wild summer steelhead considering their

10- to 12-month sojourn back to their natal rivers before spawning. In other words, given the fluvial ecology in the Pacific Northwest as we know it, if two-salt/four-year-old summer steelhead in the Umpqua Basin did need to feed in fresh water to survive, they would most likely die of starvation. Compared to the rich productivity of the marine environment, the nutrition available in fluvial systems doesn't amount to much.

If our fluvial systems did compare in productivity to the ocean, *then* resident rainbows and cutthroats in fluvial systems (trout naturally propagated and living naturally) could grow as big as steelhead, and probably just as fast. But this doesn't happen. They don't even get close. Even after living twice as long as their sea-run cousins, resident-trout size is not in the same ball park. A summer steelhead that is six years old and has spent four years at sea may measure close to 40 inches and weigh around 20 pounds. A six-year-old fluvial cutthroat or rainbow in the North Umpqua River has a reasonable chance of measuring 16 inches and weighing maybe 1½ pounds. So, it takes the lavish availability of food in the marine environment to allow steelhead to enter their natal streams with sufficient reserves to make it through the spawning process. Mother Nature assists, and ocean productivity allows adult summer steelhead and spring chinook to accumulate 20 percent more fat in their bodies by the time they leave the ocean for their spawning runs.

Saying that wild steelhead do not eat, however, is not to say that they are not drawn instinctively to the chase. In my first 12 seasons sitting at Big Bend Pool, I documented 2,300 steelhead as they approached 1,092 items, including bugs, crawdads, and small fish (see the table below). Of these approaches, 88 (3 percent) involved steelhead chasing small 2- to 4-inch fish. Not one of these chases resulted in the capture of the small fish in question and in virtually every case, the steelhead seemed to give up the chase and turn away. (Note that most of the rises I see in the pool are carried out by the steelhead, so that they can get a look above the surface of the pool; the second most common reason to rise is to get air for their air bladder. These two reasons probably make up well over a thousand rises each season. This is part of the reason why I prefer to call the active positive attention of a steelhead in the pool an "approach" and not a rise. Another thing to bear in mind is that in the 12 seasons covered in this table, I have spent 2,456 days on the pool.)

Nor does any of the information presented above in this paper mean a goddamn thing with reference to behavior of hatchery fish. Thus, the idiosyncratic data of items found in the stomachs of steelhead or observations of steelhead feeding need to be further examined to

APPROACHES IN BIG BEND POOL
1999–2010

Items approached	May	June	July	Aug	Sep	Oct	Nov	Dec	Total	%
Mayflies*					8	21	26	5	60	5
Caddisflies			1	2	12	6			21	2
Crawdads		1		8	5	4			18	2
Other arthropods		1	6	24	66	22#	14		133	12
Leaves	7	4	10	29	128	180	13	4	375	34
Plant down				14	15	1			30	3
Miscellaneous items	4	5	9	49	127	93	6	1	294	27
Unknown items	35	2	1	2	16	15	2		73	7
Subtotal	46**	13	26	127	367	348	67	10		
Small 2- to 4-inch fish chases***				11	23	52	1	1	88	8
TOTAL	46	13	26	138	390	400	68	11	1,092	100
%	4	1	2	13	36	37	6	1	100	
No. of steelhead observed approaching items	46	15	44‡	289	960	854	85	16	2,309	

Note: When more than one fish approaches an item, that item is counted only once.

Miscellaneous items: Feathers, area of a trout rise, otters, kingfisher, alder cones, mergansers, beavers, unknown plant parts, dead sticks, pieces of wood, bats, Styrofoam, bark, bubbles, fungus on a steelhead tail, fir needles, immature fir cones (reddish), sugar pine needle bundles, lichened sticks, cedar branchlets, lichens, leaf stems, blue-green algae, squirrel, stick with plant down attached, lichened bark, 6- to 8-inch cutthroats, broad-leaved maple seeds, steelhead skin flap, parr with an autumn caddis, minnow carcass, 6-inch ring-necked snakes, racers and garter snakes, scales from a fir cone, alder catkins, large pink mushroom, spiders dragged by their airborne webs.

* 22 of these approaches occurred during November of 2002.

** 43 of these approaches occurred during May of 2002 and they were carried out by 2 winter steelhead.

*** These are chases only, and they were first counted during 2002. The mature steelhead in question always turn away before getting to the 2- to 4-inch-long fish. No steelhead has yet been observed to take a small 2- to 4-inch fish. During 2002 and 2009, 48 of these small fish chases occurred.

10/10/09, 2:35 p.m.: the first and the only time I ever saw a steelhead jump to take a flying insect out of the air during my first 11 years at Big Bend Pool.

‡ 43 of these 44 steelhead were repeated rises to different items by 2 winter steelhead observed in the pool during 2002.

determine whether the fish in question was a hatchery fish. Also pay attention to whether the things found in steelhead stomachs are food or not. Think about it: Do the dippers found in steelhead represent feeding on the part of the fish? The point I am making is that, regardless of what are probably idiosyncratic incidents of feeding, present species and populations of Pacific salmon—including steelhead—have evolved life habits that do not require them to eat to make it through the spawning process. Surviving to complete the spawning process does not, however, mean that such a reproductively lucky steelhead will make it all the way back to the ocean. Only the ocean contains enough food to bring a fasting steelhead back from the brink of starvation, and relatively few of the steelhead that survive spawning make it back to the ocean.

The table above documents that only 21 percent of the items approached could be considered food items, and only a small fraction of those were actually taken and kept in the fishes' mouths. By far, the most common

ON FLY DESIGN AND PRESENTATION: Q&A WITH LEE SPENCER

Q: What do you think about when you are crafting a fly?

A: Trying to get the best materials I can, tying sparsely, and dispensing with the superfluous. In my case—as a person who has been tying one fly, a moose-hair Muddler for the last 15 years—is the moose hair spinning well enough to fill out the head of the fly, yet still produce a sparse fly?

Q: When you are swinging a fly?

A: Is my fly leaving a wake? Is it swinging neither too fast nor too slow?

Q: How has your experience as a steelhead observer influenced your approach to fly tying?

A: Not much really. My decision go pointless had been made the winter previous to Sis and my first full season at Big Bend Pool. My choice of a moose-hair Muddler was made two seasons prior to that. My time at the pool has probably reinforced the pointless decision, however.

Q: What elements of the fly and its presentation do you think matter most for triggering an approach? A strike? Are the triggers different?

A: I think that most or all of this is in the mind and daily, if not hourly, inclinations of the steelhead. Most important, and most serendipitous, is the inclination of the angler matching the inclination of the fish.

Q: Are we wasting our time overanalyzing?

A: Yes, I believe we are overanalyzing, but so what? Ignorance can be bliss—as long as we are careful about our generalizations, so that they don't interfere with our compassion for the steelhead.

Q: I like to imagine that steelhead react to lively fly patterns the way they might react to a sculpin or crayfish crossing their path. What do you think?

A: Based on what I see steelhead pay attention to each season at the pool, what I would be trying to represent would be a small, thin, long-dead twig with some sparse lichen on it. If I were trying to imitate the movement of this item, I would be fishing it dead-drifted. Would I make this imitation anyway? You bet I would, a nice, clean, smooth wake with no pumping. Do I think that pumping a fly works? Certainly it does . . . too. It all works. There is not a fly that a steelhead will not rise to sooner or later.

Their reaction to a lively fly pattern might be the same as to a sculpin or crawdad. If the small fish chases mentioned in the table (see page 35) and the essay above are representative of how steelhead might approach a fly representing a small fish, the steelhead would quite probably turn away from the fly well before making contact with it. ∎

Lee's legendary Burnt Toast with the hook point clipped and filed smooth to prevent harm to the fish. He has been fishing pointless for 20 years and counting.
ROB RUSSELL PHOTO

things that steelhead in the pool rise to are leaves, twigs, and lichens. Interestingly, the most common of the leaves approached each season is a Pacific dogwood leaf that contains large amounts of the dogwoods' unique red hue. This red, for my money, is the most similar to the reds that develop on the gill plates and lateral stripes of metamorphosed male steelhead. So, is a red fly risen to in the late summer and early fall because it resembles the red of spring chinook eggs or the red of a fully metamorphosed male steelhead? Or something else?

If, as I believe, the approaches made by steelhead to items in the refuge pool are the equivalent of their approaches to flies in the fly water, then success in getting a steelhead to take a fly in the North Umpqua River is mostly a matter of showing a fly to a steelhead that is willing to have its curiosity aroused—and to showing the fly to that steelhead without spooking it. Thus, *success in raising steelhead seems to have much more to do with the predisposition of the steelhead in question than it has to do with a fly and its presentation by an angler*. Even with hundreds of steelhead present in the refuge pool, it is quite a rare thing for a steelhead to show enough interest in an item to provoke an actual approach, much less an actual take.

In autumn—without question the best time to cast flies for summer steelhead—there are more summer steelhead present in the 150 or so named runs in the fly-water zone of the North Umpqua River than at any other time. This probably grossly translates to an average of two to six steelhead per run. Even in autumn, it is the rarity of finding a curious steelhead that makes fly fishing so problematic. Would we love them as much if they regularly roused themselves to our flies?

My experiences, along with the stories of friends, are replete with accounts of anglers making every possible mistake, yet still having steelhead take their flies. Are steelhead the anti-Murphy? I think that if a steelhead woke up in a curious mood, it would rise to a fly despite the bungling of an angler, and no matter what cast, line, or fly the angler used.

That said, curious steelhead can also be strangely selective. I see this every season when the first woolly bear caterpillar or the first woolly bear caterpillar *with long white guard hairs* is approached by the steelhead in the pool. The pool steelhead also clearly show an interest when the first of the colored leaves of the various riparian trees or bushes show up on the pool. Familiar items that do something different can also catch the attention of pool steelhead. In the late summer of 2002, four steelhead immediately rose to two green alder leaves that had just been caught and blown upstream by afternoon breezes. Note that these four steelhead that rose to the skating leaves belonged to a pod of 270 steelhead at that time.

During the early fall of that same season, an autumn caddisfly was unable to rise from the surface film on the pool. A dozen steelhead made abortive approaches in the neighborhood of the caddisfly. Then a small steelhead porpoised up and confidently took the fly at the surface. I watched through my binoculars as this steelhead swam in small circle champing its jaws. When it had come around and was facing me, the steelhead spit out several pieces of the caddisfly. With a suddenness that surprised me, I watched as several steelhead rapidly crossed in front of the steelhead to take these pieces. I was reminded of feeding bluefin tuna footage I had once seen. At this time, there were 454 steelhead present in the pool.

Now, if the ball is in the steelhead side of the court, if this is an accurate assessment of the fly and steelhead situation—that only a very small proportion of any group of steelhead are likely to be interested in any item/fly at any given time—wouldn't the anglers for this only-occasionally-rising fish be able to make up whatever rules resonated in their own minds and still manage to catch steelhead *now and then*? Would it make any difference how outlandish these rules were in relation to the reality of the steelhead? And, jumping Jesus, when you add to this the erroneous, pan-human tendency to assume in any given situation that they are being objective or that their personal experience has yielded up a representative sample, is it surprising that we have been unable to find a single steelhead that has been swayed by any theory propounded by any angler?

I find it very interesting that the dominant conceptualization for why steelhead rise to take flies is their innate aggression, anger, or fear. This, I believe, says more about us than about the steelhead. It seems that anger and aggression are easier behavioral inferences for us to connect with emotionally than simple curiosity. Is it possible that the term *angler* is not derived from a piece of bent metal, but derives from the human emotional term *anger*, that is, *anger* + L = *angler*? Wouldn't it be something if steelhead actually rose to our flies out of compassion for us? How would that change things?

In the back eddies of our awareness, are we all simply gravitating to whatever theories please us? Like the steelhead, are we aware of anything more than the obvious triggers that build our confidence in a fly? And is it this confidence that is at the heart of the thing?

For my part, I believe that it is curiosity that roused virtually all of the more than 2,300 steelhead I documented as they approached items in the pool. I do not mean to imply, however, that curiosity is the same for steelhead as it is for us. My use of the term simply means it is the best description that I have yet some across for the behavior I see every season. It was over 40 years ago that the great Washington State fly angler

Lee on the Sustut in 2014 posing with a steelhead that took his pointless fly. LEE SPENCER PHOTO

Enos Bradner came to a similar conclusion, and he is, I believe, generally recognized as the father of the curiosity theory for why these sea-run rainbows would approach a fly. (I first read of this theory in his 1971 book, *Fish On! Everything You Should Know about Steelhead Including How to Catch 'Em*.)

Is this curiosity merely a way for steelhead to exercise their desire to stay in touch with changes in their environment? One of the things that has been most evident to me in my time on the pool is that steelhead—if they are not sleeping—are quite attentive to even minor changes in their environment. Steelhead also appear to feel vulnerable while holding in the refuge pool. This is evident in the spooking that even the slightest shadow can produce when it passes over a pod of fish.

In this regard, it is worthwhile to consider that in the years since they left the North Umpqua River, adult steelhead are more than 100 times the mass and at least 5 times the length they were when they left the river on their journey to the ocean. With the same increase in length, I would be at least 30 feet tall. Perhaps even more important to these fish is the change from living in an effectively bottomless, shoreless marine environment to the confines of a river. How would you feel returning to your old high school as a 30-foot giant?

To sum up my thoughts on these questions I will quote a passage from one of Joseph Conrad's books. It applies to the steelhead, to me, to you, and potentially to the cosmos: "Belief does not necessarily imply understanding."

7

MODERN MATERIALS:
BETTER THAN THE OLD STUFF?

By Jay Nicholas

We are driven by hope. Some have called it faith. It's the thing that gives us the motivation to step out the door into the darkness, into the cold, the wind, rain, heat, whatever. And one of the things that can spark a bit of that hope is an exciting new fly-tying material. Anyone who grew up tying flies 50 or 60 years ago has witnessed a proliferation in the variety of tying materials that are easily accessible to everyone who ties flies, not only to the pros or the elite tiers with connections in the industry. Starting with

Great steelhead flies require great materials. These prime ostrich plumes were handpicked for tying Intruders.
KEN MORRISH PHOTO

the hooks, shanks, and tubes upon which we build our modern flies; progressing through the threads we use; and including every imaginable natural and synthetic material we add to make our flies—our palette has grown enormously. Some of the new generation may take our contemporary array of materials for granted. Even the most seasoned among us may not give a second thought when lashing 8 or 10 different materials on a shank, concocting recipes that would have been impossible in the 1960s. It's only natural.

From butt to head, we have at hand the raw materials with which we may tie flies that are fundamentally different, if only in subtle ways, from the flies most of us were tying in the 1960s, '70s, and '80s. But if we are able to tie differently than was usual 50 years ago, are we really able to tie better flies, flies that are more effective fish-catching lures? Pose the question like this: Are any of our modern material alternatives superior in their fish-catching powers to chenille and rooster feathers?

Answer: I think so, but perhaps in ways that are subtle and require explanation and context. On the surface, I'd venture that all the fancy new material alternatives are irrelevant, because I can combine fur, feather, and chenille—go steelhead fishing—and catch as many fish as anyone tying their flies with new-age materials and adorned with names that sound like they came from a punk rock band. But if I think about it, even my simplistic "retro" steelhead fly is tied on a modern shank, with a tiny stinger hook, using arctic fox fur for tail and wing, and adding the subtle but striking sparkle of Mirage Lateral Flash on both sides of the wing. None of this stuff was available to me 50 years ago, or if it was, I didn't know it. These might seem to be subtle differences, but in my mind, the fly I tied to swim in front of winter steelhead in 2015 was worlds more exciting than the Thor I tied in 1970.

I learned to tie flies in about 1962, with little help from a Herter's manual and much inspiration and mentoring from Audrey Joy, when she tied flies at a small station in the Meier & Frank department store in downtown Portland, Oregon. Within a few years I was tying for Norm Thompson's. Most of the flies I tied were parachute-style dry flies, but in short order, my tying skill-set expanded, and I began tying all manner of flies for Wayne Doughton's hardware store in Salem, Oregon. By the late 1970s I had begun tying for Randall Kaufmann at his Tigard, Oregon, fly shop. Each of these stages in my growth as a fly tier involved new patterns, nuances in proportions, and style, but on the whole, the basic materials I used varied little.

- **Hooks.** I tied with Mustad and Eagle Claw hooks. Steelhead flies were tied on the Eagle Claw 1197B or the Mustad 36890. The Eagle Claw 1197N or 1197G

were used on occasion but were exceptions to the traditional use of the 1197B bronze hook.
- **Thread.** I tied with Nymo thread. Period. Nymo in many colors, but all Nymo, all the time. Wooden spools.
- **Body materials.** These included chenille, yarn, and a few animal furs, notably muskrat, otter, and baby seal.
- **Hackles.** With the exception of nymphs, most flies I tied included a tail of hackle fibers and a collar hackle of rooster neck or saddle feather. Dry flies used less webby feathers; wet flies and steelhead flies used feathers with more web, if these were available.
- **Hook sizes.** Considering the steelhead flies I tied from the 1960s through the 1990s, I'd venture that winter steelhead flies were principally tied on size 4 hooks; summer steelhead flies were principally tied on size 6 hooks. Flies larger or smaller than these were by far the exception in my orders.

While I was tying my steelhead flies using materials noted above, other tiers were creating steelhead flies that looked quite different from those I crafted, using more exotic hooks, threads, and materials. Looking back on my development as a tier, I would say that I was focused on production rather than innovation, and on producing quantity of simply-tied flies as quickly as possible.

I remember meeting Dave McNeese at some point during my early days tying steelhead flies. I was more than a little intimidated by the elegant flies Dave crafted. He used hooks with a different curve, different colors, different proportions. And the materials were so exotic! I think I turned and ran as fast as I could back to the security of my world, surrounded by my chenille spools, mountains of calf tails, and pounds of strung saddle hackles.

Dave McNeese was one of those rare fly tiers who distinguished himself through innovation. He explored exotic materials, dyed his own unique colors, sought out different hooks, threads, tinsels, and hackles. Spey-style flies were not on my production list, and I knew next to nothing of flies tied with heron and various exotic plumage. For decades while I was focused on cranking out 50 dozen size 6 Skunks, tiers like Dave were crafting 50 different patterns, varying the hooks, sizes, body materials, wings, hackles, tinsels, and so forth. I looked at the flies Dave produced all those years ago and felt envious. (Honestly, I still do today.) I didn't know what he was using for hooks, tinsels, various body materials, hackles, and so forth. I recognized polar bear and jungle cock, but I didn't have any on my bench. I tried tying a few complex steelhead flies with my Eagle Claw hooks and Nymo threads, but they were ungainly and looked nothing at all like Dave's elegant flies, so I quickly retreated to the safety of my Green Butt Skunks and resumed work on my list of flies to tie for the next order.

I think it is fair to say that the steelhead flies I tied for decades were much like the earliest patterns developed by the pioneers of fly fishing in California from the 1920s to the 1950s. My Thor, Skunk, and Polar Shrimp flies were much like the simple Boss flies developed and fished in coastal California rivers—Dave's steelhead flies were West Coast derivatives of Atlantic salmon flies: elegant, multihued, complex patterns tied on graceful hooks with slim heads.

I can remember times when I'd produce 50 dozen Skunks, all in size 6s on Eagle Claw 1197B hooks. My production rate was perhaps 10 or 12 Skunks per hour, and I was paid something like $3.75 per dozen at the time. I'd whip these orders out in the evenings and mornings, during the odd hours of each day when I wasn't on duty as a biologist. These commercial shop flies were all tied to the specifications and proportions set by Wayne Doughton, a harsh taskmaster. Over time I received rave reviews from customers who fished the Deschutes, Umpqua, Rogue, Klamath, and even north into British Columbia—relating stories about steelhead they caught on my flies, the size of the fish, and so forth. Great feedback and wonderful validation—my flies caught fish and made customers happy.

Funny thing, though. I remember settling in with a different mind-set whenever I tied flies to fill my own boxes. Whether tied before the season or the night before a trip, my personal flies always had a little extra something added to them. I should rephrase that. Sometimes my own flies had a little more, but sometimes they had a little less than the flies I tied for the hardware store stock. A shorter body, perhaps, or a slimmer body with a sparser wing. Maybe I'd use polar bear instead of calf tail. I might concentrate on forming a neater head, blend two hackle colors in the tail, take more care to select an extra webby feather for the collar hackle, add a topping of Krystal Flash, spin on a dubbed seal fur body. At some point I began blending three or more colors of dubbing to achieve a body color unlike any I had ever seen in a fly shop or catalog. I might even have thrown on a pair of jungle cock cheeks.

The point is—I had to make my flies somehow different, somehow better, than the flies I already knew worked just fine. Why the fuss? Because I, like every other fly tier, am bent on creating magic at our fly vises, nothing less.

So, back to the question: Are our modern steelhead flies really different, and are they really better than the steelhead flies that people like Dave McNeese (on the fancy end of the scale) and me (on the simple end of the scale) were tying back in 1970?

Monte Ward's dining room table becomes an artist's palette of color, contrast, and movement—helpful inspiration for steelhead tying. ROB RUSSELL PHOTO

Yes. Our boxes today are stocked with flies that are different, and, yes, they are better. A few of our modern steelhead flies may be virtually identical to flies that were being fished 45 years ago. That's fine and will probably never change. But when I look across the entire portfolio of flies submitted by our tiers, I see a vast evolution. On the whole, and with the usual caveats and qualifiers, today's steelhead flies are more diversely colored, flashier, and exhibit more motion than the flies most commonly fished 45 years ago. And many of them are much larger than anything we fished 20 or more years ago. A few are actually smaller, which follows the theme of "diversity." All this diversity affords the steelhead angler better options to fish effectively under more diverse water conditions than ever before. High water. Low frigid flows. Big-water steelhead that must be located in runs that are 200 yards long and 200 feet wide. These are places where some of the largest, flashiest, wiggliest, and most colorful flies can excel in searching out a willing steelhead.

And how about the buggy nymphs in our portfolio? I never considered that such an array of dead-drift trout bugs might be effective steelhead flies back when I was filling orders of Skunks for the hardware store. Meanwhile, nymphing scenes were building steam all around me, in Northern California, on the North Umpqua, in British Columbia, and, of course, throughout the Great Lakes tributaries. These nymphs aren't just dead-drifted. Many are swung as wet flies or presented in some combination of dead-drift and swing. Today's steelhead nymphs fill niches that were overlooked by many experienced steelheaders in the past, and they add a lot to the modern fly box.

The Modern Palate

The materials we have at hand are like the spices a chef uses to enhance a meal.

Some tiers are satisfied with salt, pepper, and sugar, but other tiers reach for an array of spices I'm not even capable of naming when creating a meal. I hear chefs speak of layering spices, and how the consumer discriminates the various spices and nuances of taste. This is all fascinating to me but is, at the same time, mysterious. So I'm compelled to think it's irrelevant. My taste buds detect salt, pepper, fat, and sugar. I'm oversimplifying to illustrate a point, but generally, the nuances of a finely seasoned meal are lost on me, a guy who is likely to eat a meal in about 30 seconds, start to finish, so I can get back to tying, fishing, writing, or sleeping. I was the same way with my steelhead tying until the last few years. Thanks to a new fascination with modern fly styles, and

Jay Nicholas is surrounded by light and color at his tying desk in Corvallis, Oregon.

to my many encouraging friends, I'm happy to say that has changed. And an ironic twist of fate has thrust me to the bleeding edge of new fly materials.

YARN

I start this section under the heading of yarn, because it's hard to come up with a better heading for the many types of spun furs and synthetics we steelheaders use for the bodies of our flies. The practical old-time fly patterns developed by anglers fishing California coastal rivers for steelhead and salmon relied heavily on yarn for the fly's body. Chenille was a fancy new alternative to yarn when it hit the scene. Innovative tiers began experimenting with natural and dyed furs, usually underfur. Baby seal fur was one of the most popular materials used by artisan-class steelhead fly tiers of my era. In the 1970s I learned to combine seal fur with polar bear underfur for the body of steelhead flies. These were specially dyed in a variety of brilliant colors. The flies tied with these furs had more sparkle than those with yarn and chenille bodies, and we learned to use the term *translucence* to describe their seemingly magical properties.

Translucence, vibrancy, mobility. These terms were associated with the new dubbed body materials but never with yarn or chenille, materials that seemed inflexible and dull by comparison.

In the last few years a similar sea change has occurred as fur dubbings have been replaced with flashy synthetics like Senyo's Laser Dub, Senyo's Fusion Dub, Ice Dub, and SLF Prism. And as much as I'd like to say that these materials are no better than my old chenille, the steelhead have indicated otherwise. The eye-catching sparkle of these new dubbings appears to catch steelhead as well as they catch fly tiers.

Here's a reference list that illustrates some of the wonderful choices the modern steelhead tier has at his disposal.

NOT JUST CHENILLE

We don't just have chenille these days. Oh, no. We have . . .

Pseudo Herl	Ice Chenille
Afterglo Chenille	Krystal Flash Chenille
Trilobal Antron Chenille	Ice Dub Chenille
Variegated Chenille	Cactus Chenille
Velvet Chenille	Midge Cactus Chenille
Ultra Chenille	Holographic Cactus
Vernille	Chenille
Krystal Tinsel Chenille	Polar Chenille
EZ Magic Dub	UV Polar Chenille
Frizzle Chenille	New Age Chenille
Speckled Crystal Chenille	Estaz

NOT JUST BABY SEAL

Back in the 1970s, the use of seal and polar bear underfur, dyed in exotic colors, was a huge enhancement to those tiers of elegant steelhead flies. It's hard for most of us to access seal and polar bear dubbings these days, and I'm not sure we'd want to, but look at what we do have:

STS Trilobal Dub	Hare-Tron Dub
Ice Dub	Krystal Dub
Scud Dub	Creepy Crawley Ice Dub
Quick Descent Dub	Hare's Wiggle Dub
Angora goat	Hare's Ear Plus Dubbin
SLF Dub	Senyo's Fusion Dub
Cohen's Carp Dub	Senyo's Laser Dub
Whitlock SLF Dubbing	Senyo's Shaggy Dub
Polar Dub	

Modern synthetic dubbings offer the tier a staggering variety of color, texture, and sparkle.

NOT JUST ROOSTER FEATHERS

The simple steelhead and salmon flies developed on the West Coast rivers of California usually incorporated a collar or ring hackle of rooster neck or saddle feather. As modern steelhead flies have evolved to incorporate more materials and grown in size, fly artisan anglers have learned to incorporate many natural and synthetic products that add to the fly's fish-attracting powers.

While I was satisfied for decades to tie my steelhead flies with rooster neck and saddle feathers, many innovative anglers/tiers/artisans fishing steelhead waters were incorporating heron, marabou, turkey, pheasant, guinea, and other natural feathers to create elegant Spey-style flies. Here are some examples of materials that are often featured in today's steelhead flies:

Guinea
Ringneck pheasant
  body feathers
Ringneck pheasant tail
  fibers spun in a loop
Rhea
Lady Amherst pheasant
  tail fibers clumped
  or spun in a loop
Ostrich tail plume fibers
Ostrich body feathers
Barred ostrich plume
Craft fur (barred or
  solid colors)
Golden pheasant tippet
  feathers (natural or dyed)
Emu feathers
Silver pheasant
  body feathers
Marabou plumes
Turkey flats

Senyo's Aqua Veil Chenille
Schlappen
EP Foxy Brush
EP UV Minnow
  Head Brush
Grizzly Fiber, EP Senyo
  Chromatic Brush
EP Sommerlatte's Brush
EP Sparkle Brush
EP Anadromous brush
Senyo's Predator Wrap
Senyo's Wacko Hackle
Senyo's Freckled
  Predator Wrap
Senyo's Barred
  Predator Wrap
Senyos's Predator Wrap
Pseudo Hackle
Sparkle Pseudo Hackle
Chocklett's Body Wrap
Minnow Body Wrap

FLASH AND WIGGLE

Not to be satisfied with one type of flash and a few colors, the number of flash materials has grown dramatically in recent years, and today I can list roughly three dozen flash products, each with a similar number of color options one may pick through to find the perfect enhancement to a wing, tail, or body of a steelhead fly.

My first Skunk and Polar Shrimp flies had a white calftail wing, no more. I don't remember the exact year,

but sometime in the late 1980s or early '90s, Gordon Nash created the Street Walker—just a Purple Peril with Flashabou for a wing. That spawned a flash invasion, and today it's unusual to tie a steelhead fly without at least some kind of reflective material. Rubber legs and curly tails came a bit later, culminating in flies like Scott Howell's Squidro (page 144) and Barrett Christiansen's Lowly Glowly (page 169).

Wiggle Mostly

Perfect Rubber
  silicone legs
Cohen's Attractor tails
Fine grizzly barred
  rubber legs
Medium round rubber legs
Silicone flutter legs
Fly enhancer legs
Grizzly barred rubber legs
Rainbow shimmer legs
Magnum predator legs
Grizzly micro legs

Grizzly flutter legs
Barred Crazy Legs
Loco legs
Buggy nymph legs
Aqua Glow Crazy Legs
Barred and speckled
  Crazy Legs
Crazy Legs
Hot tipped Crazy Legs
Daddy Long Legs
Life Flex

Flash Mostly

Krystal Flash
Glow in the dark
  Flashabou
Fuchsia Haze Holographic
  Flash Fivers
Purple Haze
  Holographic Fibers
Flashabou Accent
Fluorescent Neon Flash
Grizzly Flashabou
Iceabou
Mirage Accent Opal
  Midge Flash
Polar Flash
DNA Holo Fusion
DNA Holo
  Chromosome Flash
UV Minnow Belly
Flashabou Mirage
  Split Fringe
1/69 Opal Mirage
  Lateral Scale

Lateral Scale
1/16 Opal Mirage
  Lateral Scale
Lateral Scale solid colors
Fire fly tie
Holographic Fly fiber
Flashabou
Pearl Flashabou
Mirage Flashabou
Micro Flashabou
Holographic Magnum
  Flashabou
Holographic Flashabou
Flashabou Predator
Flashabou Predator
  Holographic
Saltwater Flashabou
Magnum Flashabou
Ice Dub Minnow Back
  Shimmer Fringe
Ice Dub Shimmer Fringe

NOT JUST HAIR

My production steelhead flies tied in the 1960s, '70s, and early '80s were characterized by wings of very simple composition: calf tail or bucktail deer. The calf tail (we called it "kip tail" for a time) was white, red, or orange, depending on the pattern. The bucktail was white or natural brown, the latter taken from the center of the tail. I knew that other tiers were working with brown bear, black bear, and polar bear, and some may have worked with fox tail hair, but if so, I didn't know about it. Exotic winging materials included squirrel, ringneck pheasant tail fibers, and peacock herl. Today, the steelhead tier has many options within easy reach that alow the composition of superior wings and tails. Here is a short list:

Extra Select Craft Fur	Pro Sportfisher
Pro Sportfisher Marble fox	American possum
Pro Sportfisher	Moose body
Finn raccoon	

These materials may not comprise a long list, but they are wonderful winging materials, they compress well and allow us to make slender heads on our flies, and they are available in a wide variety of colors that steelhead find attractive.

Finnish raccoon is one of the sexiest materials on earth. The long guard hairs reflect light much like polar bear, and it comes in some fishy colors.

THREAD

Danville's
Lagartun
UNI
Ultra
Veevus

The thread one chooses these days does matter, and some great new brands and styles are available. The strength-to-diameter quality of a thread is crucial, and some newer threads are stronger than warhorses of similar diameters. Diameter is important, whether the thread is round or flat. A standard for decades, 6/0 UN-Thread is round, while 6/0 Danville is flat. Round thread supposedly offers minor advantages for certain things, like dubbing or spinning hair. But a couple of our most authoritative production tiers pointed out that round thread makes it hard to get a tight, small head on a fly, and that such threads tend to twist up in whip-finishes. Bjorn Beech went so far as to say he would never use anything but flat thread. And that's coming from a guy who ties more big steelhead flies than just about anyone.

One thread brand that has recently taken off is Veevus, and it seems to offer a nice compromise. This incredibly strong, somewhat flexible thread is round but will flatten out under pressure, allowing for very fine finish work.

TRENDING TOWARD SYNTHETICS

It's possible that future tiers will look back on this as the era when natural materials were supplanted by synthetic materials as the dominant feature of a fly.

The use of natural body materials, like silk floss and wool yarn, shifted to Antron yarn and chenille many years ago. Dubbings of baby seal, polar bear, and otter, to name a few, were replaced with insanely popular synthetic materials like STS Trilobal Dub, Ice Dub, SLF Dub, and at least a dozen others. The new synthetic dubbings have allowed us to produce bodies on our steelhead flies with more sparkle, translucence, and bugginess than the naturals, and in every imaginable color.

Synthetic materials that substitute for, or function as, hackles are relatively new on the scene, but they are probably crucial elements in the steelhead flies people will be fishing decades from now. Three factors influence the availability of natural feathers for our flies: (1) the difficulty/ethics associated with obtaining natural feathers and fur from animals, (2) the difficulty of raising healthy animals, especially birds, in captivity, and (3) competition between the fly-tying-materials wholesalers and the clothing fashion industry.

The first factor is illustrated by the decimation of wild jungle cock birds. Whether it be material like wild bird feathers, temple dog, or polar bear fur, none of us want to contribute to the demise of wild creatures in order to tie pretty flies. Or as Jeff Hickman says when he sees me tying with arctic fox, "Ozzy doesn't think that's cool."

The second factor refers to the fact that raising domesticated animals in confined habitats puts them at risk of infection, particularly various forms of bird flu that have the potential of devastating commercial

Synthetics like Craft Fur can produce flies that are just as lifelike as those made with natural materials. Workingman's Intruders, Sandy River, Alaska. ROB RUSSELL PHOTO

feather production. The third factor is illustrated by considering the example of ostrich. Any of us who tie with ostrich know that it is difficult to purchase consistently high-quality ostrich plumes. Why? Because Vegas showgirls and the fashion industry are first in line to purchase first-rate ostrich, and they are willing to pay top dollar for the best plumes. Then there's the auto industry, which uses ostrich to sweep dust from car parts before painting. They are actively buying up futures on ostrich, which could eventually spell the end of its availability for fly tiers. We fly tiers must be satisfied with the ostrich plumage that fails to meet the standards of higher-paying markets.

Another painful example of the fashion industry making cuts in our feather supply line was the virtual hijacking of grizzly saddles in 2011. We had become accustomed to using these long, slender saddle feathers in our Skagit Minnows and Intruders. But when Aerosmith lead-singer Steven Tyler went on television with feather implants in his hair, he launched a craze that ate up virtually all the grizzly saddles formerly reserved for fly tying. Thankfully the situation has eased somewhat as of 2015, but the supply is nowhere near what it was in 2010. Reliable unnamed sources in the fly-materials

industry caution me that there is no assurance that there will ever be the same plentiful access to long grizzly saddles that we might like to see.

Standing between the bird flu and the fashion industry, a wide variety of new synthetic materials offers hope to the creative steelhead fly tier. Many of the flashy, wiggly, flowy materials we are tending to use these days (stuff like Craft Fur, Polar Chenille, Senyo's Aqua Veil, and Predator Wrap) have been borrowed from the textile and handicraft industries, as well as the Christmas-decoration business. They are proving to be both attractive and effective, and have earned our trust in composing steelhead flies that possess vivid color, translucence, flow, sparkle, and wiggle: all characteristics we have come to expect.

Bottom Line: Look to Synthetics

If there is one admonition I hear from my friends in the materials industry it is this: Look to synthetics as the foundation for the future of fly tying. As attractive as natural feathers, fur, and hair might be, many issues threaten the continued flow of natural materials to the fly tier.

8

HOOKS, SHANKS,
AND TUBES

By Jay Nicholas

For three decades, from the 1960s through the 1980s, I only tied on two hooks: the Eagle Claw 1197 and the Mustad 36890. Old news. Not such great hooks. Then, along with everyone else, I migrated to the TMC 7999 and the TMC 700 hooks and found them much more to my liking. They were sharper, with a nicer profile. I will say, however, that the curve of the Eagle Claw 1197

hook is elegant in its own right and unlike any steelhead fly hook I can find these days.

This brings up an important matter for discussion: The hook's shape and wire diameter have great influence on the fly that we are able ultimately to create. One may have at hand the same pile of dubbing, chenille, winging, tinsels, hackles, and threads, but the fly one produces

Blending classic materials with space-age tube fly components produces a beautiful effect. JAY NICHOLAS PHOTO

will have an entirely different look and may also swim very differently, depending on the hook one uses for a foundation. The most extreme example of this is to look at the same pattern tied on a traditional hook, on a tube, and on a shank. No question that these flies will look and fish differently. But even when tying on hooks, the shape and the wire diameter, in addition to the eye and its general proportions, make a world of difference to the fly's character and performance. Whether the fish care or not is a matter of conjecture, and results will vary depending on circumstances. But there can be no doubt that many steelheaders are very particular about how their flies look, and that their hook choice is a key element of their creative process.

Here's a reference list of the most widely available hooks currently in use for most steelhead fly tying:

Alec Jackson

2050 Bronze Spey Fly Hook
2051 Black Spey Fly Hook
2052 Nickel Spey Fly Hook
2055 Gold Spey Fly Hook
2059 Blue Spey Fly Hook
2060 Heavy Wire Spey Fly Hook Bronze
2061 Heavy Wire Spey Fly Hook Black
2061 Heavy Wire Spey Fly Hook Nickel
2065 Heavy Wire Spey Fly Hook Gold
Alec Jackson's Black Steelhead Irons
Alec Jackson's Gold Steelhead Irons
Alec Jackson's Nickel Steelhead Irons
Alec Jackson's Black Steelhead Irons

Daiichi

2571 Boss Hook
7131 Double Salmon Hook
2151 Curved Shank Salmon Hook
2450 Short Shank Salmon Hook
2412 Low Water Salmon Hook
2117 Van Klinken Bomber Hooks
2441 Traditional Salmon Hook

Gamakatsu

Octopus
B10S Stinger
C14S Glo-Bug
L11S-3H Traditional Salmon Steelhead
T10-3H Salmon Fine Traditional
T10-3H Salmon Traditional
Sc15 Wide Gap

Olympic Peninsula Skagit Tactics (OPST)

Swing Hook

Owner

SSW, Needle-Point
SSW, Cutting-Point
SSW Straight-Eye

Partridge Salmon & Steelhead Hooks

Adlington & Hutchinson Blind Eye
Bartleet Blind Eye
Bartleet Single
Bartleet Supreme
Bartleet XL Blind Eye
Bomber Ring Eye
Heavy Salmon Single
Inline Single
Low Water Salmon
Low Water Salmon Single
Wilson Salmon Heavy Double
Low Water Double
Nordic Dow-Eye Double
Nordic Up-Eye Double
Outpoint Double
Wilson Double
Patriot Double Up-Eye
Patriot Single
Salar Double
Salar Single

Partridge Shanks

Intruder Shank
Waddington Shank
Waddington SS Shanks

Partridge Tube Fly Hooks

Intruder
Patriot Nordic Tube Double
Patriot Nordic Tube Single
Patriot Stinger Barbless Single
Patriot Stinger Tube Single
Salar Tube
Salar Tube Double
Salar Tube Treble

TMC

105
700
7999
7989

Favorite Tube Fly Hooks

2557 Daiichi Intruder, black
2553 Daiichi Intruder, red
1650 Daiichi Heavy Wire Tube Fly Hook
1648 Daiichi Alec Jackson's Tube Fly
Gamakatsu Octopus
Owner SSW, Needle- or Cutting-Point
Owner SSW Straight-Eye
Owner Tube Fly Ring Eye
OPST Swing Hook

Shanks and Tubes

Back when I was tying my simple traditional steelhead flies on so-called normal hooks, I would use between a size 2 and a size 6. Orders for steelhead flies smaller than a size 6 were rare. Even the flies tied on size 2 hooks were a small proportion of a year's production, reserved for the extremes of winter steelhead fishing. I remember reading about people fishing for winter steelhead at that time. They were using size 3/0 (and larger) hooks in an effort to get their flies down to the fish. I never filled an order for such large flies, but I did fish them myself in the mid-1960s and again in the late '70s.

I especially remember reading about a mysterious fellow named Bill McMillan, who reportedly fished giant Paint Brush flies tied on bronze, heavy-wire Mustad hooks, fished on a dead drift upstream. No strike indicator, just old-school nymphing, with a swing at the end. Bill was doing his part to pioneer methods for winter steelhead, fishing weeks on end without connecting to a steelhead. Nevertheless, he persisted and eventually saw rewards from his efforts. McMillan was the source of my inspiration to tie and fish size 3/0 and 4/0 Green Butt Skunks and Golden Demons for the winter months on Oregon's Big Elk Creek during the late 1960s. I tried the technique again on the Elk River in 1978 and 1979. I remember the thrill and surprise of hooking steelhead in both rivers with my "giant" flies, although I didn't land any. Those 3/0 and 4/0 Mustads provided significant weight and a great foundation for flies with a large profile, but the heavy-gauge wire made them difficult to set into a steelhead's mouth. Looking back on it now, those flies would seem quite small by today's standards, but our new technologies have eliminated the need for such heavy-wire hooks. Shanks and tubes have finally come into their own in the steelheading world. After more than 20 years of steady input from the Atlantic schools of fly tying, and thanks largely to the Internet and global markets, North American fly tiers are nearly in step with their Atlantic salmon brethren. Today it is routine to tie a fly of nearly any length and profile, without the burden of a giant ungainly hook. Even the most enormous steelhead flies, say 3 or 4 inches long, can be coupled with a small (say size 2), light-wire, short shank hook.

Let's Talk Shanks for a Moment

The earliest use of flies tied on shanks appears to have come from the fly-trolling schools of the British Isles and took hold along the Eastern Seaboard. Since trollers were not limited in their fly size by having to cast, they could create flies that matched the size of their piscine prey.

They connected hooks with loops of wire and cord, not bothering to break off the points of the forward hooks, since gathering food was a primary consideration. These giant flies were then trolled through lakes and estuaries behind human-powered canoes and dories.

The Waddington Shank was popularized by Richard Waddington during the 1940s and 1950s. These shanks were models for today's modern products, like Greg Senyo's Articulated Intruder Shanks and the Partridge brand Waddingtons. More Intruder-specific varieties, like the shanks from OPST, Dave McNeese, and Scott Howell, have subtly redefined the genre, although they can also be seen as the equivalent of a sacrificial hook. But as simple as they are, they are providing some return flow of inspiration from the Pacific Coast back to Europe as they are adopted by Atlantic tiers.

Many innovative steelhead tiers have opted to build their flies on spinner wire. Talk about a cheap and reliable shank—there are no downsides. Piano wire is another great source of shank material, available at most hobby stores in 3-foot lengths. *Note:* Make sure you have a top-notch pair of wire cutters if you decide to work with piano wire.

As a small-scale, part-time commercial tier/angler from the 1960s through 1980s, I was oblivious to tube and shank-tied flies of any sort rigged with short shank trailer hooks. Both of these fly styles would certainly have been superior in fish hooking and landing power than the flies I tied and fished on 3/0 hooks—and both were certainly being tied and fished by others, even though I was still tying and fishing in the dark, so to speak.

Olympic Peninsula Skagit Tactics (OPST)

OPST is a small company dedicated to providing specialized tying and fishing products oriented around the use of Intruder-style flies and Skagit-style casting with single- and double-handed rods. That sounds like a broad brush for a niche product line, but their offerings are impressive. Jerry French, Ed Ward, and Ben Paull run the business and develop the products—unique mono running lines, super-short Skagit heads, steelhead shanks, dumbbell eye shanks, swing hooks, a dubbing spinner, signature barred ostrich plumes, dotted Intruder plumes, junction tubing, and trailing hook wire.

I prefer by far to tie on these OPST steelhead and dumbbell eye shanks versus tying on a traditional hook and using wire cutters to cut off the hook at the end of the process. The OPST shanks are straight, there is nothing to cut off—no sharp metal that begs to be smoothed with a file or hone—and the dumbbell eye shanks offer a secure base for lashing on weighted eyes. Check out their business listing on page 308.

Tubes

Tube flies tipped with short-shank hooks seem to have been developed and popularized during the 1930s and were sold by Mrs. W. Morawski, a professional fly dresser in Scotland. Her flies were tied on the hollow quill of a bird feather, which seems consistent with an assertion that a similar form of tube fly was used by American Indians (an Internet reference I've not been able to verify), predating the availability of metal fish hooks.

As with shanks, the adoption of tubes by steelheaders lagged far behind that of Atlantic salmon and saltwater anglers. It wasn't until the 1990s that Northwest anglers like Bob Clay and Lani Waller popularized and adapted tubes to their steelhead applications. I had read about tying tube flies on empty ballpoint pen ink tubes and cotton-tipped swabs. The swab option sounded cleaner to me, less dangerous than the ink cartridge route. I also explored bulk tubing sourced from a laboratory supply company but was never sufficiently commited to tying on tubes to justify taking this plunge. In the process of shooting videos for the *Oregon Fly Fishing Blog*, I've explored several varieties, sizes, and materials for tube flies, including soft and hard plastic, aluminum lined and unlined tubes, copper tubes lined and unlined, tapered metal tubes, painted metal tubes, and plastic tubes of most any diameter and color one can imagine.

These options represent the range of prepackaged products offered by companies like HMH, Frödin, Eumer, the Canadian Tube Fly Company, and Pro Sportfisher. While this list may seem comprehensive, I'm sure I'm missing a few. All of these manufacturers offer excellent products that perform well and allow one to tie great tube flies. Denmark-based Pro Sportfisher and its representative in the States, Bruce Berry, deserve a lot of credit for demystifying the process of tying tube flies. Their products and supporting YouTube videos have made tying on tubes accessible and understandable for most fly tiers to such an extent that the style will undoubtedly spread far, wide, and fast in the coming years. Pro Sportfisher upped the ante in the highly competitive fly-tying materials market by offering a dizzying array (no exaggeration) of tube-fly components, all of which fit together beautifully. This means that every cone they make fits on the basic tubes they offer—same with their hook guides (junction tubing). Now imagine what it is like to walk up to a pegboard wall in a fly shop and look at 60 (a made-up number to illustrate the point) different colors and sizes of coneheads, assured that every one of the pretty little things will fit on the tube you have purchased. And every hook guide in every color will fit on the same tube, accommodating the largest to the smallest hooks.

Then imagine the 60 shapes, sizes, and colors of weights that all fit perfectly with your basic tube. Suddenly, tying a tube fly becomes a worry-free venture wherein one need only decide whether or not to add weight, what colors to use, and what sizes of weights and cones and junction tubes to use. Pro Sportfisher also supplies materials including dubbing, hair for wings, hair for dubbing brushes, imitation jungle cock, shellbacks for little trout flies and giant tarpon flies, soft heads for saltwater streamers, and is now venturing into the musky and pike arenas with extra-large, extra-heavy tubes and tabbed eyes that seem likely to be attractive to all manner of predaceous species.

Overall, the ability to mix and match all of the essential components of tube flies make the Pro Sportfisher brand an easy sell to tiers who want the assurance that the components they purchase will actually fit onto the tube properly. That said, many tube-fly designs are simple enough that they don't require anything more than a length of tube and a short bit of junction tubing.

9

TRAILING LOOPS AND
STINGER HOOKS

By Rob Russell

The current trend of using a stinger hook loop has some of the same disadvantages of the extra-long shanks we used to use. Not so much because of leverage, but because of swing weight. And if the fly is big and the stinger hook loop too long, it's possible to hook fish poorly and in some damaging places like the eyes, or gill plate, or deep in the throat or tongue. When I use a stinger hook loop, I make a point to keep it as short as possible.

—*Jerry French, 2015*

The question of how best to rig a trailing hook deserves some attention given the variety of solutions in use today. There are four main decisions to make: 1) loop material, 2) loop length, 3) the type and size of hook, and 4) the method by which the loop material is secured to the fly. A properly balanced rigging holds the hook precisely where you want it under all current speeds. That means if you like to swing soft

When a steelhead "dog bones" a large fly with a trailing hook, the results can be unfortunate. This small Umpqua hen was lucky the hook didn't go into her eye. ROB RUSSELL PHOTO

water, or if you like to let every swing marinate slowly through the last delicious little bit, you need a fairly stiff material for your loop. As Jerry warns in the quote above, trailing hooks can end up dropping below the horizon of the fly, dragging the fly down. And, most troubling of all, long or limp riggings are more hazardous to fish.

We'll cover the pros and cons of some top materials below, but—spoiler alert!—all you really need to know is that a stiff monofilament or wire loop of about 1 inch is the ticket. In our pseudoscientific tests between 2011 and 2016, Maxima brand monofilament from 20 to 25 pound emerged as the lightest, stiffest, most reliable loop material. Surflon and other steel wires came in a close second and were only downgraded because of their relative weight. When a little added weight is warranted, wire loops are a great choice. The sturdy trailing loops that mono and wire provide not only keep the hook in the strike zone but also prevent fouling—that annoying phenomenon when a trailing hook catches on the fly or tippet and hangs backward. Fouling usually happens during casting, as our flies are being jerked around at impossible speeds and ripped through the riparian vegetation. But fouling can also be caused by a missed strike from any number of fish species. Any strike that doesn't connect can cause the line to spring back, flipping the hook up toward the head of the fly. Few things are

worse than reeling up at the end of a run to find out you weren't even fishing, especially if you had a couple of good tugs.

One thing that is much worse than missing a strike is reeling in a fish that is bleeding from the gills, or has had its eye torn out by a bad hookup. Some bad hook-ups can't be helped—they are one of the risks in our sometimes bloody sport. But there is general agreement among experienced steelheaders that long trailing loops are hazardous to a fish's health. So, in addition to using a stiff material, it's a good idea to keep trailing loops as short as possible. That directive butts up against one of the great benefits of trailing loops: the ability they give us to replace hooks as needed. To allow for the replacement of hooks, the minimum loop length is between 2.3 and 3 cm (⅞" and 1³⁄₁₆"). That range is based on Gamakatsu Octopus hooks from size 4 up to size 1/0. A 2.5 cm (1") loop is a good standard, and a nice fit for size 2 hooks. The 2.5 cm (1") loop is a tight fit for size 1 and too small for 1/0. Straight-eye hooks are not a good fit for stiff trailing loops. Up-eye or down-eye hooks are required in order to align the hook shank parallel to the fly shank. Even with up- and down-eye hooks, some bending of the trailing loop around the curvature of the hook eye is required in order to get the best possible parallel alignment.

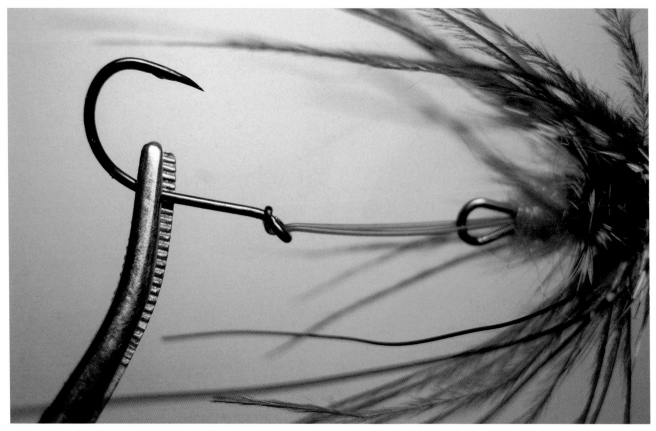

Proper hook alignment can be achieved with a mono loop. Just bend the monofilament around the eye of the hook until it rides the way you want it. ROB RUSSELL PHOTO

Securely fastening a loop to a fly shank falls in the category of "critical" steps for obvious reasons. We offer a couple of step-by-step descriptions of the trailing loop process on pages 55 (Decoteau's Fifth Element) and 67 (Hickman's Fish Taco). The canyons of our great rivers reverberate with the tortured screams of those who fall down on this step. They feel the grab, feel the pulse of adrenaline, a quick yank, and nothing. In the half second before the fish turned to run, when time stood still, they thought back to the night before. Did they remember to glue the thread wraps?

Solid trailing loops must always involve three steps: 1) a base layer of thread, 2) the securing of the loop material along the entire length of the fly shank, then doubled back and lashed down the shank again in the opposite direction, and 3) a couple drops of Zap-A-Gap or superglue over the thread wraps. It does not pay to skimp on any of those steps. For added strength some fly patterns run the loop through the eye of the fly shank. It's a great idea, but it requires using a fly shank with a large eye to accommodate for the loop material. Check out Mr. Fox's Sleech on page 201 for an example of this technique.

Fireline Loops

Berkeley's Fireline in the 30-pound-test weight has been the reigning king of trailing-loop material for commercial fly producers over the last few years. It is the best option among the many braided and gel-spun lines due to its superior stiffness. It is commonly doubled or even quadrupled for added strength and stiffness on salmon and steelhead flies. It comes in green, black, white ("crystal"), and chartreuse ("high-vis"), giving the tier a choice of complementary colors to choose from. The only downside to Fireline is that its stiffness wears out quickly—often within a couple of hours of steady casting and swinging. Once the finish is worn off, the material gets quite limp, which can lead to more fouled hooks.

Charles St. Pierre settled on Fireline as his preferred loop material years ago, and he stands by it today.

"The one thing I've learned, though," Charles said, "is that even as stiff as Fireline is, the longer your loop, the more likely your hook will foul. It's important to keep your trailing loop as short as you can—just long enough to loop a hook onto."

Monofilament Loops

Mono loops made from Maxima Ultragreen and Chameleon performed exceptionally well in our field tests from 2011 to 2016, leading us to prefer them over all others. Jeff Hickman deserves a lot of credit for the widespread use of 25-pound Maxima Chameleon as a loop material, and he has demonstrated its advantages for over a decade. The downside is its diameter. Doubled-over 25-pound Maxima can be hard to force into the eye of an Octopus or SSW hook. As we describe on page 68, getting a mono loop through the eye of a hook often requires crimping with pliers, which can compromise the strength of the loop if overdone. Stepping down to 20-pound makes the process go smoothly, but the resulting loop may not hold up to many hook changes before becoming worn and weak.

When asked whether his Chameleon loops have ever failed, Jeff smiles: "I've never had one break on me. There were a couple of times I was worried, but it's never happened."

Wire Loops

Bjorn Beech was among the first commercial steelhead tiers to introduce steel wire to his flies. Back in the 1990s, he picked through catalogs in search of the perfect material and landed on Surflon, which he still uses today. Similar products can be found in craft and fabric stores, usually sold for beading. Recently Greg Senyo developed a specialized line of colored Intruder wire, as has Olympic Peninsula Skagit Tactics (OPST). The only downside to wire loops is their weight, but if added weight is desirable, wire is perfect. Field testing so far has proven wire loops to be trustworthy, even for the biggest, hottest fish. Like monofilament, the stiffness of wire requires careful crimping with a pair of pliers before threading it through the eye of the hook.

10

TYING AND FISHING
MODERN STEELHEAD FLIES

Text by Rob Russell. Photos by Jon Jensen, unless otherwise noted.

Decoteau's Fifth Element

Mike Decoteau is one of the shining stars of the Great Lakes fly-tying scene. Hailing from Columbus, Ohio, Mike has developed his own original fly patterns for just about every species of fish that swims. Smallmouth bass tend to dominate the watery world he calls home, but he devotes many hours tying flies for resident trout, lake-run browns, freshwater drum (or sheep's head), and steelhead. He's one of the more prolific commercial tiers working today, rivaling the production of Bjorn Beech and Greg Senyo. His fantastic fly patterns are showcased on the blog *Steelhead Alley Fly Tying* (steelheadalleyflytying .blogspot.com).

The Fifth Element combines classic style with modern techniques and materials. The result is pure perfection.

Tying materials for the Fifth Element in blue and purple.

I worked up the Fifth Element to serve as a high and dirty water fly for Great Lakes tributaries. I wanted a fly in my box that I could go to when relying more on vibration than on visibility. The bulk in the head is primarily created by the collar of fox that is center tied with the butt ends folded back and hollow tied. The head on this fly displaces a fair bit of water, resulting in lots of movement in the wing trailing behind.

Although designed for dirty water, I have tied it in a variety of weights for different situations and had success pretty much everywhere I have fished it. As a matter of fact, my friend Jasper fished a white version Maine for a season, almost exclusively for landlocked salmon and brook trout, with much success. I brought pink ones to Alaska for coho [see attached photo].

—Michael Decoteau, September 1, 2015

FIFTH ELEMENT, BLUE/PURPLE

- **Shank:** 25 mm Senyo's Articulated Shank, black
- **Stinger loop:** Senyo's Intruder wire, purple, 2.5 cm (1") loop
- **Thread:** 6/0 UNI-Thread, purple
- **Weight (optional):** Small lead eyes
- **Rear dubbing ball:** Ice Dub, steelie blue
- **Body:** Flat Diamond Braid, pearl
- **Wing:** In four parts, from back to front: 1) arctic fox tail, kingfisher blue; 2) Mirage Flashabou, pearl; 3) arctic fox tail, purple; 4) Master Bright dubbing, purple, brushed out long (or Angel Hair, purple)
- **Collar:** In three parts, from back to front: 1) Senyo's Laser Dub, purple; 2) golden pheasant tail fibers; 3) ringneck pheasant rump feather dyed black
- **Topping:** Holographic Flashabou, purple haze
- **Head:** SLF Kaufmann Blend, black stone
- **Cheeks (optional):** Jungle cock nails
- **Hook:** #4 Gamakatsu Octopus, blue
- **Special tools:** None needed

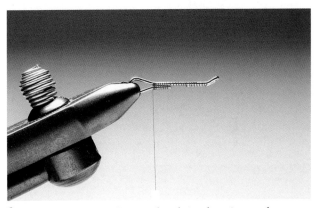

1. Secure a 25 mm Senyo shank in the vise and lay down a base layer of thread from front to back, stopping the thread at the rear.

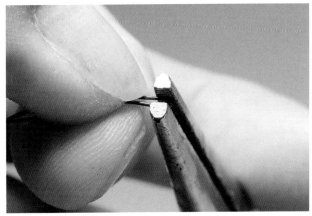

2. Cut a 3-inch piece of Intruder wire and fold it in half. Crimp the loop gently with a pair of needle-nose pliers.

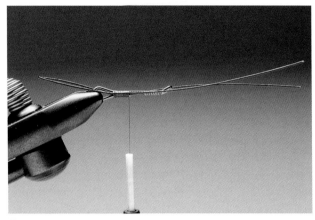

3. Tie in the wire on either side of the shank, lashing each side down to the front of the shank's rear loop.

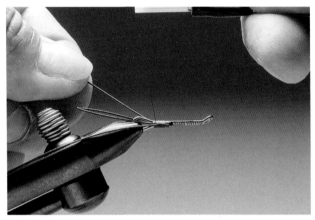

4. Fold the tag ends back underneath the shank and secure. Trim the ends flush and Zap-A-Gap the connection point.

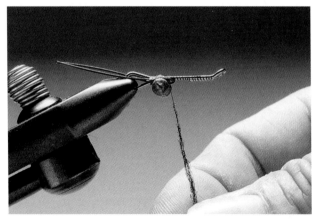

5. Tie in the lead dumbbells eyes on the underside of the shank as shown.

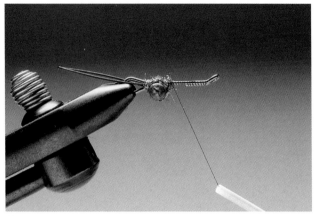

6. Dub a ball of steelie blue Ice Dub around the weight.

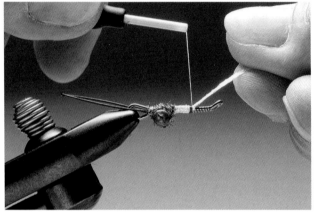

7. Tie in the pearl Diamond Braid and take two or three wraps around the shank just to the end of the return eye. Tie it off and leave a ¾-inch tag of the Diamond Braid sticking up.

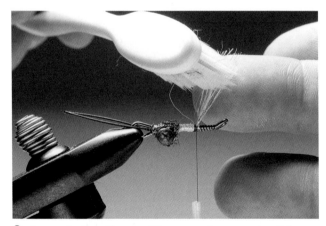

8. Separate the fibers with your scissors or bodkin, or just brush them out with a toothbrush.

9. Cut a bunch of kingfisher blue arctic fox fur for the wing. Pull the smallest fibers from the bunch and discard. Pull the guard hairs out and set aside.

10. Tie in the fox hair and add the guard hairs directly on top.

11. Double over six strands of pink Mirage Flashabou and tie in on top of the fox hair.

12. Cut a small bunch of purple arctic fox tail. Remove the guard hairs from this bunch and discard. Tie the hair in so that it spreads out evenly around the shank. The butt ends should be sticking out beyond the eye.

13. Fold the butt ends back and wrap over them slightly to hold them back. Brush out the ends and sculpt with scissors as needed to eliminate the "chopped" look of the squarely cut ends. These ends will help create bulk in the head of the fly.

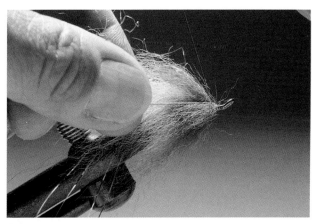

14. Fold and tie in a bunch of purple Master Bright (or Angel Hair as substitute).

15. Center-tie a clump of purple Senyo's Laser Dub on the top and another on the bottom of the shank.

18. Double-over four strands of purple haze holographic Flashabou and tie in on top.

16. Advance the thread ahead of the clumps, pull the dubbing back, and make several wraps to hold it back. Brush lightly.

19. Tie in a black ringneck pheasant body feather by the tip and wrap around the shank creating a collar.

17. Cut 16 to 18 long fibers from a golden pheasant tail and separate them into eight or nine parts consisting of two fibers a piece. Tie these evenly around the shank.

20. Center-tie clumps of black stone Kaufmann SLF Blend at the head, one on top and one on the bottom.

21. Advance the thread ahead of the clumps and make several wraps.

22. Tie in the jungle cock nails on either side of the fly. Before cutting the butt ends, fold them back and tie over them to secure them in place and prevent them from pulling out.

23. Zap-A-Gap or lacquer the head and attach a blue #4 Gamakatsu Octopus hook.

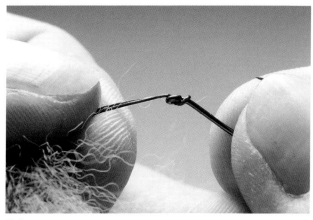

24. Roll the wire loop over the hook wire to kink it slightly so the hook runs parallel to the shank.

FISHING THE FIFTH ELEMENT

Decoteau's Fifth Element is equally at home swinging broad, even runs or poking through pocket water. It has enough weight to be dropped into slots and swung through fast water, but wherever it's fished, it maintains a full bait-fish profile. Like so many of the most effective Great Lakes patterns, the Fifth Element displaces water as it moves and takes on the physical traits of a fleeing goby or sculpin.

The Fifth Element dresses up every fish it catches, not least this fresh silver salmon.
MICHAEL DECOTEAU, RED SPOT FLY, PHOTO

Fergus's Mother of All Leeches (MOAL)

Derek Fergus has received worldwide acclaim as the originator of the MOAL, as well as the Strung Out series of steelhead, trout, and salmon flies. When considering which of the hundreds of modern steelhead patterns should be featured in our step-by-step section, the MOAL was an easy choice. The technical innovation alone, as simple as it may seem, rivals the Intruder for its ingenuity and for its impact on the steelheading landscape.

Fergus has been fishing the MOAL since the late 1990s, when he first came up with the idea for a different kind of bunny leech. String leeches had become very popular in that period, and they were deadly effective. Trey Combs had shared his initiation to the pattern in his masterwork, *Steelhead Fly Fishing*, in 1991. In the years that followed, the fly had become a commercial hit. But Derek didn't like the limitation of having the fur on just one side of the leather strip. He felt like the typical cut strip of rabbit fur was too angular and tended to ride like a piece of tape instead of something natural. He started experimenting with ways to build a bunny-strip fly with 360-degree fur, and soon he was lining up two vises on his bench to create tandem-hook flies connected by loops of soft Dacron cord. When he first applied a drop of superglue to the leather strip, the light went on, and a fly was born. Derek made up a bunch of early prototypes, fished them hard, and got results. He was pumped, not just by the way steelhead hit them but by the way they stayed hooked. Over the next couple of seasons, he refined the technique until he had prototypes that were ready for commercial production. Derek flew to Vietnam to set up a production facility, and soon the MOAL was filling bins in fly shops around the world.

"The goal was to come up with a fly that didn't have a rudder in the back and moved as freely as possible," Derek said, weaving a MOAL through the air. "This fly looks alive from every angle."

Other tiers caught on quickly and created their own versions, but the MOAL held its position in fly shops. (One of the best-known variations of the MOAL is Mr. Fox's Sleech, incorporating Polar Flash and trout beads. You can find the illustrious Mr. Fox in the gallery on page 202.) "When we started mixing multiple colors and other materials like ostrich, that's what really set the MOAL apart. We could add colors at any point in the fly!"

A big-water MOAL in purple and pink with a tungsten bead head for getting down in strong current.

As for why steelhead love the MOAL, Derek has his ideas. "Fish love leeches. I really think it goes back to the whole squid thing," Derek said. "Steelhead don't hesitate with this fly. They just eat it!"

Fergus has gone on to develop hundreds of fly patterns using his Strung Out technique. He is brimming with stories of short-striking steelhead that drove him crazy until he showed them a Strung Out Somethin-or-Nother. Wherever he goes he talks up the benefits of a small-shanked hook positioned squarely at the rear of the fly.

We're stoked to have a handful of Derek's other fantastic creations in the fly gallery on page 195. We chose to share here a two-tone version of the MOAL that is held in very high esteem in our home waters of Northwest Oregon.

Materials for tying the MOAL in purple and pink.

TWO-TONE MOAL, PURPLE/PINK

- **Front hook:** Any straight-eye hook with a large enough eye to accommodate doubled-up Dacron; #2 Tiemco 811S shown
- **Rear hook:** #2 Gamakatsu Octopus, red
- **Thread:** 6/0 UNI-Thread, red
- **Underbody:** 20- or 30-pound Dacron backing
- **Bead:** 3.8 mm Hareline Plummeting Tungsten bead, painted pink
- **Overbody:** Crosscut rabbit strips, pink and purple
- **Glue:** Tear Mender
- **Flash:** Mirage Flashabou
- **Collar:** Ice Dub, purple
- **Special Tools:** Secondary vise, bobbin threader, wire cutters, file

Set up two vises. Clamp-style will allow you to keep the underbody at maximum tension, but you can get away with heavy pedestal vises.

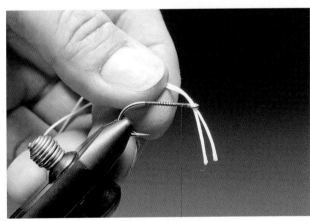

1. Place the front hook in the front vise and lay down a base layer of thread from the eye of the hook to the bend of the hook. Cut a 15.2 cm (6") long section of 30-pound-test backing and fold it in half. Wet the ends and thread them through the eye of the front hook, or use a bobbin threader to pull the Dacron through in the opposite direction.

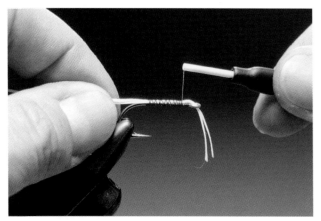

2. Measure the Dacron loop so it extends to a total fly length of 7.6 cm (3") and bind it down along the shank of the front hook with your thread.

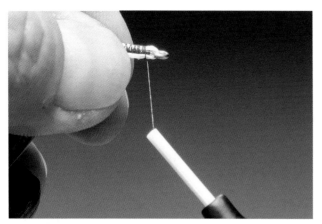

3. Pull the tag ends back along the underside of the hook shank and wrap them down, trimming off any excess.

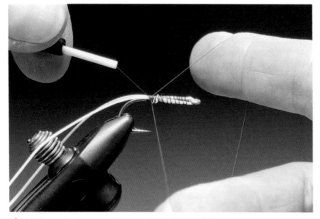

4. Whip finish and trim the thread flush.

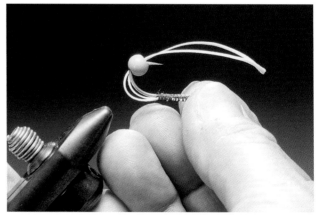

5. Remove the hook from the vise and slide a Plummeting Tungsten bead onto the Dacron loop, then onto the hook. Make sure you lead with the small-diameter end so it ends up snugging up to the eye of the hook.

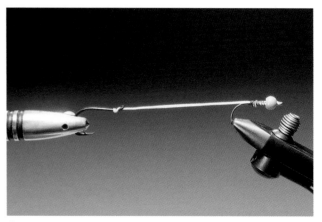

6. Thread an Octopus hook onto the Dacron loop until you can open the loop enough to give it a half twist and pass it back over the hook. This securely attaches the rear hook in a figure eight. Place the rear hook in the second vise as shown. We used two pedestal vises here, meaning we could not keep the Dacron very tight, but it did allow us to move the vises around as needed without any fuss. If you're using clamp-style vises, the following couple of steps may need to be modified slightly.

7. Bring the rear vise forward a couple of inches to loosen tension, then open up the figure-eight Dacron loop just enough to slip the end of your pink crosscut rabbit strip into the gap. It's critical that the bare skin or leather side is facing the hook with rabbit hair pointing backward. Pull the rear vise back until it's a tight as you can get it. You can start your thread again near the eye of the front hook, or you can wait until you've nearly finished with the rabbit strips. Gently squeeze out a tin bead of Tear Mender glue along the first inch of the Dacron and wrap the pink bunny strip forward the same distance. Gently fold the fur back as you wrap, being careful to trap as few fibers as possible.

8. Cut the rabbit strip and slip the end of it between the two strands of Dacron.

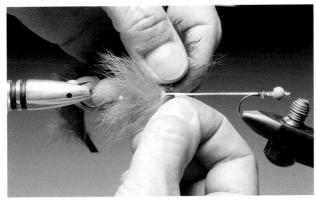

9. Slide the end of the purple crosscut rabbit strip in the same gap, again making sure that the fur is pointing toward the rear of the fly.

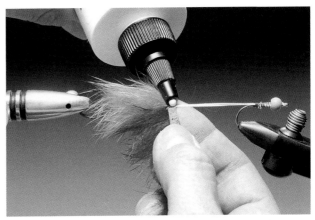

10. Apply a drop of glue to the gap and wrap the purple rabbit strip forward one turn, covering the junction of the pink and purple strips.

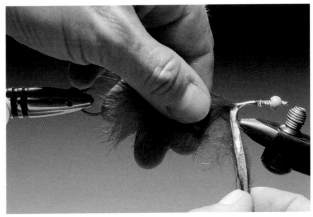

11. Apply a thin bead of Tear Mender along an inch or so of the rabbit strip and wind forward, gently folding back the fur as you go. Do not overlap your wraps at all, but keep each precisely in front of the last. Use the minimum amount of glue to avoid dripping.

12. With your thread secure on the front hook, continue gluing and wrapping the rabbit strip until it nearly butts up to the back of the bead. Tie off the bunny and trim the end flush.

13. Add two or three strands of Mirage Flashabou on either side and trim them so they are the full length of the fly.

14. Wrap a thin collar of purple Ice Dub over your thread wraps. Whip finish and cement.

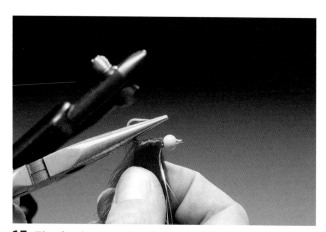

15. The final stage of building a MOAL is to clip off the front hook at the bend using strong wire cutters and file the end smooth. The filing step is optional, but a sharp edge can end up cutting through the Dacron in extreme circumstances (like a big, crazy steelhead).

FISHING THE MOAL

The MOAL we've tied here is a dredger, sporting a large tungsten bead. But MOALs can be constructed using any cone or bead you prefer. You may need a drill to widen the holes in some beads and cones in order to fit them over your front hook of choice.

Since this MOAL is so heavy, it's a great fly for dropping and dredging in heavy water, focusing on the first half of a swing. There are always a few runs where we know there are plenty of fish, but our typical swinging tactics won't get us down into the zone. Let's face it, we're talking about jig water, and this fly can get you there. You don't need a heavy tip, just 10 or 12 feet of type III or type VI. Cast the fly across and slightly upstream and throw a mend upstream. This allows the fly to drop very quickly. Trust your gut—you'll probably know instinctively when you are getting too deep and need to tighten up and swing the fly. If you don't have those instincts, you'd better have a pile of flies to get your through your education. Swing the MOAL as far inside as you dare without hanging up, then try it again, this time taking one or two steps downstream after the mend. The ultimate place for this technique is any deep slot on the far bank. You can get to depth almost instantly by taking off all tension, with either a mend, a step, or by paying out line. Then direct the swing with your rod tip, bringing it across at whatever speed you desire. Some people would haggle over whether this is truly fly fishing, others would categorize it under the "dark arts." We're not afraid to say it's jig fishing with a fly rod, and sometimes, when you're really jonesin' for steel, it's just what the doctor ordered.

Hickman's Fish Taco

I asked Jeff Hickman about the origins of his now iconic Fish Taco while I rowed him and his father, Scott, down the river one drizzly May morning. We were sneaking in a half-day float through the Tillamook Dairylands, looking for whatever species of fish happened to be swimming by. Scott, a critical member of the broodstock that created Hickmanimal back in the day, was learning to roll cast for the first time. Don't ask me how that was possible. Jeff is one of the most gifted casting instructors around; how had the two of them never gotten around to casting lessons? It dawned on me that Jeff had probably found his love for fly fishing without the usual paternal steerings.

It felt strange asking Jeff about his flagship fly for the purposes of the book project. But weeks earlier, thinking I could write the chapter off the top of my head based on my experience with the fly and its creator, my cluelessness was stunning. After all the years, all the fishing, all the whiskey-drenched geek fests, I couldn't explain how or why Hickman first authored his ostrich herl masterpiece.

"It grew out of Mister Hankey, actually," Jeff said, doing his best to reach back to his first year with Idylwilde Flies. "I remember Jon Covich was repping Idylwilde and had somehow heard about my foam mouse pattern. At the time there were a lot of guides in Alaska and Russia who were concerned about the high mortality of rainbows caught on mice. I was one of them, and had I come up with a drowned-rat sort of thing with a trailing size 4 Gamakatsu hook on the end. I think it was the first time I ever used Maxima Chameleon for a stinger loop, and I really liked how it was working. Rainbows weren't getting hurt, and the hooking-to-landing ratio seemed to improve." Sales of Hickman's Mister Hankey took off that summer. Instantly Jeff had the attention of Chris Conaty, the head of product development at Idylwilde. Chris asked him to submit some new flies for the coming season, and Jeff got to work.

"At that time I was guiding quite a bit, but also working a couple of days a week at Countrysport," Jeff recalled. Countrysport, the only fly shop in downtown Portland at the time, was a great home base for a skyrocketing steelhead guide. "The only good-size commercial flies we had were either too heavily weighted or they just didn't move the ways I wanted. I loved Intruders but

The Fish Taco is quick to tie, and offers all the profile and movement of a full-dress Intruder.

Jeff is a bit of a rock star in the fly-fishing world.
You should tease him about it whenever possible.
ROB RUSSELL PHOTO

Right: Duffy reused some of those purple Tacos all
frigging season, and they just kept getting better.
Miss that guy. ROB RUSSELL PHOTO

wanted something quick and easy to tie. So I started
messing around with quick-tie variations on an ostrich
herl Intruder. I wanted a short, buggy body and a stinger
loop that stayed straight in all current speeds."

And so the first Fish Taco passed to Idylwilde and
then to the world. As usual, it took a while to catch on.
One thing that helped drive fly sales right out of the gate
was the preseason order from Larimer Outfitters. Jeff
guided the Clackamas and Deschutes for Tom Larimer,
along with Mike Duffy. Those guys ran a lot of trips and
burned through box after box of Tacos in purple, black,
red, and pink, in roughly that order of popularity.

Jeff's quick-tie Intruder, in all the 15 minutes it took
to tie, had just about everything a long-form fly could
offer. The long ostrich did every bit of its job, catching
the eye with crazy undulation, unencumbered by the
rest of the materials. The fat, dubbed body palmered

with bristly saddle hackle looked buggy as hell and pushed the fly's tentacles outward ever so slightly. The Flashabou, while over the top by my standards, looked great and somehow didn't seem to dominate the fly. It was beautiful, and somewhere between that moment and the subsequent moment when Hickman aimed me directly at a pile of steelhead and said, "Try a cast over there," I was sold.

Jeff's confidence in the monofilament trailing loop at the rear end of the fly is absolute, and I test him on it constantly to see if there's any hint of doubt in the deepest recesses of his mind. Early in my experience with the Fish Taco, I really didn't like how the Chameleon loop tended to cock the hook off at a weird angle (more on this geeky-but-important topic of trailing loops on page 51). I soon learned I could easily remedy this problem by rolling the mono over the hook eye until the angle was perfect.

There is one last feature of the Fish Taco that everyone comes to realize, but it's worth mentioning: The Fish Taco happens to be one of the most durable flies imaginable. The older they get, the more faded the colors, the sexier they look. It's pretty incredible, actually. Check out more of Jeff's flies on page 222 in our fly gallery.

Materials for tying a black Fish Taco.

FISH TACO, BLACK

- **Shank:** .040" diameter spinner wire, with 1 cm (⅜") folded over to create eye
- **Thread:** 6/0 UNI-Thread, red
- **Stinger loop:** 25- or 30-pound Maxima Chameleon, 2.5 cm (1") loop
- **Butt:** Ice Dub, red
- **Body:** Ice Dub, purple, palmered with grizzly saddle hackle
- **Rib:** Small wire, copper or brass
- **Hackle:** Ostrich herl, black, 32 fibers
- **Flash:** Holographic Flashabou, black, 25 to 30 strands
- **Collar:** Jumbo guinea hen, natural
- **Hook:** #2 Gamakatsu Octopus
- **Special tools:** Fine-nose hackle pliers or electrical wire test clips (shown)

Fish Tacos may be tied on any kind of shank or tube, but in the interest of documenting Jeff's preferred method, we've gone with the spinner wire. You can find it in bundles of a billion or in little packets of 10 or 20. Might as well get a billion.

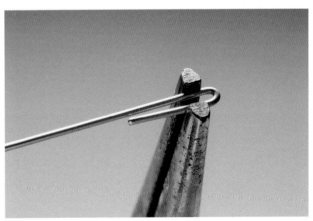

1. Start with a 7.6 cm (3") section of .040-inch-diameter spinner wire. There should be no pretwisted eyes on either end. File one end smooth to avoid it cutting your thread later. Using a pair of needle-nose pliers, or whatever bendy tool you have, bend 1 cm (⅜") of the smooth end over on itself and crimp it. Be careful not to crimp so hard that you close the loop. This may take a few practice sessions to nail down. You've just created the eye of your fly. Now put a 90-degree bend perpendicular to the eye in about the middle of the remaining shank. This angle will help to hold the shank steady in the vise during tying. With

the shank secure, start your thread about 3 mm (⅛")
back from the eye end, then wrap back 2.5 cm (1").
Wrap forward to the butt end of your wire loop, then
back to the rear. This extra layer of thread will help
bind the trailing loop to the shank.

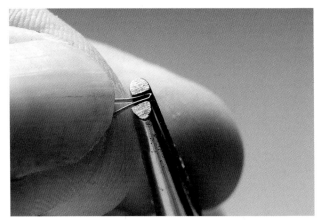

2. Cut a 7.6 cm (3") section of 25-pound-test Maxima
Chameleon. Fold it in half and use your pliers to
lightly crimp the loop. It will need to be well crimped
in order to fit through the eye of the Octopus hook.
Test the first few to make sure you are comfortable
you can get your loops through a size 2 hook. Some
people fudge and go down to 20-pound Chameleon;
others go with Owner hooks, which have slightly
larger eyes. The downside to the Owner hook is its
added weight, which can dog the fly and prevent it
from swimming to the best of its abilities. If you're
gonna fudge, go with the lighter mono, but don't
come crying to us if a mega steelhead busts you off
someday. We're teaching you the right way.

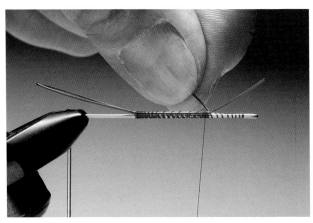

3. Measure out a 2.5 cm (1") loop, tie it down at the
back of the fly, and wrap forward just shy of the eye.
Bend the ends of the mono back tightly, crimping the
bend with your thumbnail. Wrap the thread back over
the doubled-up monofilament to the end and clip the
ends close.

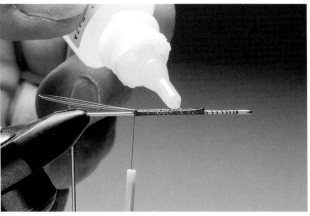

4. Added wraps of thread will help secure the mono
loop, but a dab of superglue or Zap-A-Gap brings real
assurance. You do not want to feel the horror of losing
a great fish and coming back with a loop-free fly.

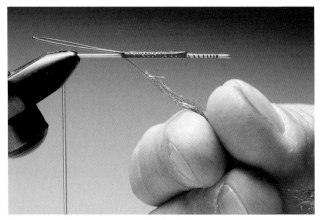

5. Grab a hefty pinch of red Ice Dub and twist a
chunky-but-tight butt on that Taco.

6. Secure your brass wire immediately forward of the
butt and let a few inches hang off the end of the fly
for later use.

7. Grab a double pinch of purple Ice Dub and dub a nice, fat, even body to within 3mm (⅛") of the eye.

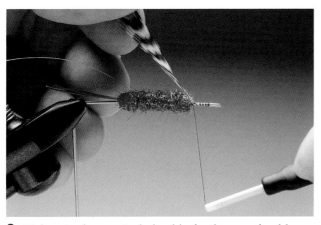

8. Pick out a long grizzly hackle feather, preferably with long fibers. Tie in at the front of the body.

9. Palmer the hackle backward evenly and tie off by counterwrapping the brass wire back to the front of the fly. This requires holding the end of the wrapped hackle feather tightly with one hand while using the other hand to wrap the wire in the opposite direction. The result is an evenly palmered body with the minimum of hackle fiber caught under the ribbing.

10. Select a black ostrich feather with good looking herl. There is a lot of variation in the size and stiffness of these feathers. Big, stiff herl makes a statement and is incredibly alive in the current. The more tapered the ends, the more natural the fly appears. Thin, whispy herl creates its own magic. The commercial versions seem to use whatever is lying around, and they tend to work fine. Once you've found the right feather, pinch together a group of 16 herl pieces and cut them away from the feather. You may want to lay them out on the bench and line the ends up if they seem wildly uneven. But by no means do they need to be even. Tie the entire bunch of herl down around the lower half of the shank, just ahead of the first wrap of grizzly hackle, so that the ends are 5 cm (2") long. Your wraps have to be good and tight. Prepare an identical bunch and tie them down on the top of the shank. Trim the ends away leaving just enough space for the guinea hen hackle (a few millimeters). This is a good time to gently pull the ostrich fibers around so they flare out evenly around the shank.

11. Select 25 to 30 strands of black Flashabou and tie them in around the ostrich. To conserve materials, you can also use half as many fibers and double them over.

12. Tie in a jumbo guinea hen feather and create a collar with two or three turns.

13. Create a head on the fly and give it two whip-finishes for added durability. Zap-A-Gap makes an excellent head cement for a fly that may fish for multiple seasons.

14. Remove the wire shank from your vise and clip it off with about 2 mm (⅟₁₆") tag end.

15. Loop on a Gamakatsu Octopus hook and bend the mono loop just enough to get the hook to ride in line with the wire shank rather than canting off at an angle, which it will want to do naturally.

FISHING THE TACO

Jeff swings the Fish Taco for steelhead 12 months out of the year—anytime he wants to show a large profile and tons of movement, which includes the summer and fall seasons on the Deschutes River. Like several of our most successful steelhead-fly designers, Jeff is a big believer in unweighted flies. He relies on short leaders and sink-tips to regulate this fly's depth on the swing and hang down. In rare cases when the Taco is fished on a dry line, leader length extends to 6 feet or more.

Hickman's Flash Taco is an effective variation of the Fish Taco for those times when you need extra power crystals.

Ingi's Motion Prawn

Jon Ingi Agustsson was recruited by Targus Fly Company at the dawn of the 21st century to join its European pro staff. Jon had built a reputation as a stellar salmon guide in Iceland and had shown great promise as a fly designer. He was among the first Atlantic tiers to seriously explore the potential for "faux fur" in fly tying. He sought out the highest quality material he could find, with a particular eye toward finding specimens with long, flowing fibers. In 2002 he designed the Motion Prawn, and later that same year it appeared in the Targus catalog.

> When I designed the Motion Prawn, I had been pondering over a new type of very long and mobile Craft Fur I had just sourced in Thailand. I had always been highly influenced by the General Practitioner pattern, and it didn't take much experimentation to come up with this striking hybrid. I strived to let the "barring" show as well as possible, with the exception of the Black Motion Prawn, where the cerise strike butt plays the key role in luring the take.
>
> Another thing I wanted to achieve was to get some weight into the fly, but without compromising the classic look and flow. The final design incorporated a tungsten bead or cone, which was slid onto the hook and fitted in the last [front] section of the dubbed body. The result was a good balance and enough weight to allow the fly to dive forward and jig whilst pulsating the fly. This way the fly has a lot of motion, hence the name "Motion Prawn."
>
> —Jon Ingi Agustsson, March 19, 2012

Targus Fly Company managed to gain a fair distribution to fly shops in Steelhead Country, including a solid position in the bins of the Fly Shop in Redding, California. But the Targus business model was decidedly geared toward volume and the big-box chains. Within only a few years, Motion Prawns were more likely to be found in the bins of large sporting-goods stores than in specialty pro shops. By the late 2000s, the Motion Prawn was on its way out. Its commercial demise was the result of a collision of forces: sales and marketing decisions that alienated the mom-and-pop fly shops, a surge in new steelhead patterns that made bin space highly competitive, and a general shift away from patterns with their hooks buried in the middle of the fly. With the onset of trailing-hook flies had come a flood

No fly is fishier or has better action in the water than a Motion Prawn.

We were super-stoked to get a box of originals from Jon's office in Thailand. These were the real thing!

of magazine articles and product promotions warning about the "short-strike."

As we collected and reviewed flies for this book, it was with a twinge of nostalgia that we elected to single out the Motion Prawn. It seemed a shame that such a relevant, revolutionary fly should suffer from the whims of marketing and distribution. Especially when one of the drivers of those whims was the mass insecurity of a generation of steelheaders who lay awake at night worrying they might miss a grab because their hook wasn't squarely at the end of their fly. We hope that readers will reconsider this excellent invention. We guarantee that if you experiment with barred Craft Fur tails on your prawn and baitfish patterns, you'll be hooked. Check out the color plate on page 148 to see a range of color combinations.

MOTION PRAWN, ORANGE

- **Hook:** #8 to #1/0 Tiemco 7989
- **Weight:** 4 mm (⁵⁄₃₂") tungsten bead for heavy flies, brass beads or cones for lighter flies (brass cone shown)
- **Thread:** 8/0 UNI-Thread, orange
- **Tag:** Mylar tinsel, medium (shown), or a few strands of Mirage Flashabou covered with a thin coat of Bug-Bond Lite UV cure resin
- **Tail:** In two sections, bottom to top: (1) short bunch of orange Krystal Flash, (2) pinch of orange Craft Fur barred with black Sharpie permanent marker (applied after fly is finished)
- **Body weilings & hackles:** The same pattern is repeated three times in three sections: 1) SLF dubbing, orange, followed by a ring hackle of saddle, orange, topped with a bunched golden pheasant neck feather, dyed orange; 2 and 3) SLF dubbing, orange, followed by a ring hackle of saddle, range, topped with bunched golden pheasant neck feather, dyed orange

Materials for tying the Motion Prawn in orange.

- **Wing (roof):** Golden pheasant shoulder feather, natural (or pair of feathers)
- **Flash:** Krinkle Mirror Flash (shown) or Mirage Flashabou, one strand per side
- **Special tools:** None needed

Tiemco 7989 is a semi-light-wire steelhead and salmon hook typically used for dries and low-water wet flies. Here the light wire helps to magnify the jigging action created by the added weight. As noted above, you can go with a tungsten bead or cone if you want a heavier fly; use a brass bead or cone for lighter versions. In most of the places we fish this fly, a brass cone ends up adding just the right amount of weight, and we will tie a few with no weight for slower, shallower runs.

3. The two-part tail begins with a small bunch of Krystal Flash tied in on top of the shank and trimmed about 1.3 cm (½") long. The Craft Fur tail is tied in directly on top of the Krystal Flash so that it is held up away from the hook bend to minimize fouling. Wait to bar the tail with a permanent marker until the fly is finished.

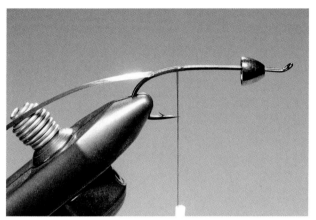

1. Slide a bead or cone onto the hook, making sure the smaller-diameter opening is facing forward toward the eye of the hook.

4. The body of the Motion Prawn is divided into thirds. Each of the smaller sections is known in Atlantic salmon fly parlance as a "weiling," and in this case they are repeated to create the illusion of a segmented shrimp. Start by dubbing a small pinch of orange SLF and wrapping it evenly over the rear third of the shank.

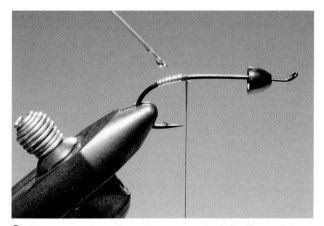

2. Start your thread at the rear end of the fly and lay down a thread base for the tag. Tie in Mylar tinsel or Mirage Flashabou, wrap forward, tie off, and trim the end.

5. Add two or three turns of orange saddle hackle.

6. Wet a golden pheasant tippet feather completely. Use your fingers to pull the wet feather tight so all the fibers are bunched together, then tie it in on the top of the rear weiling.

7. Repeat steps 4–6 to complete the second weiling.

8. The third weiling will include the bead or cone weight, which is sandwiched between two bumps of SLF dubbing; otherwise it is identical to the first two. Make the first bump of orange dubbing.

9. Push the cone had back so it fits over the first dubbing bump and add another bump in front. Use enough wraps/dubbing to hold the cone firmly in place.

10. Add another two or three turns of orange saddle hackle, preferably with slightly longer fibers than the previous weilings. Add another golden pheasant tippet, again making it slightly longer than in previous sections.

11. The wing, or shellback, of the Motion Prawn is a golden pheasant shoulder feather (or a pair of them) that is long enough to cover the entire body. I recommend starting by tying in the wing in reverse, then pulling it back to secure in its final position. This greatly increases durability. If you have trouble getting your feather(s) to lie down flat, a good trick is to use pliers to flatten the stem of the feather(s) before tying in.

12. Tie in your preferred flash, just one strand per side, and trim so the strands reach about 1.3 cm (½") past the bend of the hook. Finish the head of the fly, whip-finish, and apply a drop of head cement.

13. The final step in creating the Motion Prawn is barring the tail. With the fly still in the vise, hold

all the tail fibers tight in one hand, and use a black permanent marker to draw bars at whatever intervals you prefer. I like to try and match the distances between the weiling tippets in the tail to create lifelike segmentation.

FISHING INGI'S MOTION PRAWN

As previously mentioned, it's a good idea to tie the Motion Prawn in a variety of weights to fit differing scenarios. Jon's original tungsten version is great when you really need to get down, or if you're rapidly stripping the fly to get a lot of jigging action, but it drops out in most easy-swinging situations. Lightly weighted and unweighted versions are key in most "classic" steelhead water.

While it's fun to imagine steelhead responding to the Motion Prawn based on memories of saltwater feeding, there's an even more likely association: crawfish. Steelheaders tend to overlook the prevalence of crawfish, both as food items and as a general irritants or stimulants to steelhead. On the Pacific coast, many of us fantasize about the ocean creatures we might be imitating and forget those that are right under our boots. This lesson really came home one early-fall day on the Clackamas River. I had hooked and landed a couple of fresh-run steelhead in the first pool above reach of tide using large purple prawn/squid fly. I marveled at the willingness of these fish to chase and eat such a massive offering over 100 miles from the ocean. Then a loud knocking sound caught my attention. A pair of gulls was frantically tearing apart some unlucky food item on a flat rock nearby. One of the birds took off, hovered above, then dropped something from its beak. Both birds fell on the remains, pecking at the food and each other in a frenzy. I waded over to the rock and was amazed to find a large, live crawfish and the mutilated pieces of several others littering the rock. Seeing the crawfish was one revelation. Why hadn't I thought about crawfish as a potential focus for steelhead? But the second revelation came from the colors scattered over the rock. These crawfish were purple with blue, red, and orange highlights. I immediately thought of John Shewey's Spawning Purple—that was the color spectrum before me.

Since that day I have grown fond of shrimp and prawn flies in darker shades, and I try to channel the ubiquitous crawfish as I swing the riffles, pools, and tailouts of my home waters.

Koertge's Fur Burger

This incredible little tube Intruder is a hybrid between Dave Pinczkowski's Bad Hair Day and Ed Ward's original Intruder design. Jason Koertge (pronounced KER-chee) is the fly's creator, and a couple of his Fur Burger variations are featured in the Fly Gallery on page 239.

"When I got serious about steelhead fishing back in Wisconsin, there were only a couple of guys who fished two-handed rods," Jason said. "We sorta came together and became friends just because we ran into each other a lot. Dave was a sort of spiritual leader for a bunch of us back in the late '90s and early 2000s. Still is today, actually."

Pinczkowski was seriously into Craft Fur, constantly cooking up new patterns and new ways to take advantage of this cheap, durable material. At some point Dave was introduced to the Temple Dog pattern, one of the great Atlantic salmon designs from Europe. When he saw the way Temple Dog wings were made, with layers of fur tied in reverse and pulled back, the light went on. He started tying Craft Fur in reverse, and the effect was amazing. Dave started tying baitfish patterns with big, full-bodied profiles using nothing but a few reversed clumps of Craft Fur and some flash around the outside. One of the early patterns, designed primarily for smallmouth, was the Bad Hair Day. "It was the simplest thing ever," Koertge said. "But it moved in the water like nothing I'd ever seen."

Jason got a pack of Frödin tubes and started messing around with the technique. It wasn't long before the Fur Burger was born. He quickly figured out how Craft Fur could be used to create a profile that supported whatever outer materials are added around it. In this case the Craft Fur supports ostrich herl and Angel Hair, but it also makes an equally good base for marabou, rhea, peacock, pheasant tail, or turkey. And the key is tying it in reverse.

Another more subtle concept introduced here is the use of saddle hackle for the rear station of the fly. Much like our two Intruder examples coming up (pages 121 and 128), the Fur Burger minimizes the rear hackle, opening up the view to the fly's inner layers. The saddle hackle is folded and wrapped tightly against a bump of Ice Dub to ensure that it flares strongly, and it ends up supporting the split-tail quite effectively.

Koertge's Fur Burger blends the mobility and durability of Craft Fur with the design of a tube-style Intruder.

FUR BURGER, BLACK & BLUE

- **Tube:** Frödin medium tubing cut to 3.2 cm (1¼") long
- **Thread:** 6/0 UNI-Thread, fluorescent orange
- **Butt:** Senyo's Laser Dub, blue
- **Rear hackle:** In two parts, back to front:* 1) Saddle, kingfisher blue; 2) ostrich "split-tail," black, 10 fibers per side
- **Body:** Flat Diamond Braid, blue
- **Front hackle/wing:** In two stages, back to front:† 1) Craft Fur, black and blue, tied in reverse and pulled back, 2) 15 strands of ostrich herl, dyed kingfisher blue
- **Flash:** Angel Hair, blue
- **Collar:** Guinea hen, kingfisher blue
- **Junction tubing:** 2 cm (¾") section of Frödin small tubing inserted in the rear (ouch!)
- **Special tools:** Tube vise or a tube-tying tool for standard vise

* The Fur Burger shown here has one minor difference from the version shown in the gallery on page 239. This one does not have guinea hen in the rear hackle station.
† This Fur Burger also uses ostrich herl in the front station, which the gallery version does not.

Materials for tying a Fur Burger in black and blue.

1. With your tube locked securely in the vise, start the thread about 6 mm (¼") in from the rear of the tube. Lay down a few wraps of thread, form a 10 cm (4") long dubbing loop, and wrap the thread forward a few turns. Spread out a small pinch of blue Laser Dub in the loop and spin tight. Brush out the spun Laser Dub to free most of the fibers, then fold and wrap forward like a wet-fly hackle. Make sure each wrap is tight to the one before it to maximize the density of the dubbing bump. This will give structural support to the hackle.

2. Tie in a kingfisher blue saddle hackle feather by the tip and strip off the marabou, leaving a clear stem to hold onto while wrapping forward.

3. Fold and wrap three or four turns of hackle, keeping the wraps tight to one another. Tie it off and trip the end flush to the thread.

4. Select and prepare 10 strands of black ostrich herl for the first side of the split-tail. Tie them in so they flare out slightly to the side. Repeat this step on the opposite side.

5. Cut a 10 cm (4") section of blue flat Diamond Braid and tie it in directly on top of the last thread wraps that hold down the tail fibers, then wrap your thread forward to within 6 mm (¼") of the front end of the tube.

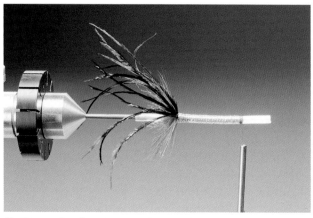

6. Wrap the flat Diamond Braid forward to the thread and tie off. Trim flush.

7. Pinch a small section of black Craft Fur from the skein and clip it at the base. Tie it down in reverse, with the butt ends pointed at the rear of the fly. Just a few turns of thread are needed.

8. Pinch another small section of blue Craft Fur and tie down directly on top of the black. Again, just a few turns of thread are needed.

Jason Koertge (right) and Jeff Hickman (left) hamming it up on the Kanektok River, Alaska. ROB RUSSELL PHOTO

9. Wet and push back the Craft Fur while wrapping your thread in front of the Craft Fur. Spit works, but you can keep a small cup of water on the bench for this purpose if you don't like slobbering on your flies.

10. Pull a few fibers of blue Angel Hair from a skein and tie them in just in front of the Craft Fur. The preferred method for doing this is to tie the fibers down in the middle and pull the ends back. One or two additional wraps of thread will keep the fibers trained back. Jason usually puts a few of these sparse bunches of Angel Hair around the outside of the Craft Fur in a semi-symmetrical fashion.

11. Select, pinch, and trim 15 strands of kingfisher blue ostrich herl and measure them to the desired length.

12. Tie them down in reverse, directly on top of the tube. Wet the herl fibers and slick them back, wrapping the thread a few turns in front to keep them from pushing forward.

13. Select a large or jumbo guinea hen feather dyed kingfisher blue and tie it in by the tip. Strip away the webby marabou from the base.

14. Wrap the hackle forward a few turns, folding it as you go so that all of the hackle fibers are directed backward. Trim the ends flush and finish the head with a few thread wraps. Give it a whip-finish and apply a drop of head cement.

15. Once the head cement is dry, trim the front end of the tube so that only a few millimeters are extending beyond the head of the fly. Using a lighter, carefully apply heat to that end until a small bead develops around the end.

16. Let it cool down completely, then remove your fly from the vise. Trim 3 mm (⅛") from the butt end of the tubing.

17. Insert a 2 cm (¾") section of Frödin small tubing in the rear as far as it will go. This smaller-diameter tubing is just big enough to pull your hook knot into, but tight enough that it will stop where you set it.

FISHING THE FUR BURGER

This is Jason's go-to pattern for winter and spring steelhead, when the water has at least a little bit of color. He sometimes slides a bullet weight onto his tippet for added sink, but usually he relies on a short leader and a sink-tip to set the depth of the fly.

The small-diameter tubing at the rear works perfectly with 12-pound-test Maxima as tippet material. One little advantage of this design is the increased chances the fly will come back when you break off a hook. Because the knot is firmly set in the tubing, the fly won't slide off the tippet if the hook pops off. If you need to step up to 15-pound-test, you'll have a hard time forcing the resulting knot into the small tubing. Instead, remove the small junction tube and seat your knot directly into the medium tubing. Lefty's No-Slip Mono Loop is a good knot for this allowing you to leave perpendicular tag end that will help to hold the knot tight.

Without any added weight, the Fur Burger remains fairly buoyant when not under tension. This can be a real asset when you're working ledges and boulder fields, where a heavier fly would hang up. In this case, the sink-tip is the only weight being manipulated by the angler, and the fly can be expected to follow the trajectory of the sink-tip with a delay of several seconds. That means the fly is usually slightly shallower than the deepest part of the sink-tip, allowing it to skim over obstructions.

Reverse Marabou Tube

Marabou tubes are a steelheader's best friend. They are amazingly quick to tie and highly effective, and they can be stacked to create composite flies of any color combination and any length. A sandwich baggie full of short tubes, a few hooks, and a handful of bullet weights can replace the need for all other flies and fly boxes. The one perceived downside is the tendency for the marabou to collapse down to nearly nothing when wet. Tiers have come up with techniques to help support marabou from behind, including bumps of chenille or dubbing, ring hackles (usually saddle hackle), and dubbing loops spun from various materials. Trey Combs documented the rise of marabou as a tying marterial in *Steelhead Fly Fishing*; in the chapter "New Steelhead Fly Patterns," Combs touched on the development of marabou hackling techniques. He described a lineage influenced by the great master of the Atlantic salmon fly, Poul Jorgensen. John Farrar, legendary Skagit guide and fly designer, was among the first Northwest steelhead tiers to integrate marabou into his Spey flies starting in 1980. Farrar gives credit to his colleague Bob Aid for settling on the most widely used marabou-hackling technique—simply wrapping the feather directly on the shank of the hook. Tying the feather in by the tip and wrapping forward has won out as the preferred technique to the present day, and that's what Jason does in the following step-by-step.

In the mid-2000s, Tom Larimer told me about a concept he was working on to improve marabou steelhead flies. He had started tying his flies in reverse. That is to say, he was starting his marabou flies at the head and working toward the back. As he wrapped materials, he pulled the fibers forward, toward the eye of the hook. Applying the materials in reverse order allowed him to slightly overlap the edges of each successive material as it was applied. This forced the marabou to stand away from the shank of the tube, creating the fullest possible profile with almost no materials. "I'm telling you, man, it's like magic. It doesn't seem like a wrap or two of hackle and a turn of chenille should do it, but the marabou stands up straight on these flies." A couple of years later, Larimer's Reverse Marabou Intruder hit fly shops, and the idea was launched into the mainstream.

Fast forward a few winter steelhead seasons: I was sitting at a rickety table in a wonderfully musty beach house. Koertge and I were guzzling Rainiers and cranking out bugs under a small desk lamp. He was super excited about his new Reverse Marabou Tubes, and the fact that they were pinning fish everywhere he went. "Dude, you won't believe it. They are so effing easy to tie, and they look badass in the water!"

Koertge had whittled Larimer's Reverse Marabou down to its essence—nothing but a few turns of marabou,

Proof that even the smallest, sparsest flies can give off a major profile. There is nothing to this fly, but it makes a huge impression.

Right: It's hard to argue with the supreme fishiness of marabou flies. KEN MORRISH, FLY WATER TRAVEL, PHOTO

a few turns of hackle, and two turns of chenille. The whole fly fit on a ½ inch of tubing and weighed about as much as thistle down. A sneeze would send a pile of these things flying around the room. And it didn't take him long to throw down a dozen of them.

The next vise over, I was tying shank-style Intruders, and I finished my first fly for the evening. I gazed skeptically at Jason's little marabous and got the creeping feeling that I was missing out on something. Then, like a mild electric shock, I had a vivid flashback to the Kanektok River. It was my first day on Bug Island, and Jeb Hall handed me a quart-size ziplock with two dozen multicolored tubes. "These will save your life," he said, deadpan as always. He walked away without another word, leaving me to figure out the details. In the days and weeks that followed I was instructed by my fellow guides in the subtleties of stacking short marabou tubes for king salmon. Jeb's words proved prophetic, and I came to rely almost exclusively on double and single tubes for their practicality and results. So why was I having trouble doing the same for steelhead?

Just last season I fished for a couple of days with Jeff Hickman on my home river. Jeff didn't usually hang down in the floodplain where I liked to fish, but he was willing to brave the hordes for a chance at some tide-fish. As we loaded rods in the boat, I was amazed to see both of his rods rigged with small, unweighted tubes. This was the guy who made a living swinging 3" long Fish Tacos for Deschutes summer steelhead. And here he was fishing tiny flies for coastal winters?

"Oh, man, I love them!" Jeff said. "I've caught so many fish on these this season." I could feel my stubborn streak percolating. I silently vowed to fish my Intruders all day as a pseudoscientific test. I knew my fish, and they loved the black Intruder. But by the end of the day, I was zero for one, and Jeff was two for two. So much for home-court advantage.

REVERSE MARABOU TUBE, PINK

- **Tube:** Frödin medium tubing, clear, cut about 2.5 cm (1") long
- **Thread:** 6/0, fluorescent pink
- **Collar:** Guinea hen, pink
- **Flash:** Flashabou, pearl or pink
- **Hackle:** Marabou, pink
- **Underhackle:** Saddle hackle, yellow
- **Butt:** Medium chenille, fluorescent pink
- **Junction tubing:** Frödin small tubing of desired length
- **Special tools:** Tube vise or tube converter tool

Materials for tying a Reverse Marabou Tube in pink and yellow.

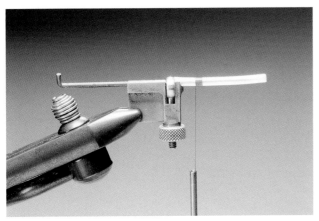

1. Cut a 1-inch-long section of tubing and fit it tightly in the vise. Start your thread toward the rear and wrap forward about ⅛ inch for a base layer.

2. Tie in a pink guinea hen feather by the tips and wrap forward, folding the hackle backward as you go.

3. Add two or three strands of Flashabou, tying them in at their centers and directing the ends down either side in a V formation.

4. Prepare a marabou quill by stripping away the fibers from the fat butt section of the feather. Then pinch the tips in one hand and gently pull the marabou fibers back toward the butt end.

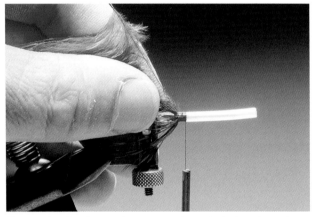

5. Tie the feather in by its tip, directly behind the last wrap of guinea hen hackle. Wrap the feather forward, folding backward as you go, keeping each wrap tight to the one before it.

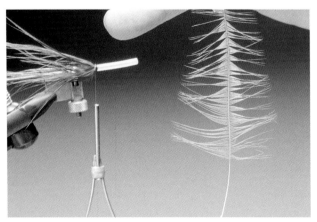

6. Wet the marabou hackle and pull it back out of the way. Prepare a yellow saddle hackle feather by stripping away the webby marabou from the butt and pulling the remaining fibers back as shown.

7. Tie the saddle feather in by its tip, directly on top of the last wrap of marabou.

8. Make the first forward wrap of yellow saddle hackle over the last wrap of marabou, then fold and wrap forward another three times and tie off. This overlapping is the key to this pattern's extreme outward flare.

9. Cut a 3-inch-long section of fluorescent-pink medium chenille, pull away a few of the pink fibers from one end, exposing the thread core. Tie in the chenille by the exposed threads to minimize bulk.

10. Wrap forward two turns, making sure the first wrap of chenille slightly overlaps the last wrap of saddle hackle. Whip-finish, apply a dab of head cement, and allow to dry.

11. Remove the tube from your vise, turn it around, and pull all the materials backward so that the guinea hen becomes the collar of the fly. Trim the front of the tube so that only a few millimeters of clear tubing extend out from the hackles.

12. Using a lighter or other flame, carefully heat the head end of the tube until it beads up slightly. Trim the butt end of the tube as needed; 1.3 to 2 cm (½ to ¾") is standard.

13. Fit a short piece of small-diameter tubing into the butt end of the fly. This will act as junction tubing, which will hold a knot tightly and prevent slipping once your hook is looped on.

FISHING THE REVERSE MARABOU TUBE

Rigging is a key consideration when fishing short marabou tubes. They work best with small, Octopus-style hooks whose upturned eyes can be threaded neatly onto a loop of tippet. This rigging keeps the hook riding parallel to the tube regardless of the current speed, and it allows you to set the hook precisely where you want it by adjusting the length of your mono loop. Most of the time a loop of 1.3 to 2 cm (½ to ¾") is optimum. Size 4 hooks are usually plenty, but bigger fish may call for a size 2.

Frödin's small-diameter tubing is just big enough to take a knot made of 12-pound-test Maxima tippet. The knot will slide tightly into the tubing and stop where the small and medium tubing overlap. If you need a little more strength, step up to a 15-pound-test Maxima tippet and remove the junction tubing. A no-slip mono loop will seat directly into Frödin's medium-diameter tube, though it helps to leave a tag end of at least a couple of millimeters to hold the knot tight.

One big reason for the growing popularity of small marabou tubes is their neutral buoyancy. On a short leader, these flies are pulled quickly to the depth of the sink-tip when under tension, but they don't drop out during a mend or a downstream step when tension is removed. This allows the angler to weave and bob the fly around boulders and over submerged ledges, fishing everything in between.

Bullet weights are a great way to apply more grains when needed. This can be particularly helpful when trying to fish slots on the far side of the river. But experience with this fly has demonstrated that it is more effective overall to let go of one's reliance on added weight and trust that steelhead will move the extra few inches to take the unweighted offering. Over the last couple of seasons, I've seen this firsthand and have become a believer.

Lambroughton's Moose Hair Skater

Like most of the steelheaders of my generation, I first saw this otherworldly fly in one of David Lambroughton's *Fly Fishing Dreams* calendars. The photo is still etched in my mind—a perfect, bright hen with a disk-shaped fly squarely in the corner of her mouth. It must have been from the Dean or the Copper River.

Lambroughton first came up with his Moose Hair Skater in 1993 after experimenting with elk hair spiders. He was having trouble finding elk hair that was long enough to make a wing case and long forward wing. Then he found moose hair, and his vision was realized. The fly became an underground hit in the BC steelheading set, but was rarely seen in the Lower 48. Eventually Umpqua Feather Merchants brought Lambroughton on as a signature tier and offered the Moose Hair Skater to the public, though it's still a rare sight in the fly bins.

It was on a long-distance call to New Zealand some 20 years after he devised the pattern when I finally talked with David and heard the story behind the fly. I had to call near midnight to make up for the 19-hour difference in time. I caught him just as he slouched into his couch, a place he calls the "Leather La Brea Tar Pit."

"It's where I like to take a nap before I go to bed," he said, sounding a bit groggy.

I had sent him a set of photos for his critique, the results from my first attempt to tie his skater. One key problem: My version was made from elk hair. Another key problem: I had no idea what I was doing.

"The whole thing is just two clumps of moose hair and a little bit of dubbing," he said. "Moose is the only hair that will hold up. The hump is even more durable because I add a few drops of flexible head cement. You can fish that thing all day and it will hold together great. The amber-colored Ice Dub body probably doesn't matter. But there are a lot of October caddis around, so I'm a big fan of orange in the fall."

The front-loaded shape of the fly is designed to plow water. "It leaves a huge wake but casts nice because there's nothing to it!"

David regaled me with stories of perfect hens sipping dry flies and cartwheeling into the sunset, and I became intensely aware of the parochial life I had lived, even with my modest travels. After talking with David, I made a vow to visit Skeena Country as soon as the book was finished. Maybe I'd even close the loop and swing a Moose Hair Skater to a perfect BC hen, just like in the calendar.

Lambroughton's Moose Hair Skater is well known among the jet-setting steelhead elite, though few of them have any idea how to tie one. Hopefully this helps! DAVID LAMBROUGHTON PHOTO

LAMBROUGHTON'S MOOSE HAIR SKATER

- **Hook:** #6 Tiemco 105 (#4 is too big, #8 is too small)
- **Thread:** 10/0 Veevus, brown
- **Tail:** Moose body hair
- **Body:** Ice Dub, orange
- **Wing case:** Moose body hair
- **Wing:** Moose body hair
- **Special tools:** Long-hair hair stacker; bodkin or long needle; flexible head cement

Materials to tie Lambroughton's Moose Hair Skater.

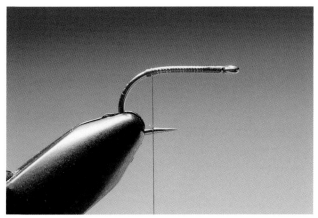

1. Lay down a base layer of thread along the whole shank of the hook.

2. Starting at the bend, tie in a stacked clump of moose body hair for the tail. Keep the tail short, as you would for a Humpy or Royal Wulff. Wrap the thread forward ⅔ of the length of the shank as shown, keeping the butt ends of the moose hair pulled forward as you go. The reliable strength of the Veevus thread comes in handy any time you're compressing deer, elk, or moose hair.

3. Tie in a second, larger clump so the tips are at least twice the length of the tail and pointing backward, toward the rear of the fly.

4. Firmly wrap the thread forward along ⅔ of the shank, just as you did for the first clump. This creates the base for dubbing the body.

5. Dub the body with orange Ice Dub.

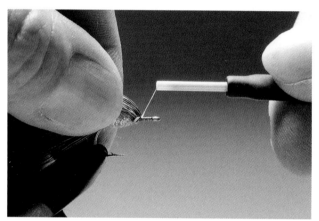

6. Pull the butt ends of the moose fibers back and stand them up with a few firm thread wraps.

7. It's optional to add a couple of turns of dubbing to stand up the butt ends even more.

8. Turn your vise so that you are looking at the fly from the front and divide the moose hair ends into two wings. Pull the wings to either side of the fly to prepare for the next step.

9. At the rear of the fly, use a bodkin or needle to separate the longer moose fibers from the shorter tail fibers.

10. When you have them clear of one another, pull the long moose tips forward while keeping the butt ends down and to the sides. This is pretty simple, but it will take some practice, so don't be surprised if your first couple attempts don't go so well.

11. Tie down the long fibers just behind the eye of the hook and secure tightly so the wing won't rotate around the shank.

12. Pull the new wing backward and add a couple of thread wraps behind the eye of the hook. Whip-finish and apply head cement to the head and the moose hair hump for added durability.

13. Pull the butt ends of moose hair forward, shaping them into two radiating wings.

14. Trim the side wings to shape as shown.

FISHING THE MOOSE HAIR SKATER

"Basically, I do the same thing wherever I fish for steelhead," David said. "The first guy goes through with the Moose Hair Skater, and the second guy goes through swinging a rubber-legged stone. I use a dry line and a 14- to 15-foot leader."

Lambroughton contends that he has never felt the need for a longer shank or a trailing hook. "When they want it, they don't miss," he explains.

Mishler's Prawn

This exquisite prawn pattern represents a specific period in the evolution of Jeff Mishler's fly tying, though you'd have to dig to find this version in his fly boxes today. That's because Jeff, like many of us, is always changing his flies depending on his latest obsession. As you can see on page 248 of our Fly Gallery, Jeff's more recent interests involve using hair for hackles rather than feathers. But a few years earlier, Jeff was fishing prawns like the one featured here, and he gave me a couple to try. I loved them, and immediately started tying my own. As I pieced my own versions together, I came to recognize the influence of Ed Ward's Intruder in the DNA of Mishler's new bug. Here was a compact little prawn displaying toned-down elements of the Intruder's best design traits. Its feather hackles were supported by sparse fur dubbing loops, it was built with two distinct hackle "stations," and it displayed an exceptional amount of movement and contrast. It dawned on me that he had devised a hybrid between a General Practitioner, which Jeff fished religiously in his early years, and an Intruder, with which Jeff was also intimately familiar.

Soon after receiving Jeff's prawn prototypes, I started working with Stackpole on this book, and I knew I wanted to feature the pattern prominently. I tied a dozen or so variations and fished them hard with excellent results. A couple of years later, as I was writing the book, I called Jeff to talk with him about the fly. To my dismay, he seemed to have forgotten all about it.

"Wait, are you talking about that little prawn tube with the beady eyes?" he asked. "I think I remember that. Didn't I give you a couple?"

Yeah, dude. Duh! And you sent me some sweet shots of fish with the prawn hanging from their mouths.

"Oh, sure, I know what you're talking about. But I don't tie those any more. Check out these new ones!"

What can I say? The guy just doesn't sit still for long. He moved on to other patterns, but I'm still stuck on this fly. So I'm pleased to share it here, with a couple of my own little tweaks. It's an excellent study in tying technique, and it's a pattern that should live on, even if Jeff has left it in the dust.

Mishler's Prawn is a detailed study in fly design, borrowing from traditional prawns like the General Practitioner and from modern styles like the Intruder.

One of Jeff's original prawns tied on a light hook shank. Such a beauty! JEFF MISHLER PHOTO

MISHLER'S PRAWN, PINK/ORANGE (IMPROVED)

- **Tube:** Small HMH tube, clear, burned on both ends, or Pro Microtube, clear (shown)
- **Thread:** UTC 140-denier, red
- **Rear hackle in two parts, back to front:** 1) arctic fox tail, pink, spun in a dubbing loop; 2) ringneck pheasant tail, dyed orange, spun in a dubbing loop
- **Tail:** Bucktail, pink, topped with a small amount of red and two strands of pink Krystal Flash or Flashabou
- **Rear shell:** Golden pheasant neck feather, dyed red
- **Eyes:** Mono crab eyes, red, with black irises applied with Sharpie permanent marker
- **Legs:** Grizzly barred rubber legs, orange
- **Body:** Flat Diamond Braid, orange, palmered with Chinese saddle, pink
- **Rib:** Small-diameter wire, red
- **Front hackle:** Arctic fox tail, cerise, spun in a dubbing loop
- **Underwing:** Finnish raccoon, pink
- **Throat:** Guinea hen, natural, pink, or orange
- **Shellback:** Four tips of grizzly saddle hackle, orange, tented in pairs
- **Head:** Hard Head lacquer, red
- **Junction tubing:** Pro Hookguide, orange

Materials for tying Mishler's Prawn in pink and orange.

- **Special tools:** tube vise or tube-converter tool, dubbing loop tool (Vergara's Wishbone Dubbing Whirler shown), dubbing brush or medium toothbrush.

1. Starting at the front of the fly, lay down a base layer of thread and stop at the rear. Form a 10 cm (4") long dubbing loop with your thread. Clip off a pinch of pink arctic fox tail and spread it out in the dubbing loop. Spin the loop, brush out the fox fibers, and wet them back for hackling.

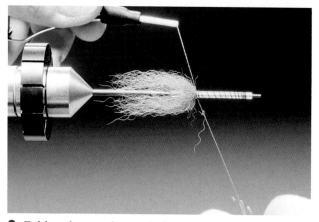

2. Fold and wrap the arctic fox to form a tight hackle. Tie it off with your thread and trim flush. Brush the fibers back to make way for the next dubbing loop. You may want to wet them slightly to keep them down.

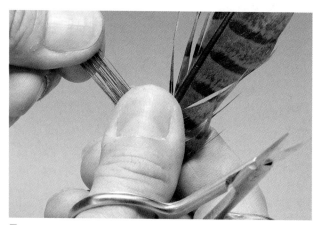

3. Form another 10 cm (4") long dubbing loop and let it hang. Trim about ½ inch of fibers from a ringneck pheasant tail feather dyed orange.

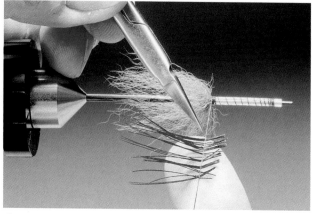

4. Keeping the pheasant fibers aligned, carefully place them in the dubbing loop and hold them tight by placing a finger behind them and pulling on the thread with the opposite hand. Use a bodkin or the tips of your scissors to arrange the fibers evenly within the loop.

5. Spin the dubbing loop tight, then fold and wrap the pheasant fibers back as you would a wet-fly hackle.

6. Pinch a small clump of pink bucktail fibers and cut them fairly long. Tie them in on top of the tube, directly over the previous thread wraps.

7. Apply an even smaller bunch of red bucktail on top of the pink, then top with two strands of pink Krystal Flash or Flashabou.

10. Cut a 10 cm (4") long section of small-diameter red wire and tie in just forward of the rubber legs. Then cut a 10 cm (4") long section of orange flat Diamond Braid and tie it down in the rear.

8. Select a golden pheasant shoulder feather, dyed red, and tie down directly over the tail at the same length as the pheasant tail hackle.

11. Wrap forward to within 3 mm (⅛") of the front of the tube. Tie down and trim flush.

9. Tie in red mono crab eyes on either side so they stick out at a 45-degree angle from the tube. Add a pair of orange barred rubber legs just above the crab eyes and trim to your desired length.

12. Prepare a pink saddle hackle feather by stripping the webby marabou portion from the stem. Tie the feather in by its base, directly over the front end of the Diamond Braid body.

13. Palmer the hackle backward in even wraps, then counterwrap with wire back to the front. Tie off the wire with a couple of extra wraps for strength, and trim the wire flush.

14. Form your final 10 cm (4") long dubbing loop. Cut off a pinch of cerise arctic fox tail and spread it out in the loop.

15. Spin the fur and brush it out with a dubbing brush or toothbrush to release the trapped fibers. Fold and wrap the fur hackle forward, then tie off and trim the loop ends flush.

16. Pinch a small piece of pink Finnish raccoon and cut it long. Leave all the guard hairs intact—they are one of the best features of this amazing material! Tie down the raccoon fur in reverse, giving a few extra thread wraps for security.

17. Trim the butt ends and pull the wing back tightly. Apply a few thread wraps directly in front of the wing so it stays back. You may also want to wet the wing, which will help keep it out of your way.

18. This next step can be a real challenge, so take it slow, and don't be afraid to untie steps that you aren't happy with and try them again. Select two pairs of 5 cm (2") long orange grizzly hackle tips for the shellback. You may wish to tie in these feathers facing backward, but I recommend the extra step of tying them in so they aim forward, then pulling them back into their final position. It makes the wings much more durable. To do this, take one matched pair, with the bright side of each facing the same direction, and tie it down with the tips pointing forward. Bend the feathers back and tie them down. Repeat this step on the opposite side, creating two slightly tented pairs of feathers that will ride together in the current. If the stems of the feathers are preventing you from lining them up properly, you can flatten them with a pair of needle-nose pliers before tying them down. Or you can try a lot of different orientations until you find one that works. It's annoying and frustrating, but if you do it enough, you will have a breakthrough.

Jeff likes to wrap red wire over the thread to create a metallic head. It looks really cool, but I went for a slightly different effect with a coat of red Hard Head lacquer. It makes a nice "hot spot" on an already red-hot fly.

FISHING MISHLER'S PRAWN

This fancy little Spot Prawn is weightless and, despite its length of over 7.6 cm (3"), casts effortlessly. It takes no effort to rig and goes well with any straight-eye hook of appropriate size. The size 4 Gamakatsu B10S matches it beautifully for summer steelhead. Try a size 2 of the same style for winter and spring steelhead. Fish it just subsurface on a dry line, in the upper column on a light sink-tip, or get it down with a heavy tip. Shorten your leader as you go deeper, since this fly will want to creep upward if given the chance.

19. Select an orange guinea hen feather, strip off the webby marabou portion from the stem, and tie it in by the tip. Fold and wrap the hackle back a few turns and tie off. Trim the ends flush and form the head with a few more wraps of thread. Whip-finish and cut the thread flush.

We've written elsewhere about the prominence of crawfish in our steelhead rivers—see Fishing Ingi's Motion Prawn on page 75. It's a bit of an indulgence, since we know of no solid evidence that steelhead munch on crawfish. You could call the prevalence of crawfish tails as summer bait a compelling clue. The point is, what we call prawn flies may be taken as crawfish, and this particular version pushes all the buttons. Double up the rubber legs, leave them a little longer, and you have yourself a full-fledged mudbug. Perhaps the similarities help to explain why prawn flies seem to work so well when presented broadside to the fish, with a downstream mend and a few seconds of hyperacceleration. Who knows? But it's fun to think about when you're working your way down a broad tailout with big fish on your mind.

Jay's Muddler Simplicity

By Jay Nicholas

The name "Muddler" is about as clear as mud these days. It could mean one of a hundred or so variations. There are weighted and unweighted Muddlers, Steelhead Muddlers, Muddlers for skating, Marabou Muddlers, Zonker-Strip Muddlers, and Strung-Out Muddlers, each dressed in an endless variety of sizes, shapes, and colors. Oh yes, and let's not forget the Rolled Muddlers. But even with the myriad possibilities, I have an image in my mind when I hear the name. It's a vision that has evolved over time, as I'm sure it has for every steelheader. I've seen a huge variety of Muddlers over the last 50 years, and the enduring aspects of these mental images are of a fly with a spun deer hair head and a wing that also includes some deer hair. That's in spite of the fact that many of the variations I've seen had only the spun deer hair head in common with the original Don Gapen Muddler Minnow tied back in the mid-1930s.

The Muddler Minnow is a fly that I have admired since I saw the pattern back in the early 1960s—classic flies tied with turkey tails and wings. These flies were works of art with fine mottled markings and perfectly tapered, tightly packed deer hair heads. As much as I admired the look of these classic Muddlers, I was usually short on courage when it came time to sit at my vise and re-create flies that were as nicely crafted as the ideal.

For my first 40 years as a fly tier, my experience with Muddlers was strained at best. Reluctantly, I tied Muddlers on a small commercial scale for Doughton hardware back in the 1970s and produced the two versions that follow.

WAYNE DOUGHTON'S TROUT MUDDLER (AKA MALHEUR MUDDLER)

- **Hook:** #8-14 Mustad 9671 or 9672
- **Tail:** Clump of dark mottled turkey wing feather fibers
- **Body:** Mylar tinsel, gold
- **Wing:** Clump of dark mottled turkey wing feather fibers
- **Head:** Deer body or rump hair—secured mostly on top of the hook, similar to an Elk Hair Caddis, but a little more bulky and ragged.

Note: When I say "clump," I mean just that, nothing fancy, just a wad of mottled turkey wing fibers tied on top of the shank, not the perfectly matched and formed wings I picture on a classic Muddler.

Jay's distillation of the myriad Muddler Minnow mutations that have emerged since the 1930s. This one is specifically designed to draw steelhead from their shadowy summer lies.

WAYNE DOUGHTON'S STEELHEAD MUDDLER

- **Hook:** #4 and #6 Claw 1197B
- **Tail:** Clump of dark mottled turkey wing feather fibers, upright and neat
- **Body:** Mylar tinsel, gold (about half of these flies were weighted with lead wire under a metallic gold embossed tinsel purchased on 1-ounce spools)
- **Wing:** Clump of dark mottled turkey wing feather fibers, upright and neat
- **Head:** Deer body or rump hair—spun and clipped into a cone shape tapered narrow to hook eye

I didn't mind tying the messy Malheur Muddler, because it didn't require full-on spinning of the deer hair head and the wing was just a messy clump of turkey wing fibers. Wayne swore by that fly for trout fishing. But the Steelhead Muddler was agony. It required a higher set of skills to form the wings and deer hair head, skills I had not yet perfected. The feedback I received from Wayne's customers—the people who fished my Trout and Steelhead Muddlers—taught me that the flies I found a disappointment were nevertheless well received by boatloads of fish.

Four decades later, I'm still not up to a perfectly crafted, classic Muddler Minnow, but my Muddler tying is relaxed and confident, because my appreciation for the fly and my personal vision for the fly's essential character have evolved to a place where the image matches my tying skills.

Long story short: Over the years I've come to see certain qualities of the Muddler as essential, and other features as elements of artistic expression. Here, for example, are characteristics I tend to examine and categorize when I see a fly.

COLOR

I've seen Muddlers tied in color shades that range from very pale gray to very dark brown, and these are all tied with natural deer hair. The color of the fly seems a fundamental characteristic to me, but I have encountered many anglers who seem color-blind, as is my dear friend and Muddler aficionado, Frank Moore. I see a pale gray deer hair Muddler as a completely different fly compared to a dark brown deer hair Muddler, unless it is very early or late in the day, and at these times I think that color is irrelevant. The availability of purple, brown, chartreuse, and pink Muddlers, to name a few, is something that is great for keeping the fly-fishing industry solvent, and I'm convinced that color can definitely affect a fish's response to a fly, but during the lowest light conditions, I think that factors other than color are far more important.

SIZE

Size matters with Muddlers, as with most flies. People who have caught far more steelhead than I on Muddlers tell me that there are times when a 7.6 cm (3") Muddler will bring steelhead to eat on the surface—and other times when a 1.3 cm (½") Muddler is the only fly a steelhead will grab. I have experienced this size sensitivity myself and believe that the smaller Muddlers are superior on the warmest days of the summer steelhead season and when fishing over steelhead that have been lying in the river longer, reverting back to trout-like feeding behaviors.

TAIL

Most Muddlers you will see in fly shops have a tail of some sort. I've come to view that tail as an element of artistic expression, not essential to a steelhead's response to the fly.

WING

I need to distinguish between a wing composed of turkey wing quill versus a wing composed of deer, elk, or moose hair. While the artist in me is drawn to the turkey quill wing feather as the most graceful and attractive, I've come to believe that a wing composed entirely of hair is every bit as attractive and effective as the turkey quill wing—and for me these hair wings are far simpler to tie. Sure, this could be a case of being influenced by wishful thinking, but my bottom line is that I believe that the turkey quill wing is nonessential to the fish-catching powers of the Muddler. In defense of this rationale, I note Muddlers tied with wings of wood duck, squirrel tail, moose body hair, marabou, and Zonker strips as examples of effective flies that lack the turkey quill.

I suppose that if I had access to perfect oak mottled turkey quills and the skills to tie perfect wings, I would do so. But that isn't the case, and I find myself perfectly content tying and fishing Muddlers with only a hair wing.

FLASH

Adding a few strands of Krystal Flash is something I usually do, but I do not think it is an essential feature of an effective Steelhead Muddler. I'm sure that steelhead can find our fly without the flash.

HEAD

The head is crucial to the Muddlers I tie, and I like to vary the head considerably, depending on what I'm trying to achieve with my fly.

HOOK

I really like the Daiichi 2141 hook in sizes 2, 4, and 6 for my Steelhead Muddlers, but will then go to TMC 5262 when I tie sizes 8, 10, and 12. I really need to try a Strung Out Muddler but just haven't found the courage to do so.

Encounters and conversations with many people over the years have influenced my thinking on the Muddler. One such incident was a story told by a far more experienced angler than I; he talked of watching a man on the Deschutes who was catching summer steelhead with a hunk of deer body hair looped onto an up-eye bait hook. As I recall the story, the man just jammed a wad of deer body hair into the bait loop after he snelled the hook, resulting in a mess of tips and butts pointing in every direction. He then proceeded to cast this mess out into the river and let it swing. Well, as you might have guessed, the steelhead ate it with total abandon.

One fellow I met on the Deschutes in the mid-1960s fished nothing but Muddlers. Seriously. He showed me several of his fly boxes. They were stuffed full of flies that ranged from a good 13 cm (5") long to flies that were probably in the size 14 class. All of his Muddlers were on the dark brown side of the color scale, and had very rough cut heads, with a thrown-together look about them. He told me that he fished from Montana to the Pacific, Northern California to Canada, and always with the same basic pattern. I was too young and inexperienced to ask him more about his rationale and presentation style, but I do remember those magical Muddler boxes. He was satisfied that one fly, in one color shade, was sufficient in waters across the Western North America.

My thinking on the Muddler was also influenced strongly by an experience fishing with Lee Clark on Oregon's Metolius River back in the 1970s. I was fishing a fully hackled, absolutely gorgeous Langtry Stone—a fly that was tied with the best saddle hackles, a high rider that quivered and danced on the water. I floated it over the pool and got no respect, only a look or two from a very large trout that rose up to reject my fly. Lee opened his Perrine aluminum fly box to proudly show me

Materials for tying Jay's Muddler Simplicity.

an assortment of his now famous Clark's Stones. In my way of seeing, they had crappy hackles, skimpy wings, and were roughly (a nice way of saying "amateurishly") tied. He handed me a fly from his box and invited me to tie it on my leader. Politely, I did so, convinced that no trout that had rejected a fly endowed with my superior craftsmanship should take one of Lee's nasty looking, bedraggled creations.

That was one of many humbling lessons I learned over the years. My first cast with Lee's fly brought that big Metolius trout up to leisurely engulf his fly. I was shocked. Thinking this had to be a terrible coincidence, I cast again after releasing the fish and was met with another willing taker. This went on with Lee standing nearby, obviously enjoying the fact that his fly was so effective compared to mine. To me, this story relates directly to my evolving perception of the Muddler, and what I judge to be essential versus nonessential features.

I should also add that my friend Steve Perakis provided the icing on the cake in adding a final dash of Muddler-confidence late in my fly-tying career. Steve's Muddler, featured in our gallery on page 265, is simply tied, with a few strands of Krystal Flash, an emphasized deer hair wing, and rough, blocky heads. I'm sure you'll see his influence in my Muddler Simplicity below.

—Jay Nicholas, March 2015

MUDDLER SIMPLICITY

- **Hook:** #2-6 Daiichi 2141
- **Thread:** Whatever
- **Tail:** None
- **Body:** Flat braided tinsel, gold
- **Wing:** No turkey quill—only a wing of moose mane, with a few strands of Krystal Flash underneath
- **Head:** A spun head that is on the large side, blocky more often than rounded, intended to make waves and create disturbance

3. Cut a small section of moose mane for the wing, pulling out the underfur. You may want to even up the ends using a hair stacker (shown), but it's not critical. Measure the wing out so that it extends at least 6 mm (¼") past the rear of the hook.

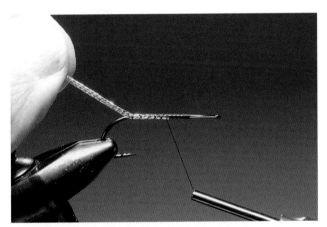

1. Start your thread behind the eye and lay down a base layer to the hook bend. Cut a 10 cm (4") long section of flat braided gold tinsel and tie in at the rear, then wrap your thread forward ⅔ of the shank, leaving the front ⅓ open for the spun deer hair head.

4. Trim the butt ends to the desired length.

2. Wrap the gold tinsel forward, tie off, and trim flush. Then tie in a few strands of Krystal Flash by their midpoint and pull all the ends back. Secure with a few wraps of thread and let the ends hang off the back of the hook. We'll trim those after the wing is set.

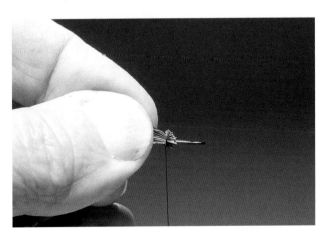

5. Tie the wing down firmly so it doesn't eventually loosen up and fly away.

6. Hold the Krystal Flash tight and trim it slightly longer than the wing.

7. Prepare a healthy pinch of deer body hair by cutting it from the skin, pulling out the underfur, and trimming off the brown tips as shown.

8. Lightly wrap your thread around the center of the bunch two times.

9. After the second wrap, pull tight on the thread and wrap tightly around the middle three or four more times to secure the hair. You don't need to be precise with your wraps.

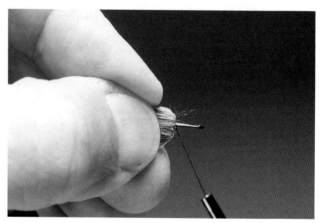

10. Pull all the deer hair back to reveal the hook shank and make a few wraps of thread right up tight to the deer hair.

11. Applying a second bunch of deer hair, repeating steps 8–10. If your proportions are right, it will seem like the deer hair is overtaking the eye of the hook. That's because you haven't compressed the deer hair yet.

12. Pinch the hook eye between your left thumb and forefinger. Push backward on the deer hair head, rotating your hand slightly as you go. The rotating action allows the deer hair to even out around the hook shank as you compress the head.

13. Pull the deer hair back and have plenty of space to make a thread head and either whip-finish or half hitch to finish. Once the thread is secure, trim the thread flush and dab with a drop of head cement.

14. Once the cement has dried, shape the head, either with sharp tying scissors or with a razor blade. Keep the head large and blocky so it cuts a big swath in the current.

Jay's Steelhead Simplicity

By Jay Nicholas

The process of writing about a fishing fly should be at once mechanical and straightforward, in a word, easy. Most certainly, however, it is not, and this is especially so when the fly is a very dear, very old companion, friend, and confidante. Such is the case with my Simplicity series of summer steelhead flies.

Back in the mid-1980s, I tied some steelhead flies for friends. The flies were rather Spartan compared to the standard flies they were in the habit of fishing. I called them Simply Purple and Simply Olive. My friends held these flies in the palm of a hand, raised their eyebrows, and said they'd give them a try.

The Simplicity series of summer steelhead flies represents a unifying fly style, tied in a variety of color phases, and is based on the fact that summer steelhead often respond well to sparsely dressed, wet flies. This fly style is my interpretation of a virtual sea of steelhead flies that were marketed and fished over the last half century; the Simplicity, at heart, is a working-man's fishing fly: a no-frills, aesthetically pleasing fly that swims true in all flows and catches summer steelhead consistently.

I tied the earliest version of the Simplicity series after my flies had been repeatedly rejected by summer steelhead over an extended period on the Deschutes and Santiam Rivers. I had read about and was intrigued by a fly tied to entice spring and summer steelhead in Washington rivers; the fly in question emphasized subtle olive color hues. I don't even remember if the article had a photo of the fly, but the image of a subtle olive fly, if only vaguely referenced in whatever article I had read, was my first inspiration for the Simplicity series.

I went to the vise and tied a fly as follows.

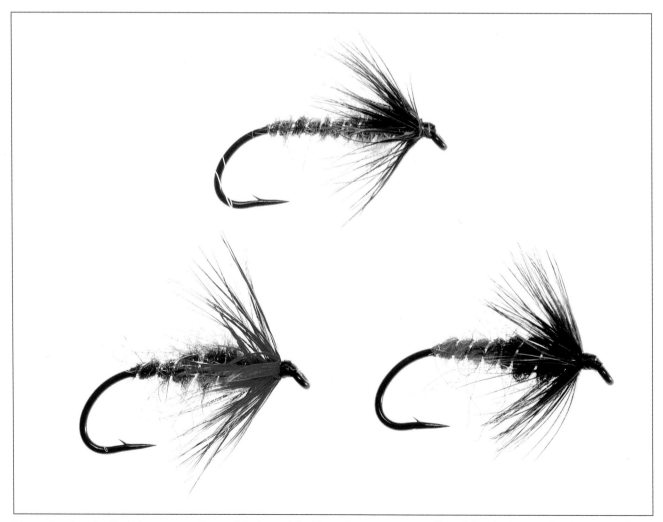

Here, Jay has boiled down a century of fads and fashions in summer steelhead fly design to the features that matter. In a world of gimmicks and gizmos, Steelhead Simplicity is a breath of fresh air.

JAY'S STEELHEAD SIMPLICITY

- **Hook:** #4 TMC 7999
- **Tail:** Pheasant rump, short
- **Butt:** Seal fur, chartreuse, slender
- **Body:** Angora goat, olive-brown, slender
- **Rib:** None
- **Wing:** Polar bear underfur, white, guard hairs removed
- **Hackle:** Chinese neck hackle, brown, webby, moderate length, relatively sparse

This fly was readily accepted by a slug of summers as soon as I was able to fish it, on both the Deschutes and Santiam, and my fondness for the fly grew with each steelhead's take.

The Simplicity's style evolution progressed shortly thereafter when several friends were heading across the Cascades to the Deschutes; they wanted a few flies to fish for summer steelhead. Instead of grabbing a handful of the usual Skunk and Purple Peril flies stuffed into quart canning jars and available for just these occasions, I tied up a half-dozen flies along the lines of the olive fly I had found so effective myself.

I had only a few evenings available for tying before their departure, if I recall it right, so I improvised as follows.

OLIVE STEELHEAD FLY

- **Hook:** #4 TMC 7999
- **Tail:** Two strands Krystal Flash, chartreuse, 6 mm (¼") each
- **Butt:** None
- **Body:** Seal, olive-brown, slender, short
- **Rib:** Oval silver, fine
- **Wing:** Polar bear underfur, white, guard hairs removed, two strands of Krystal Flash over top
- **Hackle:** Chinese neck hackle, brown, webby, moderate length, sparse, tied collar-style in front of wing

PURPLE STEELHEAD FLY

- **Hook:** #4 TMC 7999
- **Tail:** Two strands Krystal Flash, chartreuse, 6mm (¼") each
- **Butt:** None
- **Body:** Seal, slender, short
- **Rib:** Oval, silver, fine
- **Wing:** Polar bear underfur, white, guard hairs removed, two strands Krystal Flash, chartreuse, over top
- **Hackle:** Chinese neck hackle, purple, webby, moderate length, sparse, tied collar-style in front of wing

My buddies came back with rave reviews. What are those flies, they asked. Dunno, I replied, as usual; then I said, "I call them Simply Olive and Simply Purple." As my color variations grew, the style soon came to be known as *Steelhead Simplicity*.

INSPIRATION

A number of experiences fueled the development of the Simplicity series: first, commercial-scale production of steelhead flies; second, frustration at claims of fly superiority tagged on a rapidly expanding offering of commercially marketed flies; third, a natural tendency to challenge authority; fourth, field-testing by myself and hundreds of anglers who fished my flies; and finally, good old-fashioned inspiration.

Commercial-Scale Fly Production

My roots as a fly tier began with an effort to tie a decent Bucktail Caddis in the early 1960s. Slowly, painfully, I progressed to an adequate representation of the caddis and other traditional flies like the Adams, Royal Coachman Bucktail, Mosquito, and Blue Upright. When I say adequate, I mean that they held together mostly and caught trout much of the time I fished them. The learning process was hampered by a scarcity of good fly-tying books at that time. Herter's instruction booklet was my only source of guidance, because it was all I had. I tied alone, read and reread the book, and tied on and on. The Herter's book, for all it helped, failed to describe the process of creating a palmered body, and this most fundamental aspect of creating of a Bucktail Caddis remained elusive for years. Sad but true.

Not too much later, I learned about the parachute dry-fly style, fished these flies, and became enamored with the parachutes. My earliest phase of tying and fly fishing revolved around trout flies. As I progressed from casual tier / avid fly angler to part-time commercial tier, I also tied hundreds of dozens of steelhead flies before I ever fly-fished for steelhead. I would characterize these as hardware-store flies tied with Nymo thread on Eagle Claw 1197B hooks. I mimicked flies I had been given by Wayne Doughton. These flies were consistent with the most common of the low-price steelhead fly styles; in retrospect, they were drab and clumsy in comparison to flies being crafted by people like Dave McNeese and other steelhead anglers/tiers featured in Trey Combs's fine book *Steelhead Fly Fishing*.

This period of my development as steelhead angler consisted mostly of fishing for trout with flies, fishing steelhead with bait and sideline, and commercial-scale tying of both trout and steelhead flies.

It's true. My best work as a tier was focused on trout flies. I tied trout flies for Kaufmann's Portland fly shop, and Randall kept them under the counter for his best customers. My steelhead flies, though, were not quite as nicely tied. At some point, I remember offering to expand from tying trout flies and include steelhead flies in the selection of my flies sold at Kaufmann's. Jerry Swanson took a quick look at one of my steelhead flies in the palm of his hand, grabbed its wing in a set of pliers, pulled the wing out, tossed the fly on the glass display case, and shook his head. No thanks, he said.

So I drove home, pulled up to my bench, and resumed tying great trout flies and subpar steelhead flies.

Fly Frustration

My definition: The frustration of seeing barely changed versions of last year's fly patterns displayed in catalogs and fly shops from year to year, with corresponding claims of their new fish-luring power, and something relatively new on the scene, the emergence of the royalty fly. Royalty flies, in my opinion, were a means of selling new materials, promoting a fly shop, and carving off a few cents per fly to the creator of the fly in question. Having created a few fly patterns myself and seeing these and flies innovated by other tiers taken, claimed as original patterns by another tier, was a stinging experience. In retrospect, I was more than a little snippy at the time.

I looked at the ocean of steelhead flies that were being popularized in the literature, in the fly shops, and decided I was fed up with hype and personal superstition being passed off as objective truth. Here's an example. I remember well some of the fly catalogs I once browsed to develop my image of good steelhead flies. For years and years, fly shops and catalogs showcased flies that trended toward the slimmer and sparser. Then there was a marketing shift, and from one season to the next, I was seeing steelhead flies tied with big, bold, bushy marabou wings and full chenille bodies. I distinctly remember reading about certain flies that were being characterized as crossover patterns; this phrase made me quiver with anticipation, as wholesalers and retailers intended, but the rational side of my brain was laughing at my own gullibility.

Challenging the Fly Authoritarians

I have a tendency to challenge conventional wisdom, perceptions, and tradition.

Case in point: I tied many dozen winter steelhead flies for Doughton hardware, including a pattern called the Sally fly. This fly consisted of a bright flame egg-like puff at the front of the fly, silver tinsel body, and white acrylic yarn tail. "Steelhead think the sperm is chasing the egg," I was told. I didn't buy this rationale for an instant and decided the steelhead were responding to the flame yarn as much as anything else, and then, too, I recalled how effective the Black Boss fished for winter steelhead in muddy water. So I promptly tied up a few dozen Sally flies with a black yarn tail and went fishing. Of course the fly was at least as effective as the white-tailed fly fished for winter steelhead.

Another Fly Convention Challenge

Several of my summer steelhead fly fishing friends during the 1980s were excruciatingly devout promoters of a certain fly style. Hooks had to be the TMC 7989, not the 7999. Bodies had to be short and slim, starting well forward of the hook point. Fine oval tinsel rib was another requirement, and more than three turns on the body was sure to destroy the fly's effectiveness. Throat hackles must be shorter than the depth of the hook gape, tied as a beard, and extend only downward from the body, opposite a short kip-tail wing, a fly with a thin horizontal profile.

These guys were respected trendsetters, keepers of the holy book of fly patterns, creators of secret, supereffective summer steelhead flies. Their flies and opinions shaped the thinking of many steelhead tiers of the day.

I studied these flies closely, nodded my head politely, and mentally concluded that these fly dictates were nonsense. The flies I tied consistently for one of the Deschutes's most accomplished guides were anything but elegant and flouted these precisely dictated rules for constructing effective summer steelhead flies.

Jay hard at work field testing his flies. Look at the concentration he puts into it! ROB RUSSELL PHOTO

Field Testing

The need to field- or river-test steelhead flies, like any other fly, is by no means trivial. The limited time I was able to devote to personal testing was more than offset by the fact that I had *hundreds* of fly testers who diligently reported back on the performance of flies I tied for them. While I fly-fished the Deschutes and Santiam for summers, my virtual army of fly tester/anglers fished the Rogue, Klamath, John Day, Grand Ronde, and a slew of rivers whose names I don't recall across Oregon, Washington, and British Columbia.

From them I learned that certain color combinations were effective without having to test them myself. I was tying flies for guides who devoted their entire summers to steelhead fishing on the Deschutes. My flies were fished by guides and clients five or six days a week, from July through October, and this racked up thousands of days during periods when fishing was easy and periods when fishing was slow. My cadre of fly testers fished and fished, came back to report when certain fly sizes and colors really made a difference in the steelhead's receptivity to the fly, when the fish ate everything they were offered, and when the fish rejected every fly. I tied flies to their specifications and received constant feedback on each fly's performance. On a smaller scale, I fished the flies myself, and these were the magic moments when I had an opportunity to integrate every secondhand story within my brain and body.

I fished my flies in classic steelhead tailouts, frog water, and high in too-swift riffles, dawn to dark, clear and muddy water, cold and hot water, from season's start to finish. As steelhead fishing goes, I caught summers on some occasions and didn't on others. Years of experience fishing for steelhead with bait and fishing with friends who were extremely talented anglers compiled a sense for recognizing effective fishing styles and techniques, baits, lures, and flies.

This combination of first- and secondhand experience fishing flies and conventional gear are all part of the experience that founded the creation of the Simplicity series of summer steelhead flies.

Finally, Pure Inspiration

The Simplicity series is a product of my effort to create a *quintessential* summer steelhead fly. That's a bold claim, but why the hell not say it, because I really believe it, and in the end, the truth is what each of us believes. Here is how you will see the term *quintessential* defined: "representing the most perfect or typical example of a quality or class." This isn't to say I think no other fly style is effective or desirable to angler or summer steelhead. On a purely mechanical basis, the Simplicity series is a fly style that has been proved effective and pleasing to fly fishers pursuing summer steelhead for roughly three decades. The durability of this fly style's effectiveness is so deep and extensive over that time that it merits serious consideration by any angler fly-fishing for summer steelhead, or similar anadromous fish worldwide.

I wanted to create a summer steelhead fly that could earn a personal, unshakable allegiance. This meant, at first, a fly that caught fish, year after year. From that fundamental requirement followed more fly qualities on my wish list, fueled no doubt by many personal quirks. I wanted a fly that was easy to tie; swam true in quick and tepid flows, smooth glides and riffles; emphasized presentation in the upper few feet of water; hooked and held fish well when barbless; and covered what I considered the vital color and size spectrum for summer steelhead fishing.

I wanted to be able look anyone in the eye and claim this series of summer steelhead flies as my own. I could have continued to mimic and tweak flies crafted by better tiers and anglers than me, but I was inspired, excited, optimistic, and wide-eyed, determined to rethink, recraft, and build on the work of others to create a Nicholas *signature* summer steelhead fly.

I think it fair to say that the Simplicity series of summer steelhead flies is, indeed, a distinct fly style and includes body material and color options that are part and parcel associated with the fly style, and that these flies are at least as effective—and, in some cases, are more effective as any of the related fly styles out there, past and present. Is it different? Sure, it's different, but clearly, it is based on the work of thousands of tiers and steelhead anglers whose opinions and experience have influenced me over my own relatively short years as steelhead fly tier and fisher.

It was 2007 when I solidified my search image for the Simplicity.

Then came the Simply Olive and the Simply Purple, followed by so many others. Over time the style has morphed a little, as follows:

- Rely principally on the TMC 700 rather than the 7999
- Longer body, extending well behind the barb
- Oval tinsel wound along the entire length of the body
- Reliance on rooster saddles instead of pheasant rump or Chinese neck hackles, tending to include a fair amount of web
- Shorter hackles than the Simply Purple fly; collar hackles now are about the width of the hook gape
- Omission of a wing, except for a few strands of Krystal Flash or Flashabou
- Body dubbing that consists of unique color blends, incorporating several shades of STS Trilobal Dub and metallic shades of Ice Dub.

As I've said before, these are genuinely effective fishing flies, not show flies. These are the working-fishing flies tied by a local old boy, rather than in an offshore factory. Not fancy, just effective and proven over time. Cookie-cutter-perfect industrial-scale flies are usually of the highest quality these days; my own ties offer a unique if imperfect style, made for utility above all else. The

evaluation of several friends in the fly marketing industry is that the Simplicity series is a commercial failure as far as *bin appeal* goes. For readers who don't already know the phrase, *bin appeal* refers to an aura, an appearance, a dazzle that increases the fly-shop customer's tendency to reach out and grab one particular fly over another. A fly that more often tends to be selected over another, a fly that sells more dozens, a fly that catches the eye and imagination of the purchaser, this fly has "bin appeal." Fly patterns that are more often overlooked, passed over, less often purchased, and less reached for come up short on the bin-appeal scale.

First, these flies lack the tail and wing that fly tiers and consumers have come to expect of a good fly. Why on earth would anyone pay three bucks, or two bucks for that matter, for a steelhead fly that's incomplete, in a sense for half a fly? The tail and wing are so much an emotionally necessary part of our traditional steelhead flies that their omission seems tantamount to insult. Second, their names are most unglamorous, especially in this era when a fly's name is expected to conjure dramatic imagery, hint at secrecy, or drop the name of an influential personality in the industry. The Black/Grizzly Simplicity falls flat off the tongue. Mention the Stargate Blue Simplicity and all you get is a blank look. The Mack's Simplicity comes close to perking up a prospective fly buyer, but it sounds too much like the old pattern, and everyone's boxes are already full of the Max Canyon anyway. Another problem with the Simplicity series: Their dubbed bodies are such that hooks and bodies tend to get all balled up and tangled in the fly-shop bins. It isn't easy, always, to pull out a single fly and look at it. It is more common to reach in and withdraw a half dozen Simplicity flies all hooked together. And finally, there is the *no-name, no-glory* aspect of the Simplicity series. Our modern fly-fishing world swirls with language intended to excite the imagination and maintain a steady flow of cash through the fly-fishing industry. Of recent years, the flies in our boxes are graced with names like Hoser, Closer, Last Light, Fish Taco, Squidro, and so on. These flashy names inspire steelhead anglers standing in front of a fly display case: Steelhead Simplicity just lacks the pizzazz of the trendy new flies.

Instead of traditional hair or hackle-tip wings, my Simplicity flies typically employ a few strands of Krystal Flash, Opal Flash, Mirage Flash, or the like. Wet flies tied without traditional wings sink easily, swim true, and are another proven example that less is more. These flies might fish well on most occasions without the flash, but I find the extra sparkle personally attractive, and I have no indication that a few strands of flash ever detracts from the fly's acceptance by summer steelhead.

Notes on body length and ribbing: I start the body about as far back on the hook as I can; well to the rear of the hook barb. This is contrary to the style of most summer steelhead flies that begin the body even with or ahead of the hook barb. I like the longer body in part because it diverges from tradition, partly because it offsets the lack of a wing, and mostly because I prefer the look of a long body on these flies. Note that building this fly on a TMC 700 and omitting a wing adds to the potential length one can achieve with any fly. For ribbing I use Lagartun small (medium on the size 2) silver oval tinsel to rib these flies. It not only looks good, it adds integrity to the dubbed body. I doubt that the rib is essential to induce the steelhead's take, but I like it, and as I said, it dresses up an already minimalist fly style.

On hackle type and length: The Simplicity series is based on the use of rooster saddle hackles, rarely on hen capes. The intent is to obtain moderately webby hackles to form a collar about the width of the hook gape. A little wider or narrower is okay, as long as the hackles are not so full or stiff that they interfere with the fly's swim in fast water on a shallow swing.

On the use of the TMC 700: This often-overlooked hook is as reliable as any ever fished. The down-eye is reminiscent of the old Eagle Claw 1197 series, the points are sharp, the point configuration is such that it can be sharpened easily if it is nicked on a rock, the barbs are low, the hook swims true, and the wire diameter is a perfect weight to achieve a subsurface swing without precluding the option of riffle hitching the fly and skating it across the surface. The old Eagle Claw 1197 hook series offered a delightful shape and appropriately sized wire in the size 6. The sizes 2, 4, and 8 hooks in this series were not so nicely proportioned in shape or wire diameter, and all the 1197 hooks required sharpening before fishing. When I am out of 700s, I will tie the fly on a 7999 and fish it with full confidence. It's just that the Simplicity-style recipe calls for the 700, so I fish that whenever I can. In some measure, I go to the 700 just to buck the trend to market flies tied on turned-up, loop-eye hooks like the Alec Jackson and 7999. Remember, I'm fundamentally an anticonvention tier.

I find that the size 4 is effective more often than not, but on occasion, steelhead will nip the 4 and eat the 6. For the coolest waters, I would choose the size 2, especially during the earliest and latest weeks of the seasons. On days when rivers are at their warmest and fish are more likely to just nip at a fly, I reach for the smaller size 8.

COLOR VARIATIONS

The Simplicity series of summer steelhead flies has proven its fish-attraction power in several key color combinations, all tied with a blend of STS and Ice Dub materials. Key color combinations include the following:

- Blue body, black hackle
- Purple body, purple hackle
- Orange rear body, black thorax, black hackle
- Black body, kingfisher blue hackle
- Orange full dressed body, black hackle
- Green butt, black body, grizzly hackle

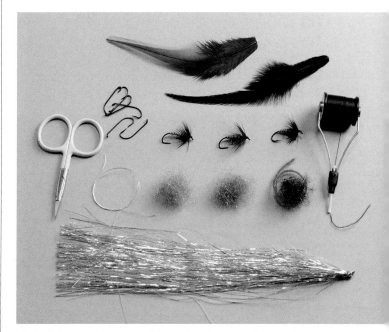

Materials for tying a couple of color variations of Jay's Steelhead Simplicity.

Steelhead Simplicity

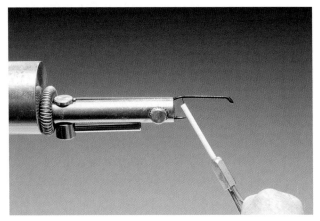

1. Prepare a TMC 700 in your vise and lay down a base layer of thread. We tied this fly on a Norvise, because it renders the process of spinning a dubbed body as clean and quick as one can imagine.

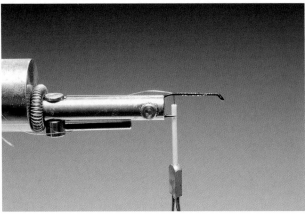

2. Tie in a 6-inch length of Lagartun small oval silver tinsel to the rear of the hook and let it hang back out of the way.

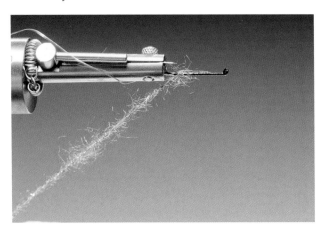

3. The body of the fly should be started as far back on the hook shank as possible, without actually extending down the bend of the hook. Tradition calls for low-water steelhead flies to be tied with short bodies, starting above the hook point or even

a smidge forward of the hook point. The Steelhead Simplicity series diverges from this convention in that it is based on a long slim body.

We will not go into details of how to spin a dubbed body with a Norvise here, except to say that our blend of dubbing materials works slightly better than dubbing pure STS dub, because of the addition of very small amounts of Ice Dub. The latter material just adds to the stickiness of the dubbing. Note also that we do not need to wax the thread when spinning dubbing with a Norvise. Finger or dubbing-loop bodies are best accomplished with a touch of Hareline Touch Dub Wax.

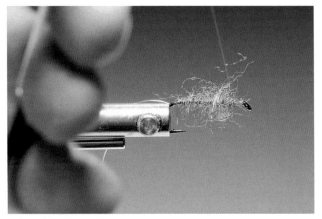

4. Spin the body in any manner you choose, but make the body relatively slim and long. Since this fly uses only a sparse Flashabou wing, you will not need very much space at the front of the fly to finish the head, so you can build a body that is a little longer than you would if using, for example, a chenille body.

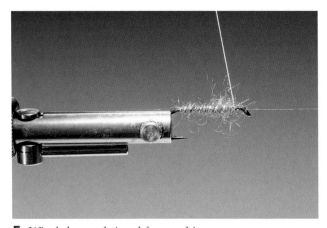

5. Wind the oval tinsel forward in even wraps over the body, tie off, and trim flush. The use of oval tinsel is a personal preference. You may use flat tinsel if you prefer. The use of metal tinsel is definitely preferable to Mylar tinsel, because the metal tinsel, either oval or varnished flat metal, significantly enhances the durability of the fly body. Steelhead eat these flies, and the tinsel helps improve the longevity of the fly's body, without detracting from the fuzz of the body.

6. Tie in and wind the hackle from the tip. I use all sorts of hackles on my Simplicity flies: rooster saddles, rooster neck hackles, Metz wet fly hackles, hen neck feathers, strung saddles, and strung schlappen. The feather qualities we strive to incorporate include proper length, a little web, and the color we are seeking.

7. The main thing is to avoid over-hackling these flies. Three or four turns of hackle in the collar will allow these flies to sink well and swim true.

8. Tie the Flashabou wing facing forward over the hook eye; this is not essential but a nice touch to increase the fly's durability.

9. Fold the Flashabou back, tie it off, and with a dab of cement, your first Steelhead Simplicity is finished.

On the Zowie Dub blends used in the Simplicity series: Straight-off-the-peg dubbings are perfectly functional, and a great selection is available. But I wanted more from my dubbing. More what? More variety. Different color shades. Dubbing that incorporates complex color highlights. More sparkle. Greater allure. I wanted to create a series of colors to call *mine*; colors that no one else could pull off a peg in a fly shop.

Marcos Vargara at Hareline Dubbin understands the strategy of fly-materials marketing. He told me the dubbing needed a name to set it apart from the hundreds of options on the market; "How about *Zowie Dub*?" he asked. Wow, Marcos, what a great idea. There you have it. And here is a list of recipes which have gone on to become the most popular Zowie Dub blends:

King Salmon Green

- Chartreuse STS
- Kingfisher Blue STS
- Fluorescent Shrimp Pink STS
- Steelie Blue Ice dub

Voluptuous Violet

- Purple STS
- Cream STS
- Kingfisher Blue STS
- Fluorescent Yellow STS
- Steelie Blue Ice Dub

Hypnotic Blue

- KF Blue STS
- Black STS
- Fluorescent Flame STS
- Purple STS
- Steelie-Blue Ice Dub

Ultimate Black

- Black STS
- Purple STS
- Kingfisher Blue STS
- Fluorescent Flame STS
- Silver Ice Dub

Perilous Purple

- Purple STS
- Seal Cream STS
- Gold Ice Dub
- Highlander Green STS
- Red-Cast Pearl Ice Dub

October Orange

- Hot Orange STS
- Fluorescent Shrimp Pink STS
- Fluorescent Orange STS
- Red STS
- Fluorescent Yellow STS
- Copper Ice Dub

Irresistible Egg

- Fluorescent Shrimp Pink STS
- Fluorescent Flame STS
- Fluorescent Cerise STS
- Fluorescent Yellow STS
- Gold Ice Dub

FISHING JAY'S STEELHEAD SIMPLICITY

Steelhead are steelhead, whether they ascend rivers in Oregon, the Great Lakes, Alaska, Argentina, Norway, BC, or the Russian Far East. These are not audacious Intruders or full-dress flies. The Simplicity series is best suited to conditions when anadromous fish are responding to a relatively slim, clean fly that swims well in every flow from very slow to very brisk, in the top several feet or several inches of the water column. These flies also dead drift and swing within a foot of the bottom, but they are not principally intended to be fished in this manner.

Fish these flies on a full dry line or add an intermediate PolyLeader so that the fly swims a few inches under the surface across tailouts or high in riffles. Hitch your fly and skate or drag it on a tight line across a riffle or tailout. Speed up the fly's swing with a strong mend to the nearshore; slow the swing with a strong mend to center river. Swing your Steelhead Simplicity on a sink-tip across boulder fields, along the edges of bedrock ledges, and across fish-holding tailouts. We usually fish these flies in the top foot or so of the water column, and often in the surface film or top 5 cm (2"). That said, this series of flies is also effective fished on sink-tips swinging them close across the river bottom.

A final application is to fish these flies on a dry line, cast upriver to the river's near side, and dead-drift them downriver toward you, as you would dead-drift a nymph. This is not the principal intention for this fly style, but if you're out there on the river, have fished the Simplicity in more intended ways, and still think there are steelhead present, you're free to give dead-drifting this fly a go; it works.

It is important to remember that the Steelhead Simplicity is the opposite end of the fly spectrum from a big Steelhead Intruder. There are times when a steelhead will move a considerable distance to take a look at an Intruder, might even nip at such a big fly but won't eat it. This same steelhead is sometimes more likely to take a modestly proportioned Simplicity into its mouth confidently, which is why this fly will often outfish more widely recognized, fully dressed traditional flies and the newly popular Intruders.

Choose either a traditional tapered leader of 2.7 to 4.6 m (9 to 15'), in 6- to 12-pound strength, depending on water clarity, fly size, and river structure. An Airflo PolyLeader in floating, hover, or intermediate is an excellent choice for Spey and switch rod presentations.

St. Pierre's Hoh Bo Spey

One whiskey-soaked night on Alaska's Kanektok River, I sat with Charles St. Pierre in his tent cabin, sharing stories and getting the scoop on his Hoh Bo Spey. Charles is a renowned Spey-casting instructor, having introduced hundreds of budding steelheaders to the art through his company, Northwest Speycasting. He's also the creative mind behind a number of steelhead fly patterns that modern anglers are likely to take for granted. The Hoh Bo Spey ranks as chief among his commercial offerings and has become one of the most widely acclaimed steelhead flies of all time. Other well-known St. Pierre patterns include the GP Spey, the Foxee Dog, and the Foxee Prawn. Check out our color plate featuring an array of his flies on page 285.

"It all started with George Cook," Charles said. It was a familiar refrain—George Cook has been the engine behind many of the world's most successful commercial flies going back to the mid-1980s. "I was working with George on his Spey-casting classes, and he was asking me if I had any fly patterns to submit to Solitude Fly Company." George had a long, successful history with

Solitude, both as a sales rep and as one of its signature tiers.

"I took George's invitation seriously," Charles said, "and started doing my homework to create a commercial steelhead fly that would rise above the clutter. I studied old Atlantic salmon fly plates, tied a lot of prototypes, and tested them on the water."

Charles noted how different sizes and weights of flies casted and fished. He watched how they acted underwater and how steelhead responded. Over the next couple of years, he came up with a formula for what he hoped would be a steelhead fly for all seasons. His criteria, after all of his testing and tweaking, boiled down to a few key pillars. He wanted a lightly dressed fly of medium-size profile with maximum movement and no added weight. A trailing hook was desirable, both to minimize short strikes and to allow for switching out dulled hooks. And in addition to lifelike movement, the materials needed to provide contrast and a sense of translucency.

Around the year 2000, Charles gave George a dozen Hoh Bo prototypes to test.

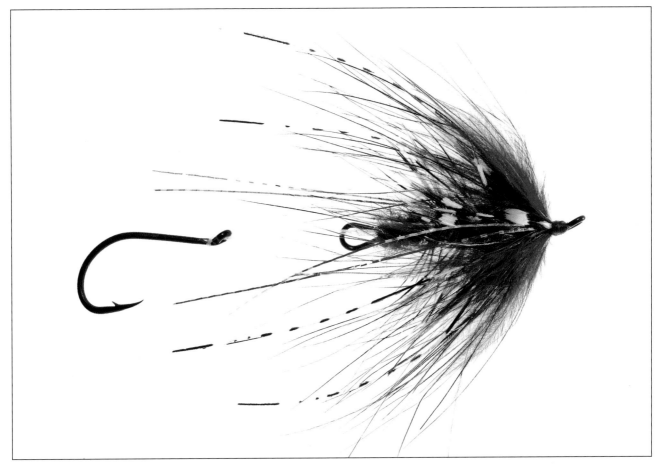

The Hoh Bo employs Lady Amherst pheasant tail fibers to glorious effect, catching the eye of steelhead and the people who chase them.

Charles enjoys a break from teaching on a lovely winter's day. RINGO NISHIOKA PHOTO

"The next time I saw George he had this shit-eating grin on his face," Charles remembers. "He took me aside and told me that he had caught a ton of fish on those flies. Rainbows on the Kenia and steelhead everywhere."

George asked Charles for some color options, samples were sent back and forth, and soon the Hoh Bo Spey went into production. Sales built slowly, but fly shops immediately recognized they had a perfect "dude fly," a fly that anyone could throw, that was light enough to stay off the bottom, and that had the right profile to attract steelhead 12 months out of the year.

"Early incarnations had grizzly hackle tips instead of Lady Amherst. But I finally settled on the Amherst fibers because the barring matched that of the palmered jumbo guinea hen in the body. And it was so light—it's barely there!"

Today the Hoh Bo Spey ranks among the best-selling steelhead flies on the market. It's also a big hit among chinook anglers in larger sizes. Favorite color combinations include black/blue, orange/pink, chartreuse/blue, and purple/orange. We've included his original dressing of black/claret, known commercially as "wine."

HOH BO SPEY, WINE

- **Shank:** 45 mm Waddington shank, or equivalent (Senyo Articulated Shank shown)
- **Thread:** 140-denier, red
- **Stinger loop:** 30-pound Fireline or equivalent, 2.3 cm (⅞") long, crystal (white)
- **Butt:** Blended Angora goat (shown) or Ice Dub, wine
- **Body:** Blended Angora goat (shown) or Ice Dub, black, palmered with jumbo guinea hen
- **Hackle:** Marabou, black, and marabou, wine, ringed with six fibers of Lady Amherst pheasant center tail, natural
- **Flash:** Krinkle Mirror Flash
- **Hook:** #1 Gamakatsu Octopus barbless, nickel

Materials to tie the Hoh Bo Spey.

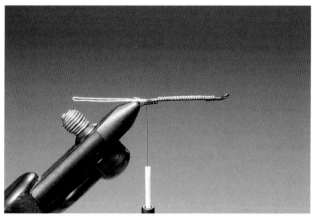

1. Wrap a base of thread over the entire shank, then wrap back to the rear of the fly. Cut a 3- or 4-inch section of 30-pound-test Fireline. Fold the Fireline in half and pinch the loop tight. Measuring your loop so it extends 2.3 cm (⅞") back, tie the Fireline down and wrap forward to the eye of the hook. Pull the butt ends back, folding them over the top of the first layer, then wrap the thread back to the rear. Trim the ends and apply a sparse bead of Zap-A-Gap or equivalent glue.

2. The butt of the Hoh Bo Spey can be dubbed simply by spinning the dubbing to the thread, but for added durability, a dubbing loop is preferred. Form a loop of thread a few inches long and spread a pinch of wine-colored Ice Dub or Angora goat inside the loop.

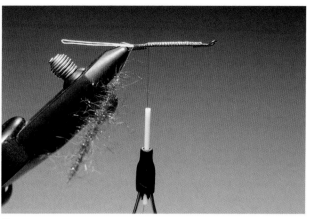

3. Using a dubbing loop tool, spin the loop so that the dubbing is locked in.

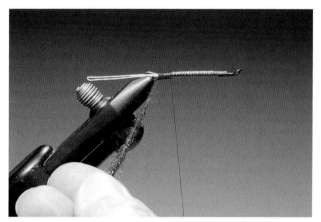

4. Compress the dubbing further with your fingers to tighten it up before wrapping.

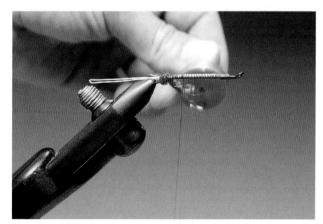

5. Wrap forward while pulling back the hair from previous wraps.

6. Tie in a 7.6 or 10 cm (3" or 4") section of wire for ribbing, then prepare another longer dubbing loop for the body. You'll need roughly three times the dubbing for the body as was used for the butt. Spread the black dubbing out within the thread loop and spin the dubbing loop tool to the desired tightness. Wrap forward evenly and tie off 2 mm (1/16") behind the eye of the fly.

7. Select a jumbo guinea hen feather, the longer the better. Strip off the marabou from the butt of the feather and tie in at the front end of the dubbed body, still leaving a 2 mm (1/16") gap between it and the eye of the hook. Using hackle pliers, fold and wrap the guinea hackle back with plenty of space between wraps. Four wraps is optimal.

8. Holding the end of the guinea feather tight with one hand, use the other hand to counterwrap the wire ribbing forward. Tie off the ribbing and trim excess guinea and wire.

9. Choose a premium black marabou feather and prepare it for hackling by stripping the lowest fibers away from the fat part of the stem. Hold the tip of the feather and pull the rest of the fibers back so you can tie in the tip without catching the longer fibers. Holding the fat stem of the marabou feather, wrap forward two or three turns and tie off.

10. Select and prepare a wine-colored marabou feather and repeat the previous steps, creating a sparse two-tone marabou hackle.

11. Cut six fibers from a Lady Amherst center tail feather and separate them for individual application. Tie them in one at a time so they are evenly spaced around the fly. One or two tight thread wraps per fiber are plenty. Trim the ends flush.

12. Tie in a couple of strands of Krinkle Mirror Flash on either side and shape the head of the fly.

13. Jungle cock eyes are optional, but they are recommended for sex appeal. Whip-finish and apply head cement. The hook is looped on later. You can shorten the loop by adding a figure-eight twist when applying the hook.

FISHING THE HOH BO SPEY

This remarkable fly was designed as a pattern for all seasons and all waters, and it really delivers. Large enough for turbid water and small enough for gin-clear water, its midrange profile is always appropriate. It fishes beautifully on a dry line with a long leader and can be taken down deeper using sink-tips and short leaders. Charles notes that he does occasionally tie the Hoh Bo Spey with extra-small lead eyes for situations where he feels the need to break through strong surface currents. He emphasizes that he's never really trying to "get down," just counteract natural drag that can lift the fly.

The thing about materials like Lady Amherst fibers is that they accentuate movement. A still photo can't do it justice, but we think it's still an interesting perspective.

The Silveynator

Perhaps the most diabolical steelhead fly to come along in our lifetimes is Brian Silvey's Silveynator. It's the nuclear option, for those times when you want to collect specimens like an old-time ichthyologist. The Silveynator's dressing borders on the simplistic, but that simplicity allows the best properties of each material to shine though. The bead head provides serious sinkiness when needed but is easy to cast. And for those anglers with nymphing tendencies, the extra grains offer complete and total control over the depth of the fly, even in really fast water. Step up to a tungsten bead and you can walk your fly along the bottom, but such weight is seldom necessary or prudent. Even with the brass bead, the Silveynator can require some slow stripping at the end of a swing, or whenever the current runs out, to avoid hanging up. But that is another double fake of this design, because those little stripping sessions will get you grabs.

Brian came up with the pattern in 2010, but it didn't hit fly shops until the following year. Unlike so many patterns that build slowly in popularity, the Silveynator blew up in 2012 and has been a staple ever since. Silvey says the pattern pretty much created itself:

"Yeah, it's pretty simple," he said, in his humble, almost sheepish way. "I was fishing a small river in the fall, and I kept cutting down my Tandem Tubes to make smaller flies. With the bunny strip that short, it didn't need anything else—it fished great. That winter, after a little playing around at the vise, it just clicked."

It's probably impossible for most of us to fathom the zone that Brian Silvey inhabits. Here's a guy who swings flies for steelhead somewhere around 200 days a year and has been doing so for well over three decades. For most of that time he has been guiding on the Deschutes and Sandy Rivers and tying flies like a madman. He holds a degree in fish biology and fisheries management, is a Federation of Fly Fishers (FFF)-certified casting instructor, and is among the most prolific signature tiers in the history of the fly industry. At the risk of embarrassing Brian, we thought it important to illustrate how a fly as elemental as the Silveynator didn't just roll off someone's vise. This fly was no accident. It was the product of decades of experience and thought. See more of Brian's creations on page 295 of the Fly Gallery.

They're going to make these illegal, so you'd better stock up.

SILVEYNATOR, BLACK/ORANGE

- **Tube:** Small-diameter tubing cut about 4 cm (1½") long
- **Thread:** 6/0 UNI-Thread, fluorescent orange
- **Tail:** Rabbit strip, black, from 2.5 cm (1") for short flies to 5 cm (2") for longer flies
- **Legs:** Ostrich, black
- **Flash:** Angel Hair, peacock
- **Hackle:** Schlappen, black
- **Collar:** Ice Dub, peacock
- **Bead:** Painted brass or tungsten bead, 5 to 6 mm (³⁄₁₆" to ¼") diameter, fluorescent orange (hole should be 2 mm [¹⁄₁₆"] diameter)
- **Junction tubing:** Small vinyl tubing, 1.3 to 2 cm (½" to ¾") long
- **Special tools:** Tube vise or tube-converter tool, 2 mm (¹⁄₁₆") drill bit, lighter

Note: Commercially tied Silveynators are built on a section of small, clear, rigid tubing (shown), but it can be easily adapted to any type of tube, including the old standby, the plastic stem of a cotton-tipped swab.

Materials for tying a black Silveynator. (You can still turn back!)

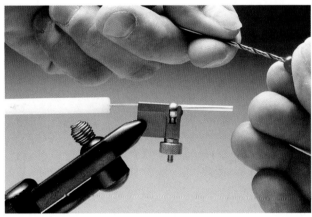

1. Cut a section of small-diameter rigid tubing about 4 cm (1½") long. Fit the tubing onto a tube-tying vise or a tube-converter tool. Select a painted brass or tungsten bead and make sure it will slide onto your tubing. Often the hole will need to be lightly bored out with a 2 mm (¹⁄₁₆") drill bit to remove the touch of paint that has caused the hole to narrow. Slide the bead onto the front end of the tube so that 2 mm (¹⁄₁₆") is sticking out the front.

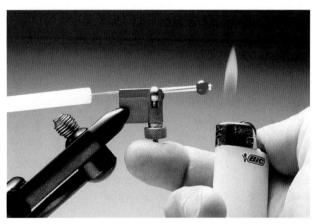

2. Carefully melt the end of the tubing with a lighter or candle to create a ridge that will hold the bead in place.

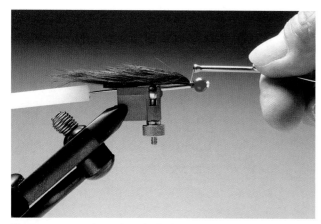

3. Start your thread right behind the bead and wrap back about 3 mm (⅛")—believe it or not, this is all the shank you'll need to create this amazing fly! Cut a section of black bunny strip from 2.5 to 5 cm (1" to 2") long and tie in over the thread base.

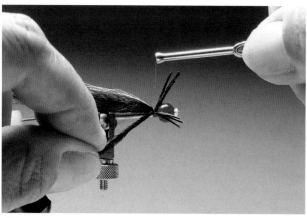

4. Center tie a small pinch of gold Angel Hair and pull back, wrapping down into a single sparse wing directly over the bunny strip. Then tie in three or four strands of black ostrich herl on either side of the body (optional but nice).

5. Tie in a black schlappen feather by the butt or the tip and wrap forward until your wraps are fitting tightly to the bead. Tie down and trim flush.

6. Dub a small pinch of peacock Ice Dub and wrap into a narrow collar directly behind the bead.

7. Two whip-finishes replace the need for head cement, and your Silveynator is ready for a short section of flexible junction tubing.

FISHING THE SILVEYNATOR

By Rob Russell

As mentioned earlier, this fly gives the angler complete control over the depth at which it rides through the current. For anglers who like to work weighted flies into narrow slots and pockets, borrowing from our jig-fishing brethren, there is nothing better.

My introduction to this game-changing fly came from my good friend Mariusz. He had driven down to the coast one early spring evening with a box full of freshly tied Silveynators. That night we sipped cocktails and huddled around the tying table.

"Rob, do you fish the Silveynator?" Mariusz asked.

"Never have," I replied. "Seems like they're always sold out when I go by the fly shop."

"Oh, man. You are going to love these," he said, handing me a small, clear plastic box full of little egg-sucking bunny leeches.

It felt like a drug deal. I could see there was a twinge of guilt behind Mariusz's eyes. And there was something in the way he handed me the box. He almost seemed to pull it back away from me with a look that said, "Careful!"

Each fly was a perfect steelhead confection, with its candy-coated bead. Mariusz had tied them in some beautiful color combinations, and I was instantly mesmerized.

"Rob," he said, looking around as if someone might be listening, "it's like jig for fly rod." His Eastern European accent made it feel like we were engaged in Cold War fishing espionage.

There was a long pause as I considered his words. I fit a size 4 Gamakatsu B10S hook into the junction tubing of a black-and-blue Silveynator and bounced it around in the palm of my hand. I felt like it would drop like a rock. The bunny strip was long enough to display great movement, but short enough that it didn't require a trailing loop or a secondary tie-down. The long shank of the B10S put the hook just inside the tip of the bunny—perfect! The whole thing was feeling very jiggy.

"Is this still fly fishing? I asked.

"I don't know, but I love it," Mariusz replied.

The next day we fished our favorite river and had the luxury of hitting many places where I had seen fish congregating the day before. With Mariusz swinging his switch rod from the bow of the boat, I would describe the spot where a fish had been the day before and hold the boat 40 or 50 feet above the site. Mariusz would cast across the fish's path, a few feet upstream. When the fly hit the water, he would drop some line, taking tension off the fly and drifting it down toward the fish. When the fly seemed to be just ahead of the steelhead's position, Mariusz pinned the line in his fingers and lifted the rod slightly to get the fly moving. One thousand one, one thousand two, bang! Fish on!

This scene repeated itself a couple more times before we pulled over for a break. It just so happened that this "break" put us on my favorite bar on the whole river,

You have to admit it's kind of "jiggy." But sometimes you just want to catch some fish.

One hell of a Tillamook rainbow at 37" x 19". I'm still shaking! MARIUSZ WROBLEWSKI PHOTO

and I was having evil thoughts as I grabbed Mariusz's new Beulah Onyx 6-weight. He had it rigged with a Skagit Switch line, a short custom sink-tip of T11, and a few feet of 12-pound tippet. At the end of all that was a gorgeous little black and blue Silveynator that I knew was going to get bit.

"You are gonna love that rod, man. Would you like a smoke before you go?"

We each burned a Marlboro and watched the water. I blathered on about all the amazing steelhead that had been caught from this particular run over the years. So many memories of snow-bellied chromers flying through the air—it was just one of those magic spots.

"After you, mister," Mariusz said with a knowing smile.

I waded into the riffle, then turned and angled upstream as I went. As great as the run below us looked, the narrow green slot coming from the tailout above looked like the place where my fish was hiding. With a fly like the Silveynator, I could easily lob it into the slot, take a couple of steps downstream to sink the fly, then lead it through the fast water at just the right depth. I finally made it into position, cast the fly to the very edge of the willows on the other side, and dropped a couple feet of line. When the current pulled my line tight, the swing came across slowly, with just the right amount of tension. I looked over at Mariusz, and he was looking

at me. I made a second cast, stepped down, and gently lifted the rod to start the swing. I heard Mariusz let out an involuntary "Oh, man . . ."

The fly stopped and pulled back with a heavy jerk. Mariusz started laughing, and the fish turned directly downstream and ran full speed away from me. It felt really heavy, but I wasn't used to the rod, so I couldn't be positive.

It was my second cast with a Silveynator, and all of my evil plans were coming true exactly as I had imagined. The fish held its ground, and I came to realize it was, in fact, a big one. A couple of minutes later, as it held in the fastest, deepest water and refused to move, I thought I might even have an early spring chinook. As that thought flitted through my mind, the fish started to show some fatigue, then it rolled to the surface, showing thick sides and the wide, pink stripe of a spring buck. It took a few more minutes to wear him down, but we finally brought him to hand and put the tape to him: 94 cm (37") long, 48 cm (19") around, and one I will remember as long as I live. *Thanks, Brian and Mariusz!*

P.S. Brian's preferred program is 91 to 122 cm (3' to 4') of leader, period. And 10-pound for summer fish, 12-pound for winter fish. Keep it simple, he says. I can't do it, but you probably should.

Ward's Shank-Style Intruder

We discussed the history of the Intruder earlier (see chapter 4, The Intruder Revolution). Here we offer a personal variation developed over five seasons of heavy fishing and tying with only Intruders. The Nightmare Intruder is named for the black/red/white color combination made famous by the Nightmare Jig. This evil jig pattern was born on the Cascade River of Washington State. From there it leaked to the coast, then to the lower Columbia, where it rocketed to fame. In the years since, many fly anglers have borrowed the color scheme to design their own Nightmare flies.

This version of the Intruder incorporates one minor modification to Ed's original design—it doesn't have a hackle or dubbing loop in its rear section. This style emerged over time, as I came to feel that the rear hackle obstructed the view deeper into the fly. So one day I simply left out the rear dubbing loop of arctic fox. Suddenly the rear view of the fly was wide open. And it was one less dubbing loop to worry about. Ken Morrish addressed the issue of "opening up" the fly in his Intruder designs (page 254) by trimming away some of the rear hackle.

There are a lot of ways to tie and rig Intruders, but the "sacrificial hook" method is the original. That term refers to the fact that you'll be transforming a perfectly good hook into a shank, which some see as wasteful. Today you don't have to mutilate perfectly good hooks since there are several brands of prepared shanks to choose from. I still enjoy tying them on an Alec Jackson Spey hook. I love the curvature of the shank, the "just right" diameter of the wire, and the small, finely crafted eye. But for the utilitarian purpose of building an Intruder, you can get away with any upturned-eye hook of the desired length. You can also create a shank from scratch by bending spinner or piano wire.

A subtle but critical feature of the original shank-style design is the tiny monofilament loop built in at the back end. This adds resistance to support for the wire insulation that holds the tippet to the shank. Without it, repeated casting will work the insulation off the end of the shank and eventually the tippet will tear through the insulation. Many a beautiful Intruder has been tied without this loop, either accidentally or on purpose, and most have ended up as cat toys or worse.

Shank-Style Intruders are a blast to tie and fish. But be careful, they can take over your life!

NIGHTMARE INTRUDER, SHANK-STYLE

- **Shank:** #1/0 Alec Jackson Spey hook
- **Thread:** 140-denier, red
- **Weight:** Small lead eyes painted white
- **Tag:** Flat Mylar tinsel, gold side up
- **Butt:** Small chenille, fluorescent red or cerise
- **Rear eyes:** Jungle cock nails
- **Split-tail:** Ostrich herl, black, topped with Lady Amherst pheasant tail
- **Rib:** Small copper wire
- **Body:** Flat Diamond Braid, fluorescent red, palmered with hot orange saddle hackle
- **Front hackle:** In three parts, back to front: 1) arctic fox tail, fluorescent red, spun in a dubbing loop, 2) 15 to 20 strands of ostrich herl, black, spun in a dubbing loop, 3) 12 to 15 strands of Lady Amherst pheasant tail, natural, spun in a dubbing loop
- **Wing:** Pair of black-laced American hen hackle tips dyed red
- **Flash:** Two strands of Krinkle Mirror Flash doubled over
- **Special tools:** Medium toothbrush, wire cutters, file, hackle pliers, dubbing loop tool (Vergara's amazing Wishbone Dubbing Whirler shown)

Materials for tying a shank-style Nightmare Intruder.

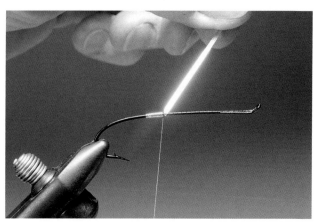

2. Start your thread just behind the eye of the hook and wrap back 4.5 cm (1¾") for your base layer. Tie in a 7.6 cm (3") long section of medium flat Mylar tinsel, gold side down. Bring your thread forward 6 mm (¼"), then wrap the tinsel forward, gold side up, to the thread. Tie off and trim flush.

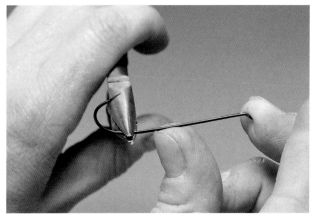

1. It's optional whether you want to take some of the bend out of the hook before you lock it in the vise. As much as I love the curve of these hooks, too much curve will aim your trailing hook down at an angle. I prefer to straighten the shank just a little to keep the hook from aiming too far down. The trouble with this approach is that it orients the hook point at an unusual angle and can cause tiers to hurt themselves. *Please be careful!*

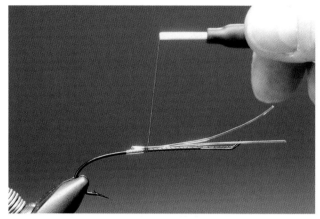

3. Cut a 10 cm (4") section of 30-pound-test Maxima Ultragreen or its equivalent. Bend it in half and pinch the bend tight. Lay the mono loop down over the top of the Mylar tag with the butt ends pointed toward the front of the fly. Measure it out to roughly 5 mm (³⁄₁₆"), or slightly shorter than the tag, and secure with a few tight thread wraps.

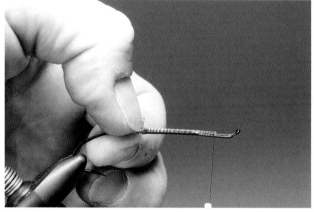

4. Wrap the thread forward, keeping the monofilament tags lined up evenly on top of the shank. Stop your thread wraps 5 mm (³⁄₁₆") behind the eye of the hook and give a few more turns in that position to lock down the end. These precise measurements seem a little silly, but they can be helpful when you're starting out. If you don't have a ruler, you can always eyeball it using our photos for reference.

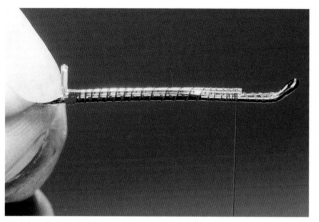

5. Trim the mono butt sections flush to your last wrap of thread. Use your thumbnail to forcefully bend the remaining mono loop forward toward the front of the fly. Bring the loop back so it stands up perpendicular to the shank.

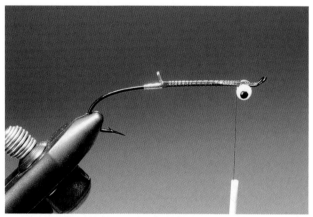

6. Tie in the dumbbell eyes under the shank with alternating thread wraps across the center in an X pattern until they feel firmly in place. Give the eyes a few more wraps of thread in a figure-eight pattern, then a few more in the X pattern. Alternate these until the eyes feel solid, then wrap the thread back to the rear of the fly.

7. Tie in one or two tight turns of small-diameter fluorescent-red chenille, secure, and trim. Select two jungle cock nails and tie them in tightly on either side of the chenille bump. The closer your thread wraps are to the chenille, the more the eyes will stand out from the shank—a 45-degree angle is optimum. Clip six full-length strands of black ostrich herl from a feather, pinch them together at their base and wet them with either spit or water. The strands will stick together, making them easy to handle. Tie in the first bunch on one side of the fly, then repeat the steps and place a second bunch on the opposite side. The classic split-tail flares out at 45-degree angles on the top side of the tube.

8. Top each side with three strands of Lady Amherst pheasant tail, being careful to maintain the 45-degree flare of the tail. Tie in a 10 cm (4") section of copper wire and lay back over the vise for later ribbing. Tie in a 10 or 13 cm (4" or 5") section of flat braid and wrap forward to within 3 mm (⅛") of the dumbbell eyes. Tie off and trim flush. Select a hot orange saddle hackle with long fibers for the inner skeleton of the fly. Remove the marabou from the butt end and tie in at the front.

9. Palmer the hackle back and counterwrap with the copper wire. This means holding the hackle tip tight with one hand and counterwrapping the wire with the other.

10. Make a dubbing loop roughly 10 cm (4") long for the first stage of the front hackle. Select a healthy pinch of fluorescent-red arctic fox tail and remove the guard hairs. Place the clump of hair in the dubbing loop and spread it out evenly.

11. Spin the arctic fox, then brush until it is clear enough to wrap without bunching up. A medium toothbrush is a perfect tool for this. Take your time and brush gently until almost every trapped fiber comes free.

12. Wet the fibers and fold them to one side of the thread as you would a wet fly hackle. Wrap forward, folding as you go, keeping each wrap tight to the one before.

13. Tie off the dubbing loop, trim flush, and brush the hackle forward and backward until it is clear of clumps and trapped fibers.

14. Wet the hackle once more and pull it back out of the way, then make another 10 cm (4") long dubbing loop. Select 15 to 20 strands of black ostrich, bunch them together, and hold them over your Intruder. You'll be spinning these fibers in the dubbing loop to create the second layer of the front hackle, so you'll

want to measure out the appropriate length and trim them all flush. With the ends butt ends all lined up evenly, place them into the dubbing loop and press the thread against your index finger to pin down all the fibers. With the fibers held under pressure, you can use a bodkin or the tips of your scissors to separate each fiber so they spin into an even hackle.

15. Once they are separated by 1 or 2 mm (about $\frac{1}{32}$"), spin the loop tight and lightly brush to free any trapped fibers.

16. Wet and fold the fibers back to prepare for wrapping the hackle.

17. Wrap forward to finish the front hackle, then make your final 10 cm (4") dubbing loop. Select 12 to 15 strands of Lady Amherst tail and repeat the steps above to spin and hackle the Amherst fibers. If your measurements are perfect, your last wrap of hackle will fit tightly behind the dumbbell eyes. But don't worry if it takes a few attempts to get a handle on all the dimensions that go into this fly.

18. For your wings, pick out a matching pair of black-laced American hen cape feathers dyed red. Measure them out over the fly and strip all excess fibers from the stems. Tie in the first hackle tip in reverse, then bend back. Depending on the feather you may need to cross the hackle tip diagonally over the top of the tube in order to have it lay back in a "tented" position. Or you may need to just pull it straight back on the same side as it was tied in. Take your time and try a couple of different tactics until you get the feather to sit at the angle you want. Repeat those steps on the other side so you end up with a nicely tented pair of wings. This can be the most difficult step, as the quills of different feathers have different shapes, and can end up folding back inconsistently. Tie in two strands of Krinkle Mirror Flash on one side, then double them back and tie down so they run along the other side. Give it two whip-finishes and apply head cement.

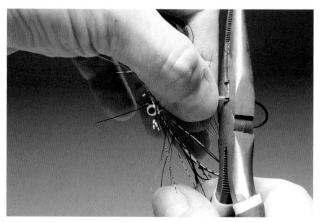

19. To finish the fly, you'll need to wait until the head cement is completely dry. Then, use a pair of wire cutters to cut the hook from the shank, about 3 mm (⅛") behind the tag.

20. Gently pull all of the fly's materials to the front of the fly and get a good grip on it with one hand. With the other hand, use a file to smooth the end of the hook wire. It's critical that there be no sharp edges left that could abrade or cut your tippet while fishing.

Once the end is filed smooth, you're ready for the final test. . . .

THE BOWL TEST

As Ed Ward explains in the Intruder tying sequence of the first *Skagit Master* video, the bowl test reveals whether an Intruder has been successfully constructed. Tie the hook-less fly to a short piece of tippet material and give it a swim in a bowl of water. Are the materials standing out and creating a full profile? Is the split-tail flaring away from the shank, or just hanging behind the fly? Are the wings lying back the way you planned? Then pull the fly out of the water and observe how it collapses. Does it compress into a pencil, or does it retain some of its shape? Over time you will learn a lot from your bowl tests, and your Intruders will evolve and improve.

It's important to point out here that even a properly constructed Intruder can fail due to unexpected variances in materials. Arctic fox tail, or whatever substitute you decide to use, is usually the key. Stiffer arctic fox holds it shape, while the soft stuff collapses when wet. Sometimes a batch of fox tail will seem fine but end up not performing, while others that seem questionable surprise you. It can be a moving target, so don't beat yourself up if a fly doesn't meet your expectations. Just tie another one.

To the uninitiated, the bowl test seems like an indulgence, like a victory lap. But when you are engineering these flies for specific traits, the bowl test helps you see how different materials interact when wet.

FISHING THE SHANK-STYLE INTRUDER

To fish this fly you'll need a hook and a section of small flexible tubing from 6 to 9 mm (¼" to ⅜") long. Gamakatsu's B10S is a good choice, but you can use many different hook styles. For the tubing, Ed Ward settled on a section of insulation from 16-gauge electrical wire for his Intruders. You can also find flexible vinyl tubing that fits the task. It just has to be small enough in diameter to hold tightly to your shank.

Rigging the Intruder is similar to rigging a tube. Run the terminal end of your tippet through the eye of the hook and again through the tiny monofilament loop at the rear end of the fly. Slide it up the leader, then slide a section of insulation or tubing up the leader. Tie on a hook using Lefty's No-Slip Mono Loop. Slide the insulation and fly back down to the hook, then push the insulation onto the smooth-filed end of the hook wire. As you tighten the tippet down, you can adjust the hook so that it rides upside down. This will help your fly avoid hanging up on rocks and wood when it's on the swing.

Shank-Style Intruders, at least the longer ones, are notoriously difficult to cast. That said, a sparsely tied fly of moderate length (like the one featured here) will cast quite well using a compact Skagit-style head. The length of your sink-tip is another major factor in how this rig will cast. Through winter and spring, a 3 m (10') section of T-14 is the perfect tip for casting. There may be times when you need 3.7 or 4.3 m (12' or 14') to cut through turbulence, and you will feel a big difference in casting. In the summer, a 3 to 4.3 m (10' to 14') section of type III sink-tip is usually plenty.

Keep your leader fairly short. In normal winter and spring conditions where there's at least a little turbidity, 1 to 1.2 m (3' or 4') of leader is sufficient. For clear water you may want to lengthen your leader to 1.5 or 1.8 m (5' or 6').

Most of the original Intruder clan typically cast the fly at a 90-degree angle, make one full mend to reset the angle a little lower, and let it swing. In heavy flows where they want the fly to drop down early in the swing, they'll take their downstream steps immediately after their mend. This accentuates the mend, allowing the fly to drop before it comes under tension. As with any fly, make sure your Intruder swings all the way to the end, then let it hang for a couple of seconds. If you're bottoming out, lighten up your sink-tip and try again. When you've hit the sweet spot, you'll be able to sink the fly when you want to, but you should always be able make it all the way through the swing without hanging up.

Remember, this fly was not designed to dredge the bottom. The weight in an Intruder is usually intended to break through the surface current. As Ed relates in

Dec Hogan's masterwork, *A Passion for Steelhead*, "People think I must be fishing them right on the bottom when they see the lead eyes, but I'm lucky if they sink a foot or two. Without the lead, they would skate on the surface."

One final note on fishing Ed's original rigging: Where your tippet goes through the eye of the shank, and again where it's held to the butt end of the shank by the wire insulation, a certain amount of abrasion is to be expected. Check your tippet for abrasion every hour or so and retie whenever you can feel noticeable roughness.

Ward's Tube-Style Intruder

Tube-Style Intruders have become popular owing to the ease with which they can be tied, rigged, and fished. They are generally lighter to cast, as long as they are not weighed down with excess materials. While Shank-Style Intruders are generally more durable and deeper sinking, they require additional accessories and rigging time compared to a simple tube. Ed Ward discusses the pros and cons in the first *Skagit Master* video as he ties a Tube-Style Intruder for the camera. He notes that the tube version is especially good for Intruders that are tied "in the round," with no distinct top or bottom. We've found that most tubes can be stabilized enough to maintain the desired attitude if materials are applied carefully, and the hook and eyes are positioned to provide adequate keel. That said, even the most careful designs can end up riding at an angle or even spinning. This is at least partly because of the tendency for the tubes themselves to bend under the pressure of many thread wraps. Tying on some of the softer tubes will train you to be sparing with thread wraps and even with thread pressure to avoid bending or crushing them. This variability makes the bowl test a helpful exercise for correcting problems at the tying bench rather than out on the water.

This wild little thing incorporates slender grizzly hackle tips to accentuate movement and contrast. And the chartreuse saddle hackle at the center glows like a tiny lightbulb.

The "Fire Tiger" color scheme, ranging from green to chartreuse to hot orange, is a study in contrasts and a fun combination for an Intruder. We chose it here to illustrate how contrasting shades and colors can create layers within an Intruder with the absolute minimum of materials. Notice how the orange arctic fox and the chartreuse saddle hackle glow from within the heart of the fly. Meanwhile the hot-pink grizzly hackle tips and natural gray ostrich shape the outer profile. This is a fly that is sure to be visible to a fish no matter what part of the color spectrum is dominating because of light conditions. Its profile is large, but the illusion is created with a few whisps of ostrich and a couple of narrow hackle tips. This fly won't absorb water, making it easy to cast despite its size.

Materials for tying the Fire Tiger Intruder on a Pro Tube.

TUBE-STYLE INTRUDER, FIRE TIGER

- **Tube:** Pro Flexitube 40/10, clear
- **Thread:** 140-denier, red
- **Weight:** Small lead eyes painted white
- **Butt:** Small chenille, cerise
- **Rear hackle:** Guinea hen, natural
- **Rear eyes:** Jungle cock nails
- **Split-tail:** Ostrich herl, natural gray, topped with grizzly hackle tips dyed cerise
- **Rib:** Small copper wire
- **Body:** Flat Diamond Braid, fluorescent red, palmered with chartreuse saddle hackle
- **Front hackle:** In two parts, back to front: 1) arctic fox tail, fluorescent red, spun in a dubbing loop; 2) 15 to 20 strands of ostrich herl, natural gray
- **Tentacles:** Two grizzly saddle hackle tips, dyed cerise, positioned to flare out from the sides of the fly
- **Wing:** Pair of grizzly hackle tips, natural
- **Flash:** Single strand of Krystal Flash doubled over

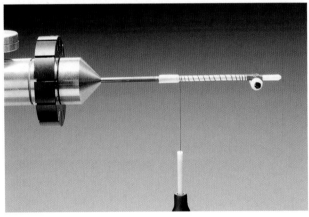

1. Lay down a base layer of thread on the front end of the tube where the dumbbell eyes will be secured. Tie in the dumbbell eyes with alternating thread wraps across the center in an X pattern until they feel firmly in place. Give the eyes a few more wraps of thread in a figure-eight pattern, then a few more in the X pattern. Alternate these until the eyes feel solid, then wrap the thread back to the rear of the fly.

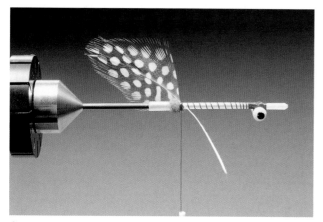

2. Tie in two tight turns of small-diameter cerise chenille, secure, and trim. Select a large guinea hen feather, strip its marabou from the thick end of the stem, and tie in at the base.

3. Wrap the guinea forward two or three wraps. Tie off and trim.

4. Choose two jungle cock nails and tie them in on either side of the tube. Once strongly secured, fold them all the way forward, then back so they stand out at 45 degrees from the tube with the guinea hackle.

5. You'll want a cup of water on the bench for this next trick: Clip six strands of ostrich herl from a feather and pinch the ends tight between your thumb and index finger. Dip the ends in the water and use your other hand to squeeze the water off. Those six light strands of ostrich are suddenly transformed into a single unit that can be easily tied in at the tail. The classic split-tail flares out at 45-degree angles on the top side of the tube; tie in the first bunch on one side of the fly, then repeat the steps and place a second bunch on the opposite side.

6. Top each side with a long, narrow grizzly hackle tip, dyed cerise.

7. Tie in a 10 cm (4") section of copper wire and lay back over the vise for later. Tie in a 10 or 13 cm (4" or 5") section of flat braid and wrap forward to within 3 mm (⅛") of the dumbbell eyes. Tie off and trim flush.

8. Select a chartreuse saddle hackle with long fibers for the inner skeleton of the fly. Remove the marabou from the butt end and tie in at the front.

9. Palmer the hackle back and counterwrap with the copper wire. This will mean holding the hackle tip tight with one hand and counterwrapping the wire with the other.

10. Make a dubbing loop roughly 10 cm (4") long for the first stage of the front hackle. Select a healthy pinch of fluorescent-red arctic fox tail. If the guard hairs are too crazy, you can pull them out, but leaving them in will add some stiffness to your fur hackle. Place the clump of hair in the dubbing loop and spread it out evenly. Give the mat of fur a slight diagonal angle within the thread loop as shown, so that the length of the finished fibers tapers from shorter to longer.

11. Spin the arctic fox, then brush until it is clear enough to wrap without bunching up. A stiff dubbing brush is okay, but a standard medium toothbrush is optimal. Take your time, brush gently, and feel every trapped fiber come free.

12. Wet the fibers and fold them to one side of the thread as you would a wet fly hackle. Wrap forward, folding as you go, keeping each wrap tight to the one before. Tie off the dubbing loop, trim flush, and brush the hackle until it's clear of clumps and trapped fibers.

14. With the butt ends all lined up evenly, place them into the dubbing loop and press the thread against your index finger to pin down all the fibers. With the fibers held under pressure, you can use the tips of your scissors to separate each fiber so they are lined up.

13. It will help to wet the fox hackle and pull it back out of the way for the next step. Make another 10 cm (4") long dubbing loop. Select 15 to 20 strands of natural gray ostrich, bunch them together, and hold them over your Intruder. You'll be spinning these fibers in the dubbing loop to create the second layer of the front hackle, so you'll want to measure out the appropriate length and trim them all flush.

15. Spin the loop tight and lightly brush the ostrich fibers to free any that were trapped.

Dries & Skater, page 2. Top row, left to right: Davidchik's Lil O'Muddler, Mia's Metalhead Muddler, Mystery Marabou Muddler. Second row: Brett's Obie Waker, Bjorn's Tom Thumb, Lambroughton's Moose Hair Skater. Third row: Jay's Muddler Simplicity, Spencer's Burnt Toast, Perakis's Crude Muddler. Fourth Row: St. Pierre's Greased Liner, Pinch's Craftober Caddis, Pinch's Indie Skater Tube. Fifth row: Morrish's Pompadour Skater, Quigley's Dragon Gurgler, Karnopp's Shade Chaser. Sixth row: Finnerty's Steelhead Skater, Barrett's Riffle Plow, Davidchik's Skater Kiss.

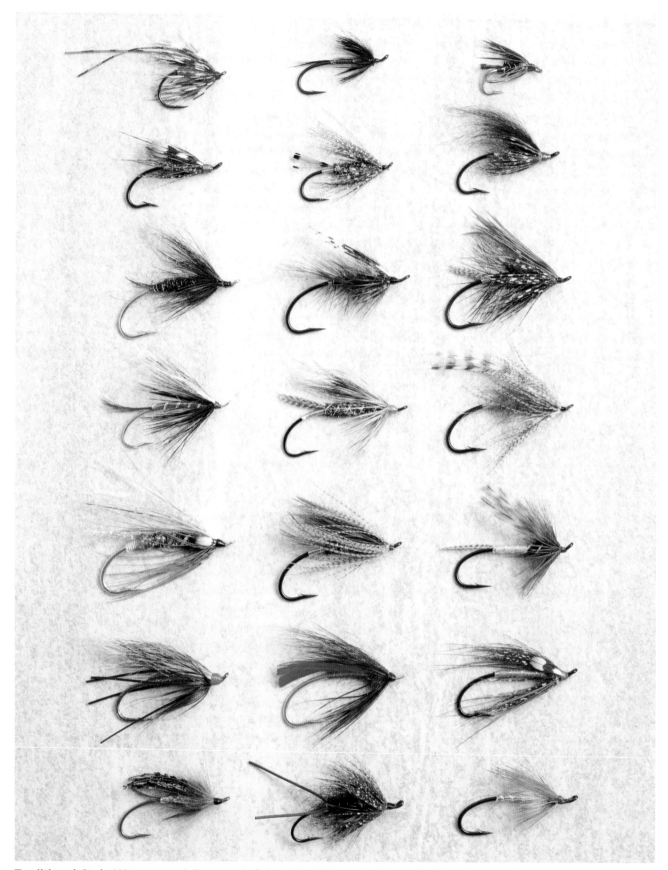

Traditional-Style Wets, page 1. Top row, left to right: Hickman's Dinner Bell, Perakis's Holo Gnat, Davidchik's Lil Double Coachman. Second row: St. Pierre's Steelhead Pupa, Hartwick's Skinny Spratley, St. Pierre's Fox Wing. Third row: Mia's Black Diamond, Klara's Railbird 2001, Hartwick's Silent Assassin. Fourth row: Hazel's Engagement, Bennett's Halo, Hartwick's October Hilton. Fifth row: Ramsey's Hüsker Dü, Hartwick's Duck Turd, Perakis's Green Cree Hilton. Sixth row: Karnopp's Kortge Closer, Sheppard's Rednecks' Revenge, St. Pierre's Steelhead Soft Hackle. Seventh row: Davidchik's Autumn Error, Fitzpatrick's Steelhead Stone, Davidchik's Moe.

Traditional-Style Wets, page 2. Top row, left to right: Jay's Steelhead Simplicity, Klara's Bluesbreaker, Silvey's Lucky Charm. Second row: Bennett's Last Light, Ewing's Punk Rock Girl, Ramsey's Blue Meanie. Third row: Chou's Dawn Patrol, Ewing's Chrome Snatcher. Fourth row: Vokey's Classy Hooker, Fitzpatrick's Seahawk. Fifth row: Pink & Purple Bin Fly, Hazel's Green-Butt Lum Plum, Silvey's Snow Cone, purple. Sixth row: Barrett's Pink Angel, Perakis's Flood Cab, Silvey's Snow Cone, black and green. Bottom: Davidchik's Fallout.

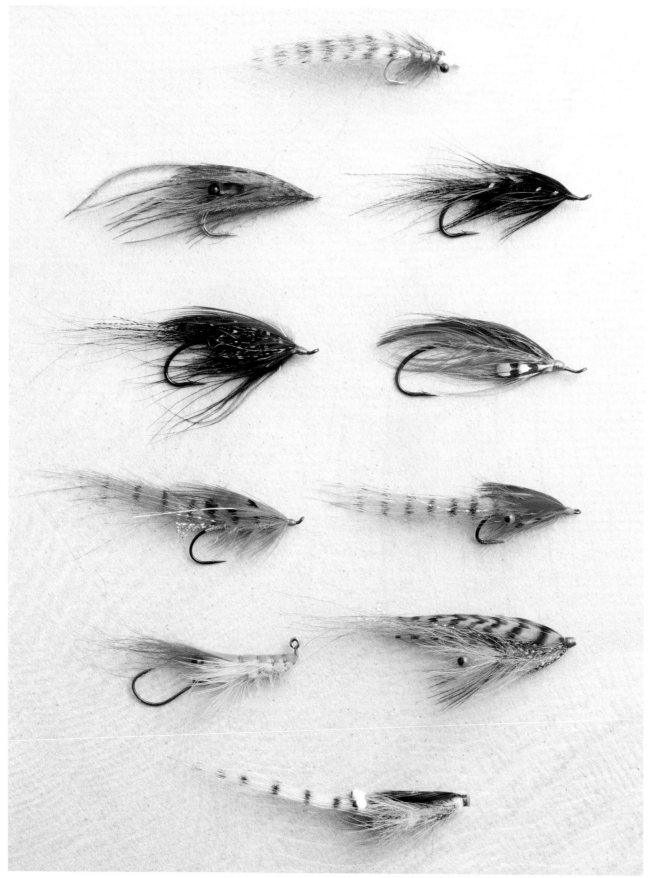

Shrimp & Prawns, page 1. Clockwise from the top: Russell's Motion Krill, Perakis's Santiam GP, St. Pierre's Ribbon Spey, Russell's Quick Prawn; Mishler's Prawn, Koertge's One-Off Prawn, Mikey's Shrimp, Ingi's Motion Prawn, St. Pierre's GP Spey, Morrish's Simple Prawn.

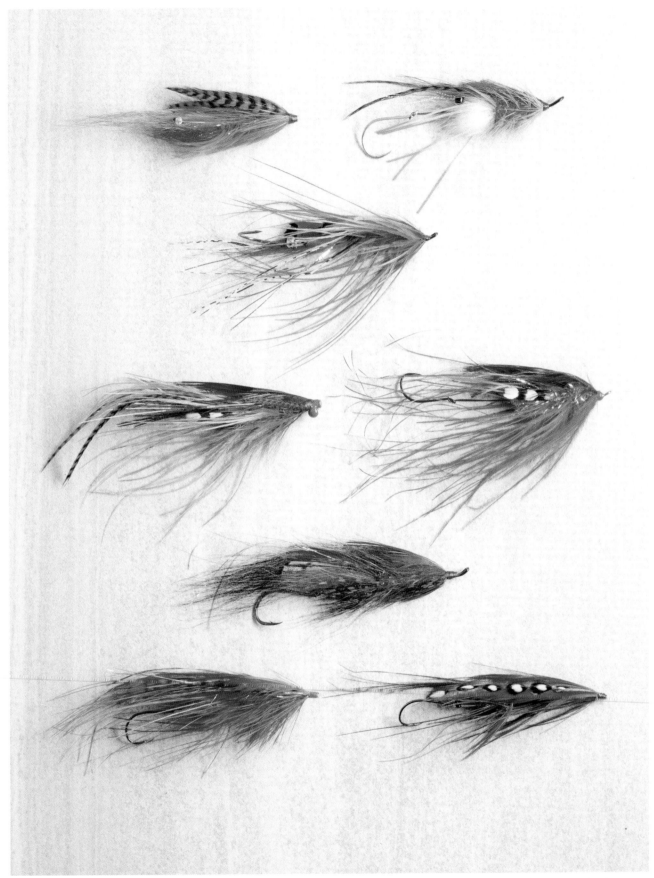

Shrimp & Prawns, page 2. Top row: Mishler's Prawn, Mikey's Prawn. Second row: Goodis's BC Prawn. Third row: Justin Miller's Rusty Prawn Tube, Paul Miller's Super Spey Prawn. Fourth row: St. Pierre's Foxee GP. Fifth row: Styskal's Sauk River Prawn, Styskal's Trago Satyr.

Half-Chickens, page 1. Top row: Mishler's Hairwing Intruder, Howell's Signature Intruder. Second row: Paul Miller's Super Spey Phantom. Third row: Hickman's Fish Taco, Workingman's Intruder. Fourth row: Vokey's Navy Deceiver. Fifth row: Feenstra's Grapefruit Leech, Senyo's Artificial Intelligence.

Half-Chickens, page 2. Clockwise from the top: Niagara Intruder, Gwyn's Fly, Stu's Intruder, Bjorn's Overdressed Hooker, Goodis's Muppet Intruder, Koertge's Fur Burger, Zellman's Intruder, French's Intruder, Justin Miller's Blue Steel Intruder, Mikey's Blue Intruder.

Half-Chickens, page 3. Top row: Howell's Squidro, Mikey's Mini-Intruder. Second row: Fergus's Strung Out Beach Bum, Fitzpatrick's UV Polar Intruder. Third row: Pinch's Intruder, Piette's Intruder. Fourth row: Morrish's Ostrich Temptress, Morrish's Intruder. Fifth row: Ewing's Hoh Special, Bjorn's Jumbo Critter.

Tubes, page 1. Top row: Nickel's Zebra Tube, Hazel's Fruit Stripe. Second row: Pinch's Eat a Peach Leech, Marty's Metal Detector. Third row: Koertge's Fur Burger, Hartwick's Hoser. Fourth row: Ingi's Turbo Cone, Barry's Rambulance.

Motion Prawns in five delicious colors; a space-age Turbo Cone, bottom.

Bjorn Beech

Bjorn Beech is a prolific custom fly tier and the mad scientist behind several iconic steelhead and salmon patterns. He's also the proprietor of one of the greatest fly shops in Steelhead Country, the Fly Fisher in Lacey, Washington. Bjorn's Jumbo Critters and Super Stinger Prawns have been the leading "big flies" on the market for the last decade or more. He says he learned the basics from his dad, starting with his first fly when he was four years old. "My biggest influences since Dad would have to be Syd Glasso and Poul Jorgensen," he said. "They had a wonderful eye for detail and perfection." Today Bjorn ties hundreds of dozens of steelhead flies each season for the jet set, and his touch is unmistakable. Steelhead and salmon guides the world over recognize and admire his flies when they find them in a client's box. When we asked him how many flies he ties each year, he couldn't pin down a number. "Well, let's put it this way. . . . I've gone through 257 spools of thread in the last six months."

Many of Bjorn's flies are built using wire dubbing loops, a technique that has become one of his trademarks.

"The thing I do that gets the most questions is spinning loops with my Makita drill," he said. "It's the quickest and most durable way to go." He's developed a brilliant system involving minimal tools, and he's happy to help other tiers get started. He also sells fly components, including his own Intruder shanks in multiple sizes, custom cone-heads in many sizes and colors, and an amazing Big Bore bodkin that makes picking out dubbing a breeze. To purchase some of Bjorn's specialized components and tools, look up the Fly Fisher's business listing on page 307.

Over the course of our interviews for the book, there was one topic that brought out the most emotion in Bjorn, and it's one to which we can relate: "Like many of us, I started tying on Mustad hooks," he said. "For years we begged and pleaded them to make a sharper, stronger hook. They didn't. When the Japanese hooks hit the market—Tiemco, Gamakatsu, Owner, Daiichi—I threw all of my Mustads in the garbage, where I hope they burn in hell." Amen, brother.

Bjorn doing a little harvesting down the road from his shop in Lacey, Washington. If you love great fly shops, check out the Fly Fisher. BJORN BEECH PHOTO

RUBBER LEGGED TOM THUMB

- **Hook:** #4 Tiemco 760
- **Thread:** UTC 210- or 280-denier, fluorescent orange
- **Tail:** Elk rump
- **Body:** Thread
- **Back and wing:** Elk rump
- **Legs:** Perfect Rubber, brown

Notes: Bjorn says he encountered this pattern while exploring Canadian lakes. He added the rubber legs and started using it as a steelhead skater.

OCTOBER CADDIS SPEY

- **Hook:** #4 Tiemco 777 or 9395
- **Thread:** 140-denier, black
- **Body:** Stretch tubing, amber, filled with olive oil
- **Hackle:** Sparse Angora goat hair spun in a dubbing loop
- **Collar:** Widgeon
- **Wing:** Mallard, brown
- **Head:** Ice Dub, peacock

Notes: This is tied low-water style, leaving about 3 mm (⅛") of the shank exposed in the back.

HEAD KNOCKER

- **Hook:** #2-6 Tiemco 777 or 9395
- **Thread:** 210-denier, tan
- **Tail:** In two parts, bottom to top: 1) grizzly chickabou, tan; 2) rabbit strip, sculpin olive
- **Body:** Flat Diamond Braid, gold
- **Belly/throat:** Grizzly chickabou, tan
- **Wing:** Rabbit strip, sculpin olive, flanked by grizzly neck feathers, olive
- **Head:** Sculpin Helmet
- **Eyes:** 5 mm adhesive, red

BOTTLE BRUSH LEECH, BLACK

- **Hook:** #2-6 Tiemco 777 or 9395
- **Bead:** Black, sized to desired weight
- **Thread:** 210-denier, black
- **Tail:** Marabou, black, with holographic Flashabou, purple
- **Body:** Stretch tubing, black, filled with olive oil, and palmered with Whiting Dry Fly saddle, black
- **Hackle:** Several additional turns of the Whiting Dry Fly saddle, black

Notes: Bjorn says that his most memorable steelhead of his life came to a Bottle Brush Leech. "It was a 41-inch buck that took the fly in about a foot of water. I was stripping in for the next cast, the water exploded, and hell was released!"

SUPERMAN

- **Shank:** The Fly Fisher Shanks by Bjorn, 2.5 cm (1")
- **Thread:** 210-denier, red
- **Stinger loop:** 26.4-pound Surflon-coated wire, 2.8 cm (1⅛") long
- **Weight:** Reversed cone, red
- **Tail:** Polar bear, red, tied sparse
- **Body:** Polar Chenille, kingfisher blue
- **Collar:** In two parts, back to front: 1) rhea and Flashabou, both blue, twisted in a wire dubbing loop; 2) guinea hen, kingfisher blue
- **Cheeks:** Jungle cock nails
- **Hook:** #1 Gamakatsu Drop Shot

Notes: Bjorn says the original name for this fly isn't clear, indicating it is a pattern he picked up somewhere along his steelheading career.

PIXIE BITCH, PINK

- **Shank:** The Fly Fisher Shanks by Bjorn, 2.5 cm (1")
- **Thread:** 210-denier, fluorescent orange
- **Stinger loop:** 26.4-pound Surflon-coated wire, 2.8 cm (1⅛") long
- **Weight:** Large reversed cone, red
- **Body:** UV Polar Chenille, pink
- **Collar:** In two parts, back to front: 1) polar bear or bucktail, pink, twisted in a wire dubbing loop; 2) silver Flashabou spun in a dubbing loop
- **Hook:** #1 Gamakatsu Drop Shot

Clockwise from top: Bottle Brush Leech; October Caddis Spey; Rubber-Legged Tom Thumb, Head Knocker.

BJORN'S SUPER STINGER PRAWN, BLACK/BLUE

- **Shank:** The Fly Fisher Shanks by Bjorn, 4.5 to 5.7 cm (1¾" to 2¼")
- **Thread:** 210-denier, black
- **Stinger loop:** 26.4-pound Surflon-coated wire, 3.2 cm (1¼") long
- **Weight:** Medium nickel-plated lead eyes secured behind front marabou hackle
- **Tail:** Bucktail, black, topped with Flashabou, silver and metallic blue
- **Rear hackle:** Marabou or Spey plume, royal blue
- **Body:** Small chenille, black
- **Shellback:** Scud back, clear
- **Front hackle:** Marabou or Spey plume, black
- **Wing:** Three American hen neck feathers laid flat, 5.4 cm (2⅛") long
- **Hook:** #1 Gamakatsu Drop Shot

Notes: The original Bjorn Super Prawn was one of the first large commercial marabou streamers to hit the shop bins in the 1990s. At the time, it was tied on large Tiemco 7999s, and it was offered in a bunch of great color combos. Then, as the collective consciousness of Northwest steelheaders began wading through a period of short-strike insecurity in the late '90s, the market called for revision, and the Super Stinger Prawn was born. The geeks among us will note that the commercial variety relies on Fireline for its stinger loop (usually doubled), while Bjorn's custom ties sport his famous Surflon loop.

Bjorn points out that the true origins of the Super Prawn date back to the 1980s, when he and other Cascadia steelheaders were starving for flies with more profile and attitude. Steelheaders on the Cowlitz, Kalama, Skykomish, and Skagit were faced with massive water and volatile winter and spring flows. It was the dawn of a marabou streamer revolution—a prelude to the Intruder revolution that would begin a decade later. And the Super Prawn ranked as the Che Guevara of the marabou uprising.

BJORN'S JUMBO CRITTER, PINK/ORANGE

- **Shank:** The Fly Fisher Shanks by Bjorn, 4.5 to 5.7 cm (1¾" to 2¼")
- **Thread:** 210-denier, red
- **Stinger loop:** 26.4-pound Surflon-coated wire, 3 cm (1³⁄₁₆") long
- **Eyes:** Small to medium brass, gold finish

- **Weight (optional):** Reversed cone head under front collars for larger profile
- **Tail:** Polar bear or DNA Frosty Fish Fiber, pink, twisted in a wire dubbing loop
- **Flash:** Krystal Flash, pink
- **Body:** Angora goat hair, dubbing loop
- **Rib:** Large oval tinsel, silver
- **Collar:** In two parts from back to front: 1) polar bear of DNA Frosty Fish Fiber, pink, twisted in a wire dubbing loop; 2) Lady Amherst pheasant center tail, twisted in a wire dubbing loop
- **Head:** Angora goat hair, orange, dubbed with fingers
- **Hook:** #1 Gamakatsu Drop Shot

Notes: Another of the workhorses of the commercial trade, this fly is responsible for a staggering number of landed fish due to its pervasive distribution to lodges in BC and Alaska. While the Super Stinger Prawn has dominated when a weighted fly is needed, the Jumbo Critter fills the role of unweighted mega fly. Not that Bjorn ever intended it to be unweighted. The fact that commercial production of the Jumbo Critter incorporated bucktail instead of polar bear or Frosty Fish Fiber, and opted against an added cone weight, resulted in a surprisingly buoyant fly. But this feature came in handy when water conditions called for something light. Perhaps the biggest factor in the widespread use of both the Prawn and the Critter was the prominence of their sales rep, the inimitable George Cook.

OVER DRESSED HOOKER, BLACK/BLUE

- **Shank:** The Fly Fisher Shanks by Bjorn, 4.5 cm (1¾")
- **Thread:** 210-denier, black
- **Stinger loop:** 26.4-pound Surflon-coated wire, 2.8 cm (1⅛") long
- **Eyes:** Small to medium nickel-plated lead
- **Tail:** In four parts, each twisted in a wire dubbing loop: 1) polar bear, royal blue; (2) Lady Amherst pheasant tail; (3) Flashabou, blue; 4) silver pheasant tail,
- **Body:** Holographic Flashabou, black
- **Rib:** Medium wire, silver
- **Collar:** In five parts, from back to front, each twisted in a wire dubbing loop: 1) polar bear, black; 2) rhea herl, black; 3) Lady Amherst pheasant center tail; 4) holographic Flashabou, black; 5) Silver pheasant body.
- **Hook:** #1 Gamakatsu Drop Shot

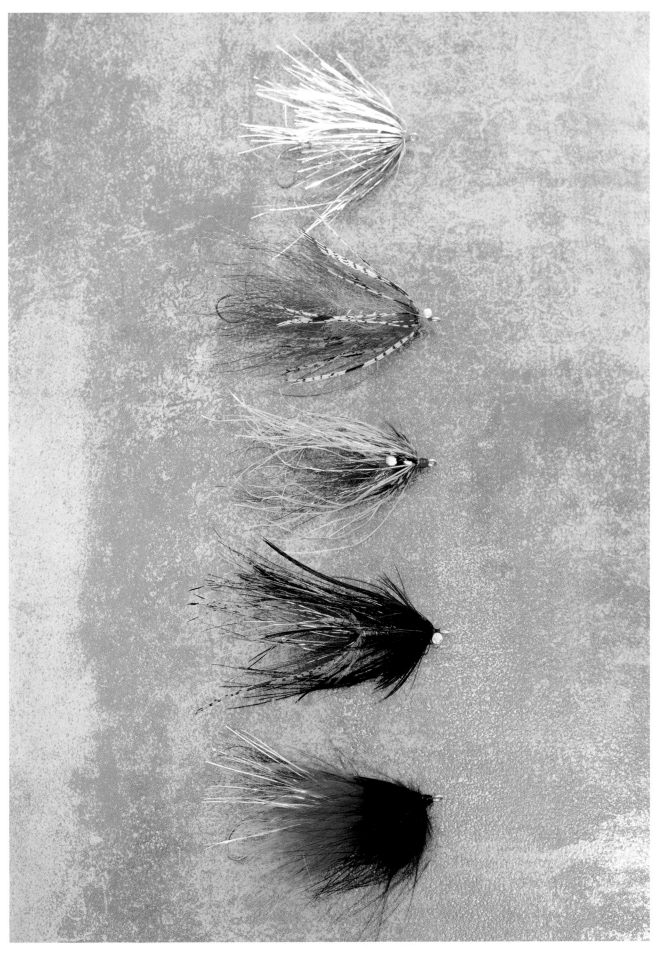

Top to bottom: Pixie Bitch, Jumbo Critter, Superman, Overdressed Hooker, Stinger Prawn.

Michael Bennett

Michael Bennett is a die-hard steelheader and owner of Pacific Fly Fishers in Mill Creek, Washington. He's an FFF-certified casting instructor and a fly designer for Solitude Fly Company. Michael grew up fishing Oregon's Rogue and Umpqua Rivers, went down to University of Southern California for college, then moved up to Snohomish County in the late '90s. He's been a fixture in the Puget Sound fly-fishing scene ever since, and his fly shop is one of the best around.

C-U SKATER

- **Hook:** #3 or #5 Daiichi Alec Jackson Spey, black
- **Thread:** 6/0 Danville, orange
- **Tail:** Krystal Flash, pearl dyed purple
- **Shellback:** Strip of 2 mm foam, black, 9 mm (⅜") wide by 35 mm (1⅜") long; rear end has a V trimmed out of it to give it a forked tail, and the front end has the corners trimmed off
- **Body:** Ice Dub, purple
- **Collar:** Guinea hen, natural
- **Wing:** In three parts, bottom to top: 1) Krystal Flash, pearl; 2) deer body hair; 3) calf tail, chartreuse
- **Head:** STS Trilobal Dub, orange

BENNETT'S HALO

- **Hook:** #3 or #5 Daiichi Alec Jackson Spey, black
- **Thread:** 6/0 Danville, start with white, then switch to orange for head
- **Tip:** Extra-small French oval tinsel, silver
- **Tag:** Flashabou, pearl dyed peacock
- **Tail:** Teal flank, natural
- **Body:** Extra-long Peacock herl spun with a strand of extra-small French oval tinsel, silver, for added strength
- **Rib:** Medium French oval tinsel, silver
- **Collar:** Grizzly saddle hackle
- **Wing:** In three parts, bottom to top: 1) Midge Flash, pearl; 2) Lite Brite, holographic gold; 3) squirrel tail, natural gray

Notes: Michael recommends this fly for times when the sun is on the water or anytime during the day when the water is very clear.

Michael enjoying some fall fishing in the Great White North. MICHAEL BENNETT PHOTO

Top row, left: Bennett's Halo; right: Bennett's Last Light. Below: C-U Skater. Bottom three: Exasperators in three color combinations.

BENNETT'S LAST LIGHT

- **Hook:** #3 or #5 Daiichi Alec Jackson Spey, black
- **Thread:** 6/0 Danville, start with white, then switch to purple for head
- **Tip:** Extra-small French oval tinsel, silver
- **Tag:** Flashabou, light blue
- **Tail:** Saddle hackle fibers, purple
- **Body:** Ice Dub, black, mixed with Lite Brite, purple haze
- **Rib:** Medium French oval tinsel, silver
- **Collar:** Chinese saddle, black, followed by guinea hen, purple
- **Wing:** In three parts, bottom to top: 1) Midge Flash, pearl; 2) Lite Brite, blue; 3) squirrel tail dyed black or equivalent

Notes: Michael recommends this fly as his go-to for the first and last light of the day.

EXASPERATOR, BLACK/BLUE

- **Shank:** 20 mm Waddington
- **Stinger loop:** 30-pound Fireline, 3.2 cm (1¼") long
- **Thread:** Danville Monocord, black
- **Eyes:** Medium (1/24 ounce) painted lead eyes, white
- **Tail:** Flashabou, silver, 8 to 10 strands, topped with Lite Brite, deep blue, both extending 5 cm (2") from the end of the shank
- **Body:** Lite Brite, deep blue, spun in a dubbing loop and wrapped forward to cover the rear half of the shank, then picked out with a bodkin
- **Pectoral fins:** In two parts, back to front: 1) rabbit fur, black, spun in a dubbing loop and wrapped forward two turns; 2) two bunches of stacked bucktail, black, tied in and wrapped at their bases to create distinct pectoral fins protruding at a 45-degree angle from shank
- **Wing:** Rabbit strip, black, 8.3 cm (3¼") long, tied in just behind lead eyes
- **Head:** Rabbit fur, black, spun in a dubbing loop, wrapped around eyes and finished just behind the eye of the shank (trim away excess as needed to form the thread head)
- **Hook:** #1 or #2 Gamakatsu Octopus, blue, with a small bump of thread wrapped directly behind the eye and lacquered to protect the stinger loop from abrasion

Notes: The word exasperate is defined as "to irritate or provoke to a high degree." Michael's goal in designing this highly provocative creature was to maximize movement. He cites three main inspirations for the final design, beginning with Bob Hull's original String Leech, illustrated in Trey Combs's *Steelhead Fly Fishing*. The String Leech maximized movement by allowing the long rabbit strip to move freely. Next, Michael cites Larry Dahlberg's Flashdancer. The idea behind the Flashdancer is to create a large, bulky head that produces a vortex as water rushed around and behind it. This kicks the rabbit strip and the underlying Lite Brite around violently. Finally, when considering how best to finish the fly, Michael credits Ken Morrish and his Morrish Sculpin for the idea of using a dubbing loop rather than a crosscut rabbit strip. This retains the desired movement of the material without overcrowding the head of the fly.

First designed for a trip to British Columbia, the Exasperator has become Michael's go-to big fly everywhere he goes. It makes up of the bulk of his winter, spring, and early summer fly selections for one simple reason: It gets results. And steelhead aren't the only fish that have fallen prey to this electric sculpin pattern. As Michael says, "The Exasperator has taken its share of big chinook in Chile and Alaska, largemouth and smallmouth bass, giant browns in eastern Washington, and lots of Alaska rainbows." Other favorite colors for steelhead include black/purple, purple, and olive. And try natural brown for trout and bass!

Bruce Berry

Bruce Berry is a phenomenal fly tier who has earned a reputation as one of the leading designers of tube-style flies in the Pacific Northwest. As a rising industry rep in the early 2000s, Bruce connected with Denmark-based Pro Sportfisher and helped them set up distribution to US fly shops. Since then he has produced dozens of fly-tying videos, sharing his super-fishy patterns and extolling the virtues of tubes. He is a Montana Fly Company signature tier, and his patterns are widely available through fly shops.

RAMBULANCE, SHRIMPISH

- **Tube:** Pro Nanotube, clear
- **Hook Guide/Junction:** Pro Hookguide, large, fluorescent orange
- **Weight:** Pro Drop Weight, medium, or Pro Raw Weight, small
- **Butt:** MFC Berry's Fish Dope Dubbing, sunkissed orange
- **Rear Hackle:** Golden pheasant tippet, dyed fluorescent orange
- **Rear Wing:** Craft Fur, flame orange
- **Rib:** Small Lagartun, silver

- **Body:** Salt Water Flashabou, pearl over black thread
- **Body Hackle:** Saddle Hackle, fluorescent orange
- **Dubbing Bump:** MFC Berry's Fish Dope Dubbing, sunkissed orange
- **Prop:** Pro American Opossum, hot pink twisted into dubbing loop, or Pro Soft Sonic Disc, medium
- **Front Wing:** Craft Fur, fluorescent pink
- **Lateral Lines:** Krinkle Mirror Flash, dyed pink
- **Front Hackle:** Marabou, pink
- **Flash:** Mirage, pink (tied in like horns)
- **Collar:** Schlappen, pink
- **Cheeks:** Pro Jungle Cock HD, magenta

The Rambulance has proven itself as a top producer of steelhead year-round since it came on the scene in 2008. Bruce shared the story of how he came up with the pattern:

> Berry's Rambulance is not a new fly, per se, but when compared to something like a Green Butt Skunk, a Polar Shrimp, or a Starlight Leech, it seems like a fly that is hot off the vise. Those who pay

Berry tying at the Northwest Fly Tying Expo. JAY NICHOLAS PHOTO

Clockwise from upper left: i-fli, black and green; i-fli, black and red; Rambulance, shrimpish; Rambulance, pink; Rambulance, blue and purple; Tube Leech, black and blue; Big League Leech, blue; Marabou Madness, orange; Marabou Madness, blue; Marabou Madness, pink.

attention to fly-shop blogs, newsletters, and videos may know about it, or may have even fished it.

When I first sat down to design the "perfect" marabou fly, I started by asking myself, "Does the world really need a new steelhead fly?" Mark Bachmann always told me, "It's all just fuzz on hook until you show me a picture of it in a steelhead's jaw." In today's commercial fly world, there is something to be said for a statement like that. Working for a commercial company myself [Montana Fly Company], I am sure there are more than a handful of flies each season that make catalogs without having had the chance to get wet first! The difference in my world of "fuzz on a hook" and a fly worth talking about is this: I don't like to even name a fly until it has taken fish. That said, I have a hard time staying tuned into a certain fly, even of my own creation, until it produces consistently, on different waterways, in different times of the year for steelhead or trout. Past that, if the fly is fun to tie, aesthetically pleasing, and easy to cast . . . now we're onto something worth talking about! Of course, the world needs another steelhead fly!

Tying a fly, to me, basically means wrapping common sense, experience, and trial and error around a hook [or in this case, a tube]. Sometimes it is an involved process going through stages of development including multiple tries, other times it is simple. After all steelhead eat pink rubber worms . . . right!

The Rambulance started shortly after—and I mean as the credits were rolling—watching an Oregon Public Broadcasting program back in 2009. Long story short, biologists and OPB crew members wanted to watch the spawning habits of *Oncorhynchus mykiss* to see if that information would yield any clues to the protection and ongoing efforts to restore the numbers of our beloved steelhead in the Pacific Northwest. Observing what happens in the wild while humans were mucking about was impossible. The solution: specially designed waterproof cameras strategically placed around pre-spawn and spawning habitat where the fish would act like fish without the interference of man.

The video results were amazing, in particular a group of "sneaker" fish, as OPB termed them, worked in teams to agitate and move steelhead. The male steelhead took the bait multiple times, moving off his bed to chase off potential competition. The male obliterated one sneaker, later on giving chase to another, while a third 3- to 3½-inch fish ducked under the adult female and took care of the job of inseminating the eggs.

Wow, small immature-looking trout are sexually mature? Steelhead hate these little bastards? Man . . . I bet if I can imitate "sneakers" in basic size, shape, color, and movement, I can catch a lot of fish . . . off the spawning beds, of course!!! Okay, show's over. I wish I would have recorded this one. Now off to the tying room.

Meanwhile, like most other fisherman chasing steelhead, I was taken in by the Intruder from the first time I saw that fly in Dec Hogan's *A Passion for Steelhead* on the two-page spread. I had a box loaded with them, in sizes from 3 inches to about 7 inches long. I found the rabbit-infested flies, among other materials, hard to cast at best—almost impossible in tight casting situations. In open water where I could make a full D loop, the soon-to-be-doomed-to-the-garbage-can flies would lazily waffle their way across and fizzle out mid-stream. I also felt like a lot of flies were in a constant struggle. What struggle is that, you ask? The struggle was the loads of T14 needed to get a fly down! But the over-dressed flies did not want to go down.

This fly was going to be different: large 3- to 3½-inch profile, colors that will represent these fish, easy to cast, a fly that will allow the tip to get it to the desired fishing depth efficiently, and tied on a tube. That way, if the hook becomes fouled or I want to change hook size, it would be quick and easy to replace the hook and keep the fly. Sounds easy, right?

Actually, it was easy! The first attempt just showed that the wing lengths needed a little tweak in order to keep its wiggle and boogie from the softest to the hardest currents you would encounter steelhead with a fly. From there, I tied it with Iceland sheep, arctic fox, temple dog, Finn raccoon, and Craft Fur. I settled on Craft Fur simply because the dyes were consistent and colorfast. At the end of the day, you could stuff the wet flies in a jacket pocket, and they wouldn't transfer any color to the jacket. Also, the material would not bend up in all sorts of contorted angles while drying out and riding around in my jacket, hip pack, or boat bag. The alternate material that comes in a close second is marble fox.

Rambulance has evolved into three color options: The original blue is for fishing from clear to optimal conditions both in late summers and winters. My second version is a two-toned hot orange / blaze orange that shows up well in all conditions, from "steelhead green" to glacial-tinted winter steelhead streams. The last color is another two-toned hot orange / hot pink version that I call "Shrimpish."

Like most fishermen, when I am catching fish, I am not too worried about the color. When I am not catching and watching guys come in behind me and stick a fish with a pink rubber worm or pink- or orange-dyed shrimp, it pisses me off. At first it was disheartening to know that a majestic fish like a steelhead could be so easily fooled and taken readily on such simple piece of rubber, popped out of a mold to look like a worm. On second thought, it is about 3½ inches, plus or minus, it wiggles, and pink and orange are good colors!

So, bam, that is all three Rambulance flies in a nutshell. The fly is not really Scandinavian-style, not really an Intruder, it's a "Rammer." That said, if conditions were routinely optimal, I would probably just tie up a few dozen in the original blue color and fish confidently on all my normal haunts. Unfortunately, steelhead fishing is hardly ever optimal, and in the winter, optimal is a rarity.

—Bruce Berry, 2014

I-FLI, BLACK/RED

- **Tube:** Pro Nanotube, black or clear
- **Hook guide/junction:** Pro Hookguide, fluorescent red, large
- **Weight:** Pro Drop Weight, medium, or Pro Raw Weight, small
- **Butt:** Berry's Fish Dope Dubbing, maraschino red
- **Rear hackle:** Golden pheasant tippet, fluorescent red
- **Rib:** Lagartun, silver, small
- **Body:** Saltwater Flashabou, pearl over black thread
- **Body hackle:** Saddle hackle, red
- **Dubbing bump:** Berry's Fish Dope Dubbing, maraschino red
- **Prop/throat:** Pro American Opossum, hot red twisted into dubbing loop, or Pro Soft
- **Sonic Disc, medium**
- **Front wing:** Craft Fur, black
- **Lateral lines:** Krinkle Mirror Flash, pearl
- **Front hackle:** Marabou, black
- **Flash:** Flashabou, Black holographic (tied in like horns)
- **Collar:** Schlappen, black
- **Over wing:** Four dyed red grizzly rooster saddles, tied tented over the top
- **Cheeks (optional):** Pro Jungle Cock HD, orange

MARABOU MADNESS, BLUE

- **Tube:** Pro Tube Flexitube, cyan blue
- **Hook guide/junction:** Built into injection molded stepped tube
- **Weight:** 10 or 15 mm Pro Flexiweight, or Pro Raw Weight, small or medium
- **Prop/throat:** Pro American Opossum, Cyan Blue, twisted into a dubbing loop, or Pro Soft Sonic Disc, medium or large
- **Hackle 1:** Marabou, royal blue
- **Hackle 2:** Marabou, royal blue
- **Hackle 3:** MFC Ostrich, kingfisher blue, clumps of four tied in top, bottom side, and side
- **Flash:** Krinkle Mirror Flash, dyed blue
- **Collar:** Schlappen, black
- **Cone:** Pro Ultra Sonic Disc, metallic purple, 9 mm
- **Cheeks (optional):** Pro Jungle Cock HD, natural

BIG LEAGUE LEECH, KATHI'S FAVORITE (BLURPLE)

- **Tube:** Pro Microtube, fluorescent orange
- **Hook guide/junction:** Pro Hookguide, black, large
- **Weight:** 10 or 15 mm Pro Flexiweight, or Pro Raw Weight, small or medium
- **Body:** Polar Chenille, purple
- **Wing:** Pro American opossum, hot purple (taper cut)
- **Flash:** Flashabou, rainbow
- **Collar 1:** Pro American opossum, hot cyan blue twisted into dubbing loop
- **Collar 2:** Schlappen, royal blue
- **Cheeks (optional):** Pro Jungle Cock HD, natural

Jeff Bright

Jeff Bright is a celebrated author, freelance writer, photographer, travel specialist, and host of steelhead and salmon angling adventures around the world. He conducts business activities from his home in San Francisco, but he always keeps one foot firmly planted in Skeena Country. Jeff was good enough to send us samples of his flies in 2011, when this book project was just getting started. Since then, Jeff says his tying has evolved toward tube flies almost exclusively. His new stuff is a hybridization of European salmon styles with steelhead styles from the Pacific Northwest. The Hilton, Siren, and Squid patterns featured here served him well for about a decade, and we are pleased to share them. Check out Jeff's business listing on page 308 to track down his latest work.

SIREN, PINK

- **Shank:** #2 or #4 Tiemco 9395 or equivalent straight-eye hook
- **Stinger loop:** 30- to 50-pound Fireline, 2.5 cm (1") loop
- **Thread:** 6/0 UNI-Thread, fluorescent pink
- **Eyes:** Small nickel-plated lead eyes
- **Tail:** Krystal Flash, two strands each of silver and metallic cerise
- **Butt:** Angora goat, cerise
- **Rear hackle:** In two parts: 1) marabou, pink; 2) marabou, cerise
- **Body:** Small Cactus Chenille, white, palmered with schlappen, cerise
- **Front hackle:** Marabou, cerise
- **Tentacles:** Grizzly hackle tips, cerise, tied long
- **Topping:** Ostrich herl, pink
- **Throat:** Ostrich herl, pink
- **Collar:** Extra-large guinea hen, pink
- **Flash:** Krystal Flash, two strands each of silver and metallic cerise
- **Head:** Angora goat, cerise
- **Hook:** #1 Gamakatsu Octopus, red

SIREN, BLACK/BLUE

- **Shank:** #2 or #4 Tiemco 9395 or equivalent straight-eye hook
- **Stinger loop:** 30- to 50-pound Fireline, 2.5 cm (1") loop
- **Thread:** 6/0 UNI-Thread, fluorescent pink
- **Eyes:** Small nickel-plated lead eyes
- **Tail:** Krystal Flash, two strands each of silver and metallic blue
- **Butt:** Angora goat, red
- **Rear hackle:** In two parts: 1) marabou, kingfisher blue; 2) marabou, purple
- **Body:** Speckled Chenille, Midnight Fire, palmered with schlappen, black
- **Front hackle:** Marabou, black
- **Tentacles:** Grizzly hackle tips, red, tied long
- **Topping:** Ostrich herl, black
- **Throat:** Ostrich herl, black
- **Collar:** Extra-large guinea hen, blue
- **Flash:** Krystal Flash, two strands each of silver and metallic blue
- **Head:** Angora goat, red
- **Hook:** #1 Gamakatsu Octopus, red

Jeff shows off a gorgeious Dean River steelhead that fell for one of his creations.
JEFF BRIGHT SUPPLIED THE PHOTO, SHOT BY APRIL VOKEY

Top to bottom: Siren, pink; Siren, black and blue; Boreal Squid, pink; Boreal Squid, black and blue; Northern Hilton, pink and orange.

NORTHERN HILTON, PINK/ORANGE

- **Shank:** #4 or #6 Tiemco 9395 or equivalent straight-eye hook
- **Stinger loop:** 50-pound Fireline, 2.5 cm (1") loop
- **Thread:** 6/0 UNI-Thread, fluorescent orange
- **Butt:** Ice Dub, pink
- **Rear hackle:** In two parts: 1) marabou, pink; 2) saddle hackle, orange
- **Body:** Diamond Braid, pink
- **Front dubbing ball:** Ice Dub, pink
- **Front hackle:** In two parts: 1) saddle hackle, orange; 2) guinea hen, orange
- **Wings:** Grizzly hackle tips, one pair of orange and one pair of pink, tied Hilton-style
- **Flash:** Krystal Flash, orange
- **Hook:** #1 Gamakatsu Octopus, red

BOREAL SQUID, PINK

- **Shank:** #2 or #4 Tiemco 9395 or equivalent straight-eye hook
- **Stinger loop:** 30- to 50-pound Fireline, 2.5 cm (1") loop
- **Thread:** 6/0 UNI-Thread, fluorescent pink
- **Eyes:** Small nickel-plated lead eyes
- **Body:** Diamond Braid, pink
- **Dubbing ball:** Ice Dub, pink
- **Hackle:** In two parts: 1) Baitfish Emulator, Fluorescent Fuchsia; 2) short ostrich herl, pink
- **Flash:** Krystal Flash, pink; holographic Flashabou, pink
- **Tentacles:** In three parts, all 13 cm (5") long: 1) eight thin saddle hackle tips, cerise; 2) four thin grizzly hackle tips, cerise; 3) eight pieces of ostrich herl, pink
- **Collar:** Guinea hen, pink
- **Head:** Ice Dub, pink
- **Hook:** #1 Gamakatsu Octopus, red

BOREAL SQUID, BLACK/BLUE

- **Shank:** #2 or #4 Tiemco 9395 or equivalent straight-eye hook
- **Stinger loop:** 30- to 50-pound Fireline, 2.5 cm (1") loop
- **Thread:** 6/0 UNI-Thread, orange
- **Eyes:** Small nickel-plated lead eyes
- **Body:** Diamond Braid, blue
- **Dubbing ball:** Ice Dub, orange
- **Hackle:** In two parts: 1) Baitfish Emulator, black; 2) short ostrich herl, kingfisher blue
- **Flash:** Krystal Flash, blue; metallic Flashabou, blue
- **Tentacles:** In three parts, all 13 cm (5") long: 1) eight thin saddle hackle tips, blue; 2) four thin grizzly hackle tips, blue; 3) eight pieces of ostrich herl, black
- **Collar:** Guinea hen, blue
- **Head:** Ice Dub, orange
- **Hook:** #1 Gamakatsu Octopus, nickel

Notes: Jeff has created a series of working flies here that really get the job done for steelhead and king salmon. Nothing fancy, just solid, brightly colored flies with ample movement, contrast, and profile. His Giant Squid series makes brilliant use of long hackle tips, taking Brian Kite's Pick 'Yer Pocket design to an extreme. These flies are pure frenetic movement in the water!

Hogan Brown

Hogan Brown was born and reared in Sacramento, California. As a kid, his fishing excursions involved begging for a ride or making the long walk to the lower Yuba River, his nearest trout fishery. His love for steelhead grew organically from his trout fishing, and the two have somewhat blurred together ever since. His early fly-tying influences were Northern California greats, especially Andy Burke, Mike Mercer, and Bob Quigley. Of those influences, Hogan says, "I could see they really looked at what they were imitating and worked on the parts of the bug that triggered the fish or that they key on."

Once he started guiding, Hogan's main influence became day-to-day necessity, and he has since created some of the buggiest nymphs of all time. Like many California steelheaders, Hogan fishes his nymphs both dead-drifted and swung, often in the same cast.

Today he runs his guide service, HGB Fly Fishing, from his home in Chico, California. He chases trout, steelhead, stripers, and bass, depending on the time of year. Many of his fly patterns are tied commercially and can be found in fly shops around the world.

Hogan and his little fishing buddy on the home waters. HOGAN BROWN PHOTO

HOGAN'S CHUBBY COUSIN

- **Hook:** #6-10 Tiemco 3769
- **Bead head:** Medium or large brass
- **Thorax bead:** 5 mm glass, root beer
- **Thread:** 70-denier, gray or dun
- **Tail:** Ringneck pheasant tail tied short with barred silicone rubber legs, tan, tied in on either side
- **Rib:** Large wire, copper
- **Abdomen:** Thread base with a pair of turkey biots pulled over and ribbed forward
- **Thorax:** Ice Dub, golden brown, wrapped behind and in front of glass bead
- **Collar:** American hen hackle, brown
- **Legs:** Two pairs of barred silicone rubber legs, tan, tied in on either side X style
- **Dubbing collar:** Ice Dub, cinnamon

HOGAN'S ROCK 'N' ROLLER, GOLD

- **Hook:** #6-10 Tiemco 2302
- **Thread:** 70-denier, cinnamon
- **Weight:** .020" or .025" lead wire, wrapped over the length of the shank, leaving some space for a head; additional straight sections of lead wire lashed to sides to create a wide, flat base for the body
- **Tail:** Turkey biots, brown, with barred silicone rubber legs, tan, tied in on either side
- **Rib:** Large wire, copper
- **Abdomen:** Ice Dub, peacock, with three turkey biots, brown, pulled over and ribbed forward
- **Rear collar:** American hen hackle, brown, with barred silicone rubber legs, tan, tied in on either side
- **Thorax:** Angora goat dubbing, blend of orange, yellow, red, and claret
- **Front collar:** American hen hackle, brown, with barred silicone rubber legs, tan, tied in on either side
- **Wing case:** Segment of turkey tail feather, natural, coated with a bead of epoxy (apply epoxy at the end)
- **Antennae:** Turkey biots, brown

Top row: two Chubby Cousins. Bottom row, left: Rock 'n' Roller, brown; right: two Rock 'n' Rollers in gold.

HOGAN'S ROCK 'N' ROLLER, BROWN

- **Hook:** #2-6 Tiemco 2302
- **Thread:** 70-denier, black
- **Weight:** .025 lead wire, wrapped over the length of the shank, leaving some space for a head; additional straight sections of lead wire lashed to sides to create a wide, flat base for the body
- **Tail:** Turkey biots, black, with round rubber legs, black, tied in on either side
- **Rib:** Large wire, black
- **Abdomen:** Holographic Flashabou, purple haze, with three turkey biots, brown, pulled over and ribbed forward

- **Rear collar:** American hen hackle or partridge, dark brown, with round rubber legs, black, tied in on either side
- **Thorax:** Angora goat dubbing, blend of black, dark brown, and purple
- **Front collar:** American hen hackle, brown, with round rubber legs, black, tied in on either side
- **Wing case:** Segment of turkey tail feather, natural, coated with a bead of epoxy (apply epoxy at the end)
- **Antennae:** Turkey biots, black

Brian Chou

Over the last dozen years or so, Brian has become one of the Pacific Northwest's leading product designers and testers. A patient yet enthusiastic casting instructor, he is a genuinely kind soul with a heart to help others. His relaxed holistic approach is woven into everything he does, whether raising a family, partnering with his wife in their health and wellness business, consulting for fly-fishing manufacturers, or tying steelhead flies. He's a signature tier for Montana Fly Company, adviser with Thomas & Thomas, contributing writer and photographer to the Portland-based magazine *Steelheader's Journal* and board member of Soul River Runs Wild, a nonprofit that helps veterans and at-risk youth discover the outdoors through fly-fishing and education. His humility, positive attitude, and respect for the big picture set a great tone and example for future generations of steelheaders. Brian's flies are a fun mix of art, engineering, tradition, and innovation.

SZECHUAN SHRIMP, GREEN/BLACK

- **Thread:** UTC waxed 70-denier, fluorescent green
- **Tubing:** Pro Microtube, black
- **Junction tubing:** Pro Hookguide, green, large

Chou contemplating a modern version of the Red Winged Blackbird called "Rip City." CHAD BROWN PHOTO

- **Eyes:** Nickel-plated brass, (5 mm) ³⁄₁₆″
- **Dubbing:** Ice Dub, caddis green, wrapped in figure-eight around dumbbell eyes
- **Lower rear wing:** Calf tail, black
- **Hackle 1:** Golden pheasant neck, dyed green
- **Hackle 2:** Hareline American Speckled Hen Back, caddis green
- **Pincers:** Green-dyed golden pheasant tippet under chartreuse-dyed Lady Amherst center tail
- **Upper rear wing:** Arctic fox, black
- **Hackle 3:** Lady Amherst head, highlander green
- **Body:** Ice Dub, olive, palmered with grizzly saddle, chartreuse
- **Front wing:** Arctic fox, black
- **Outer wing:** Grizzly hackle, chartreuse
- **Flash:** Angel Hair, baitfish color
- **Collar:** Hareline American Speckled Hen Back, caddis green
- **Hook:** #5 Gamakatsu Drop Shot 1/0 or Partridge Salar Tube Double (pictured)

SZECHUAN SHRIMP, ORANGE

- **Thread:** UTC waxed 70-denier, red
- **Tubing:** Pro Microtube, clear
- **Junction tubing:** Pro Hookguide, orange, large
- **Eyes:** Nickel-plated brass, (5 mm) ³⁄₁₆″
- **Dubbing:** Ice Dub, pink, wrapped in figure eight around dumbbell eyes
- **Lower rear wing:** Calf tail, red
- **Hackle:** Golden pheasant tippet feather, dyed red
- **Pincers:** Lady Amherst center tail, dyed red
- **Upper rear wing:** Arctic fox, red
- **Body:** Ice Dub, pink, palmered with grizzly saddle, red
- **Front wing:** Arctic fox, orange
- **Outer wing:** Grizzly hackle, red
- **Flash:** Angel Hair, red and gold mixed
- **Collar:** Guinea hen, red
- **Hook:** #5 Gamakatsu Drop Shot 1/0 or Partridge Salar Tube Double (pictured)

Clockwise from upper right: Mooshoo Muddler, green and black; Dawn Patrol; Mooshoo Muddler, red; Szechuan Shrimp, orange; Szechuan Shrimp, green and black.

MOOSHOO MUDDLER, RED/BLACK

- **Shank:** Any straight-eye gold shank
- **Stinger loop:** 15 lb/.021" d15bl Berkley Steelon nylon-coated wire, black
- **Thread:** 6/0 UNI-Thread, black
- **Tail:** Golden pheasant tippet, dyed red
- **Rear body:** Flat Mylar tinsel, gold side up
- **Thorax:** Spirit River Brite Blend, red/black, brushed out and palmered with red-dyed grizzly saddle
- **Rib:** Ultra Wire, red, medium
- **Undercollar:** Golden pheasant tippet, dyed red
- **Flash:** Angel Hair, red
- **Wing:** Tented pair of red-dyed grizzly saddle tips
- **Head:** Elk belly (coarse), black, spun and trimmed
- **Hook:** #4 Gamakatsu Big River Bait

MOOSHOO MUDDLER, GREEN/BLACK

- **Shank:** Any straight-eye gold shank
- **Stinger loop:** 15 lb/.021" d15bl Berkley Steelon nylon-coated wire, black
- **Thread:** 6/0 UNI-Thread, black
- **Tail:** Golden pheasant tippet, dyed green
- **Rear body:** Flat Mylar tinsel, gold side up
- **Thorax:** Spirit River Brite Blend, green, brushed out and palmered with chartreuse-dyed grizzly saddle
- **Rib:** Ultra Wire, green, medium
- **Undercollar:** Golden pheasant tippet, dyed green
- **Flash:** Angel Hair, green and silver mixed
- **Wing:** Tented pair of chartreuse-dyed grizzly saddle tips
- **Head:** Elk belly (coarse), black, spun and trimmed
- **Hook:** #4 Gamakatsu Big River Bait

DAWN PATROL

- **Shank:** Any straight-eye gold shank
- **Stinger loop:** 15 lb/.021" d15bl Berkley Steelon nylon-coated wire, black
- **Thread:** UTC waxed 70-denier, light blue
- **Tail:** Golden pheasant tippet, dyed green
- **Tag:** Seven turns of oval gold tinsel (medium), with four turns through the body
- **Underbody:** Ice Dub UV, black, palmered with natural blue-eared pheasant, stripped off on one side
- **Collar:** Guinea hen, dyed teal
- **Wing:** Peacock sword
- **Eyes:** Jungle cock nails
- **Hook:** #4 Gamakatsu Big River Bait

Barrett Christiansen

Barrett Christiansen is a steelhead, trout, and salmon guide based in Eugene, Oregon. He's also a busy custom fly tier, which can have him tying tarpon, largemouth bass, and trout flies in addition to his steelhead and salmon patterns. He's lucky to call the North Umpqua one of his home rivers, but he spends most of his fishing days on the Willamette and McKenzie. Barrett operates Calypso Guide Service, which is included in our Business Listings on page 307.

In the category of "the dark arts," Barrett gets credit for being the first we know of to add a curly tail to a heavily weighted Glo-Bug. He called the resulting fly the Lowly Glowly, after the Lowly Worm in Richard Scarry books.

"It slayed in off-color water," Barrett said, "to the point that I started fishing on days I never would have considered before. It was that productive. Same with the Vernille Worm—big, nasty water suddenly became fishable."

Barrett's diverse collection of flies is indicative of the unpretentious, pragmatic vibe of the Eugene steelhead scene. It's a region where skaters, swingers, and nymphers live in peace and harmony. Maybe it's because they spend so much of their year trout fishing and don't have the luxury of developing a hang-up about nymphing.

From the top: Pink Angel; Clear Goo Baitfish; Floating Comet; Riffle Plow; Lowly Glowly; Vernille Worm.

RIFFLE PLOW

- **Hook:** #4 Tiemco 700
- **Thread:** 120-denier, black
- **Tube:** Small HMH tubing, with one end melted and pressed into an oval-shaped foot
- **Body:** Thin fly foam, orange
- **Thorax:** Ice Dub, black
- **Legs:** Round rubber legs, black
- **Wing/head:** Elk hair lashed down tight to the HMH tubing; butt ends are shaped with Zap-A-Gap and cut to shape once dried

Notes: Tie the HMH tubing in first, tying the body materials over the top of it. Lighter wire hooks can be substituted for the Tiemco 700 when targeting smaller steelhead.

PINK ANGEL

- **Hook:** #1-6 Partridge Bartleet Single, black
- **Thread:** 70-denier, hot pink
- **Tag:** Small or medium French oval tinsel, silver
- **Body:** Floss or thread, hot pink
- **Rib:** Small or medium French oval tinsel, silver
- **Thorax:** UV Ice Dub, light pink
- **Hackle/collar:** Guinea hen, pink
- **Wing:** Angel Hair, pink

Notes: When trimming the Angel Hair wings to length, feather the ends rather than just cutting them all the same length. This makes for a more natural-looking wing.

CLEAR GOO BAITFISH

- **Hook:** #6 Gamakatsu C14S
- **Body:** Angel Hair, kingfisher blue and white, feathered at the ends
- **Head:** Clear Cure Goo
- **Eyes:** 2 mm adhesive eyes

FLOATING COMET

- **Hook:** #4 Gamakatsu L11S-3H
- **Thread:** 120-denier, chartreuse
- **Eyes:** Large plastic nymph eyes
- **Tail:** Calf tail, chartreuse
- **Body:** Diamond Braid, silver
- **Hackle/collar:** Saddle hackle, chartreuse

LOWLY GLOWLY

- **Hook:** #6 Gamakatsu C14S
- **Thread:** 120-denier, fluorescent orange
- **Weight/eyes:** Nickel-plated dumbbell eyes, medium or large
- **Tail:** Curly fly tail, pink
- **Butt:** Estaz Chenille, pink, medium
- **Body:** Glo-Bug yarn, shell pink

VERNILLE WORM

- **Front hook:** #4 Mustad 3406, or any cheap ring-eye hook
- **Thread:** 120-denier, fluorescent orange
- **Weight/eyes:** Medium or large nickel-plated dumbbell eyes
- **Rear hook:** #6 Gamakatsu C14S
- **Connector loop:** 50-pound Tuf-Line or equivalent; start with 2¾"-long loop between hooks
- **Tail:** Vernille or Ultra Chenille, pink, twisted with a short clump of cerise marabou tied in at the tip Body: Two strands of Vernille or Ultra Chenille, pink, braided with the Tuf-Line loop
- **Head:** Continue wrapping the body strands onto the front hook shank and around the dumbbell eyes

Jason Cichy

Jason is a fixture on the steelhead waters around Eugene, Oregon. Like most center-state steelheaders, he's at home swinging and nymphing, as the water and seasons dictate. Most nights he falls asleep at the vise, waking up in a pile of dyed feathers and shuffling off to bed sometime in the wee hours. His flies are a beautiful balance of modern and traditional, especially his Willamette River summer series featured here.

OLD WORLD HILTON

- **Hook:** #1-8 Tiemco 7999, black
- **Thread:** 6/0 UNI-Thread, blue
- **Tag:** Medium holographic tinsel, silver
- **Tail:** Saddle hackle fibers, kingfisher blue
- **Butt:** Ostrich herl, black
- **Rear body:** Floss, chartreuse
- **Front body:** Angora goat dubbing, black, picked out with a bodkin
- **Rib:** Medium French oval tinsel, silver
- **Hackle:** Grizzly hen hackle
- **Wings:** Tented pair of grizzly hackle tips
- **Flash:** Krystal Flash, pearl dyed fluorescent chartreuse
- **Cheeks:** Jungle cock nails

Notes: The Silver Hilton is still a standard steelhead fly in the upper Willamette and McKenzie Rivers, and every guide has his own variation. Cichy's offers beautiful color highlights, a webby hackle, and just a hint of flash.

WILLAMETTE SUNRISE

- **Hook:** #5 or #7 Daiichi Alec Jackson Spey, nickel
- **Thread:** 8/0 UNI-Thread, fluorescent orange
- **Tag:** Holographic Flashabou, green
- **Body:** Hareline Dubbin, red for the back half, black for the front
- **Rib:** Medium French oval tinsel, silver
- **Wing:** Arctic fox tail, yellow, topped with a small tuft of arctic fox tail, orange
- **Hackle:** Spey hackle, orange
- **Cheeks:** Jungle cock nails
- **Collar:** Light furnace hackle

Jason with a decent winter fish from the Oregon Coast. Memorable day, that one. ROB RUSSELL PHOTO

Clockwise from the top: Old World Hilton; Willamette Sunrise; Willamette Motion Prawn in four color combinations; Midnight Darkness; Bloody Skunk.

BLOODY SKUNK

- **Hook:** #3 or #5 Daiichi Alec Jackson Steelhead Iron, black
- **Thread:** 6/0 UNI-Thread, black
- **Tag:** Medium holographic tinsel, silver
- **Tail:** Saddle hackle fibers, red
- **Body:** Angora goat dubbing, black
- **Rib:** Medium French oval tinsel
- **Wing:** Bucktail, black, mixed with Grizzly Krystal Flash, red, and Krystal Flash, pearl dyed black
- **Collar:** Saddle hackle, black
- **Cheeks:** Jungle cock nails

MIDNIGHT DARKNESS

- **Hook:** #3-7 Daiichi Alec Jackson Spey, black
- **Thread:** 6/0 UNI-Thread, black
- **Tag:** Medium holographic tinsel, silver
- **Tail:** Saddle hackle fibers, red
- **Body:** Angora goat dubbing, black, palmered with schlappen, black
- **Rib:** Medium French oval tinsel
- **Flash:** Grizzly Krystal Flash, red, mixed with Krystal Flash, pearl dyed black
- **Throat:** Marabou, black
- **Collar:** Guinea hen, red
- **Wings:** Stripped goose, black
- **Cheeks:** Jungle cock nails

WILLAMETTE MOTION PRAWN, BLACK GOLD

- **Hook:** #1-4 Daiichi 2451, black
- **Thread:** 8/0 UNI-Thread, black
- **Tag:** Medium holographic tinsel, silver
- **Tail:** In three sections, bottom to top: 1) short bunch of red Krystal Flash, 2) pinch of yellow Craft Fur barred with black Sharpie permanent marker, (3) American hen hackle, black
- **Body weilings:** In three sections, back to front: 1) Angora goat dubbing, followed by a ring hackle of orange saddle, topped with American hen hackle, black; 2) same as the first; 3) Ice Dub, black, followed by a ring hackle of schlappen, black, topped with a pair of golden pheasant shoulder feathers dyed black
- **Flash:** Flashabou, red, one strand per side
- **Cheeks:** Jungle cock nails

Notes: Cichy's Willamette Motion Prawns are very close to Ingi's Motion Prawn (page 147), but with no added weight and no golden pheasant tippets. Here, the weight comes from the heavier gauge hook.

EMULATOR PRAWN, PURPLE/PEACOCK

- **Hook:** #1-4 Daiichi 2451, black
- **Thread:** 8/0 UNI-Thread, black
- **Tag:** Medium holographic tinsel, silver
- **Tail:** In three sections, bottom to top: 1) short bunch of Krystal Flash, pearl; 2) Baitfish Emulator, purple, barred with black Sharpie permanent marker, mixed with a few fibers of Micro Flashabou, pearl; 3) golden pheasant neck, dyed purple
- **Body weilings:** Repeat three times: Ice Dub, peacock, followed by a ring hackle of black saddle, topped with golden pheasant neck dyed purple
- **Collar:** Guinea hen, purple
- **Wing:** Golden pheasant neck, dyed purple
- **Flash:** Holographic Flashabou, purple haze, one strand per side
- **Cheeks:** Jungle cock nails

Notes: Basically the same as the Willamette Motion Prawn (page 173), this incorporates Baitfish Emulator for added sparkle.

Trey Combs

This guy really needs no introduction, but just in case there are a few folks who don't know about Trey, he is the master scribe and storyteller of our church. He is probably best known as the author of *Steelhead Fly Fishing* (1991), which has been the bible for all serious steelheaders since it was published. Trey is also a wonderful fly designer, and we're honored to have his new SteelFlash series featured here. Thanks, Trey!

BLUE STEELFLASH

- **Eyes:** 1/40 ounce chrome-plated lead barbell eyes coated with red glitter paint and sealed with 5 Minute Epoxy
- **Body:** Holographic Mylar tinsel, kingfisher blue
- **Tail:** Trilobal dubbing, kingfisher blue, mixed with Ice Dub, blue steelie. Shoulder with several strands of Flashabou, blue pearl, on each side.
- **Skirt in two parts:** 1) Dubbing loop of Ice Dub, black, mixed with Ice Dub, Blue Steelie. Pick out; 2) Ice Wing, dark purple (this is "black/purple.") Shoulder with Flashabou, first blue and then purple pearl.
- **Topping:** Holographic Mylar Flashabou, blue and purple
- **Dorsal:** Holographic Mylar Flashabou, fuchsia

Trey field-testing his new flies on the OP. So far, so good! TOMO HIGASHI PHOTO

PURPLE STEELFLASH

- **Eyes:** 1/40 ounce chrome-plated lead barbell eyes coated with red glitter paint and sealed with 5 Minute Epoxy
- **Body:** Holographic Mylar tinsel, purple
- **Tail:** Trilobal, purple, mixed with Ice Dub, blue steelie.
- **Skirt in two parts:** 1) Dubbing loop as with tail, for underskirt; 2) Ice Fur, purple, for skirt
- **Shoulder with mixed strands of blue and purple pearl Flashabou.**
- **Topping:** As in Blue SteelFlash, holographic Mylar tinsel in blue, purple, and fuchsia

Notes: All shouldering and topping is doubled when tied in, which makes the fly extra durable. For summer-run steelhead Trey alternates the blue with the purple. He ties them on shanks from 15 mm to 25 mm and Daiichi hook 2557 in #6 or #4.

BLACK STEELFLASH

- **Eyes:** 1/40 ounce chrome-plated lead barbell eyes coated with blue glitter paint and sealed with 5 Minute Epoxy
- **Tail:** Ice Dub, black, mixed with Ice Dub, steelie blue. Apply several strands of Dyed-Pearl Flashabou, blue, to each side.
- **Skirt in two parts:** 1) Black Ice Dub, black; 2) skirt over, Ice Fur in black mixed with Ice Dub, steelie blue.
- **Shoulder with holographic Mylar Flashabou, black; sides, midline:** Flashabou, blue pearl. Dorsal: Flashabou, black first, then blue and fuchsia holographic Flashabou.
- **Head:** Ice Dub, black

ORANGE STEELFLASH

- **Eyes:** 1/40 ounce chrome-plated lead barbell eyes coated with hot pink nail polish and pearl glitter paint, then sealed with 5 Minute Epoxy
- **Body:** Holographic Mylar tinsel, orange
- **Tail:** Ice Dub Shimmer Fringe, fluorescent hot pink.
- **Skirt in two parts:** (1) Dubbing loop with Ice Dub, flame; (2) Ice Fur, fluorescent orange; Shoulder with Flashabou, orange pearl.

Steelflash flies offer a big profile with extra helpings of flash and wiggle.

Shoulder with holographic Flashabou, orange.
Dorsal: Holographic Flashabou, red
- **Head:** Ice Dub, hot orange

HOT PINK STEELFLASH

- **Eyes:** 1/40 ounce chrome-plated lead barbell eyes coated with red glitter paint and sealed with 5 Minute Epoxy
- **Body:** Holographic Mylar tinsel, pink
- **Tail:** Ice Dub Shimmer Fringe, fluorescent hot pink
- **Skirt in two parts:** (1) Trilobal dubbing, flame; (2) Ice Fur, cerise. Shoulder and belly with Pink Pearl Flashabou. Dorsal: First pink, and then fuchia holographic Mylar tinsel.

Notes: On the medium and large flies, it's necessary to tie in a small dubbing loop of Ice Dub, or trilobal dubbing, under the tail to keep the tail up and flowing in the currents. The 15 mm flies are slightly over 2 inches long with the size 6 stinger hook in place. Though labor intensive, I think these tiny SteelFlash flies will fish circles around conventional hair wings. My biased opinion!

SteelFlash Flies

I developed SteelFlash flies in an effort to create a fly that neither absorbs nor traps water, has an abundance of flash, has tremendous action in the water, and both sinks well and balances perfectly with a stinger hook riding up. Underbodies of synthetic furs are sparse and carefully combed out, so that water flows through the material. This application is *not* a "bump" to help splay out skirts at the tail and at the head. Note that the holographic skirts leave much of the underbody exposed. The underbody should undulate in the currents as well at the skirt. The result is that SteelFlash flies are easy to cast, even in large winter-run sizes with a size 2 or size 1 hook. As summer-run patterns with a size 4 stinger hook, the flies can easily be cast with a 5-weight single-hand rod or a 4-weight two-hand rod.

Head weight below the shank with painted barbell eyes exceeds the leverage weight of the upturned hook. But the fly can still be led and will maintain a perfect swimming attitude throughout a broadside, greased line presentation. On the hard swing, the fly wobbles side to side, but the hook still rides up properly.

The fly patterns that follow have been extensively fished in Washington and in British Columbia's Skeena system of rivers. These trials produced stunning results. We discovered that steelhead would leave their holding station, race after the fly, and take it going away. For Kerry

Burkheimer, two Skeena steelhead nearly spooled him after taking the Blue and the Purple Steelflash patterns. Jack Mitchell, famed Japanese fly fisher Tomo Higashi, and I had identical results with the dark patterns.

All five of these patterns are superb winter-run flies, including those in the smaller summer-run size.

These SteelFlash flies are weighted but swim slightly head down, and they remain so balanced that the angler can lead the fly through soft water and give steelhead an ideal profile view.

STEELFLASH FLY-TYING INSTRUCTIONS

All flies are tied on Partridge Intruder or Partridge Waddington shanks. I use 25 mm for summer-run steelhead, and 35 mm or 45 mm shanks for winter-run steelhead.

TYING THE STEELFLASH BLANK

- **Shank:** 25 mm Partridge Intruder shank (for summer-run steelhead)
- **Tying thread:** Danville's 210-denier Flat Waxed Nylon
- **Wire loop:** Wire loop needs to test at 25 pounds or more. The loop needs to be sufficiently rigid so that it doesn't flop around with the stinger hook, catching on other parts of the fly.

Wind thread evenly from the front to the loop at the end of the shank, stopping before the rear loop. Cut the wire so that the loop will extend about 2 to 3 cm (1") and at least 1 cm (⁴⁄₁₀") in front of the eye. Tie down doubled wire with even turns until reaching the eye. Run wire ends through the eye and hold in place under the shank. Tightly lash down ends. Whip finish with four or five turns. Soak with a 50/50 solution of Hard As Hull Head Cement and thinner. You should now have a perfectly smooth body that is ready for eyes and tinsel.

Change tying thread to 6/0 UNI-Thread, silver doctor blue, or to 10/0 Veevus, black.

Turn the body upside down and secure Wapsi dumbbell plated eyes, 1/40 ounce or 1/60 ounce, with figure-eight wraps. (The weight of the eyes depends on the size and depth of water being fished.) Make sure the eyes are perfectly in line with the wire loop at one end and the eye of the Intruder shank at the other. Directly behind the eyes, tie in blue holographic Veevus Mylar, L (wide). Wind the tinsel evenly down the body and back, and tie off just behind the eyes.

Using pink fingernail polish, paint the eyes; this will dry in seconds. I then coat the eyes with red glitter paint (available in squeeze bottles in craft stores). When completely dry, I coat the eyes with 5 Minute Epoxy. These steps are labor intensive if done one fly at a time, so I'll do at least several at once, step by step. Applying the epoxy takes time as I can only apply it one fly at a time. The epoxy not only makes the eyes glow but keeps the eyes secured to the body after the proverbial thousand casts.

The epoxy should be allowed to cure overnight. Otherwise, the flies are sticky and the eyes dulled from handling. I hang the "blanks" on pins waiting to be dressed.

SteelFlash Blue

The pattern is basically black and blue, with purple highlights. Underbody is black Craft Fur with blue metallic dubbing. Both have bright red glitter eyes.

The SteelFlash pattern, and the Purple version that follows, are my best all-light summer-run patterns. Neither pattern needs to be run deep to be effective. They throw off so much flash that they are deadly simply fished on the swing using a floating—dry—tip.

SteelFlash Purple

The pattern carries a purple underbody of Craft Fur mixed with blue metallic dubbing, with blue holographic highlights dorsally. My preference is for very dark purple dubbing at the head.

Steelhead are famous for their attraction to purple. Like the Blue, above, this fly is extremely effective on either bright days or overcast days. I personally feel this is the best of all the "purples" for steelhead. And because of the upturned stinger hook, the fly swims through skinny rock-filled currents without hanging up.

SteelFlash Black

This subdued dark pattern is a super alternative to the Blue and Purple SteelFlash patterns. I especially like it under low light, or with midday's intense light on steelhead that have already been worked over. I have such confidence in this pattern that I feel that the Black can move a steelhead when other patterns have failed.

The Black has a strong silhouette. I turn to this fly when the river is discolored, or when light is low; that is, this pattern is likely to be the first and the last pattern I fish each day for summer runs. Even on deep pools with little current.

SteelFlash Pink

Among the bright steelhead patterns, pink reigns number one on most lists, especially in British Columbia, and I think this applies for both summer and winter steelhead. The SteelFlash approach adds chrome and fluorescent pink dubbing to cut through discolored water. Holographic Flashabou, mostly pink but with a mix of fuchsia, pearl, and red, partially covers a body of pink and hot fuchsia.

I'll fish the Pink in small sizes on domestic rivers with a sink-tip set up, especially if there are salmon in the river that have schooled up and have pushed steelhead from lies. The Pink will attract both chinook and coho salmon. During the winter, when no such competition exists, I fish the Pink in the larger size, swinging it on 10 feet of T-11, or even faster sink-tips when water is high and discolored. The exception comes at first light, when steelhead may be parked in a foot or two of water along the beach. The smaller Pink on an intermediate tip is a perfect approach.

SteelFlash Orange

Orange steelhead flies have been my go-to patterns for as long as I've been fishing for winter steelhead. The Orange SteelFlash pattern is tied with highly contrasting oranges: The tail of pearl orange and opal orange veil hot orange Craft Fur, creating one set of glowing oranges. The forward skirt has orange holographic Flashabou that veils pearl orange Flashabou, both over a body of hot orange Craft Fur mixed with metallic orange dubbing. This creates a deeper orange glow. The eyes, painted orange with gold glitter, provide a very different shade of orange. This is a dazzling, "shrimpy" orange fly full of semitransparent motion. There is no other orange steelhead fly remotely like it.

I fish the fly on a fast sink-tip for winter-run steelhead: Mend to reduce the speed of the swing, and then let the fly swim directly below for a few seconds before stripping in the fly. The tail gives the fly tremendous flash, a signal to steelhead when the fly is on the swing.

Jerry Darkes

Jerry is one of the most knowledgeable fly anglers in the country, with over 40 years of experience fishing, tying flies, writing, speaking, and teaching other anglers. In that time, he has sought out and mastered an incredible range of fly opportunities throughout the Great Lakes region from his home in the suburbs of Cleveland. Jerry has been deeply involved in the evolution of Great Lakes steelhead fly patterns, and the wide array of his contributions here span decades of influences from his friends and fellow anglers. His first book, *Fly Fishing the Inland Oceans: An Angler's Guide to Finding and Catching Fish in the Great Lakes*, was released through Stackpole Books in September 2013. His second book is *Fly Tyer's Guide to Tying Essential Bass and Panfish Flies* (Lyons Press, 2014).

SUCKER SPAWN

- **Hook:** Heavy wet fly or scud hook, #10-16
- **Thread:** Red
- **Body:** Cream angora yarn separated into individual piles that are then looped and tied down to the hook shank

Notes: This is considered a must-have pattern for the eastern Great Lakes. It was originally an early-season

Jerry Darkes giving his best impression of a normal person. JIMMY CHANG PHOTO

trout fly, for when trout were feeding on the roe of spawning suckers. This is the color scheme tied for this application and still the most popular for steelhead. This fly is also tied in a wide variety of colors as an attractor pattern.

BLOOD DOT

- **Hook:** #10-16 heavy wet fly or scud hook
- **Thread:** Cream
- **Body:** Cream angora yarn separated into individual piles that are then looped and tied down to the hook shank
- **Spot:** Glo-Bug yarn or McFly Foam, steelhead orange, tied down in the center of the shank and trimmed short

Notes: This Sucker Spawn variation was made popular by Pennsylania angler and tier Jeff Blood.

SCRAMBLED EGG

- **Hook:** #10-16 heavy wet fly or scud hook
- **Thread:** Orange
- **Body:** Thin length of cheese and steelhead orange Glo-Bug yarn or McFly Foam tied in so it extends back behind the hook, then is pulled over the top of the hook shank and tied down in a series of loops or bumps to the hook eye

CYCLOPS

- **Hook:** #10-14 Daiichi 1120 or equivalent
- **Bead:** Small glass bead, red or orange
- **Thread:** UTC 70-denier, orange
- **Body:** Plastic canvas craft yarn, yellow, orange, or chartreuse
- **Spot:** Glo-Bug yarn or McFly Foam, steelhead orange, tied down in the center of the shank and trimmed short

Notes: This is Jerry's personal take on an "eyed" egg pattern. "The craft yarn has a unique appearance in the water that can be more productive than regular yarn," Jerry said.

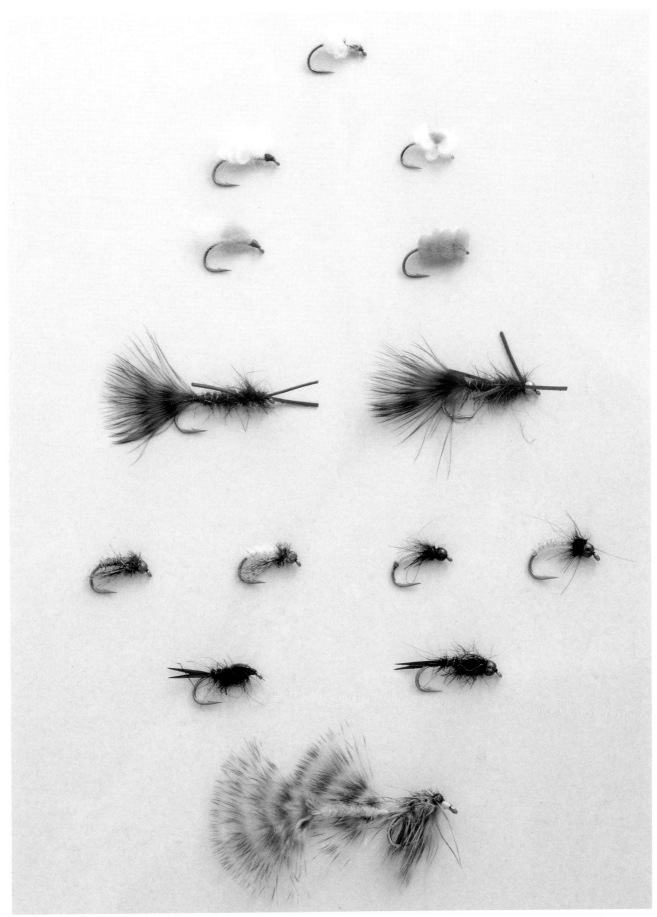

Top row: Cyclops. Second row: Sucker Spawn; Blood Dot. Third row: Nuke Egg; Scrambled Egg. Fourth row: Superior X-legs, unweighted and bead head versions. Fifth row: Dr. Mike's Caddis, dark and light; JQ's Caddis in two sizes. Sixth row: Great Lakes Simple Stone, unweighted and bead head versions. Bottom: Sexy Hexy.

Left column, top to bottom, including bottom-most fly: Emulator; four Arctic Wigglers in assorted colors; two Niagara Intruders. Right column, top to bottom: Boa Leech, black; Boa Leech, purple; Boa Minnow; Iced Rabbit Tubes in two colors.

NUKE EGG

- **Hook:** #8-12 heavy wet fly or scud hook
- **Thread:** Orange
- **Body:** Short length of bright Egg Yarn tied in just behind the eye of the hook, veiled with a thin layer of light-colored yarn surrounding the bright spot that is trimmed to extend just past the spot

SUPERIOR X-LEGS

- **Hook:** 2XL to 3XL long heavy nymph hook, #8-10
- **Bead (optional):** Copper, sized to hook
- **Legs:** Single strand of Sili Legs, brown, tied in on each side of the hook, then trimmed in proportion to hook
- **Thread:** 6/0 UNI-Thread, brown
- **Tail:** Marabou, brown or grizzly brown
- **Abdomen:** Stonefly blend, brown
- **Rib:** Fine wire, copper

Notes: "This is a go-to pattern in Lake Superior tributaries. It is particularly popular in Wisconsin and the Upper Peninsula of Michigan."

GREAT LAKES SIMPLE STONE (UNWEIGHTED AND BEAD HEAD)

- **Hook:** Unweighted—#8-14 Daiichi 1530; bead head—#8014 Daiichi 1760 (or equivalents)
- **Bead (optional):** Black, sized to hook
- **Thread:** UTC 70-denier, black
- **Tail:** Goose biots, black
- **Abdomen:** Stonefly or hare's ear blend, black
- **Rib:** Fine wire, copper
- **Thorax:** Stonefly or hare's ear blend, black, spun in a dubbing loop
- **Wing case:** Soft fibers from a ringneck pheasant tail feather

Notes: As Jerry says, "This pattern is obviously just a black Hare's Ear Nymph with a biot tail. Black stoneflies are found across the Great Lakes, and their size varies greatly. When they become active in late winter, steelhead will key on them as a food source. Using a short, heavy hook allows for a small fly that still has plenty of strength to hold a large, active steelhead."

JQ'S CADDIS

- **Hook:** #8-14 Daiichi 1120
- **Bead:** Black, sized to hook
- **Thread:** Body—UTC 70-denier, chartreuse; head—UTC 70-denier, black
- **Body:** Stretch tubing, chartreuse, with underwrap of thread for added color
- **Head:** Hare's ear blend, black

Notes: Credited to Joe Quaradillo, this caddis larva pattern imitates the *Ryacophila* genus abundant across the Great Lakes region.

SEXY HEXY

- **Hooks:** Rear—any straight-eye hook of appropriate size; front—#6-10 Daiichi 1120
- **Thread:** UTC 70-denier, cream
- **Eyes:** Small plastic bead chain, black
- **Tail:** Grizzly marabou, natural
- **Abdomen:** Hare's ear blend dubbing, dirty yellow
- **Gills:** Grizzly marabou, natural
- **Articulation:** Rear hook is clipped at the bend and the finished abdomen is attached to front hook with loop of 10-pound monofilament
- **Thorax:** Hare's ear blend dubbing, dirty yellow, palmered with grizzly hen hackle
- **Wing case:** Peacock herl

Notes: Steelhead are known to feed heavily on *Hexagenia* nymphs, also known as "wigglers," across much of the Great Lakes region. This is Jerry's simplified version of several different articulated patterns.

DR. MIKE'S CADDIS, LIGHT AND DARK

- **Hook:** #10-16 Daiichi 1120
- **Bead:** Copper, sized to hook
- **Thread:** Light—UTC 70-denier, cream; dark—UTC 70-denier, olive
- **Body:** Light—Spirit River Brite Blend, caddis cream; dark—Spirit River Brite Blend, olive
- **Throat:** Partridge neck fibers
- **Head:** Peacock herl

BOA MINNOW

- **Hook:** #1-2 Daiichi 2461
- **Thread:** UTC 70-denier, white
- **Tail:** Marabou, gray
- **Body:** Boa yarn (aka eyelash yarn or Gala Yarn), white or white-to-gray
- **Flash:** Krinkle Mirror Flash, four strands on each side, tied in extending forward from eye, then pulled back and tied down between wraps of the body material (spreads flash throughout the body)
- **Head:** Ice Wing Fiber, pearl, clumped and tied back

Notes: Boa yarn and its facsimiles are usually sold at craft stores. Some brands have very interesting color transitions, while others are a solid color. This versatile baitfish pattern is effective when swung, stripped, and dead-drifted.

BOA LEECH, PURPLE

- **Hook:** #1-2 Daiichi 2461
- **Thread:** UTC 70-denier, fluorescent pink
- **Tail:** Marabou, purple
- **Body:** Boa yarn (aka eyelash yarn or Gala Yarn), purple
- **Flash:** Holographic Flashabou, four strands on each side, tied in extending forward from eye, then pulled back and tied down between wraps of the body material (spreads flash throughout the body)
- **Head:** Ice Dub, pink, clumped and tied back

EMULATOR

- **Hook:** #2/0-2 Daiichi 2461
- **Thread:** UTC 140-denier, tan
- **Tail:** Grizzly marabou, natural
- **Body:** Emu herl, wrapped over shank then palmered with grizzly schlappen
- **Collar:** Mallard or gadwall flank, hackled spider-style
- **Flash (optional):** Krystal Flash, dark olive
- **Head:** Australian opossum

Notes: This is Jerry's version of Kevin Feenstra's legendary original pattern (see page 194). Darkes comments, "Feenstra has been an instrumental force in the use of swung flies and two-handed rods in Michigan. The Emulator has been the template for numerous variations that produce steelhead across the Great Lakes and beyond."

LUCIOUS LEECH, PURPLE/BLACK

- **Hook:** #2/0-2 Daiichi 2461
- **Thread:** UTC 140-denier, chartreuse
- **Tail:** Marabou, purple
- **Body:** Wrapped marabou, purple, then black
- **Flash:** Krinkle Mirror Flash, eight strands on each side, tied in extending forward from eye, then pulled back and tied down between wraps of the marabou (spreads flash throughout the body)
- **Collar:** Mallard flank, dyed chartreuse
- **Head:** Petite Estaz, chartreuse

Notes: This is another favorite Kevin Feenstra pattern adapted by Jerry Darkes. The potential color combinations are endless.

ARCTIC WIGGLER, EMERALD SHINER

- **Tube:** Eumer 17 mm x 4 mm ballhead tube, white
- **Thread:** UTC 70-denier, chartreuse
- **Tail/wing:** In three parts, back to front: 1) arctic fox tail, white, with guard hairs; 2) eight strands of Krinkle Mirror Flash; 3) arctic fox tail, chartreuse, with guard hairs
- **Body:** Petite Estaz, chartreuse
- **Hackle:** Schlappen, white
- **Collar:** Palmer Chenille, olive

Notes: The Eumer ballhead tube makes a versatile tying platform. The Arctic Wiggler has an exceptional baitfish profile when wet, and swim-tank tests show this fly's very tight wiggle pattern in the current. This particular color scheme imitates one of the most common Great Lakes forage species. Eyes can be added, if desired, and any short-shank, straight-eye hook can be used. The hook eye can be seated in a piece of junction tube or rigged stinger-style on a loop.

ARCTIC WIGGLER, SMELT

- **Tube:** Eumer 17 mm x 4 mm ballhead tube, white
- **Thread:** UTC 70-denier, silver gray
- **Tail/wing:** Krystal Flash, rainbow, in between two sections of arctic fox tail, gray; holographic Flashabou, blue, over the top
- **Body:** Petite Estaz, salmon
- **Hackle:** Schlappen, gray
- **Collar:** Palmer Chenille, shad gray

ARCTIC WIGGLER, OLIVE/KELLY/COPPER

- **Tube:** Eumer 17 mm x 4 mm ballhead tube, copper
- **Thread:** UTC 140-denier, olive
- **Tail/wing:** Flashabou, copper and Kelly green, in between two sections of arctic fox tail, olive
- **Body:** Petite Estaz, olive
- **Hackle:** Schlappen, olive
- **Collar:** Palmer Chenille, olive

ARCTIC WIGGLER, FLAME THROWER

- **Tube:** Eumer 17 mm x 4 mm ballhead tube, orange
- **Thread:** UTC 140-denier, orange
- **Tail/wing:** Krinkle Mirror Flash, orange, and holographic Flashabou, orange, in between two sections of arctic fox tail, orange
- **Body:** Petite Estaz, orange
- **Hackle:** Schlappen, flame red
- **Collar:** UV Polar Chenille, fluorescent orange

Notes: This color and material combination is designed for high, off-color water. It was named by well-known Ohio steelheader Joff Liskay.

NIAGRA INTRUDER

- **Shank:** Straight-eye hook or medium Flymen Articulated Shank
- **Thread:** UTC 140-denier, white
- **Eyes:** Small barbells eyes, lead or brass, depending on desired weight
- **Stinger loop:** .018″ plastic-coated craft wire
- **Hackle:** Marabou, white or gray
- **Wing:** Rabbit strip, gray or ice-blue blue
- **Flash:** Krinkle Mirror Flash, silver or pearl
- **Head:** Crystal Braid, pearl
- **Hook:** #1-2 Gamakatsu Octopus

Notes: This versatile fly is a creation of Canadian guide Paul Castellano and works well swung or stripped. It is typically tied as a baitfish imitation, but can be made in any color(s) desired. Jerry's original notes for this fly indicate that Paul sometimes used 30-pound Fireline for the stinger loop. He goes on to explain that the Fireline tended to soften, and that he has come to prefer the wire.

ICED RABBIT TUBE

- **Tube:** Medium plastic tube, 2 cm (¾″) long, melted slightly at both ends
- **Thread:** UTC 70-denier, white
- **Tail/wing:** Rabbit strip
- **Hackle:** Schlappen
- **Head:** Ice Dub or Ice Wing Fiber, clumped and pulled back

Notes: As an attractor or baitfish, color this fly as desired. This pattern is simple to tie and easy to rig, and it catches fish. Thread the hook on a loop to run it stinger-style, thereby minimizing snags.

Michael Davidchik

Steelie Mike is a Southwest Washington–based steel-header, emergency room nurse, writer, and signature tier for Rainey's Flies with a great sense for fly design. Every fly he ties has a specific purpose, playing its part in his strategic approach to catching fish. "Fishing my home waters of Southwest Washington, I'm covering water both blessed and cursed with hatchery Skamania and Chambers Creek steelhead," Mike said. "I've learned that a fly's size, profile, color, movement, and light are frequently the key to bringing these often-stale fish to the beach."

SNOT ROCKET

- **Shank:** #2 Owner SSW or Daiichi 2557
- **Thread:** UTC 70-denier, red
- **Stinger loop:** Berkley Steelon 15- or 20-pound wire, 3.2 cm (1¼") loop
- **Dubbing:** Ice Dub, hot orange
- **Underhackle:** Crosscut bunny (6.4 cm/2½" per fly), orange, spun in a dubbing loop
- **Flash:** Flashabou, gold

Mike hucks a line across his home river.
BRIAN CHOU PHOTO

- **Hackle:** In two parts, back to front: 1) Spirit River marabou, fluorescent orange; 2) Hareline Extra-Select Marabou, red (tied slightly longer than the first)
- **Hook:** #2 Owner SSW

ROCKET MINNOW

- **Shank:** #2 Owner SSW or Daiichi 2557
- **Thread:** UTC 70 denier, red
- **Stinger loop:** Berkley Steelon 15- or 20-pound wire, 3.2 cm (1¼") loop
- **Dubbing:** Ice Dub, peacock
- **Underhackle:** Crosscut bunny (6.4 cm/2½" per fly), olive, spun in a dubbing loop
- **Flash:** Flashabou, red
- **Tentacles:** Grizzly saddle tips, red
- **Hackle:** In two parts, back to front: 1) grizzly saddle marabou; 2) Hareline Extra-Select Marabou, olive
- **Hook:** #2 Owner SSW

Notes: Both the Snot Rocket and the Rocket Minnow are reminiscent of Mike Kinney's Skagit Minnow, and Davidchik gives credit where it's due. His technique of supporting the marabou's profile with spun rabbit fur is unique and effective.

FALLOUT

- **Hook:** #4-8 Daiichi 2151
- **Thread:** UTC 70-denier, pink
- **Tag:** Lagartun Oval French Mini-Braid
- **Tail:** Golden pheasant tippet, dyed pink (or red)
- **Body:** STS Trilobal Dub, fluorescent pink, or Ice Dub, UV pink
- **Hackle:** Soft hen saddle, white
- **Wing:** Mirage Flashabou, pink

Notes: Mike says the Fallout came from years of fishing Gorman's Caballero Egg and wanting a version for swinging. "Egg patterns are well-known steelhead producers under a bobber, but very underrated as swung flies," he said. "Over the years I realized that I wanted to bring a classic style to the Egg and make it mine. Not to mention that after a while I was a little embarrassed to swing a plain Glo-Bug."

Top row: Skater Kiss; Fallout. **Second row:** Autumn Error; Moe. **Third row:** Rocket Minnow.
Fourth row: Lil Double Coachman; Lil O'Muddler. **Bottom:** Snot Rocket.

SKATER KISS

- **Hook:** #4-8 Daiichi 2110
- **Thread:** UTC 70-denier, orange
- **Tail:** Golden pheasant crest, dyed red
- **Undertail:** Golden pheasant tippet, dyed pink
- **Butt:** Ice Dub, orange
- **Body:** 1 mm foam, orange
- **Body/wings:** Spun mule deer body hair

Notes: Mike designed this foam skater to move water. "Over the last decade of fishing dries, I have noticed one thing: The more water the fly pushes, the more aggressive the take." This is a great fly for chugging, popping, twitching, or just waking against the current.

AUTUMN ERROR

- **Hook:** #4-8 Daiichi 2161
- **Thread:** UTC 70-denier, red
- **Rib:** Medium Lagartun oval French tinsel, silver
- **Body:** Flat gold tinsel
- **Collar:** Dubbed bunny fur, yellow
- **Collar:** Grizzly saddle hackle, dyed yellow
- **Wing:** Polar bear, orange

Notes: "The Autumn Error was indeed an error on my part," Mike said. "One of my confidence flies in autumn is Lloyd Silvius's Fall Favorite. While sitting at the tying desk one summer, I tied several flies that I believed to be Fall Favorites. But when I sat back and looked at them, I realized that I had gotten the colors wrong." The fish didn't mind at all, and a new fly pattern was born.

MOE

- **Hook:** #5-9 Daiichi 2050
- **Thread:** UTC 70-denier, black
- **Tail:** Golden pheasant crest, dyed red
- **Body:** Sparkle braid, gold
- **Wing:** Peacock sword, six to eight fibers
- **Hackle:** In two parts from back to front:
  1) brown bunny fur, cut back and dubbed;
  2) CDC, light mallard gray

Notes: Mike created the Moe after having a Grande Ronde trip saved in the 11th hour by a fly that was given to him by a stranger on the banks of the river. "His pattern had a very neutral, drab color scheme," Mike said. "But it surprised me by catching a large hen on the last day of the trip. I took the simple color combo, changed some of the materials, and added a CDC overcollar for contrast."

LIL DOUBLE COACHMAN

- **Hook:** #8-12 Kamasan B270
- **Thread:** UTC 70-denier, red
- **Tag:** UTC 70-denier, red
- **Tail:** Golden pheasant tippet, red
- **Body:** Peacock herl
- **Rib:** Small gold wire
- **Collar:** India hen hackle
- **Wing:** Ringneck pheasant tail, red

LIL O'MUDDLER

- **Hook:** #8-12 Kamasan B270
- **Thread:** UTC 70-denier, red
- **Ribbing:** Small oval French tinsel, gold
- **Body:** Hareline Hare's Ear Plus Dubbin, natural
- **Head/collar:** Deer body hair, dyed orange, spun and trimmed

Notes: Both the Lil Double Coachman and the Lil O' Muddler are variations of classic patterns in micro sizes. "With the highly pressured water of today's world, sometimes big isn't all the ladies think it is," he said. "Especially in areas that have been worked over, you will be surprised what you can find when you drop down your fly size." The double hooks help the flies ride straight in fast water and when fishing a dry line.

Michael Decoteau

Mike Decoteau is one of the shining stars of the Great Lakes fly-tying scene. Hailing from Columbus, Ohio, Mike has developed his own original fly patterns for just about every species of fish that swims. Smallmouth bass tend to dominate the watery world he calls home, but he devotes many hours tying flies for resident trout, lake-run browns, freshwater drum (or sheep's head), and steelhead. He's one of the more prolific commercial tiers working today, rivaling the production of Bjorn Beech and Greg Senyo. To read more, check out the step-by-step on page 55.

FIFTH ELEMENT, PURPLE/PINK

- **Shank:** 25 mm Senyo's Articulated Shank, black
- **Stinger loop:** Senyo's Intruder Wire, purple, 2.5 cm (1") loop
- **Thread:** 6/0 UNI-Thread, purple
- **Weight (optional):** Small lead eyes
- **Rear dubbing ball:** Ice Dub, UV purple
- **Body:** Flat Diamond Braid, pearl
- **Wing:** In four parts, from back to front: 1) arctic fox tail, white; 2) Mirage Flashabou, pink; 3) arctic fox tail, purple; 4) Angler Hair or Ice Wing, pink
- **Collar:** In three parts, from back to front: 1) Senyo's Laser Dub, shrimp pink; 2) golden pheasant tail fibers; 3) golden pheasant body feather, dyed red
- **Topping:** Holographic Flashabou, purple haze
- **Head:** SLF Kaufmann Blend, black stone
- **Cheeks (optional):** Jungle cock nails
- **Hook:** #4 Gamakatsu Octopus, red

Notes: Michael's favorite color combinations for the Fifth Element are purple/pink, purple/blue, red/orange, and blue/chartreuse/white.

EVIL TWIN BROTHER, BLACK/ORANGE

- **Shank:** 25 mm Senyo's Articulated Shank, black
- **Stinger loop:** Senyo's Intruder Wire, red, 2.5 cm (1") loop
- **Thread:** 6/0 UNI-Thread, purple
- **Rear dubbing Ball:** Ice Dub purple
- **Body:** Diamond Braid, red
- **Rib:** Size B Ultra Wire, red
- **Body hackle:** Guinea hen, natural
- **Wing:** In two parts, from back to front: 1) arctic fox tail, orange; 2) arctic fox tail, black
- **Sides:** Lady Amherst pheasant center tail fibers, dyed orange
- **Collar:** Burnt Spey hackle, black
- **Topping:** Lady Amherst pheasant, center tail fibers, natural
- **Cheeks (optional):** Jungle cock nails
- **Hook:** #4 Gamakatsu Octopus, black

Notes: Michael's favorite color combinations for the Evil Twin Brother are black/orange, black/chartreuse, black/purple, and blue/olive/white.

Mike cranks out some wild streamers at his home tying desk. CHRIS WALKER PHOTO

Four stunning examples of the Fifth Element.

The Evil Twin Brother in four of his moods.

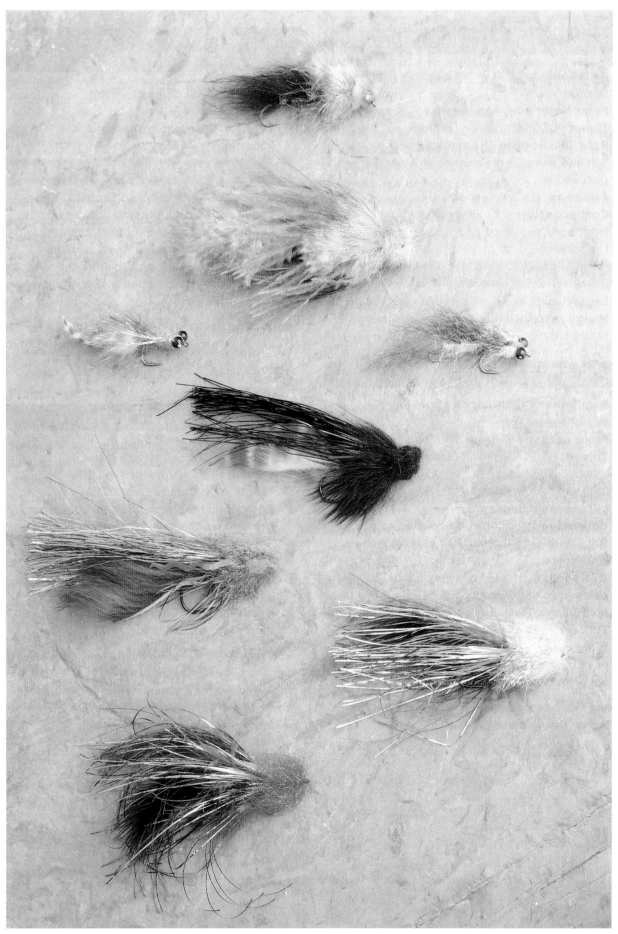

From the top: Psycho Sculpin; Emulator Sculpin; Better Than Spawn; Australian Possum Hex; Cow Killer Sculpin; Aquatic Nuisance; Grapefruit Leech in two color combinations.

Top: Strung Out Tonya Harding. Second row: Strung Out Junk-in-the-Trunk; Strung Out Beach Bum. Third row: Strung Out Rockstar. Fourth row: two MOAL styles. Fifth and sixth rows: two Marabou MOAL styles.

Dean Finnerty

Dean is one of the handful of steelhead guides who are lucky enough to call the North Umpqua River their office. He's been a dedicated steelheader since his grade school days in Gresham, Oregon, and now has over 40 years of experience tying and swinging flies throughout the Pacific Northwest. His signature steelhead patterns, several of which are featured here, are tried-and-true distillations of his many tying influences and his decades spent on the water.

FINNERTY STEELHEAD SKATER, FALL

- **Hook:** #6-8 Tiemco 7989
- **Thread:** Mono cord, black
- **Tail:** Krystal Flash, root beer, topped with a small bunch of moose mane
- **Shellback:** 2 mm foam, orange, tapered from 3 mm (⅛") wide to 13 mm (½") wide, the narrow end tied in at the rear of the fly
- **Abdomen:** Deer belly hair, spun and trimmed tight in a taper
- **Hackle:** Guinea hen, dyed purple
- **Thorax:** Deer body hair, rust, spun with tips out and trimmed on the bottom
- **Head:** Bring the foam strip forward over the back, pulling the rust deer hair tips back and to the sides, and tie down just behind the eye of the hook

FINNERTY STEELHEAD SKATER, SUMMER

- **Hook:** #2-6 Tiemco 7989
- **Thread:** Mono cord, black
- **Tail:** Krystal Flash, pearl, topped with a small bunch of moose mane
- **Shellback:** 2 mm foam, tan, tapered from 3 mm (⅛") wide to 13 mm (½") wide, the narrow end tied in at the rear of the fly
- **Abdomen:** Deer belly hair, spun and trimmed tight in a taper
- **Hackle:** Guinea hen, dyed purple
- **Thorax:** Deer body hair, rust, spun with tips out and trimmed on the bottom
- **Head:** Bring the foam strip forward over the back, pulling the rust deer hair tips back and to the sides, and tie down just behind the eye of the hook

Notes: These simple, effective skaters were developed over years of guiding on Oregon's North Umpqua and represent a distillation of many experiences and influences. Our experience suggests they perform best with a riffle hitch.

STEELHEAD SCULPIN

- **Hook:** #1-4 Tiemco 7999
- **Thread:** 140-denier, brown
- **Rib:** Large wire, copper
- **Body:** Angora goat dubbing, golden stone
- **Gills:** One turn of Angora goat dubbing, red
- **Wing/tail:** Rabbit strip, dark brown, tied in at the front and ribbed Matuka-style with copper wire
- **Eyes:** Small plastic bead chain, black
- **Pectoral fins/head:** Deer or elk belly hair, spun and trimmed to create distinct pectoral fins and a Muddler-style head

TANDEM TUBE INTRUDER

- **Tube:** Small HMH tube, red, 3.2 cm (1¼") long
- **Thread:** 140-denier, black
- **Eyes:** Small or medium brass barbell eyes, nickel finish
- **Butt:** Medium chenille, shell pink
- **Body:** Polar Chenille, UV copper
- **Hackle:** In two steps, back to front: 1) guinea hen, kingfisher blue; 2) guinea hen, natural
- **Flash:** Angel Hair, peacock, tied in on top then pulled down each side and tied down
- **Underwing:** Rabbit strip, black, with a short section of medium or large tubing, chartreuse, tied in near the rear end
- **Shellback:** Pair of grizzly saddle hackle tips tied 8.5 cm (3⅜") long
- **Head:** Rabbit fur, black, spun in a dubbing loop and wrapped behind, over, and around the eyes

From the top: Finnerty Steelhead Skater, fall and summer versions; Steelhead Sculpin; Tandem Tube Intruder; Snelled Egg Fly.

Stuart Foxall

Stuart runs his own business back in the United Kingdom but dabbles heavily in fly fishing. I had the pleasure of spending time with him on the Kanektok in 2012, and it was obvious we needed to include his flies in this book. Thankfully his patterns are now available commercially through Aqua Flies. If you don't see them in your local fly shop, ask the store manager to give Aqua Flies a call and get things rolling.

STU'S RHEA INTRUDER, METAL DETECTOR

- **Shank:** 40 mm Senyo's Articulated Shank, black
- **Stinger loop:** Senyo's Intruder Wire, silver, 3 cm (1³⁄₁₆") loop
- **Thread:** 6/0 UNI-Thread, red
- **Eyes:** Small or medium brass eyes, black
- **Butt:** Ice Dub, chartreuse
- **Rear flash:** Combination of Midge Flash, Krinkle Mirror Flash, and Mirage Flashabou, pearl
- **Rear hackle:** In four parts, from back to front: 1) arctic fox tail, chartreuse; 2) rhea herl, black; 3) Lady Amherst pheasant tail, chartreuse; 4) schlappen, black
- **Body:** UTC Mirage Tinsel, pearl or ice blue, large
- **Rib:** Ultra Wire, gold, medium diameter
- **Front dubbing ball:** Ice Dub, chartreuse
- **Front flash:** Holographic Flashabou, blue, and Krystal Flash, metallic blue
- **Front hackle:** In two parts, from back to front: 1) Rhea herl, black; 2) Lady Amherst pheasant tail, kingfisher blue
- **Collar:** Schlappen, black
- **Shellback:** Pair of golden pheasant shoulder feathers, dyed black
- **Hook:** #1 Gamakatsu Octopus, black

STU'S RHEA INTRUDER, BLACK/BLUE

- **Shank:** 40 mm Senyo's Articulated Shank, black
- **Stinger loop:** Senyo's Intruder Wire, blue, 3 cm (1³⁄₁₆") loop
- **Thread:** 6/0 UNI-Thread, black
- **Eyes:** Small or medium brass eyes, black
- **Butt:** Ice Dub, chartreuse
- **Rear hackle:** In three parts, from back to front: 1) arctic fox tail, white; 2) rhea herl, kingfisher blue; 3) schlappen, royal blue
- **Rear flash:** Mirage Flashabou, pearl
- **Body:** Large UTC Mirage Tinsel, ice blue
- **Rib:** Medium Ultra Wire, gold
- **Front dubbing ball:** Ice Dub, chartreuse
- **Front flash:** Mirage Flashabou, pearl, and standard Flashabou, metallic blue
- **Front hackle:** In two parts, from back to front: 1) Rhea herl, black; 2) Lady Amherst pheasant tail, kingfisher blue
- **Collar:** Schlappen, black
- **Hook:** #1 Gamakatsu Octopus, black

STU'S MINI INTRUDER, ORANGE/BLACK

- **Shank:** 25 mm Senyo's Articulated Shank, black
- **Stinger loop:** Senyo's Intruder Wire, red, 2.5 cm (1") loop
- **Thread:** 6/0 UNI-Thread, black
- **Eyes:** Small brass eyes, black
- **Butt:** Petite Estaz, metallic red
- **Rear hackle:** In four parts, from back to front: 1) rhea herl, orange; 2) Lady Amherst pheasant tail, orange; 3) saddle hackle, red; 4) saddle hackle, orange
- **Rear flash:** Krystal Flash, pearl
- **Body:** Diamond Braid, metallic red
- **Rib:** Medium Ultra Wire, gold
- **Front chenille ball:** Petite Estaz, metallic red
- **Front hackle:** In two parts, from back to front: 1) Rhea herl, black; 2) Lady Amherst pheasant tail, kingfisher blue
- **Front flash:** Mirage Flashabou, pearl, and Krystal Flash, pearl
- **Collar:** Saddle hackle, black
- **Hook:** #2 Gamakatsu Octopus, black

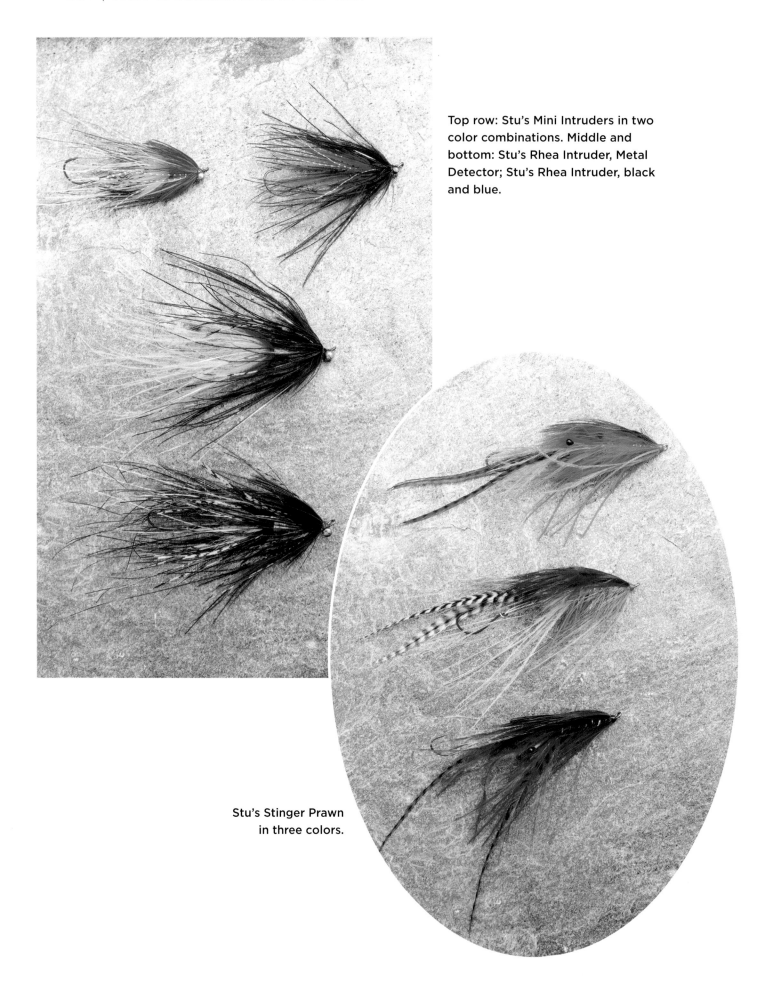

Top row: Stu's Mini Intruders in two color combinations. Middle and bottom: Stu's Rhea Intruder, Metal Detector; Stu's Rhea Intruder, black and blue.

Stu's Stinger Prawn in three colors.

STU'S STINGER PRAWN, PINK

- **Shank:** 40 mm Senyo's Articulated Shank, pink
- **Thread:** 6/0 UNI-Thread, orange
- **Stinger loop:** Senyo's Intruder Wire, pink, 3 cm (1³⁄₁₆") long
- **Rear weiling:** In eight parts, back to front: 1) Senyo's Laser Dub, pink; 2) tented pair of grizzly saddle feathers, tied 9.5 cm (3¾") long; 3) rhea herl, pink, spun in a dubbing loop; 4) ring hackle of schlappen, pink; 5) pair of silicone rubber legs, pink, tied under shank; 6) small bunch of bucktail, orange; 7) red-painted monofilament eyes; 8) topped with a pair of golden pheasant body feathers, dyed red or pink
- **Middle and front weilings:** Repeated from back to front in five steps: 1) base of Ice Dub, gold; 2) palmered with saddle hackle, pink; 3) ribbed with large oval tinsel, gold; 4) pair of silicone rubber legs, pink, tied under shank; 5) topped with a pair of golden pheasant body feathers , ascending in size
- **Throat:** Rhea herl, pink
- **Hook:** #1 Gamakatsu Octopus, black

Notes: Color variations of this exceptional fly deserve some description. The orange version, like the pink version above, also utilizes gold Ice Dub for the body but uses orange silicone legs. The purple version features a black dubbing blend for the body but uses pink silicone legs.

STU'S GRIZZLY TURBO CONE, BLACK/BLUE

- **Tube:** FutureFly medium tube, 1.8 mm diameter, blue, fitted into a 3 mm diameter tube, black
- **Cone/disc:** 8 mm FutureFly UfoDisc, silver
- **Thread:** 6/0 UNI-Thread, black
- **Butt:** Krystal hackle, chartreuse
- **Tail:** Pair of grizzly saddle hackle tips, dyed royal blue
- **Body:** Senyo's Fusion Dub, sky, palmered with saddle hackle, black
- **Rib:** Small oval tinsel, silver
- **Hackle:** In three parts, back to front: 1) arctic fox tail, light blue, spun in a dubbing loop; 2) ostrich plume, royal blue; 3) ostrich plum, black
- **Eyes:** Jungle cock nails tied in between the arctic fox and the first ostrich hackle

- **Flash:** DNA Frosty Fish Fiber, sky blue; Mirage Flashabou, pearl
- **Junction tubing:** FutureFly Soft Knot Control, clear

STU'S STEELIE PIGLET, ORANGE/GOLD/YELLOW

- **Tube:** FutureFly medium tube, 1.8 mm diameter, yellow, fitted into a 3 mm diameter tube, orange
- **Cone/disc:** Large cone head, fluorescent orange
- **Thread:** 6/0 UNI-Thread, orange
- **Butt:** Senyo's Laser Dub, hot orange
- **Tail:** Small bunch of Chinese boar bristles, dyed orange, topped with a few strands of pearl Krystal Flash
- **Rear hackle:** Schlappen, yellow
- **Body:** Ice Dub, gold (picked out and brushed after ribbing)
- **Rib:** Small oval tinsel, silver
- **Hackle/collar:** Schlappen, orange
- **Flash:** Mirage Flashabou, pearl
- **Eyes:** Jungle cock nails
- **Junction tubing:** FutureFly Soft Knot Control, clear

STU'S JUNGLE TAIL, PINK/PURPLE

- **Tube:** FutureFly medium tube, 1.8 mm diameter, pink, fitted into a 3 mm diameter tube, orange
- **Cone/disc:** 8 mm FutureFly UfoDisc, silver
- **Thread:** 6/0 UNI-Thread, pink
- **Butt:** Senyo's Laser Dub, pink
- **Eyes/tail:** Jungle cock nails, tied long
- **Rear hackle:** Schlappen, fluorescent fuchsia
- **Body:** Pearlescent flat tinsel
- **Rib:** Small oval tinsel, silver
- **Front hackle:** In three parts, back to front: 1) arctic fox tail, spun in a dubbing loop; 2) ostrich herl, pink, spun in a dubbing loop; 3) marabou, royal blue
- **Flash:** Krinkle Mirror Flash, pearl, tied in between the ostrich and marabou
- **Legs:** Silicone rubber, purple/blue flake
- **Collar:** Marabou, purple
- **Junction tubing:** FutureFly Soft Knot Control, clear

From the top: Stu's Grizzly Turbo Cones in two colors, with a third tucked in the lower half of the arrangement; Stu's Steelie Piglets in three color combos; Stu's Jungle Tails in two colors.

Jerry French

Jerry is one of the creators of the original Intruder design, and he still swears by their fish-catching power 25 years later.

"As long as you can cast them," French said. "Not everyone can put them out there, so I did finally have to come up with something smaller and easier to cast for day-to-day guiding."

Read more on that story in chapter 4, "The Intruder Revolution." As for that easier-to-cast fly pattern he had to come up with? After a lot of experimentation, it came down to the Dirty Hoh, a hybrid bunny-leech that incorporates some of the buggier elements of Intruder design. And even though Jerry was really busy guiding when we came to him looking for flies, he was kind enough to tie a set of two Intruders and two Dirty Hohs, for this book. Recipes for each style are presented here in the most general terms and without reference to specific colors.

Jerry hard at work in his "creature factory" on the Washington coast. Ben Paull, OPST.

FRENCH'S INTRUDER

- **Shank:** A sacrificed hook, heavy wire, with at least a 1½" length of tying area and an eye that's turned either up or down
- **Eyes:** Small Psuedo Eyes
- **Thread:** 220 Denier (stronger if you need it for mega-loops), white
- **Mono loop:** 15-20-pound mono, the stiffer the better, folded in a tight loop and lashed to the shank with a ⅛" loop left at the rear of the fly
- **Rear station in three or four parts, back to front:** 1) a tightly folded and brushed "composite loop" incorporating two flashy, synthetic dubbings; 2) "split tail" with 6 strands of barred ostrich herl tied long and flared out on each side of the dubbing bump; 3) two or three strands of holographic Flashabou; and 4) a pair of Jungle cock nails, optional
- **Body:** Holographic tinsel
- **Front station in three or four parts, back to front:** 1) a repeat of the rear composite loop; 2) another composite loop including a synthetic dubbing of complimentary color, synthetic hackle and 20 or so strands of barred ostrich herl; 3) two or three strands of holographic Flashabou; and 4) a small bunch of additional ostrich herl along the dorsal line of the fly, optional
- **Wings:** A matched pair of feathers, usually grizzly saddle hackle, tied long so they fan over the body of the fly

THE DIRTY HOH

- **Shank:** A sacrificed hook, medium to heavy wire, with at least ¾" length of tying area and an eye that's turned either up or down
- **Cone head:** Match desired color and sink rate
- **Thread:** 220 Denier, white
- **Braided loop:** 30-50-pound braid extending 2" back from the rear of the shank
- **Hook:** OPST Swing hook, size 3
- **Tail:** Barred bunny strip tied long, trimmed to a length of 2½", with its end attached to the hook
- **Body in six parts, back to front:** 1) composite loop of natural and synthetic dubbings; 2) Jungle cock nails on either side as eyes; 3) two flared clumps of barred ostrich herl as legs; 4) 2 or 3 strands of holographic Flashabou; 5) composite loop of synthic dubbing and synthetic hackle, tied longer than the first loop, brushed and folded as it's wrapped; 6) dubbing loop of ostrich herl
- **Collar:** Ice Dub in a complimentary color

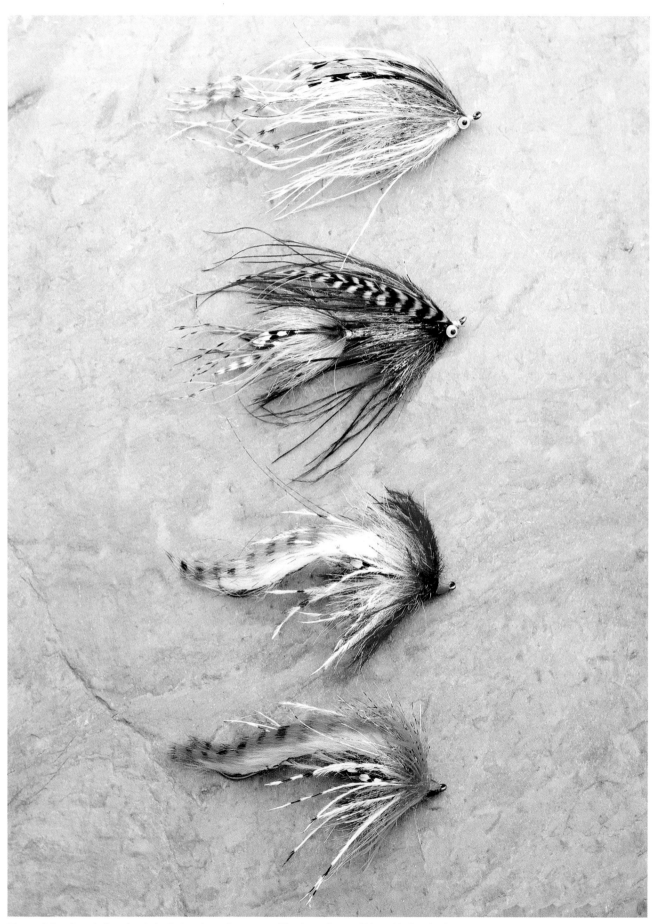

Two old-school shank-style Intruders (top two flies) and two Dirty Hohs, below.

Aaron Goodis

Aaron is a world-class photographer and adventure angler based in Vancouver, BC. His photography and flies are gorgeous, and we are pleased to be able to share these with our readers. The flies featured here are big and bold—indicative of the kind of water and the kind of fish he chases in his home waters. And he deserves a lot of credit for devising the Muppet Intruder. It stands out as a unique interpretation, and it looks amazing in the water. Learn more about Aaron and his work on his website (aarongoodisphotography.com).

SK8TER

- ▨ **Hook:** #1/0-4/0 Partridge Bartleet Traditional Light Wire Salmon Hook
- ▨ **Thread:** UTC 70-denier, black
- ▨ **Tail:** Holographic Flashabou, blue
- ▨ **Butt:** Seal fur or Angora goat dubbing, wine
- ▨ **Rear wing:** Deer belly hair, black
- ▨ **Underbody:** 2 mm round foam, black, wrapped up to within 1.3 cm (½″) of the hook eye
- ▨ **Overbody:** Seal fur or Angora goat dubbing, black
- ▨ **Front wing/head:** Deer belly hair, black, clipped Muddler-style

Notes: This fly is designed to skate high for fresh, aggressive summer and fall steelhead on the rivers of British Columbia. As Aaron says, "Essentially this is a supersize grease-liner that creates a huge wake." He recommends a riffle hitch for best results.

PINK PANTHER

- ▨ **Hook:** #1.5 Daiichi Alec Jackson Spey, bronze or black
- ▨ **Thread:** UTC 70-denier, black
- ▨ **Tail:** Krystal Flash, pink, topped with deer belly hair, hot pink
- ▨ **Rear body:** Ice Dub, hot pink
- ▨ **Rear wing:** Deer belly hair, hot pink
- ▨ **Underbody:** 2 mm round foam, pink, wrapped to just behind the hook eye
- ▨ **Overbody:** Ice Dub, hot pink
- ▨ **Front wing:** Deer belly hair, black, clipped Muddler-style
- ▨ **Head:** 3 mm sheet foam, pink, glues heavily with Flexament

A landscape photographer by trade, Aaron can usually be found hiking into wild places with his camera and tripod. AARON GOODIS PHOTO

From the top: Sk8ter; Pink Panther; Bull Muddler; BC Prawn; three versions of the Muppet Intruder.

BULL MUDDLER

- **Shank:** Mustad SL73UBLN-3690, #2
- **Thread:** UTC 70-denier, fluorescent pink
- **Stinger loop:** 30-pound Fireline doubled, 2 cm (¾") long
- **Hook:** #2 Owner SSW (looped on before tying), with hook point riding down
- **Eyes:** Small Pseudo Eyes, tied in on top of the shank
- **Tail:** Ostrich herl, olive, eight strands with a few strands of Krystal Flash, olive
- **Body:** Sparkle chenille, silver
- **Wing:** Polar Flash, green, and Flashabou, olive, topped with 12 strands of ostrich herl, olive
- **Hackle:** Large grizzly neck hackle, olive
- **Collar/head:** Deer body hair, natural, spun and trimmed Muddler-style

Notes: This flashy streamer is an Intruder-era take on the Marabou Muddler, incorporating ostrich in place of marabou. The name refers to the fact that bull trout can't leave this one alone, but it is equally effective on steelhead and coho. Aaron will often let it swing, but he also likes to strip it across the current at various speeds to elicit the most explosive grabs.

BC PRAWN

- **Shank:** #1-2/0 Mustad SL73UBLN-3690
- **Thread:** UTC 70-denier, black
- **Stinger loop:** 30-pound Fireline doubled, 2 cm (¾") long
- **Hook:** #1 Owner SSW (looped on before tying), with hook point riding up
- **Tail:** Polar bear, dyed orange (or bucktail substitute), with a few strands of Krinkle Mirror Flash
- **Butt:** Diamond Braid, orange
- **Feelers:** Lady Amherst pheasant center tail, six fibers tied in around the entire circumference

- **Eyes:** Large epoxy mono eyes
- **Rear wing:** Pair of ringneck pheasant shoulder feathers, dyed orange
- **Body:** Seal or Angora goat fur, dark orange, palmered with rhea herl or blue-eared pheasant, orange
- **Collar:** Long saddle hackle or schlappen, burnt orange
- **Wing:** Pair of ringneck pheasant shoulder feathers, dyed orange

Notes: This lifelike prawn is one of Aaron's staples for winter-run steelhead. He tends to swing it deep with a sink-tip, and he notes that it is equally effective for bull trout and resident rainbows.

MUPPET INTRUDER, PINK/GREY

- **Shank:** #1-1/0 Mustad SL73UBLN-3690
- **Thread:** UTC 70-denier, fluorescent pink
- **Stinger loop:** 30-pound Fireline doubled, 1.6 cm (⅝") long
- **Hook:** #1 Owner SSW (looped on before tying), with hook point riding up
- **Eyes:** Small Pseudo Eyes, tied in under the shank
- **Body:** Diamond Braid, pink
- **Dubbing bump:** Polar bear, natural, spun in a dubbing loop
- **Hackle:** Ostrich or rhea herl, pink, tied in above and below shank
- **Flash:** Flashabou, pearl, tied in on the sides
- **Collar:** Mallard flank, folded and wrapped spider-style
- **Wing:** Grizzly saddle hackle tips, pink

Notes: This is among the most simple, easy-to-tie Intruder styles we've seen, providing plenty of profile and movement with a minimum of materials. Aaron's other favorite color combinations include blue/chartreuse and blue/black/pink.

Jack Hagan

Jack Hagan grew up amid the unique guide culture of Oregon's Deschutes and Sandy Rivers. His parents, John and Shirley, operated the best fly shop on Portland's east side, Northwest Fly Fishing Outfitters. It was no surprise when Jack started guiding the Deschutes as a young man and eventually took over the family business. Northwest Fly Fishing Outfitters has grown with the times and remains the premier fly shop for most of the Portland metro area. Jack spends a bit more time behind the counter than he used to, but he still passes a lot of days on his home rivers. His signature flies featured here have become popular steelhead patterns throughout the Columbia River basin.

TRAIN WRECK, PURPLE

- **Hook:** #3-5 Alec Jackson Spey, nickel silver
- **Thread:** 10/0 Veevus, black
- **Tail:** Floss, purple
- **Body:** Frostbite, black
- **Rib:** Salar Microbraid, purple
- **Thorax:** Ice Dub, black
- **Wing:** Eight strands of Krystal Flash, purple
- **Hackle:** Webby saddle hackle, purple
- **Collar:** Guinea hen, purple

Notes: Jack's Train Wreck can be worked into any color or combination of colors. Like many steelhead tiers, he relied on the brilliant microbraid marketed by Lagartun for the bright colors of this series. When Lagartun closed its doors in 2014, it took a while for suitable replacements to show up. As of 2015, Salar and UNI are offering similar microbraids, though they are still somewhat hard to find in shops.

PINK PANTHER

- **Hook:** #1-3 Alec Jackson Steelhead Iron, nickel silver
- **Thread:** 6/0 UNI-Thread, fluorescent pink
- **Tail:** Marabou, hot pink
- **Body:** Large Mylar tinsel, silver side up, overwrapped with Edge Bright, fluorescent pink
- **Thorax:** Ice Dub, black
- **Wing:** Mirage Flashabou, pink pearl, eight strands
- **Hackle:** Webby saddle hackle, black
- **Collar:** Jumbo guinea hen, hot pink

GREEN LANTERN

- **Hook:** #1-3 Alec Jackson Steelhead Iron, gold
- **Thread:** 6/0 UNI-Thread, chartreuse
- **Tail:** Marabou, lime green or chartreuse
- **Body:** Large Mylar tinsel, silver side up, overwrapped with Edge Bright, green
- **Thorax:** Ice Dub, black
- **Wing:** Mirage Flashabou, pearl, eight strands
- **Hackle:** Jumbo guinea hen, chartreuse

Train Wreck, orange; Train Wreck, blue; Train Wreck, purple; Green Lantern; Pink Panther.

Jason Hartwick

Jason Hartwick owns and operates Steelhead on the Spey Guide Service on California's Klamath and Trinity Rivers. A native of Sacramento, Jason caught his first steelhead on the nearby American River and was hooked for life. Now he shares his passion with others through his guiding. He credits the influences of California's fly pioneers Lloyd Silvius and Jim Pray for his summer and fall patterns, and Walt Johnson for his use of natural materials that glow in the water.

Hartwick's Hoser has developed a major following since it debuted in the Idylwilde catalog in 2010. Today Hartwick is a signature tier for Aqua Flies, and his patterns are again finding their way into fly shops. Both Steelhead on the Spey and Aqua Flies are included in our business listing starting on page 307.

OCTOBER HILTON

- **Hook:** #3 or #5 Daiichi Alec Jackson Steelhead Iron, black
- **Thread:** 70-denier, black
- **Tag:** Flashabou, pearl
- **Body:** Angora goat dubbing, burnt orange
- **Rib:** Small wire, copper
- **Hackle:** Grizzly saddle
- **Wing:** Flared pair of grizzly hackle tips
- **Collar:** Mallard or teal flank

SKINNY SPRATLEY

- **Hook:** #6-10 Tiemco 7999, black
- **Thread:** 70-denier, black
- **Tag:** Flashabou, pearl
- **Tail:** Golden pheasant tippet fibers
- **Body:** Three or four peacock herl strands, spun before wrapping
- **Rib:** Small wire, gold
- **Hackle:** Guinea hen, natural
- **Wing:** Midge flash, golden olive

DUCK TURD

- **Hook:** #3 or #5 Daiichi Alec Jackson Steelhead Iron, black
- **Thread:** 70-denier, red
- **Tag:** Flat Mylar tinsel, gold
- **Tail:** Saddle hackle fibers, red
- **Body:** Four or five peacock herl strands, spun before wrapping
- **Rib:** Small French oval tinsel, gold
- **Wing:** Ringneck pheasant tail fibers
- **Collar:** Mallard or teal flank

SILENT ASSASSIN

- **Hook:** #3 or #5 Daiichi Alec Jackson Steelhead Iron, black
- **Thread:** 70-denier, black
- **Tag:** Flat Mylar tinsel, gold
- **Tail:** Mallard or teal flank fibers
- **Body:** Floss, black, palmered with saddle hackle, black
- **Rib:** Medium French oval tinsel, gold
- **Hackle:** Guinea hen, natural
- **Wing:** Ringneck pheasant tail fibers

HARTWICK'S HOSER

- **Tube:** Small HMH tube, pink, 5 cm (2") long to start
- **Butt:** STS Trilobal Dub, hot pink
- **Rear hackle:** Chinese saddle, hot pink
- **Body:** Medium Mylar tinsel, pearl, palmered with Polar Chenille, hot pink
- **Weight:** Large brass cone head, reversed
- **Dubbing bump:** Two turns of STS Trilobal Dub just forward of the cone
- **Wing:** In three parts, bottom to top: 1) Pseudo Hair, pink; 2) Angel Hair, UV pink; 3) two pairs of grizzly saddle hackle tips, hot pink, tented
- **Flash:** Four strands of holographic Flashabou, purple haze
- **Front hackle:** Marabou, purple
- **Collar:** Schlappen, black
- **Junction tubing:** Standard soft HMH junction tubing 1.5 cm (roughly ½") long
- **Hook:** Any #1 or #2 straight-eye, short-shank hook

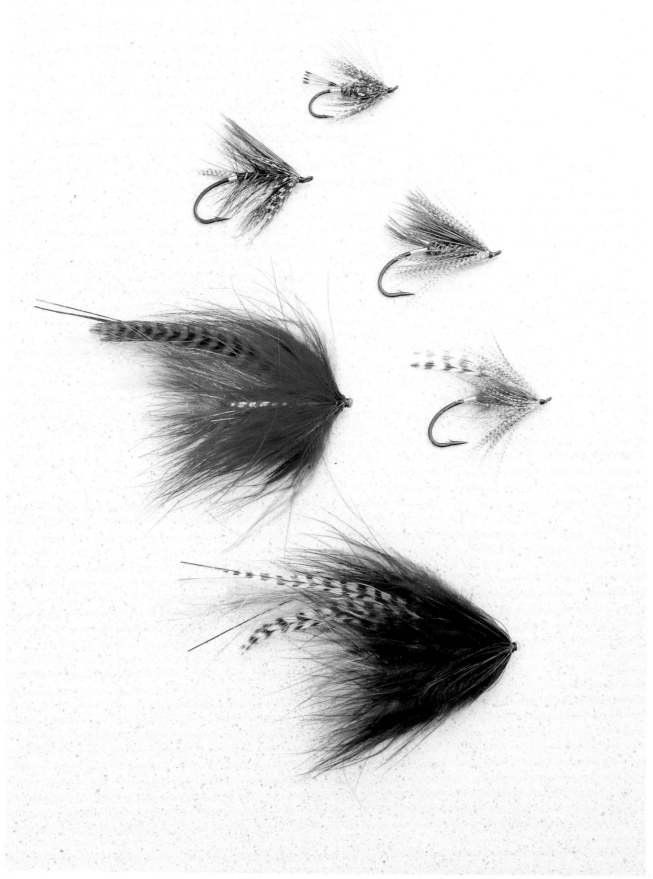

From the top: Skinny Spratley; Silent Assassin; Duck Turd; October Hilton; Hartwick's Hoser in purple and pink; Hartwick's Hoser in black and blue.

Amy Hazel

Amy is the owner and manager of Deschutes Angler in Maupin, Oregon. She and her husband have been guiding steelheaders on the Deschutes for decades, as well as teaching the art of casting and fly tying. Amy's contributions here stand out as unique, artful, and fun. And that describes her pretty well, too.

GREEN BUTT LUM PLUM

- **Thread:** 8/0 UNI-Thread, purple
- **Hook:** #3-7 Alec Jackson Nickel standard wire 2052; #3 Alec Jackson Heavy Wire 2062; or #3-9 Alec Jackson Steelhead Irons
- **Butt:** Danville's Depth Ray Nylon Wool, fluorescent chartreuse
- **Tail:** Golden pheasant tippets, dyed orange
- **Rib:** Small French oval tinsel, silver
- **Body:** Lum Plum Yarn (Punch Yarn), #815 violet
- **Hackle/collar:** Regular guinea fowl, dyed purple
- **Wing:** Natural white polar bear tied reverse-style with four strands Mirage Flashabou, opal 3005, over the top of the polar bear
- **Other wing options:** White bucktail, calf tail, white parts of a striped skunk tail, white artic fox tail

The Green Butt Lum Plum began as a collaborative effort between the three John Hazel & Company guides in 1999. Amy tells the story:

John Hazel, Dec Hogan, and I would have nightly meetings and dinner after long days spent guiding on the Deschutes. I was the rookie guide, learning tons from John and Dec both about the river and about tying flies. The fly bench was in the kitchen, so I had John or Dec leaning over my shoulder as I learned to tie the classic hairwing patterns.

Our good friend Bill Lum stumbled upon this really fine purple wool yarn at a craft store, and the color screamed steelhead. He brought us a sample, and I used it as a body material because I was pretty bad at dubbing perfectly even tight bodies back then. This stuff was so easy to tie with, I loved it right off the bat. I tied up, basically, a Green Butt Skunk with this purple body and an orange tail instead of red. I made the collar out of guinea fowl and—with good instruction from both John and Dec—learned to tie a polar bear wing in

reverse-style while still achieving a small head on the fly. This required a lot of practice and a lot of thread breaking, since I had to use 8/0 thread. As I was finishing up one of the first flies with this yarn, Dec leaned over the fly bench and declared it to be the *Lum Plum*. It has been my number-one steelhead fly in my years of guiding steelhead on the Deschutes.

I believe that two elements of this fly are key to attracting steelhead: the green butt (which glows under UV light) and the white wing. The little bit of flash over the white wing was key not only for the steelhead to see the fly but also for the guide to see the fly. Back in 1999, the Deschutes had very few brushy trees along the low banks thanks to the 100-year flood of 1996 that scoured the banks of the river. The big trees that were left standing were dead/dying with little to no foliage on them.

Amy living the dream with a fancy BC buck.
AMY HAZEL

Standing on the high bank or climbing into the dead trees gave John, Dec, and me the perfect vantage point to watch the clients' flies swim from the middle of the river into the bank. The flash and white wing can easily be seen from 100 feet out, so we got the thrill of watching the reaction of every steelhead the fly swam over. With the fly right in the surface film, we were able to watch steelhead swim 10 to 15 feet from their holding lies to the surface to grab the Lum Plum. More often than not, they ate this little fly without hesitation. We still watch the fly swing in the few areas that aren't overgrown, and the thrill of seeing a steelhead charging to the surface never gets old.

THE ENGAGEMENT

- **Thread:** 8/0 UNI-Thread, red
- **Hook:** #3-7 Alec Jackson Nickel standard wire 2052; #3 Alec Jackson Heavy Wire 2062; or #3-9 Alec Jackson Steelhead Irons
- **Tail:** Golden pheasant crest, dyed red
- **Body:** Lagartun French Mini-Flatbraid, green
- **Rib:** Medium French oval tinsel, silver
- **Hackle/throat:** Black saddle hackle
- **Wing:** Natural white polar bear tied reverse-style with four to six strands holographic Flashabou, silver 6991, over the top of the polar bear
- **Other wing options:** White bucktail, calf tail, white parts of a striped skunk tail, white artic fox tail
- **Other body options:** Ice Dub, caddis green; holographic Flashabou, green; or other tinsel

Steve Rowe, who owned the Ashland Outdoor Store in southern Oregon, was a great friend and excellent steelhead angler. He fished the Deschutes with John and Dec for many years before I came along. Steve was a bachelor when I came on the scene, but a few years later he had met the woman of his dreams and was prepared to pop the question. I was honored when he asked me to help him with his plan to surprise Renee during her first-ever steelhead trip on the Deschutes. He described the ring to me over the phone and told me that he was going to put it under one of the clips of a classic Wheatley fly box among dozens of beautiful steelhead flies. I told him that I had the champagne covered and that it would be chilled and ready for celebration at the right moment. With a flash of inspiration, I sat down at my fly bench that night and created a fly for Renee to fish, based on the elements of the ring hidden in Steve's fly box. The silver hook represented the platinum band, the emerald body nearly matched the brilliance of the large emerald, the holographic flash attempted to create the sparkle of the diamonds, and the red tail and thread symbolized, what else, love. The polar bear wing added a little class.

On the first morning of the four-day trip, I put a two-handed rod in Renee's hands and taught her how to Spey cast. Like most women, she listened to instruction and never tried to muscle the cast, and within an hour or so she was bombing out 60- to 70-foot casts. I showed her the beautiful fly that I had tied just for her and also told her that we were not allowed to name the fly until she had hooked a steelhead on it. In a long run with a riffle break at the top and another 100 yards downstream, I put Steve at the bottom and told him that I would work with Renee in the top piece. Steve was in the run below us and kept turning to look upstream to check on his gal's progress. As I stood by her side and calmly repeated the 'Give 'em the loop' mantra, I saw the surface swirl. Renee did everything right and soon the rod was doubled over, and we were shrieking like school girls. Steve whipped his head around and began high-stepping and splashing toward us while reeling in his line madly. By the time Steve made it up to the riffle, we had just netted a beautiful wild hen, shining as chrome bright as the ring in Steve's fly box. After pictures, high fives, hugs, and kisses, Steve called Renee over to the bank, and I slipped away to give them their moment. He opened his fly box, got down on one knee, and asked her to pick a fly. Shaking with adrenaline, thinking that this was some weird steelhead ritual, she saw a rather pretty fly in the box and said, "This one." Flummoxed, Steve pointed to the ring and said, 'How about *this one*?' All I heard from my hiding place in the bushes was, '*Hell yes!!*' I grabbed the champagne and glasses from the boat, and, while sipping the bubbly, we named Renee's fly.

Far left: Green Butt Lum Plum. Far right: The Engagement; middle: Fruit Stripes in three color combinations.

FRUIT STRIPES

- **Tube:** Pro Sportfisher Pro Microtube, color to match one of the bars in the barred rhea
- **Hook guide:** Color should pop and accent the barred rhea
- **Dubbing (in the rear and in the middle):** Seal or Angora goat in colors to match one of the bars in the barred rhea
- **Hackle:** Layer 1: natural pintail flank; layer 2: barred rhea tied in the round two or three pieces at a time, spaced to allow movement of 12 to 15 pieces per round
- **Weight:** Pro raw weight, small (tungsten), tied in ⅔ up the tube so the fly is a bit front heavy, with dubbing on either side of the weight
- **Hackle:** Layer 1: natural pintail flank; layer 2: contrasting color of barred rhea tied in as before
- **Front hackle/throat:** Regular guinea fowl dyed to match one of the rhea colors in the rear
- **Optional flash:** A few strands of a complementary shade of Angel Hair tied in over the top of the first layers of hackle

Notes: The rhea that I am using is from Fish Hunter ("the pro's choice"), which they dye in hot fluorescent colors. Get crazy! The color combos are fun to create.

This is a tweener fly that can be used for summer steelhead or in the winter when the flows are low and clear. It has the very natural traditional flank feathers of a pintail drake mixed with the very unnatural fluorescent-dyed barred rhea. The colors of the barred rhea reminded me of Fruit Stripe gum, which was popular in the 1970s and lost its flavor approximately 45 seconds after you started chewing it. The color combinations on this fly are endless, and they really pop, especially under UV light. The sparse materials allow the fly to sink in the current quickly, and the materials dance like crazy in the water. I tie this fly on Pro Microtubes in a variety of colors with a variety of hot-colored rubber hook guides that accent the materials in the fly. The weight in the fly is a Pro Raw Weight—which is tungsten and available in a variety of sizes. I slide the weight onto the tube one-third of the way back from the front of the fly. I find that this placement of the weight really makes the fly undulate.

—Amy Hazel

Jon Hazlett

A giant fall buck that grabbed ahold of Jon's purple Dirk Wiggler. JON HAZLETT PHOTO

Jon has been a fixture on the rivers of southern Oregon his whole adult life and has taught hundreds of people how to cast, fish, and tie flies for steelhead. He owns and operates his own guide business, Jonny on the Spot Guide Service, out of Medford. Jon's flies have been available commercially for many years, but it was a pleasure to receive a set of his originals for this project. Thanks, Jon!

DIRK WIGGLER, BLACK & BLUE

- **Shank:** 25 mm Senyo's Articulated Shank
- **Thread:** UNI Big Fly, black
- **Eyes:** Medium nickel-plated lead eyes
- **Stinger loop:** Senyo's Intruder Wire, 2.5 cm (1") loop
- **Butt:** Ice Dub, blue
- **Hackle:** In three parts, back to front: 1) turkey flat, black, palmered; 2) 10 to 12 fibers of Flex-Floss, blue, trimmed to 10 cm (4"); 3) marabou, royal blue

- **Collar:** Schlappen, black
- **Flash:** Holographic, purple
- **Head:** Ice Dub, UV black
- **Contrast bars:** Black Sharpie permanent marker in bars over full length of fly; red Sharpie permanent marker for tips of Flex-Floss

DIRK WIGGLER, BLUE & GRAY

- **Shank:** 25 mm Senyo's Articulated Shank
- **Thread:** UNI Big Fly, black
- **Eyes:** Medium nickel-plated lead eyes
- **Stinger loop:** Senyo's Intruder Wire, 2.5 cm (1″) loop
- **Butt:** Ice Dub, blue and silver-gray mixed
- **Hackle:** In three parts, back to front: 1) turkey flat, gray, palmered; 2) 10 to 12 fibers of Flex-Floss, gray, trimmed to 10 cm (4″); 3) gray marabou
- **Collar:** Schlappen, black
- **Flash:** Holographic, blue
- **Head:** Ice Dub, UV black
- **Contrast bars:** Blue Sharpie permanent marker in bars over full length of fly; red Sharpie permanent marker for tips of Flex-Floss

DIRK WIGGLER, OLIVE

- **Shank:** 25 mm Senyo's Articulated Shank
- **Thread:** UNI Big Fly, black
- **Eyes:** Medium nickel-plated lead eyes
- **Stinger loop:** Senyo's Intruder Wire, 2.5 cm (1″) loop
- **Butt:** Ice Dub, UV light olive
- **Hackle:** In three parts, back to front: 1) turkey flat, yellow, palmered; 2) 10 to 12 fibers of Flex-Floss, olive, trimmed to 10 cm (4″); 3) marabou, light olive
- **Collar:** Schlappen, black
- **Flash:** Holographic, blue
- **Head:** Ice Dub, UV black
- **Contrast bars:** Dark green Sharpie permanent marker in bars over full length of fly, red Sharpie permanent marker for tips of Flex-Floss

DIRK WIGGLER, RED & BLACK

- **Shank:** 25 mm Senyo's Articulated Shank
- **Thread:** UNI Big Fly, black
- **Eyes:** Medium nickel-plated lead eyes
- **Stinger loop:** Senyo's Intruder Wire, 2.5 cm (1″) loop
- **Butt:** Ice Dub, purple
- **Hackle:** In three parts, back to front: 1) turkey flat, black, palmered; 2) 10 to 12 fibers of Flex-Floss, black, trimmed to 10 cm (4″); 3) marabou, black
- **Collar:** Schlappen, black
- **Flash:** Holographic, black
- **Head:** Ice Dub, UV black

Notes: Jon adds contrast to the Dirk Wiggler by using Sharpie permanent markers to add strong bars from front to back. He follows with a red Sharpie for the ends of the Flex-Floss. Additionally, Jon prefers to keep the full length of the fly at about 4 inches, then trims it down on the river if he feels the need for a smaller presentation. He notes that the Dirk Wiggler is not a "fancy" fly, but a blue-collar, workingman's fly that will last "almost forever."

DEUCE WIGALO, BLUE

- **Shank:** #2 Tiemco 700
- **Thread:** UNI Big Fly, black
- **Eyes:** Small to medium lead eyes, painted red
- **Stinger loop:** Senyo's Intruder Wire, 2.5 cm (1″) loop
- **Tag:** Krystal Flash, olive, 1.3 cm (½″)
- **Rear hackle:** Grizzly saddle, chartreuse
- **Tail:** Bunny strip, blue, 4 cm (1½″)
- **Legs:** Flex-Floss, blue, 8 to 10 strands, cut to desired length
- **Flash:** Holographic, blue
- **Body:** Ice Dub, blue
- **Collar:** Schlappen or guinea hen, kingfisher blue
- **Head:** Ice Dub, blue
- **Dingleberry:** 6 mm trout bead

Notes: The Deuce Wigalo is also commonly tied in black, purple, and pink.

From the top: Deuce Wigalo in two color combinations; Dirk Wiggler in three color combinations.

Ed Hepp

Ed is an amazing artist and one of the kindest people on the planet. He developed the Underachiever years ago and dedicated himself to the pattern and the unusual material with which it is made—cashmere goat. As with a good Intruder, Ed's flies are engineered for function and durability so that every element of the fly has a purpose.

UNDERACHIEVER, RED/BLACK

- **Shank:** 35 mm Waddington, rear loop bent downward to allow stinger hook/loop to ride straight
- **Thread:** 6/0 UNI-Thread, red
- **Weight:** Small to medium lead wire wrapped over the shank, leaving 3 mm (⅛") of the shank clear at the front and back ends
- **Hook:** #1 or #2 Owner SSW, needle point

Ed shows off a brightly colored buck that fell for one of his red Underacheivers. JEFF MISHLER PHOTO

- **Stinger loop:** A loop of 30-pound Amnesia, red, tied off on the shank of the hook with a barrel knot (nail knot)
- **Tail:** Arctic fox tail, black
- **Body:** Medium Mylar tubing, copper, palmered with cashmere goat, red, spun in a wire dubbing loop
- **Underwing:** Flashabou, red, flanked by a pair of grizzly saddle hackle tips, red
- **Collar:** Arctic fox tail, black, spun in a wire dubbing loop, brushed, and folded as it's wrapped
- **Wing:** Cashmere goat guard hairs tied long

Notes: This unique pattern, featured in the well-known DVD *Skagit Master 3: Steelhead Flies Beyond the Books*, is the first we have seen to use a stinger loop that is not lashed to the shank. The loop is tied to the hook and looped through the downturned rear loop of the Waddington shank. It's also the only pattern featured in this book that uses cashmere goat, and the only one with a body that's wrapped with lead. The result of Ed's eccentric design is a fly with exceptional movement that can glide along shallow ledges and drop off into buckets without hanging up. It should also be noted that cashmere goat offers a translucence approaching that of polar bear.

A set of four Underachievers in Ed's favorite color combinations.

Jeff Hickman

Jeff is a long-time steelhead guide and fly designer based in White Salmon, Washington. He and his wife run Fish the Swing guide service in Oregon, and Kimsquit Bay Lodge on the Dean River in British Columbia. More about Jeff and his famous Fish Taco can be found in our step-by-step chapter on page 65.

DINNER BELL, NATURAL

- **Hook:** #4 Gamakatsu Octopus
- **Thread:** 6/0 UNI-Thread, red
- **Body:** 3 mm glass seed beads, orange, held in place by a bump of thread at the bend of the hook
- **Hackle:** Guinea hen, natural
- **Wing/legs:** Barred silicone rubber, tan/black flake

MCBLUBBIN, BLACK

- **Shank:** Any straight-eye hook
- **Stinger loop:** 25- or 30-pound Maxima Chameleon, 2 cm (¾") loop
- **Butt:** Ice Dub, chartreuse
- **Body:** Fun Fur yarn, black, and Polar Flash, black
- **Wing case/head:** 5 mm foam, black
- **Collar:** Guinea hen, natural
- **Legs:** Round rubber legs, black, double thick
- **Hook:** #4 Gamakatsu Octopus

Notes: Jeff's original McBlubbin samples were made from skeins of Fun Fur yarn he bought at the local craft store. When it came time to source the materials for production, the specific yarn he had used, which incorporated thin black Mylar strands, had been discontinued. The folks at Lion Brand Yarn say it may come back seasonally, so keep your eyes open. In the meantime, one can mix the standard Fun Fur with black Polar Flash to get a similar effect. Brushing out the Fun Fur with a dubbing brush will improve the bulk.

SID FISHOUS, PINK/PURPLE

- **Shank:** Any straight-eye hook
- **Weight/head:** 6 mm (¼") cone head, pink
- **Stinger loop:** 25- or 30-pound Maxima Chameleon, 2.5 cm (1") loop
- **Butt:** Senyo's Laser Dub, purple
- **Rear hackle:** Marabou, purple
- **Body:** Holographic Flashabou, pink
- **Rib:** Small wire, gold or copper
- **Dubbing ball:** Ice Wing, pink, dubbed and picked out
- **Wing:** Ostrich herl, purple, 12 fibers
- **Flash:** Holographic Flashabou, pink, 24 strands
- **Collar:** Extra-large guinea hen, pink
- **Hook:** #2 Gamakatsu Octopus

Notes: As with any of Hickman's mono loop patterns, the end of the loop must be firmly crimped (not smashed) with pliers in order to be passed through the eye of the hook.

PARTY BOY, PINK

- **Shank:** .040" diameter spinner wire, with 1 cm (⅜") folded over to create eye
- **Eyes:** Small nickel plated lead
- **Stinger loop:** 30-pound Fireline, 3.2 cm (1¼") loop
- **Body:** Polar Chenille, pink
- **Wing:** Barred rabbit strip, pink, 8 cm (3⅛") long, with a short section of large diameter tubing (pink) tied near end
- **Rib:** Medium wire, red, wrapped over rabbit strip Matuka-style
- **Flash:** Krystal Flash, metallic red
- **Collar:** Extra-large guinea hen, pink
- **Head:** Ice Dub, UV shrimp pink
- **Hook:** #2 Gamakatsu Octopus

Notes: Rigging the Party Boy requires that the Fireline loop is passed through the piece of tubing at the rear of the wing before the hook is attached.

Top row: McBlubbin' in black and purple. Second row: Dinner Bell in two colors (left and right); Fish Taco, black. Third row: Flash Taco in red and purple. Fourth row: Sid Fishous, purple. Bottom: Party Boy, pink.

FISH TACO, RED

- **Shank:** .040" diameter spinner wire, with 1 cm (⅜") folded over to create eye
- **Thread:** 6/0 UNI-Thread, pink
- **Stinger loop:** 25- or 30-pound Maxima Chameleon, 2.5 cm (1") loop
- **Butt:** Ice Dub, UV shrimp pink
- **Body:** Ice Dub, peacock, palmered with Chinese saddle hackle, red
- **Rib:** Small wire, copper
- **Hackle:** Ostrich herl, red, 32 fibers
- **Flash:** Flashabou, silver, 25 to 30 strands
- **Collar:** Extra-large guinea hen, red
- **Hook:** #2 Gamakatsu Octopus

Notes: As with any of Hickman's mono loop patterns, the end of the loop must be firmly crimped (not smashed) with pliers in order to be passed through the eye of the hook.

FLASH TACO, PINK/PURPLE

- **Shank:** .040" diameter spinner wire, with 1 cm (⅜") folded over to create eye
- **Thread:** 6/0 UNI-Thread, red
- **Stinger loop:** 25- or 30-pound Maxima Chameleon, 2.5 cm (1") loop
- **Butt:** Ice Dub, UV chartreuse
- **Body:** Ice Dub, UV shrimp pink, palmered with Chinese saddle hackle, fuchsia
- **Rib:** Small wire, copper
- **Hackle:** Angel Hair, purple
- **Flash:** Holographic Flashabou, pink, 30 or more strands
- **Collar:** Extra-large guinea hen, pink
- **Hook:** #2 Gamakatsu Octopus

Notes: As with any of Hickman's mono loop patterns, the end of the loop must be firmly crimped (not smashed) with pliers in order to be passed through the eye of the hook.

Scott Howell

Scott Howell is one of the best-known steelhead guides in the world, and his Signature Intruder is among the most commercially successful fly patterns in modern history. His fishing and fly-tying expertise is well documented, especially in volume 2 of the *Skagit Master* video series. Here we have a set of original flies tied by Scott himself, along with recipes and notes. Enjoy!

SKA-OPPER, NATURAL

- **Hook:** #2-6 Daiichi 1280 or 2110
- **Thread:** UNI Big Fly, white
- **Tag:** Flat Mylar tinsel, gold side up
- **Tail:** Krystal Flash, gold, and arctic fox tail guard hairs, orange
- **Body:** UNI-Yarn, orange
- **Legs:** Rubber legs, orange
- **Hackle:** Guinea hen, orange
- **Head and "wings":** Natural deer hair, natural
- **Wing case:** 3 mm foam, brown, tapered from 0.5 cm to 1 cm

Notes: The Ska-opper was among the first modern popper flies for steelhead. It's also remarkable for the unusual contrast and movement in its design. Regarding the name, Howell says, "For the record,

George Cook named it. I came to him with what I called a steelhead popper, and he said, 'That name will never sell.' I said, 'Call it whatever you want—you're the salesman!'" The rest is history, as they say.

SIGNATURE SERIES INTRUDER, BLACK/GREEN BUTT

- **Shank:** Howell's Steely Shank or substitute
- **Thread:** UNI Big Fly, black
- **Eyes:** Small to medium nickel-plated lead eyes
- **Tag:** Flat Mylar tinsel, silver side up
- **"Retriever" loop:** 50-pound Fireline, 2.5 cm (1") loop
- **Butt:** Ice Dub, chartreuse
- **Tail:** Black ostrich herl, 20 fibers fanned over the top of the shank
- **Body:** Flat Mylar tinsel, silver side up
- **Dubbing bump:** Arctic fox tail, black
- **Hackle:** Ostrich herl, black
- **Head:** Rabbit fur, black
- **Shellback (wings):** Grizzle saddle feathers
- **Hook:** #1 or #2 Gamakatsu Octopus

Notes: This has been Scott Howell's go-to fly for much of his guiding career—his "confidence fly" for

Top row: Signature Intruder, black and red; Ska-opper, natural. Second row: Steely Cone Intruder, purple; Signature Series Intruder, black and green. Third row: Steely Cone Squidro, black and green; Seafood Series Squidro, salmon. Bottom: Prom Dress, blue with custom Steely Cone bullet weights.

nearly every steelheading scenario. The stinger-hook rigging, what Scott calls the "retriever-style," is not his preferred rigging when compared to the original "old school" Intruder rigging discussed below in the notes for the Black/Burgundy version of the fly. The retriever rigging is considered the most practical for commercial production, but Scott feels that it can allow fish added leverage to shake the fly loose.

SIGNATURE SERIES INTRUDER, BLACK/BURGUNDY

- **Shank:** Howell's Steely Shank or substitute
- **Thread:** UNI Big Fly, black
- **Eyes:** Small to medium gold-plated brass eyes
- **Tag:** Flat Mylar tinsel, gold side up
- **Mono loop:** 30-pound Maxima Ultragreen tied along length of shank, leaving a 3 mm (⅛") loop
- **Butt:** Ice Dub, orange
- **Tail:** Ostrich herl, black, 20 fibers fanned over the top of the shank
- **Body:** Flat Mylar tinsel, gold side up
- **Dubbing bump:** Two dubbing loops: 1) arctic fox with guard hairs, red, short; 2) arctic fox with guard hairs, black, medium length
- **Hackle:** Ostrich herl, black
- **Head:** Rabbit fur, black
- **Shellback (wings):** Badger saddle feathers, dyed burgundy or red
- **Hook:** #1 or #2 Daiichi 2571 (or any short-shank, straight-eye salmon hook of comparable size)

Notes: Along with the Black/Green Butt version of the fly, this is one of Howell's most productive color combinations. In his own words, "The Black/Burgundy one is right out of my box and is rigged the way I still fish my Intruders. It is tied to be rigged 'old school' with the leader through the fly and the hook fixed to the shank with rubber tubing." The tubing he refers to is clear speaker wire insulation cut to 1 cm (⅜") length. Tube fly junction tubing is an excellent substitute; it's just important that you match your tubing with the diameter of your hook or shank wire so you have a tight connection that will hold up to casting.

STEELY CONE SERIES GUIDE INTRUDER, PURPLE/GREEN BUTT

- **Shank:** Any sturdy, straight-eyed hook with at least 4 cm (1½") of tying area

- **Thread:** UNI Big Fly, black
- **Tag:** Flat Mylar tinsel, silver side up
- **"Retriever" loop:** 50-pound Fireline, 2.5 cm (1") loop
- **Butt:** Ice Dub, chartreuse
- **Tail:** Ostrich herl, black, 20 fibers fanned over the top of the shank
- **Body:** Flat Mylar tinsel, silver side up
- **Dubbing bump:** Arctic fox tail with guard hairs, purple
- **Hackle:** In two parts, from back to front: 1) ostrich herl, black; 2) marabou, purple
- **Hook:** #1 or #2 Gamakatsu Octopus
- **Weight:** Eco Pro or equivalent tungsten worm weight, black or red

Notes: Howell's Steely Cone series marks a departure from the typical use of dumbbell eyes for weight. Here's what Scott says about this series: "The Steely Cone concept really keeps me versatile when fine-tuning depth. I understand that flies this heavy are of little use on the Skagit or other classic bar-type rivers. But down here [on the Umpqua] we deal with fish that are very reluctant to move vertically in the water column. This problem is compounded by the fact that most of our rivers are carved from basalt. No classic, bar-type runs. No soft inside edges. Just very tight-lipped fish living at the bottom of fast 6- to 10-foot-deep slots. I remember years and years ago running into Bob York on the North Umpqua in winter. He was very discouraged and was cutting his trip short because of his lack of success. At the time, I shared his frustration. We just couldn't get it done the way we had everywhere else. It has been fun for me putting the pieces of the puzzle together over the years."

Weights are added to the tippet as the flies are tied on to the leader. Here it is critical that the hook have a straight eye so that a tungsten worm weight can be mounted to the leader. Scott typically uses 1/16-, 1/8-, and 3/16-ounce weights but notes that they are available up to ½ ounce (ouch!). First Scott ties a loose overhand knot in the tippet, leaving a 2- to 3-inch tag end, just as you would if tying a standard no-slip mono loop. Then he runs the weight up the tippet, threads the fly on the tippet, and threads the end of the tippet back through the weight and the overhand knot. Finally, he completes the no-slip loop and pulls it tight. The end result is a knot that locks the bullet weight in place directly above the eye of the hook, ensuring that the weight can't slip up the leader when not under tension.

SEAFOOD SERIES SQUIDRO, SALMON

- **Shank:** Piano or spinner wire shaped to imitate an upturned-eye salmon hook
- **Thread:** UNI Big Fly, white
- **Eyes:** Small to medium nickel-plated lead eyes
- **Tag:** Flat Mylar tinsel, silver side up
- **"Retriever" loop:** 80-pound white Dacron or 50-pound Krystal Fireline, 2.5 cm (1") loop
- **Butt:** Ice Dub or Angora goat, pink
- **Tail:** Sili Legs or Crazy Legs, clear/pearl pepper flake, 20 fibers
- **Body:** Flat Mylar tinsel, silver side up
- **Dubbing bump:** Arctic fox with guard hairs, pink or salmon colored, short
- **Hackle:** In two parts from back to front: 1) silicone legs, clear/pearl pepper flake, 20 fibers; 2) marabou, pink or salmon colored
- **Hook:** #1 or #2 Gamakatsu Octopus, white finish

STEELY CONE SERIES SQUIDRO, BLACK/GREEN BUTT

- **Shank:** Any sturdy straight-eyed hook with at least 4 cm (1½") of tying area
- **Thread:** UNI Big Fly, black
- **Tag:** Flat Mylar tinsel, silver side up
- **"Retriever" loop:** 50-pound Fireline, 2.5 cm (1") loop
- **Butt:** Ice Dub, chartreuse
- **Tail:** Sili Legs or Crazy Legs, black/blue bars, 20 fibers
- **Body:** Flat Mylar tinsel, silver side up
- **Dubbing bump:** Arctic fox with guard hairs, black, medium length
- **Hackle:** In two parts from back to front: 1) barred silicone legs, black/blue bars, 20 fibers; 2) marabou, black
- **Hook:** #1 or #2 Gamakatsu Octopus

Notes: See notes for Steely Cone Series Guide Intruder (page 226) for weight and rigging instructions.

STEELY CONE SERIES PROM DRESS, BLUE

- **Shank:** Any sturdy, straight-eyed hook with at least 4 cm (1½") of tying area
- **Thread:** UNI Big Fly, black
- **"Retriever" loop:** 50-pound Fireline, 2.5 cm (1") loop
- **Body:** Flat Mylar tinsel, silver side up
- **Dubbing bump:** Arctic fox with guard hairs, blue, short
- **Hackle:** Flashabou, blue, generously applied
- **Collar:** Guinea hen, blue
- **Hook:** #1 or #2 Gamakatsu Octopus

Notes: See notes for Steely Cone Series Guide Intruder (page 226) for weight and rigging instructions.

Eric Ishiwata

Eric is a college professor in Colorado who spends a lot of time swinging flies for trout and steelhead out west. He's been a signature tier in the fly business for several years, and we are fortunate to have this set of beautiful steelhead flies to share with our readers. They are truly unique and inspiring.

VARIABLE WEIGHT GRAND MASTER FLASH

- **Tube:** Pro Flexitube 40/40
- **Weight:** Extra-small, small, or medium Pro Raw Weight
- **Butt:** Hareline Frizzle Chenille, large
- **Hackle:** Silver pheasant
- **Tail:** Ostrich herls
- **Flash:** Flashabou
- **Body hackle:** Marabou blood quill
- **Wing:** Flashabou, Speckled Flashabou, Polar Flash, ostrich herls
- **Head:** Hareline Pseudo Hair + Ice Dub + Senyo's Laser Dub

Eric puts the finishing flame to one of his fancy marabou streamers. RUSS SCHNITZER PHOTO

PROTUBE BUGGER

- **Tube:** Large Pro Nanotube + Pro Hook Guide
- **Butt:** Mirage tinsel
- **Tail:** Marabou, Mirage flash
- **Body:** Chenille + copper rib, small
- **Hackle:** Grizzly hackle
- **Collar 1:** Saddle hackle
- **Weight:** Medium Pro Sportfisher Tungsten Raw Weight
- **Collar 2:** Hareline Grizzly Soft Hackle
- **Disc:** Medium Pro Ultra Sonic

RUMP ROAST

- **Body:** Flat Diamond Braid
- **Shoulder:** Hareline Frizzle Chenille, large, and schlappen
- **Hackle:** Marabou blood quills
- **Antennae:** Ringneck or golden pheasant tail fibers
- **Body:** Hareline Pseudo Hair or Pro American Opossum
- **Flash:** Angel Hair Flash
- **Shellback:** Ringneck pheasant rump feathers, three pairs, tented
- **Weight:** Medium Hareline's Plated Lead Eyes

PETIT MEAT

- **Tube:** Pro Tube Flexitube 40/40
- **Weight:** Extra-small, small, or medium Pro Raw Weight
- **Hackle:** Schlappen
- **Antennae:** Ringneck, golden, or Lady Amherst pheasant tail
- **Eyes:** Golden or Lady Amherst pheasant tippets
- **Body:** Flat Diamond Braid
- **Wing:** Pine squirrel or mink Zonker
- **Shoulder:** Hareline Pseudo Hair and Ice Dub
- **Horns:** Ringneck, golden, or Lady Amherst pheasant tail
- **Collar:** Ringneck pheasant rump
- **Disc:** Small Pro Ultra Sonic

Top row: Petite Meat in four color combinations. Second row: Rump Roast in two colors. Third row: ProTube Bugger in three colors. Last three: Variable Weight Grand Master Flash in three colors.

Brett pauses for a quick photo at his fly-tying desk in Palo Cedro, California. He's the reigning master when it comes to spinning rabbit fur in dubbing loops, as evidenced in his beautiful Intruders

the real attention getter is the surface disturbance, and this fly creates a good one.

There is one thing I would like to mention, and I'm sure you have all heard this before: when fishing a waking fly, *the grab doesn't always come at the sweet spot in the swing.* Over the years I have hooked several fish when the fly had finished swinging and was dangling straight down. It doesn't happen often, but it does happen. So, at the end of the swing, before you start retrieving, let the fly relax for a few seconds. Make this a habit. And pay close attention to those scant few seconds when resting your fly . . . especially when fishing the first light of early morning!

—Brett Jensen

BRETT'S KLAMATH INTRUDER, BLACK AND BLUE

- **Shank:** #8 TFS #8774
- **Stinger loop:** Senyo's Intruder Wire, black, for hook #6 or smaller
- **Hook:** #6-8 Gamakatsu Octopus
- **Eyes:** Extra-small painted lead eyes, pearl
- **Body:** In two parts, back to front: 1) Ice Dub, UV peacock black; 2) Ice Dub, UV dark olive
- **Hackle:** Schlappen, kingfisher blue
- **Legs:** In two parts: 1) MFC Mini Centipede Legs, speckled white; 2) Lady Amherst pheasant tail, white, minimum two to four fibers tied in separately
- **Flash:** Krinkle Mirror Flash, blue, no more than two strands
- **Collar:** In two parts, back to front: 1) bunny fur, blue, spun in a dubbing loop; 2) bunny fur, black, spun in a dubbing loop
- **Hook:** #4-6 Gamakatsu Octopus, black

Top row: Petite Meat in four color combinations. Second row: Rump Roast in two colors. Third row: ProTube Bugger in three colors. Last three: Variable Weight Grand Master Flash in three colors.

Brett Jensen

Brett is a veteran fly tier, fisherman, and fly fishing guide in Northern California's Klamath River country. It's a place where steelhead are often seen joining in with the resident trout on a caddisfly hatch. The "troutiness" of the Klamath and Trinity steelhead shines through in Brett's understated-but-buggy fly designs. His flies possess a fun combination of trout and steelhead styles. And they are tied with a level of care and precision that helps to make up for the rest of us slouches.

BRETT'S OBIE WAKER, BLACK

- **Hook:** #5-7 Daiichi Alec Jackson Spey, black
- **Tag:** Mirage tinsel, pearl
- **Body:** Ice Dub, UV black
- **Rib:** Mirage tinsel, pearl
- **Legs:** Lady Amherst pheasant tail, natural, two fibers per side
- **Flash:** Krinkle Mirror Flash, no more than two strands per side
- **Foam lip:** Rainy's 2 mm Cross-Link sheet foam, black
- **Wing/head:** Yearling elk or deer body hair, dyed black
- **Eyes:** Jungle cock nails, tied in just under the head

Notes: Brett's Obie Waker is a short-shank version of the Klamath Waker, tied on a size 1 and size 1/0 Gamakatsu Split Shot/Drop Shot hook.

BRETT'S OBIE WAKER, BROWN

- **Hook:** #5-7 Daiichi Alec Jackson Spey, black
- **Tag:** Mirage tinsel, pearl
- **Body:** Ice Dub, UV rust
- **Rib:** Mirage tinsel, pearl
- **Legs:** Wood duck flank, natural, two fibers per side
- **Flash:** Krinkle Mirror Flash, no more than two strands per side
- **Foam lip:** Rainy's 2 mm Cross-Link sheet foam, tan
- **Wing/head:** Yearling elk or deer body hair, natural
- **Eyes:** Jungle cock nails, tied in just under the head

The performance of the Obie Waker clearly comes from the 2 mm foam lip tied right behind the eye of the hook. The hair wing adds support and helps to strengthen the fly's stability. I tie this pattern both with a short and a long body. Both patterns fish well. However, I find the short body pattern is best suited for traditional tailouts or holding water that is soft, slow, and smooth. The long-body version of this fly fishes best in soft, slow-rolling riffles, or wherever there's a delicate and gentle surface chop.

Materials used to tie this pattern are simple and easy to find, and the pattern itself is straight forward and easy to tie. For the body material, I really like UV Ice Dub. This dubbing is available in several colors, and when spun in a loop, you can easily control its thickness. Don't spin the loop too tight. I like it with just enough give or softness so the ribbing pulls in just a little and seats on a firm base. Before wrapping the body with the newly formed loop, be sure to take a dubbing needle and pick through the fibers freeing those that are trapped.

For the wing, I prefer to use elk, and finding the perfect patch can be difficult. This is not to say that deer hair doesn't make a good-looking and durable fly; it does, and I use both. But elk, especially yearling elk, is a bit stiffer with less flair. Whether you use deer or elk, closely examine each patch and select the one that best fits the proportions of the fly you are tying. And look for the texture and hair length that works for you.

Be careful when tying in the foam lip. The first few wraps of thread should be snug but not tight. You can easily weaken or even cut the foam if you overtighten. Once the lip is in place, you can then secure everything tightly with a smooth layer of thread. A smooth, even surface is easier to dub over, and it also makes a good base for securing the hair wing. Body color and wing type are up to you. Be creative!

Hooks for this fly are important and aren't cheap. The short-body Waker is tied on Gamakatsu's Split Shot/Drop Shot hook. I love this hook! It features a nice wide gape and a very modest upturned eye. Absolutely a perfect fit for this fly. The long-body version is tied on an Alec Jackson Spey. It, too, features a slight upturned eye and is of the highest quality.

Are the jungle cock eyes an important element of this pattern? Probably not, but they're a nice touch for sure. And they might stimulate a response. But

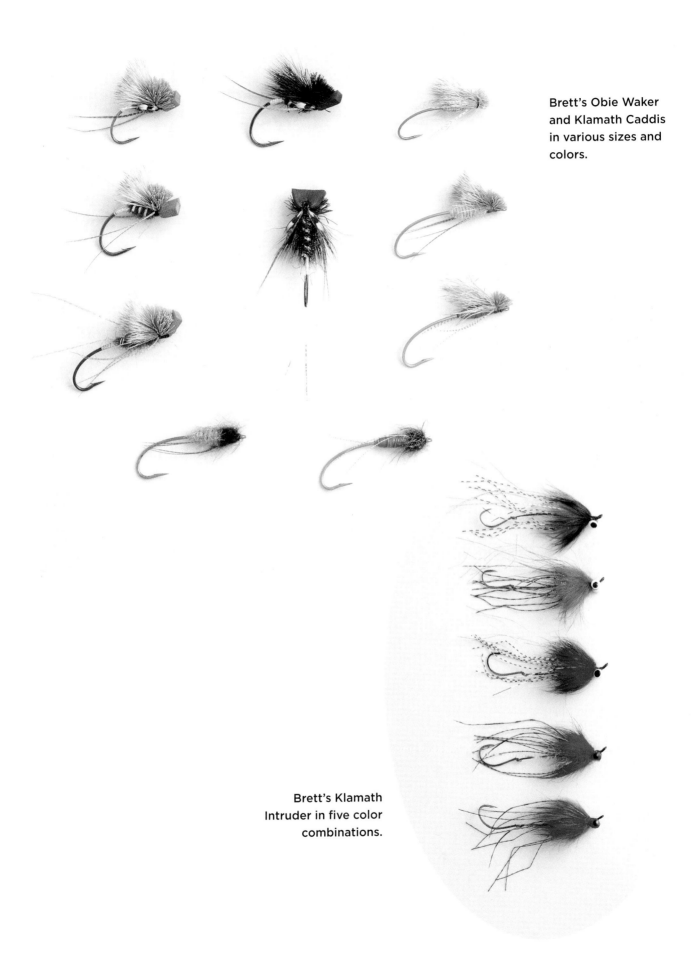

Brett's Obie Waker and Klamath Caddis in various sizes and colors.

Brett's Klamath Intruder in five color combinations.

Brett pauses for a quick photo at his fly-tying desk in Palo Cedro, California. He's the reigning master when it comes to spinning rabbit fur in dubbing loops, as evidenced in his beautiful Intruders

the real attention getter is the surface disturbance, and this fly creates a good one.

There is one thing I would like to mention, and I'm sure you have all heard this before: when fishing a waking fly, *the grab doesn't always come at the sweet spot in the swing.* Over the years I have hooked several fish when the fly had finished swinging and was dangling straight down. It doesn't happen often, but it does happen. So, at the end of the swing, before you start retrieving, let the fly relax for a few seconds. Make this a habit. And pay close attention to those scant few seconds when resting your fly . . . especially when fishing the first light of early morning!

—Brett Jensen

BRETT'S KLAMATH INTRUDER, BLACK AND BLUE

- **Shank:** #8 TFS #8774
- **Stinger loop:** Senyo's Intruder Wire, black, for hook #6 or smaller
- **Hook:** #6-8 Gamakatsu Octopus
- **Eyes:** Extra-small painted lead eyes, pearl
- **Body:** In two parts, back to front: 1) Ice Dub, UV peacock black; 2) Ice Dub, UV dark olive
- **Hackle:** Schlappen, kingfisher blue
- **Legs:** In two parts: 1) MFC Mini Centipede Legs, speckled white; 2) Lady Amherst pheasant tail, white, minimum two to four fibers tied in separately
- **Flash:** Krinkle Mirror Flash, blue, no more than two strands
- **Collar:** In two parts, back to front: 1) bunny fur, blue, spun in a dubbing loop; 2) bunny fur, black, spun in a dubbing loop
- **Hook:** #4-6 Gamakatsu Octopus, black

BRETT'S KLAMATH INTRUDER, ORANGE

- **Shank:** #8 TFS #8774
- **Stinger loop:** Senyo's Intruder Wire, orange, for hook #6 or smaller
- **Hook:** #6-8 Gamakatsu Octopus
- **Eyes:** Extra-small painted lead eyes, red
- **Body:** In two parts back to front: 1) Arizona Diamond Dub, tangerine; 2) Ice Dub, UV red
- **Hackle:** Schlappen, red
- **Legs:** In two parts: 1) MFC Centipede Legs, orange; 2) Lady Amherst pheasant tail, orange, two to four fibers tied in separately
- **Flash:** Krinkle Mirror Flash, orange
- **Collar:** In two parts, front to back: 1) bunny fur, fluorescent fuchsia, spun in dubbing loop; 2) bunny fur, hot orange, spun in dubbing loop
- **Hook:** #4-6 Gamakatsu Octopus, black

Just because it's small in size doesn't mean it's easy to tie. Like its larger siblings, the Klamath Intruder takes time to put all the pieces together. The idea of fishing a small Intruder-style fly came to me a year ago, when fishing close to the ocean for summer-run fish in late fall. The prototypes were tied with small light wire hooks. The fly itself looked great, fished great, and was proportioned nicely. But it failed miserably! The first adult steelhead straightened the hook with very little effort. Tying the fly with the right size hook proved difficult, as my mind is geared strongly to proportions. So this pattern took some time to develop. But, this past season it finally came together. My mind relaxed a bit and allowed me to use a substantial hook while keeping the physical body size at a minimum. Using the right hook along with a few other additions and modifications has turned this fly into a very productive pattern.

You should be able to find all the materials needed to tie this fly in any well-stocked fly shop that caters to the steelhead fisherman. For the body I use, Ice Dub, preferably in UV colors. The color selection is great, it is an easy material to work with, makes a solid shoulder, and has proven very durable when spun in a loop. The Centipede Legs are what gives the fly its movement, and they truly are the fly's key element. I have found that the fly performs best with no more than eight and no less than six legs that are clipped 5 to 6 mm ($\frac{3}{16}$" to $\frac{1}{4}$") past the end of the hook. And don't overdo the Mirror Flash! Two strands seems about right, and even at that, when fishing in low clear water or on bright days, it can really light things up.

All rabbit fur strips are not the same. One package might be short and thick, another package long and thin. I suggest you look at each package of hair closely before you buy and select for qualities that work best for you. When spinning the collars, be careful not to use too much fur. I use approximately a 2.5 cm (1") pinch of fur for the first collar and a little less for the second. After spinning, what you want is a nice thin brush that's even in length.

This fly takes two hooks to create. For the shank, I use a traditional salmon fly hook in a size 8. No need to buy the best, since you're clipping off the hook. For the stinger, Gamakatsu Octopus is a perfect match for this fly. The size 8 stinger hook is the standard for most of my Intruders, but there are times when I will step up to a size 6.

The Klamath Intruder has proven to be effective wherever it's been fished. It's my go-to pattern in the shoulder season of late fall, and it fishes well into the early months of winter. The color options are unlimited, and it can be tied with or without the lead eyes. A challenge to tie? Perhaps . . . but a fun one to fish!

—Brett Jensen

Justin Karnopp

Justin is a TV producer and screenwriter based in Missoula, Montana. He grew up in Oregon and credits his father for getting him started as a fly tier. Once he started hanging around fly shops, he met Paul Wolflick, one of Central Oregon's leading tiers and teachers. Paul helped Justin excel as a fly tier. "The original *Flies of the Northwest* was my fly-tying bible, and I think I tied just about every pattern in that volume."

Since those early days, Justin's career in the outdoor television world has taken him all over the globe in search of great fish on the fly. He also spends a lot of time hunting upland birds and elk, as time allows. For all of his passions, steelhead hold a special place in his heart, and he still looks forward to spending a few weeks every year on the rivers of the Pacific Northwest.

SHADE CHASER

- **Hook:** #6 Daiichi 2421
- **Thread:** 6/0 UNI-Thread, claret
- **Tail:** Flex-Floss, black
- **Abdomen:** Claret thread coated with head cement
- **Thorax:** Ice Dub, claret
- **Rib:** Mirage Flashabou, opal

Justin at home on the sticks. JUSTIN KARNOPP PHOTO

- **Hackle:** Grizzly saddle
- **Legs:** Flex-Floss, black
- **Wing case:** 2 mm foam, tan; 12 Mirage Flashabou fibers over the top

KORTGE CLOSER

- **Hook:** #6 Gamakatsu T10-6H, red
- **Thread:** 6/0 UNI-Thread, fiery orange
- **Abdomen:** Holographic Diamond Braid, red
- **Thorax:** Diamond Braid, purple
- **Hackle:** Chinese saddle hackle, black
- **Legs:** Spanflex, black
- **Underwing:** Mirage Flashabou, opal
- **Overwing:** Fox squirrel tail, natural

SNAKE EYES, GREEN

- **Hook:** #4 Daiichi 1730
- **Weight:** .03" or .035" lead wire wrapped under thorax area
- **Thread:** 3/0 UNI-Thread, black
- **Eyes:** Large nickel plated lead eyes
- **Tail:** Round rubber legs, black
- **Abdomen:** STS Trilobal Dub, highlander green
- **Rib:** Large V-Rib, chartreuse
- **Hackle:** Chinese saddle, black
- **Legs:** Round rubber legs, chartreuse
- **Wing case:** Large Scud Back, black
- **Head:** Ice Dub, black
- **Antennae:** Round rubber legs, black

BHAGWAN

- **Shank:** #1/0 or #2/0 Daiichi 3110 or equivalent
- **Thread:** 3/0 UNI-Thread, black
- **Eyes:** BallzEyes, large
- **Stinger loop:** 30-pound Dacron backing, 2.5 cm (1") length
- **Throat:** Marabou, red
- **Cheeks:** Cock pheasant neck feathers
- **Wing:** Rabbit strip, purple, cut to 7.6 cm (3") long

Notes: To hold everything together, Justin glues the rabbit strip down to the Dacron loop and the trailing hook shank with Zap-A-Gap. This keeps the hook point in line with the tail of the fly, and it provides rigidity to prevent fouling of the hook during casting.

Clockwise from top: Shade Chaser; Kortge Closer; Bhagwan; Snake Eyes, green.

Matt Klara

Matt is a talented tier who lives in Helena, Montana, and makes pilgrimages to the Pacific Northwest for steelhead. Brian Chou (page 166) introduced us to Matt when we asked him if there were any other tiers we should include in this book. "You really need to see his stuff," Brian said. "This guy gets it." We couldn't agree more. In fact, we think his Hobgoblin is one of the most innovative designs in this collection, and a great crossover into the bass world.

HOBGOBLIN, BRIGHT

- **Shank:** Any straight-eye hook with at least 2.5 cm (1") of shank for tying
- **Thread:** Size A Danville's Flymaster Plus 210 denier, fluorescent fire orange
- **Stinger loop:** 65-pound Tuf-Line XP braid, red, 4.5 cm (1¾") long
- **Eyes:** Pseudo Eyes, red, sized to fit water conditions
- **Tail:** Rabbit strip, white, with the Tuf-Line threaded through with a needle, exiting the top (fur side) of the strip
- **Body:** Mix of Angora goat and Ice Dub, orange (color to match the hot tips of the rubber legs)
- **Flash:** Flashabou, pearl, six to eight strands

Matt inspects his fly and seems happy with what he sees. IAN MAJSZAK PHOTO

- **Legs:** Hot-tipped silicone rubber legs, hot pink with orange tips, tied in with tips facing forward, one clump above and one clump below the shank
- **Collar:** Arctic fox tail, hot pink, spun in a dubbing loop (color to match the base color of the rubber legs); palmer the collar behind the rubber legs that are facing forward, tie off, and pull the rubber legs back over the collar
- **Wing:** Natural grizzly hackle tips, two tied in at the head, just in front of the eyes
- **Hook:** #2 or #1 Owner SSW Needle Point

NIGHTMARE MUDDLER

- **Shank:** Any straight-eye hook with at least 4 cm (1½") of shank for tying
- **Stinger loop:** 20-pound Surflon Micro Supreme, 3 cm (1⅛") long
- **Tail:** Bucktail, tan, from the center of a natural bucktail, tied 360 degrees around the hook shank, topped with golden pheasant tippet feather
- **Body:** Angel Hair, PMD, roughly dubbed and picked out, palmered with grizzly hackle through rear ⅔ of the body; natural golden pheasant tippet palmered through front ⅓ of body
- **Rib:** Small wire, gold, counterwrapped through the hackle for durability
- **Wing:** Grizzly hackle tips
- **Head and collar:** Natural cow elk hair, one clump, unstacked, spun and trimmed to shape
- **Hook:** #2 or #1 Owner SSW Needle Point

Notes: Matt says this pattern was inspired by the simple desire for a large Muddler variation that utilized the proven "stinger hook" concept. The name is attributed to a comment made by Marty Sheppard, who claimed to have nightmares about the fly after seeing it for the first time.

Matt adds the following homage: "Few bonds are stronger than a great friendship forged on the water over many seasons. For nearly 15 years, from Montana, to Baja, to the bonefish flats, and all those steelhead rivers in between, Niall Boggs of Bend, Oregon, has been a steadfast companion, angling inspiration, and all-around great fishing buddy. I'm sharing this fly, Niall's pattern, in his honor, and in honor of great fishing buddies everywhere."

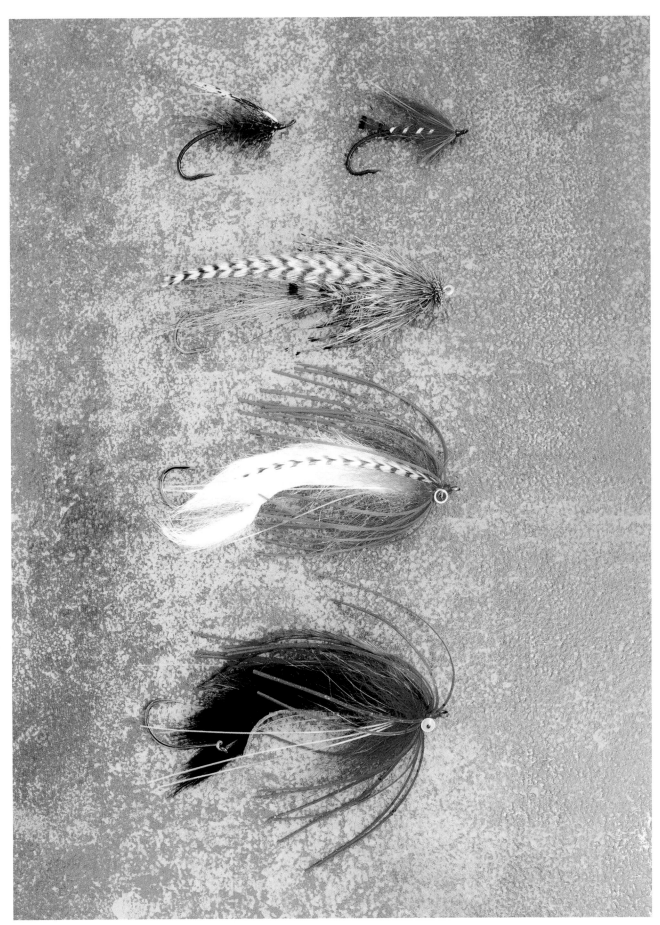

From the top left: Railbird 2001; Bluesbreaker; Nightmare Muddler; Hobgoblin, bright; Hobgoblin, dark.

BLUESBREAKER

- **Hook:** #3-7 Daiichi 2052 Alec Jackson Spey
- **Thread:** UTC 70-denier, red
- **Tail:** Golden pheasant tippet, red (or other bright color)
- **Body:** Blend of arctic fox tail fibers, royal blue, and Wapsi SLF Poul Jorgensen Dubbing, electric blue
- **Rib:** Medium holographic silver tinsel
- **Collar:** Rabbit fur, royal blue, spun into a dubbing loop and palmered, topped with two or three turns of teal blue saddle hackle
- **Wing:** Arctic fox tail, royal blue, with 8 to 12 strands of Mirage Flashabou, opal

RAILBIRD 2001

- **Hook:** #5-9 Daiichi Alec Jackson Steelhead Iron
- **Thread:** UTC 70-denier, black
- **Tag:** Small wire, copper, three or four turns
- **Tail:** Grizzly saddle hackle fibers, dyed claret
- **Body:** Angora goat dubbing, claret, palmered with grizzly saddle, also claret
- **Rib:** Small wire, copper, counterwrapped through the hackle for durability
- **Collar:** Guinea hen, yellow
- **Wing:** Lady Amherst pheasant tail, six to eight fibers

Notes: Matt discovered this fly on one of his many readings of Trey Combs's masterwork, *Steelhead Fly Fishing*, one of the great links between steelheading past and present. Matt explains, "Trey provided a recipe, but no photo, and attributed the pattern to the late John Benn [1838–1907]. My suspicion is that the original Railbird was tied with a dense, bulky palmer and a long wing on a short shank, down-eye trout hook—the common dressing style in Northern California and Southern California at that time. My version takes a sparser, low-water approach and uses an up-eye salmon-style hook along with some of my favorite materials to create a translucent, buggy look in the classic color scheme. Thank you, Mr. Benn. I wonder what you would think of steelheading if you were around today."

Jason Koertge

Jason Koertge (pronounced KER-chee) is one of an influential wolf pack of Midwest steelheaders who migrated to the Pacific Northwest in the '90s (see page 23). Every person in that group went on to make his mark on fishing culture in one way or another, though some got pulled back to Wisconsin and Michigan. Jason put down roots, married a sweet girl from Estacada, and quickly developed a reputation as a wicked-smart and secretive angler on the Oregon Coast and Willamette tributaries. But for all his fishing exploits, Jason made his biggest mark off the water, as a writer and as a fly tier. A professional ad writer in the outdoor sports trade, Jason had a well-trained skill for connecting with an audience. He came into the Northwest outdoor scene like a whirlwind, contributing to magazines and thinking up some of the most memorable ad campaigns in the history of fly-fishing. Then came Jason's experimental blog, the *Voluntary Beatdown*. It was a deeply personal, existential rampage though the inner world of a rainforest steelheader. Jason's punk-in-camo style blew stuff up,

much in the spirit of the Intruder clan. In short order the *Beatdown* came to speak for a whole new generation of steelheaders. It was a little Internet chapel, giving anglers a dose of heaven to get them through their work week until they could suit up and climb back into the river. And then, just as quickly as it had appeared, the *Beatdown* was gone. Jason pulled down the site and went back to his crittery, secretive ways. "I set a time limit of one year, and I said what I wanted to say," Koertge said unapologetically.

As a fly tier, Jason's influence might have been so much water under the bridge if we hadn't talked him into this project. He had never wanted to make a name as a tier, considering himself a student of great anglers, not a master. But as his world got fishier and fishier, he found himself in the center of a fly-design incubator, surrounded by legendary fly designers and hybridizing his styles with theirs. Over a dozen or so years, Jason's steelhead flies boiled down to three main patterns, featured here, and on pages 76 and 81.

From the top: The Criddler; Fur Burger, pink and orange; Fur Burger, black and blue.

THE CRIDDLER

- **Tube:** Small tubing, clear
- **Thread:** 6/0 UNI-Thread, red
- **Butt:** Craft Fur, black, tied in reverse, pulled back and trimmed short
- **Split-tail:** Ostrich herl, six fibers on each side
- **Body:** Diamond Braid, gold, palmered with Chinese saddle hackle, black
- **Hackle:** Chinese saddle, red
- **Collar:** Ostrich herl, white, applied like a hackle

Notes: This little critter was created to match the coloration and size of the deadly Nightmare Jig.

FUR BURGER, PINK (LARGE)

- **Tube:** Frödin medium tubing, cut to 4 cm (1½") with a 2 cm (¾") section of small tubing inserted at the rear
- **Thread:** 6/0 UNI-Thread, fluorescent orange
- **Butt:** Senyo's Laser Dub, pink
- **Rear hackle:** In three parts, back to front: 1) saddle, pink; 2) guinea hen, orange; 3) ostrich "split-tail," white, 10 fibers per side
- **Body:** Pink Diamond Braid

- **Front hackle:** In two stages, back to front: 1) Craft Fur, orange, clumped in reverse and pulled back; 2) Craft Fur, pink, tied in reverse and pulled back
- **Collar:** Pink guinea hen
- **Flash:** Angel Hair, silver

FUR BURGER, BLACK & BLUE (SMALL)

- **Tube:** Frödin medium tubing, cut to 3.2 cm (1¼") with a 2 cm (¾") section of small tubing inserted at the rear
- **Thread:** 6/0 UNI-Thread, fluorescent orange
- **Butt:** Senyo's Laser Dub, blue
- **Rear hackle:** In three parts, back to front: 1) saddle, kingfisher blue; 2) guinea hen, blue; 3) ostrich "split-tail," black, 10 fibers per side
- **Body:** Blue Diamond Braid
- **Front hackle:** In two stages, back to front: 1) Craft Fur, blue, clumped in reverse and pulled back; 2) Craft Fur, black, tied in reverse and pulled back
- **Collar:** Guinea hen, blue
- **Flash:** Angel Hair, blue

Notes: Step-by-step tying instructions on page 77.

John McMillan

John McMillan needs no introduction in the steelheading world, and we are lucky to have him represented here. His flies reflect his personality, his parentage, and the confidence of his approach. His father's iconic Muddler-ile caddis covers most summer-fishing situations just fine, but it's sensible to have a small black wet-fly as a backup plan. And, of course, everybody needs some big wiggly bugs for winter fishing. A working man's steelhead fly selection. Thanks, John!

STEELHEAD CADDIS

- **Hook:** #4 Gamakatsu T10-3H, black
- **Thread:** 6/0, black
- **Body:** Angora goat dubbing, yellow, spun in a dubbing loop
- **Wing:** Tented pair of light, mottled turkey tail strips
- **Collar/head:** Elk rump hair spun and trimmed Muddler-style

Notes: To call this pattern "modern" is probably a stretch, but given the fact that John is the modern generation of the McMillan family line, and given his modern contributions to steelhead biology and conservation, we really wanted to include these patterns.

BOTTLE BRUSH

- **Hook:** #1-4 Gamakatsu T10-6H, black
- **Thread:** 6/0, black
- **Rib:** Fine wire, gold
- **Body:** Angora goat dubbing, wine or dark purple, spun in a dubbing loop, palmered with long saddle hackle, black

ARTICULATED INTRUDER, BLACK/PINK

- **Hooks:** #1-4 Gamakatsu T10-6H, black
- **Thread:** 6/0, black
- **Rear Hook Dressing**
- **Hackle:** Ostrich herl, black, 30 to 35 strands tied in around the full circumference of the shank
- **Front Hook Dressing**
- **Eyes:** Small Pseudo Eyes
- **Hackle:** Ostrich herl, black, 30 to 35 strands tied in around the full circumference of the shank
- **Flash:** A few fibers of Micro Flashabou on the top and bottom
- **Collar:** Ostrich herl, hot pink, 15 to 20 strands
- **Head:** Angora goat dubbing, hot pink, spun in a dubbing loop and wrapped behind, around, and over barbell eyes

From the top: Steelhead Caddis; Bottle Brush; Articulated Intruders, black; Articulated Intruder, blue.

Justin Miller

In the category of "doing what you love," nobody does it better than Justin Miller, director of the Fly Shop's Kamchatka Peninsula operations. He found his calling in 2004, when he was hired as a counselor at the Fly Shop's FishCamp program and started sharing the magic of fly fishing with kids. From there he rose like a meteor through the ranks, guiding the steelhead rivers of Northern California and building up knowledge and experience for his eventual appointment in 2008 as a camp manager in Kamchatka, Russia. He has an infectious enthusiasm and more than enough skill and experience to back it up. Here he shares a few of his signature steelhead patterns and some of the thought behind them. We think his flies are some of the finest ever tied, and we hope you agree. *BIG thanks to Justin for his contributions and positive energy!*

THOMPSON CLOSER

- **Shank:** #1 TFS 8774 (The Fly Shop's proprietary brand)
- **Stinger loop:** Beadalon seven-strand coated wire, black, 2 cm (¾") loop
- **Thread:** Ultra 140-denier, fluorescent orange
- **Butt:** Medium Cactus Chenille, orange
- **Rear hackle:** In two parts, from back to front: 1) Finnish raccoon, orange; 2) turkey flat, black
- **Body:** Ultra Wire, copper, medium
- **Forward bump:** Medium Cactus Chenille, orange
- **Flash:** Flashabou, copper
- **Hackle:** In two parts, from back to front: 1) spun deer body hair, black; 2) turkey flat, black
- **Wings:** Furnace grizzly saddle hackle feathers, paired
- **Hook:** #1 Gamakatsu Split Shot/Drop Shot hook, black

PAULITO'S TDFER

- **Shank:** #1/0 TFS 8774 (The Fly Shop's proprietary brand)
- **Stinger loop:** Beadalon seven-strand coated wire, black, 2.5 cm (1") loop
- **Thread:** Ultra 140-denier, black
- **Eyes:** Medium Psuedo Eyes, black
- **Butt:** Diamond Braid, orange
- **Rear hackle:** In three parts, from back to front: 1) Finnish raccoon, orange; 2) ostrich or rhea herl, olive; 3) turkey flat, black
- **Body, rear half:** Fine Diamond Braid, green
- **Body, forward half:** Small Cactus Chenille, black; palmered with brown hen saddle
- **Flash:** Flashabou, copper
- **Hackle:** In two parts, from back to front: 1) turkey flat, black; 2) ostrich or rhea herl, olive
- **Topping:** Ostrich herl, black
- **Shellback:** Grizzly saddle hackle feathers, dark orange
- **Head:** Spun deer body hair, black, tied in on underside only
- **Hook:** #1 Gamakatsu Split Shot/Drop Shot hook, black

BLUE STEEL INTRUDER

- **Shank:** #1/0 TFS 8774 (The Fly Shop's proprietary brand)
- **Stinger loop:** Beadalon seven-strand coated wire, black, 2.5 cm (1") loop
- **Thread:** Ultra 140-denier, blue
- **Eyes:** Medium brass eyes, black
- **Butt:** Diamond Braid, blue
- **Rear hackle:** In three parts, from back to front: 1) arctic fox tail, blue; 2) ostrich herl, black; 3) schlappen, black
- **Body, rear half:** Diamond Braid, black
- **Body, forward half:** Medium Cactus Chenille, blue; entire body palmered with grizzly saddle hackle, blue
- **Hackle:** In four parts, from back to front: 1) spun deer body hair, black; 2) Lady Amherst pheasant tail; 3) turkey flat, blue; 4) ostrich herl, black
- **Flash:** Flashabou, silver
- **Topping and throat:** Arctic fox tail, blue
- **Hook:** #1 Gamakatsu Split Shot/Drop Shot hook, black

From the top: Thompson Closer; Rusty Prawn Tube; Jedi Mind Trick; Blue Steel Intruder; Paulito's TDFer. These are some of the finest steelhead flies ever tied, and they are not for show.

JEDI MIND TRICK, PINK/BLUE

- **Shank:** #3/0 Alec Jackson Spey hook, nickel silver finish
- **Stinger loop:** Beadalon seven-strand coated wire, blue, 2.5 cm (1") loop
- **Thread:** Ultra 140-denier, fluorescent pink
- **Butt:** Diamond Braid, blue
- **Rear hackle:** In three parts, from back to front: 1) Finnish raccoon, pink; 2) turkey flat, blue; 3) ostrich herl, black
- **Body, rear half:** Diamond Braid, lavender, palmered with grizzly saddle hackle, blue
- **Body, forward half:** Medium Cactus Chenille, blue, palmered with grizzly saddle hackle, pink
- **Hackle:** In four parts, from back to front: 1) spun deer body hair, black; 2) turkey flat, pink; 3) ostrich herl, black; 4) turkey flat, blue, barred with Sharpie permanent marker
- **Flash:** Krinkle Mirror Flash, silver or pearl
- **Shellback:** Grizzly saddle hackle tips, pink, tied long
- **Cheeks:** Jungle cock nails tied in below shank
- **Hook:** #1 Gamakatsu Split Shot/Drop Shot hook, black

The Jedi Mind Trick

Story and photos by Justin Miller

My first confidence fly for steelhead in BC was a blue and black Intruder-style fly. I named it Blue Steel, after the male supermodel facial expression from *Zoolander*. I fished it 90 percent of the time, and caught 90 percent of the fish on it. Some days I would switch it up though, and a pink version was my second choice, and some days pink was definitely the ticket!

One year, before I was headed over to the Russian Far East to guide the Kamchatka Steelhead Project, I started doing some experimenting at the bench. The dime-bright and plentiful steelhead of Kamchatka are the grabbiest I have encountered, making it an unbelievable testing ground for new patterns. That season I got to test and build confidence in a couple new patterns that have since become go-to flies in my arsenal and some of my favorite patterns all around the Pacific Rim.

The fly that really took off for me was just a mix of my two favorites. I had not seen blue and pink mixed together in an Intruder before, but as soon as I tied the first one, I knew it was going to be a killer. How could it not? The blue always worked, but on those days that just felt like pink, the fish would see that, too. It was the best of both.

The fish of Kamchatka did not argue, and they seemed to key in on the fly in many different conditions, and my confidence it the pattern grew quickly. The Jedi Mind Trick was my new favorite pattern. Kamchatka's aggressive steelhead helped me prove it was a slayer, and that confidence spread when I got home. Fish ate it everywhere; it just felt like it brainwashed fish when they saw it. They couldn't say no. It is still one of my favorite flies to this day.

Justin's tying desk at home in Redding, California. JUSTIN MILLER PHOTO

A fine Russian steelie fresh from the Sea of Okhotsk. JUSTIN MILLER PHOTO

RUSTY PRAWN TUBE

- **Tube:** Medium-diameter HMH tube, cut to 3.7 cm (1½″) with 2.5 cm (1″) of large-diameter HMH Hook Holder tubing
- **Thread:** Ultra 140-denier, fluorescent orange
- **Eyes:** Small brass eyes
- **Butt:** Medium Cactus Chenille, orange
- **Rear hackle:** In two parts, from back to front: 1) wood duck flank, orange; 2) ostrich herl, orange
- **Split-tail:** In two parts: 1) ostrich or rhea, black, six strands on each side; 2) grizzly saddle hackle tips, orange, tied long
- **Rear eyes:** Large jungle cock nails
- **Body, rear half:** Medium Cactus Chenille, orange, palmered with saddle hackle, orange
- **Middle hackle:** Ostrich herl, orange
- **Middle topping:** Pair of golden pheasant body feathers, dyed red
- **Body, forward half:** Holographic flat tinsel, red, palmered with saddle hackle, orange
- **Flash:** Flashabou, pearl
- **Front hackle:** Wood duck flank, orange
- **Front topping:** Pair of large golden pheasant body feathers, dyed red
- **Head:** Painted with orange Hard Head lacquer

Notes: Justin has merged the classic General Practitioner with the modern Intruder to create the ultimate prawn fly. Like all of his creations, once you take the time to tie this fly, you may be reluctant to fish it. But Justin points out that his flies are made to fish. You may just want to avoid waters with overhanging trees or large woody debris.

Paul Miller

Paul Miller is a larger-than-life personality and a prominent leader in the "big fly" movement that developed during the Intruder Revolution. He is widely credited for introducing rhea feathers to the fly-tying world back in 2000. He says, "The thing that's great about rhea is its strength. Its durability is truly remarkable and considerably better than bunny, marabou, and other common fly-tying materials." His flies, like those of Dave Pinczkowski and Kevin Feenstra on Lake Michigan, are intended to move water and create alluring vibrations, in addition to their visual impact.

SUPER SPEY PHANTOM

- **Shank:** 40 mm Senyo's Articulated Shank, copper
- **Thread:** 6/0 UNI-Thread, orange
- **Stinger loop:** Senyo's Intruder Wire, red, 3 cm (1³⁄₁₆") long
- **Rear weiling:** From back to front: 1) Estaz, orange; 2) ring hackle of long rhea herl, orange, spun in a dubbing loop; 3) jungle cock nails for eyes; 4) pair of golden pheasant body or shoulder feathers, dyed orange, 3 cm (1³⁄₁₆") long; 5) two strands each of Midge Flash and Krinkle Mirror flash, silver and/or pearl
- **Center weiling:** 1) Estaz, orange; 2) throat of long rhea herl, orange; 3) ring hackle of schlappen or large saddle, orange; 4) pair of golden pheasant body or shoulder feathers, dyed orange, tied 3.5 cm (1³⁄₈") long
- **Front weiling:** 1) Estaz, orange; 2) throat of long rhea herl, orange; 3) ring hackle of schlappen or large saddle, orange; 4) pair of golden pheasant body or shoulder feathers, dyed orange, 4 cm (1½") long
- **Shellback:** Pair of golden pheasant shoulder feathers, dyed orange, 5 cm (2") long
- **Hook:** #1 Gamakatsu Octopus, red

SUPER SPEY PRAWN

- **Shank:** 40 mm Senyo's Articulated Shank, black
- **Thread:** 6/0 UNI-Thread, black
- **Stinger loop:** Senyo's Intruder Wire, black, 3 cm (1³⁄₁₆") long
- **Rear and middle weilings:** Repeated from back to front: 1) Estaz, peacock; 2) ring hackle of long rhea herl, black, spun in a dubbing loop; 2) ring hackle of schlappen or long saddle, chartreuse
- **Front weiling:** 1) Estaz, peacock; 2) ring hackle of long rhea herl, black
- **Flash:** Several strands of Krinkle Mirror Flash
- **Collar:** Extra-large guinea hen, dyed chartreuse
- **Eyes:** Jungle cock nails
- **Hook:** #1 Gamakatsu Octopus, black

Notes: At first glance, two characteristics of these flies jump out: 1) They are huge—10 to 13 cm (4" to 5") in length, and 2) they exhibit a tremendous amount of movement. Paul says the driving idea behind his flies is the way they come to life when properly fished. He calls them "swimming flies," referring to the way they open and close during a down-and-across swing. Paul explains, "The ideal setup is type III to type VI water, where the fly is coming across at 'steelhead speed.' Early in the

Super Spey Prawn, top; Super Spey Phantom, bottom.

experimentation with these flies, we noticed that many, if not most, of our takes came at the end of the swing, or as the fly turned and slowed down. When these flies come into slower water, or water with varied current, they open up, offering a dramatically larger profile." He adds that his flies, while originally tied for steelhead, have found a growing popularity among trout guides in Argentina, where big browns can be tough to entice, and where the added lifelike movement of rhea can make all the difference. And, he points out, "People need to know that these flies will knock the daylights out of king salmon!"

Jeff Mishler

Jeff is one of the Pacific Northwest's most talented fly tiers, and he may be the most accomplished outdoorsman we've ever met. He was the first American to legally catch a steelhead in Kamchatka back in the early '90s, and since then he has gone on to create some of the finest photography, videos, and books in the history of our sport. He is probably best known as the creative genius behind the Skagit Master series of videos, and for his many contributions to leading magazines. In 2015 he published *Bent*, a book of artful essays and photographs. It took a long time to get the flies that are featured here, but we hope you agree that it was worth the wait. We never did manage to wrestle the recipes out of him for his newer flies, so we'll all have to work those out on our own. You can learn how to tie the Mishler Prawn in our step-by-step feature on page 91.

MISHLER'S PRAWN, ORANGE (ORIGINAL)

- **Tube:** Small HMH tube, clear, burned on both ends
- **Thread:** UTC 140-denier, orange
- **Butt:** Arctic fox tail, red, spun in a dubbing loop
- **Tail:** Bucktail, orange
- **Eyes:** 3 mm seed beads, chartreuse, glued to burnt ends of 20-pound Maxima Ultragreen
- **Body:** Senyo's Laser Dub, orange, palmered with schlappen or long Chinese saddle, orange
- **Rib:** Medium wire, red
- **Throat:** Two more turns of the body hackle
- **Shellback:** Four tips of grizzly saddle hackle, orange, tented in pairs
- **Flash:** Angel Hair, UV
- **Head:** Medium wire, red

Notes: This is one of the first prototypes of the Mishler Prawn, tied in the mid-2000s.

MISHLER'S PRAWN, PINK/ORANGE (IMPROVED)

- **Tube:** Small HMH tube, clear, burned on both ends, or Pro Microtube, clear
- **Thread:** UTC 140-denier, red
- **Rear hackle:** In two parts, back to front: 1) arctic fox tail, pink, spun in a dubbing loop; 2) ringneck pheasant tail, dyed orange, spun in a dubbing loop
- **Tail:** Bucktail, pink, topped with a small amount of red and two strands of pink Krystal Flash
- **Rear shell:** Golden pheasant neck feather, dyed red
- **Eyes:** Mono crab eyes, red, with irises applied with a black Sharpie permanent marker
- **Legs:** Grizzly barred rubber legs, orange
- **Body:** Flat Diamond Braid, orange, palmered with Chinese saddle, pink
- **Rib:** Small wire, red
- **Front hackle:** Arctic fox tail, cerise, spun in a dubbing loop
- **Underwing:** Finnish raccoon, pink
- **Throat:** Guinea hen, natural, pink or orange
- **Shellback:** Four tips of grizzly saddle hackle, orange, tented in pairs
- **Head:** Medium wire, red
- **Junction tubing:** Pro Hookguide, orange

Notes: See our full step-by-step feature on this fly on page 91.

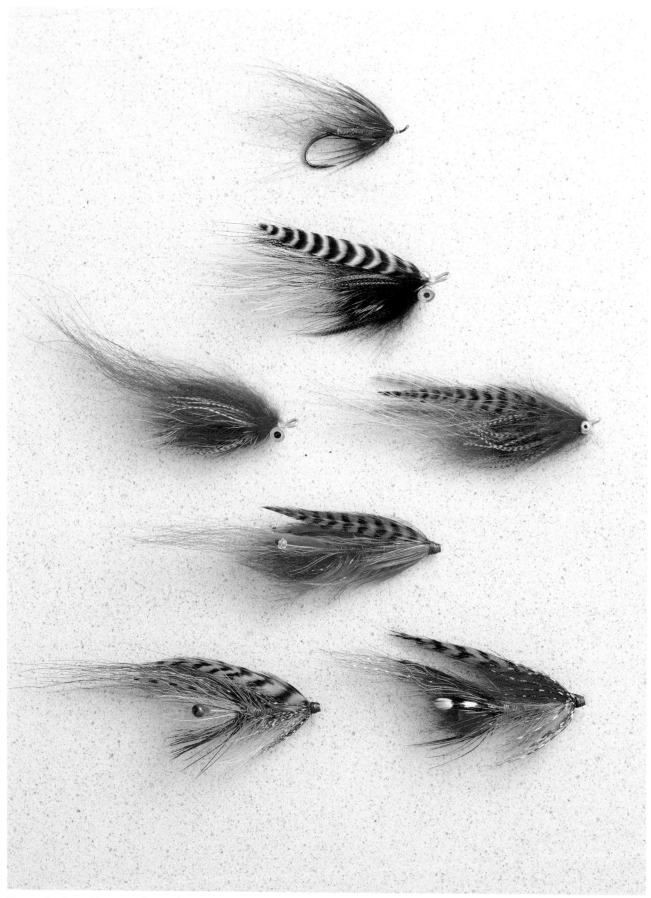

From the top: Unnamed wet fly, orange and red; Hair Hackle Intruder, black and green; two Hair Hackle Intruders in orange; Mishler Prawn, orange (original); two Mishler Prawn variations tied by RR.

Kevin Morlock

Kevin is a successful Michigan steelhead guide with decades of experience tying and swinging flies. His contributions here stand out for their sheer utility. Each one has been designed to do a specific job, and they all have served him well. We feel strongly that Kevin's unvarnished style is refreshing and hides some secrets from which all of us can benefit. So take a close look and keep an open mind.

BABY SALMON

- **Hook:** #6 or #8 Tiemco 3761
- **Thread:** 140-denier, black
- **Body:** Mirage Flashabou, opal
- **Wing:** Mallard flank
- **Head:** Build up a base of black thread, then add an accent of red thread covering the rear half of the head

Notes: From Kevin's published work on the Indigo Guide Service web site, indigoguideservice.com: "This fly is my evolution of the best spring-into-summer salmon fry pattern. From April through June, the Pere Marquette River and other Michigan streams become thick with young salmon in the 2 to 4 cm (¾" to 1½") range. They are an abundant and high protein food source that our resident trout and visiting steelhead focus on. This is a must-have pattern in my box for steelhead and trout swung behind an egg. When I'm just focusing on trout, we will use this fly to fish downstream around cover, riffles and drop-offs. Or my latest favorite is to fish it behind a larger attractor streamer. . . . 90 percent of the fish will come on the fry pattern."

4 EYES

- **Hook:** #4 Tiemco 3769
- **Eyes:** Medium brass bead chain, four beads long
- **Thread:** 140-denier, black
- **Tail:** Mirage Flashabou
- **Body:** UV Polar Chenille, any color
- **Hackle:** Schlappen
- **Head (optional):** Peacock herl twisted on thread for strength and then wrapped behind and between lead eyes

Notes: This pattern was created as a way for Kevin to use his favorite materials, Mirage Flashabou and Polar Chenille. The result is a fly that glows in the water and is a consistent producer for all the guides on the Indigo Guide Service crew.

EGG SUCKING SCULPIN

- **Hook:** #1 Daiichi 2151
- **Thread:** 140-denier, black
- **Tail:** Rag yarn, brown
- **Body:** Petite Estaz, pearl (or large Cactus Chenille)
- **Flash collar:** Flashabou, copper or red
- **Hackle:** Schlappen, mustard yellow or brown
- **Collar:** Rag yarn, brown (about a 5 cm [2"] piece fanned and tied over and under)
- **Head:** Standard Estaz, orange

Notes: This is a variation on Walt Grau's Easy Sculpin. Kevin says, "While the fly looks clunky dry, it transforms into an alive-looking imitation when wet." It imitates the prolific goby as well as a sculpin.

BASIC BUCKTAIL

- **Hook:** Gamakatsu Octopus, size #2-2/0
- **Tube:** Create a 5 cm (2") tube of double thickness by inserting a small-diameter tube into a medium-diameter tube and lightly burning the ends
- **Thread:** 210-denier
- **Body:** Standard Estaz, any color
- **Wing:** Bucktail
- **Overwing:** Flashabou

Notes: This is Kevin's go-to fly for the rivers of Western Michigan. He characterizes these rivers as "piles of snags with water running through them," thus the need for a simple pattern that he doesn't mind losing. He notes that he switched from Clousers to these tubes because the tube design allows the Flashabou to move freely without getting wrapped up in the bend of the hook. It also allows him to use a small Octopus hook, which he feels is easy on the fish and very effective at landing fish.

From the top: Four color variations on the Basic Bucktail tube; Egg Sucking Sculpin; Four Eyes, brown; Baby Salmon; Four Eyes, purple and black.

Ken Morrish

Ken is probably best known to steelheaders for his beautiful photography and popular fly patterns. He's also an outspoken environmentalist, fly-fishing instructor, consultant to tackle manufacturers, and co-owner of the Ashland, Oregon–based Fly Water Travel. Ken's images and flies have become integral parts of the foundation of modern steelheading, and we're honored to have them included here. He's also the only guy to turn in flies that imitate lizards! Cool stuff . . .

"I began tying about age 8 but got serious about it at age 10," he said. "I am now 45, so that makes 35 years at the vise so far."

Ken's father taught him the basics of tying and encouraged him to keep at it. "By the time I could tie a Brindle Bug that he was confident in fishing, he promptly stopped tying and began requesting that his boxes be kept full." By age 11, he was taking lessons at Creative Sports Enterprises in Walnut Creek, California. Steve Call, a strict protégé of Andy Puyans, drilled him on Catskill-style split duck quill wings and Humpies with split deer hair wings. "When Steve made the rounds between the students and came across subpar work, he would often torch the flies with a lighter while we were asking for advice. When the fly went up in smoke and the bobbin hit the table, we knew it was time to try again."

After Steve's tutelage, Ken graduated to tying for the main man—and owner of Creative Sports—Andy Puyans. "He spent a lot of time teaching specific techniques, and even more time helping us understand the subtle structures and properties of natural materials," Ken remembered. "It was the greatest education I could have hoped for."

Aside from his earlier teachers, Morrish credits his fly-tying inspiration to the influences of Dave Whitlock, Ed Haas, Syd Glasso, and the Intruder trio of Ward, French, and Howell. "There are lots of other tiers whose work I love, but those guys most shaped my style and interests."

Ken travels the world hosting trips with Fly Water Travel, including a few weeks each fall in Skeena Country. "The majority of my personal tying is steelhead focused, because that is what I really like to fish for," he said. "I do spend a lot of time designing flies for overseas production, and most of that tying is centered around trout flies, because they drive fly sales. I also tie and design saltwater patterns. But steelhead flies are my favorite."

OCTOBER CADDIS POMPADOUR (POM) SKATER

- **Hook:** #4-8 Tiemco 3769
- **Thread:** 140 or 210-denier, tan
- **Tail:** Krystal Flash, root beer
- **Underbody:** Krystal Flash, root beer, wrapped
- **Overbody:** 5 mm foam, tan, trimmed in a dramatic taper from 1 cm (⅜") wide at head down to 2 mm (1⁄16") wide at tail; additional trimming from bottom of tail and at corners of head
- **Throat/wings:** Deer body or belly hair, tan, spun and trimmed to create wings

Notes: Wrap a few strands of Krystal Flash around the thread when lashing down the foam. This prevents the thread from cutting through the foam, and it ends up looking great. Ken also notes that he when he secures the rear portion of foam, he posts around the base to prevent the foam from rotating on the shank.

The Pom Skater is durable, it skates high without a riffle hitch, and it cuts a nice wake. Ken says the other key consideration in designing the Pom was its attitude. "I wanted a fly that rode low enough in the back that it wouldn't get pushed away by a rising steelhead."

The pattern is also commonly tied like an "After Dinner Mint" with black foam, black deer hair and a

This perfect BC buck fell for one of Ken's Simple Prawns. Notice how the purple eyes stand out.

From the top: October Caddis Pompadour Skater; Nightshade Pompadour Skater; Monster Skater; two Steelhead Lizards, green and blue-belly.

From the top: Simple Prawn; Morrish's Medusa, black and pink; Ostrich Temptress, black and pink; Intruder, black and pink; Cold Medicine, black and gold.

green Krystal Flash body. The other popular color variation, called Nightshade, features black foam, purple deer hair, and a red Krystal Flash body.

MONSTER SKATER

- **Shank:** #4 Tiemco 9395, or equivalent straight-eye hook
- **Stinger loop:** 20-pound Fireline, flame green, doubled, 2.3 cm (⅞") long
- **Butt:** Deer belly hair, dyed hot pink, trimmed to create wings
- **Tail:** In three parts: 1) Midge Flash, chartreuse; 2) ostrich herl, pink, on the sides; 3) rabbit strip, gold, 5 cm (2") long, with guard hairs trimmed off all but the end
- **Underbody:** Petite Estaz, red, palmered with grizzly dry fly saddle, red
- **Throat/Wings:** Deer belly hair, hot pink, trimmed to create wings
- **Legs:** Grizzly barred rubber legs, white
- **Overbody:** 6 mm foam, white
- **Hook:** #2 Gamakatsu Octopus

Notes: This is the re-creation of a fly that Ken swung in British Columbia in early April 2011. It was early spring, with water temps still in the low 40s. His confidence in skated flies got the better of him, and he rose nine steelhead in one day! There's a lesson in there somewhere. . . .

STEELHEAD LIZARD, BLUE-BELLY

- **Hook:** #5 Daiichi Alec Jackson Steelhead Iron, nickel
- **Thread:** UNI Big Fly, blue
- **Body:** 3 mm foam, tan, glued to 2 mm foam, gray, trimmed in the shape of a lizard head and body, then cut down the belly to make a slot to insert the hook
- **Back/tail:** Barred rabbit strip, light brown, glued to the foam with Tear Mender
- **Legs:** Large grizzly barred rubber legs, tan, tied in bunches of three, then secured in leg positions while also securing the body to the hook
- **Eyes:** 3 mm holographic 3-D adhesive eyes, secured with superglue

Notes: With the hook in the vise, apply a small bead of superglue in the belly gap of the foam and press the foam body down on the hook. Tie in the legs while holding back the rabbit fur to make a space for the thread wraps. The finishing touches on the

Blue-Belly lizard require a blue Sharpie permanent marker. Ken colors the whole belly, and adds blue spots down each side. He offers this tip: "One of the guys at Hareline turned me on to Tear Mender to glue the hide down. It works great and is the main trick to this tie."

Typically these lizards were tied on Tiemco 700s (now discontinued), but the larger Blue-Belly was tied as described in the recipe above.

SIMPLE PRAWN

- **Hook:** #5-7 Daiichi Alec Jackson Steelhead Iron, nickel
- **Thread:** 6/0 UNI-Thread, red
- **Tail:** Polar bear or bucktail, peach or orange, with a small bunch of deer body hair, dyed orange, underneath the shank
- **Horn:** Grizzly hack tip, olive
- **Feelers:** Two strands of ostrich herl, olive
- **Eyes:** 4 mm metallic beads, purple, glued to burnt ends of 40-pound Maxima Ultragreen
- **Body:** Polar Chenille, orange, wrapped tight and folded like a hackle
- **Throat:** Ostrich herl, olive, four strands on each side
- **Shellback:** Ringneck pheasant rump feather, dyed olive

Notes: Ken ties huge trailing-hook versions of this fly as well, and he always ties them as sparsely as possible. This fly barely exists, yet casts a full profile through which the eyes can be easily distinguished.

MORRISH MEDUSA, PINK/BLACK

- **Shank:** #4 Tiemco 7999, or equivalent
- **Thread:** 6/0 UNI-Thread, fluorescent pink
- **Eyes:** Small painted lead eyes, white
- **Stinger loop:** 20-pound Fireline, crystal, doubled, 2.8 cm (1⅛") long
- **Tail:** Krystal Flash, pink, topped with a rabbit strip, black, 4.5 cm (1¾") long
- **Wings:** Tented pair of grizzly saddle hackle tips, natural
- **Hackle/skirt:** Marabou, pink
- **Legs:** Ostrich herl, black, three strands on each side
- **Ears:** Pair of hen neck feathers, black, tied so they flare away from the shank
- **Head:** Bunny fur, black, clumped and pulled back
- **Hook:** #2 Gamakatsu Octopus, red

From the top: Muddler Simplicity; three versions of Steelhead Simplicity; four of Jay's Retro series.

Notes: Ken admits he has a black-and-pink issue. But what we noticed most is that this is one of the few West Coast steelhead patterns that remind us of the sculpin patterns of the Midwest. Coincidence?

INTRUDER, BLACK/PINK

- **Shank:** #5 Daiichi Alec Jackson Steelhead Iron, nickel
- **Thread:** 6/0 UNI-Thread, fluorescent pink
- **Eyes:** Medium to large Pseudo Eyes
- **Stinger loop:** 20-pound Fireline, crystal, doubled, 2.8 cm (1⅛″) long
- **Tail:** Midge Flash, chartreuse
- **Butt:** Ice Dub, pink, spun in a dubbing loop, brushed, and folded as it's wrapped for maximum compression and flare
- **Rear hackle:** One turn of marabou, black
- **Split-tail:** Ostrich herl, pink, three strands on each side
- **Body:** Flashabou, black
- **Front dubbing bump:** Ice Dub, pink, spun in a dubbing loop, brushed, and folded as it's wrapped
- **Front hackle:** Craft Fur, black, spun in a dubbing loop, brushed, and folded as it's wrapped
- **Topping:** Ostrich herl, black, six strands
- **Collar:** Extra-large guinea hen, natural
- **Legs:** Ostrich herl, pink, three strands on each side
- **Shellback:** Tented pair of grizzly saddle hackle tips
- **Hook:** #2 Gamakatsu Octopus, red

Notes: Ken ties the sparsest Intruder we have seen, and this project has exposed us to quite a few. He likes to clip away some of the material from the underside of the fly to expose the full skeleton from underneath. His flies display a unique elegance, and a highly functional quality that can only come from immense skill and experience. Take a close look and soak it in.

COLD MEDICINE, BLACK/GOLD

- **Shank:** #4 Tiemco 9395, or equivalent straight-eye hook
- **Thread:** 6/0 UNI-Thread, fluorescent pink
- **Eyes:** Small to medium Pseudo Eyes
- **Stinger loop:** 20-pound Fireline, crystal, doubled, 2 cm (¾″) long
- **Tail:** Midge Flash, chartreuse, tied in under the shank
- **Butt:** Ice Dub, fluorescent hot pink
- **Rear dubbing bump:** Craft Fur, yellow, spun in a dubbing loop, brushed and folded as applied
- **Split-tail:** Ostrich herl, black, five strands on each side, topped with black and gold Flashabou
- **Body:** Holographic Diamond Braid tinsel, gold
- **Front dubbing bump:** Ice Dub, fluorescent hot pink
- **Front hackle:** In two parts back to front: 1) Craft Fur, yellow, spun in a dubbing loop, brushed and folded as applied; 2) ostrich herl, black, eight strands on each side
- **Topping:** Flashabou, black and gold
- **Head:** Flashabou, gold, wrapped over and around the eyes
- **Hook:** #2 Gamakatsu Octopus, red

Notes: Living somewhere between an Intruder and a Prom Dress, the Cold Medicine is Ken's flash fly. As with his Intruders, he likes to clip away some of the material to keep the underside open, showing off the innards of the fly.

OSTRICH TEMPTRESS, BLACK/PINK

- **Shank:** #5 Daiichi Alec Jackson Steelhead Iron, nickel
- **Thread:** 6/0 UNI-Thread, fluorescent pink
- **Eyes:** Medium to large Pseudo Eyes
- **Stinger loop:** 20-pound Fireline, crystal, doubled, 3.5 cm (1⅜″) long
- **Tail:** Krystal Flash, chartreuse
- **Butt:** Deer belly hair, dyed hot pink, tied in a reverse clump and pulled back
- **Split-tail:** Ostrich herl, black, four strands on each side, topped with Flashabou Polar Flash, black rainbow
- **Body:** Diamond Braid, purple
- **Front bump:** Deer belly hair, dyed hot pink, tied in a reverse clump and pulled back
- **Front hackle:** Ostrich herl, black, tied in reverse and pulled back
- **Flash:** Flashabou Polar Flash, black rainbow
- **Head:** Craft Fur, black, spun in a dubbing loop and "tamed" with Softex
- **Hook:** #2 Gamakatsu Octopus, red

Jay Nicholas

In addition to Jay's Simplicity series, which are featured in our step-by-step section starting on page 99, Jay has created a new series of shank-style flies that marry classic steelhead fly patterns with modern materials and design. He shares the story behind the development of the Retro series in the notes below.

MUDDLER SIMPLICITY

- **Hook:** #2-6 Daiichi 2141
- **Thread:** Whatever
- **Tail:** None
- **Body:** Flat braided tinsel, gold
- **Wing:** No turkey quill—only a wing of moose mane, with a few strands of Krystal Flash underneath
- **Head:** A spun head that is on the large side, blocky more often than rounded, intended to make waves and create disturbance

Notes: See our complete history and description of Muddler Simplicity on page 96.

STEELHEAD SIMPLICITY

- **Hook:** #2-6 Tiemco 700
- **Thread:** Whatever
- **Body:** Zowie Dub
- **Rib:** Oval tinsel, silver
- **Hackle:** Rooster saddle, leaning toward the webby side
- **Flash wing:** Krystal Flash or Flashabou

Notes: See our complete history and description of Steelhead Simplicity on page 102 and a list of Zowie Dub colors on pages 109–10.

JAY'S RETRO STEELHEAD THOR

- **Shank:** 25 mm Senyo's Articulated Shank or 32 mm OPST
- **Trailer line:** 30-pound Fireline, crystal
- **Hook:** #4 Gamakatsu Octopus, black or red
- **Tail:** Arctic fox, black, full
- **Body:** Medium chenille, fluorescent fire orange
- **Wing:** Pro Sportfisher Marble Fox, cream
- **Flash:** Mirage Lateral Flash, two strands each side
- **Cheek/eyes:** Jungle cock or substitute (optional)
- **Collar hackle:** Fluorescent orange saddle or schlappen
- **Thread:** 6/0 Veevus, black

JAY'S RETRO TIDEWATER SPECIAL

- **Shank:** 25 mm Senyo's Articulated Shank or 32 mm OPST
- **Trailer line:** 30-pound Fireline Crystal
- **Hook:** #4 Gamakatsu Octopus, black or red
- **Tail:** Arctic fox, Brown, full
- **Body:** Medium chenille, black
- **Wing:** Pro Sportfisher Marble Fox, cream
- **Flash:** Mirage Lateral Flash, two strands each side
- **Cheek/eyes:** Jungle cock or substitute (optional)
- **Collar hackle:** Badger cock hackle, dark, wide
- **Thread:** 6/0 Veevus, black

JAY'S RETRO POLAR SHRIMP

- **Shank:** 25 mm Senyo's Articulated Shank or 32 mm OPST
- **Trailer line:** 30-pound Fireline, crystal
- **Hook:** #4 Gamakatsu Octopus, black or red
- **Tail:** Arctic fox, Orange, full
- **Body:** Medium chenille, fluorescent shrimp pink
- **Wing:** Pro Sportfisher Marble Fox, cream
- **Flash:** Mirage Lateral Flash, two strands each side
- **Cheek/eyes:** Jungle cock or substitute (optional)
- **Collar hackle:** Fluorescent orange saddle or schlappen
- **Thread:** 6/0 Veevus, red or black

From the top: Muddler Simplicity; three versions of Steelhead Simplicity; four of Jay's Retro series.

JAY'S RETRO STEELHEAD ELEGANCE

- **Shank:** 25 mm Senyo's Articulated Shank or 32 mm OPST
- **Trailer line:** 30-pound Fireline Crystal
- **Hook:** #4 Gamakatsu Octopus, black or red
- **Tail:** Pro Sportfisher Marble Fox, hot cyan blue, full
- **Body:** Ice Dub, black, over superglue base
- **Wing:** Pro Sportfisher Marble Fox, black
- **Flash:** Mirage Lateral Flash, two strands each side
- **Cheek/eyes:** Jungle cock or substitute (optional)
- **Collar hackle:** Saltwater neck hackle, long webby, bright purple
- **Thread:** 6/0 Veevus, black

JAY'S RETRO LAST RESORT

- **Shank:** 25 mm Senyo's Articulated Shank or 32 mm OPST
- **Trailer line:** 30-pound Fireline Crystal
- **Hook:** #4 Gamakatsu Octopus, black or red
- **Tail:** Pro Sportfisher Marble Fox, royal blue, full
- **Body:** Medium chenille, fluorescent fire orange
- **Wing:** Pro Sportfisher Marble Fox, black
- **Flash:** Mirage Lateral Flash, two strands each side
- **Cheek/eyes:** Jungle cock or substitute (optional)
- **Collar hackle:** Black saddle or schlappen
- **Thread:** 6/0 Veevus, black

Notes: Jay fished all of these Retro flies with great success from January through April 2015. They are presented above in the order of the number of fish hooked on each. Jay explains the development of the pattern:

My roots back in the '60s, '70s, and '80s, tying and fishing steelhead flies, involved patterns like the Green Butt Skunk, Thor, and Polar Shrimp; flies tied with hackle tails, chenille bodies, white wings, and a saddle hackle collar. They were invariably tied on traditional hooks like the Eagle Claw 1197B at first and later on the TMC 700 and 7999. I never fished purples and blues for winter steelhead in those days, but the patterns I fished were very effective in their day, and in my heart, I've never abandoned my admiration for these flies. The Retro series featured here is the result of my attempt to reconfigure my favorite old patterns with some of the advantages of new fly-tying technology. On the water, I found these flies more effective than exact renditions of the flies I fished 30 and 40 years ago. I actually fished old-style flies tied on Eagle Claw 1197B hooks against these retro-style flies, and found the Retro series flies produced more grabs and fewer snags. I like the stinger hook much better than the traditional hook. I can rig the stinger with the hook point up, and it will slide over a lot of the twigs and sticks that I fish around. I like the very full tail and wings of arctic fox with just a tiny little pinch of flash. The wings and tails, dressed full and generously, have two seemingly contradictory properties: They are at the same time a bold profile, and they are translucent. These are nearly neutral-density flies: They sink, but they sink very slowly. They will not settle to the bottom in slow waters. On occasion I will tie these flies on an OPST (Olympic Peninsula Skagit Tactics) shank with a bead head for weight.

I have tied and fished these flies with dubbed bodies, and while I like the look of the dubbed bodies, I often keep tying with chenille rather than dubbing. Why? Because the chenille flies are every bit as effective as the dubbed flies, and I'm hopelessly convinced that chenille possesses magical and eternal fish attractant properties if one truly believes.

Flash? I always incorporate the flash, prefer the Mirage Lateral Flash over other materials, but remain unconvinced regarding whether the flash is essential or not.

Jungle cock? Purely for fun, although there are good imitations available. I'm old and have a few Jungle Cock capes in the drawer, so I'm going to put them to work before it's too late for me to enjoy them.

—Jay Nicholas, May 2015

Ethan Nickel

Ethan is one of the leading steelhead, trout, and salmon guides in Central and South Oregon, with over 20 years under his belt. Based in Eugene, Ethan is strategically located to access some of the best steelhead rivers in the world, with emphasis on the Deschutes, Willamette, and Umpqua. He's a great fly tier, and we're glad to be able to feature a couple of his more innovative patterns here.

BROKEBACK MUDDLER

- **Hook:** #4 Daiichi 1550
- **Extended head shank:** #8 Tiemco 5212
- **Thread:** 6/0 UNI-Thread, purple or black
- **Butt:** Twisted floss, red
- **Body:** Diamond Braid, purple
- **Rib:** Brass wire, extra small
- **Dubbing bump:** Ice Dub, purple
- **Legs:** Lady Amherst pheasant tail, two fibers per side
- **Flash:** Mirage Flashabou, opal
- **Wing:** Moose body hair
- **Head:** Deer body hair, dyed purple

Notes: Several innovative tiers have designed flies with extended heads to effectively eliminating the need for a riffle hitch. Ethan is the first we have encountered to take this "sacrificial hook" approach, and we can report that it skates extremely well. The added weight of the heavy-wire nymph hook helps to tilt the head upward and push the red butt below the surface. It's absolutely brilliant.

ZEBRA TUBE, BLUE/CHARTREUSE

- **Tube:** Small-diameter HMH rigid tube, cut to 2.5 cm (1") long
- **Thread:** 6/0 UNI-Thread, black
- **Underbody:** Diamond Braid, silver holographic, covering 1 cm (⅜") of tube
- **Hackle:** In three parts, from back to front: 1) Craft Fur, chartreuse; 2) Craft Fur, blue; 3) Craft Fur, black
- **Collar:** Schlappen, black, including one turn of the marabou fibers at the base of the feather
- **Flash:** Two strands of Mirage Flashabou, opal; four strands of Flashabou, pearl dyed black

Ethan displays a bruiser Oregon buck that made his winter season. ETHAN NICKEL SUPPLIED THE PHOTO, SHOT BY HIS BUDDY LES MARTIN

ZEBRA TUBE, BLACK/ORANGE

- **Tube:** Small-diameter HMH rigid tube, cut to 2.5 cm (1") long
- **Thread:** 6/0 UNI-Thread, orange
- **Underbody:** Diamond Braid, silver holographic, covering 1 cm (⅜") of tube
- **Hackle:** In three parts, from back to front; 1) Craft Fur, orange; 2) Craft Fur, black; 3) Craft Fur, black
- **Collar:** Golden pheasant shoulder feather, dyed orange
- **Flash:** Two strands of Mirage Flashabou, opal; four strands of Flashabou, pearl dyed black

From the top: Brokeback Muddler, purple; Zebra Tubes in two colors.

Mike Orlowski

Mike is very well known in the Vancouver steelheading scene and has inspired a new generation of fly tiers with his passion and creativity. He was among the first contributors to this project in 2008 and has evolved considerably since then. Even so, this collection is an authentic representation of Mike's style and of the types of flies that catch fish in Southwest British Columbia. Compare with the flies of Aaron Goodis (pages 209–10) to see some interesting parallels.

ARCTIC MUDDLER, BLACK/BLUE

- **Tube:** Small HMH tube, clear
- **Thread:** 210-denier, tan or brown
- **Tail:** In three parts, bottom to top: 1) arctic fox tail, blue; 2) Flashabou, blue; 3) arctic fox tail, black
- **Body:** Angora goat dubbing, black with blue highlights, palmered with grizzly saddle hackle
- **Rib:** Small wire, red
- **Collar:** Elk body hair
- **Head:** Elk body hair spun and trimmed tight to create a bullet-shaped head

MIKEY'S SHRIMP

- **Shank:** #1 Gamakatsu jig hook
- **Thread:** 210-denier, tan or brown
- **Hook:** #2 Gamakatsu Octopus, red
- **Stinger loop:** 30-pound Maxima Chameleon, 1 cm (⅜″) long—hook must be attached before tying
- **Butt:** Medium chenille, shell pink
- **Eyes:** Epoxy mono crab eyes, black
- **Tail:** Polar bear, orange, topped with arctic fox tail, red
- **Body:** Medium chenille, shell pink, palmered with Chinese saddle hackle, yellow
- **Rib:** 210-denier thread, tan or brown
- **Shellback:** Edge Brite, orange

MIKEY'S PRAWN

- **Shank:** 45 mm Waddington shank
- **Thread:** 140-denier, red
- **Weight:** Dumbbell eyes, painted flurescent orange
- **Stinger loop:** 30-pound Maxima Chameleon, 2.5 cm (1″) long
- **Butt:** Medium chenille, shell pink, wrapped over and around dumbbell eyes
- **Eyes:** Epoxy mono crab eyes, black
- **Rear hackle:** Rabbit fur, white tipped with orange, spun in a dubbing loop
- **Legs:** Silicone rubber legs, white with hot orange tips
- **Tail:** In three parts, bottom to top: 1) Midge Flash, pearl; 2) polar bear, orange; 3) grizzly saddle tips, orange, tied long
- **Body:** Dubbing blend, hot orange, palmered with Chinese saddle hackle, shell pink
- **Rib:** Medium wire, copper
- **Shellback:** Three pairs of golden pheasant neck feathers, dyed orange, tied in every ⅓ of body, with the last pair forming the final wing at the front end of the fly
- **Hook:** #1 or #2 Gamakatsu Octopus, barbless, nickel

MINI-INTRUDER, PINK/PURPLE

- **Shank:** 35 mm Waddington shank
- **Thread:** 140-denier, red
- **Stinger loop:** 30-pound Maxima Chameleon, 2.5 cm (1″) long
- **Butt:** Arctic fox, cerise, trimmed short and spun in a dubbing loop
- **Rear hackle:** Blue-eared pheasant or thin marabou, purple
- **Body:** Large wire, copper
- **Dubbing bump:** Arctic fox, cerise, trimmed short and spun in a dubbing loop
- **Front hackle:** Blue-eared pheasant or thin marabou, purple
- **Flash:** Midge Flash, pearl, and Flashabou, blue
- **Head:** Blend of yellow and hot orange Ice Dub, spun in a dubbing loop, brushed and folded as wrapped
- **Hook:** #1 or #2 Gamakatsu Octopus, black

From the top: Arctic Muddler, black and blue; Mikey's Shrimp; Mikey's Prawn; Mini-Intruder, pink and purple; Articulated Intruder, blue

ARTICULATED INTRUDER, BLUE

- **Shanks:** 23 mm (rear) and 28 mm (front) Waddington shanks
- **Thread:** 140-denier, black
- **Stinger loop:** 30-pound Maxima Chameleon, 2.5 cm (1") long
- **Butt:** Polar bear body hair, white, spun in a dubbing loop
- **Rear hackle:** In three parts, back to front: 1) ostrich herl, light blue; 2) schlappen, royal blue; 3) schlappen, black
- **Connector loop:** 50-pound Dacron backing material looped through eye of reach shank and lashed to front shank (and doubled over through eye of front shank for added security)
- **Eyes/weight (tied on front shank):** Small or medium brass eyes, nickel plated
- **Body:** Diamond Braid tinsel, kingfisher blue
- **Front dubbing bump:** Polar bear body hair, white, spun in a dubbing loop
- **Front hackle:** In three parts, back to front: 1) ostrich herl, light blue; 2) schlappen, royal blue; 3) schlappen, black
- **Hook:** #1 or #2 Gamakatsu Octopus, black

Jason Osborn

Within our network of obsessed steelheaders, Jason Osborn stands out for being just a little more obsessed than the rest. Even after 10 years of guiding in Washington's legendary Skamania region, Jason's fire burns bright, especially in the fall when steelhead can be found behind almost every rock in southwest Washington. He is the manager of Northwest Fly Fishing Outfitters, a family-owned shop with a friendly vibe on Portland's East Side. For all of Jason's passion and enthusiasm for steelhead fishing and fly tying, he is a quiet man who listens well and chooses his words carefully. It wasn't until 2013 that we finally got a chance to look at Jason's steelhead box, and we immediately knew he would be featured in this book. His flies embody today's modern fly styles with their seamless blending of European and North American influences but with a Pacific Northwest feel. He is very knowledgeable about new fly-tying innovations and has helped to bring new products like the Pro Sportfisher lineup (Pro Tubes) to a wider audience.

TUXEDO

- **Tube:** Pro Tube Flexitube 40/10, clear
- **Thread:** UTC 140-denier, black
- **Tag:** Small French oval tinsel, red floss
- **Tail:** Golden pheasant tippet, golden pheasant crest
- **Butt:** Ostrich herl, black
- **Body:** In two parts, back to front: 1) flat Mylar tinsel, silver; 2) Hare's Ear Plus Dubbin, black, palmered with Chinese saddle hackle
- **Rib:** Small French oval tinsel
- **Wing:** Arctic fox, white, topped with Finnish raccoon, black
- **Flash:** Angel Hair, UV white, between the arctic fox and the Finnish raccoon
- **Topping:** Four strands of peacock herl
- **Collar:** Gadwall or mallard flank
- **Eyes:** Medium Pro Jungle Cock HD, natural

9-VOLT

- **Tube:** Pro Tube Microtube, black
- **Thread:** UTC 140-denier, black
- **Weight:** Small Pro Drop Weight, black
- **Butt:** Senyo's Laser Dub, pink
- **Tail:** Ostrich herl, purple, barred with a black Sharpie permanent marker, topped with Flashabou, purple
- **Body:** Polar Chenille, copper
- **Hackle:** In four parts, back to front: 1) arctic fox tail, black, spun in a dubbing loop; 2) marabou, lavender; 3) marabou, cerise; 4) marabou, black
- **Flash:** Flashabou, copper
- **Disc:** Small Pro Ultra Sonic Disc, black chrome
- **Junction tubing:** Pro Hookguide, purple

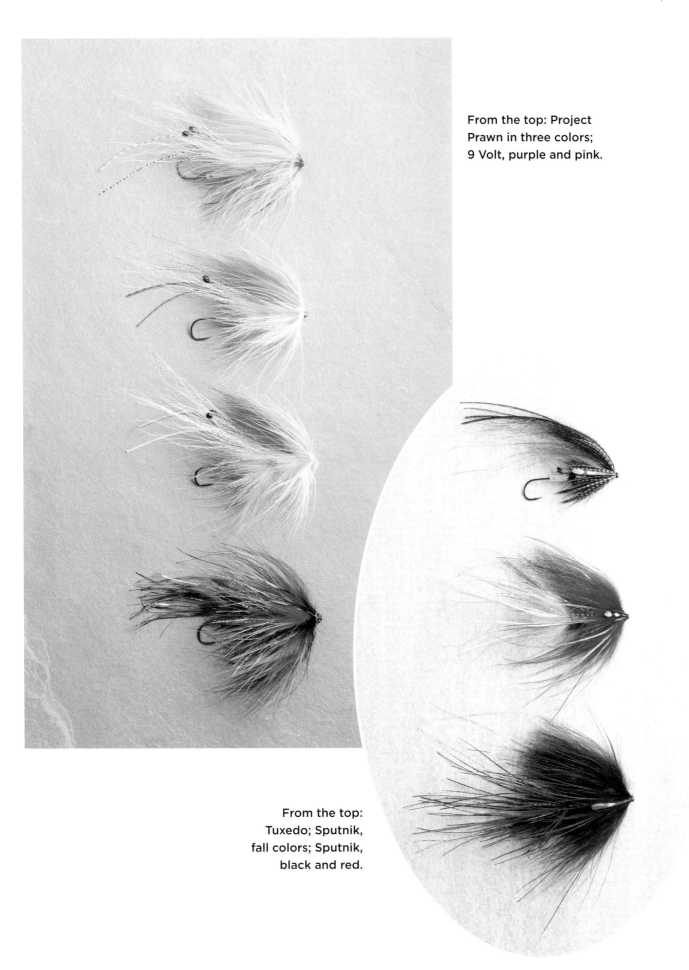

From the top: Project Prawn in three colors; 9 Volt, purple and pink.

From the top: Tuxedo; Sputnik, fall colors; Sputnik, black and red.

PROJECT PRAWN

- **Tube:** Pro Tube Microtube, clear
- **Thread:** UTC 140-denier, red
- **Weight:** Small nickel-plated lead eyes
- **Rear hackle:** In two parts, back to front: 1) arctic fox, white, trimmed short and spun in a dubbing loop; 2) marabou, peach or shell pink
- **Tail:** Bucktail, white, topped with barred silicone rubber legs, orange with black bars
- **Body:** Medium flat Mylar tinsel, opal
- **Under hackle:** Arctic fox, white, spun in a dubbing loop
- **Eyes:** Epoxy mono crab eyes, black
- **Wing:** Finnish raccoon, orange, topped with marabou, peach
- **Flash:** Angel Hair, electric shrimp
- **Hackle:** Marabou, white
- **Collar:** Schlappen, white
- **Junction tubing:** Pro Hookguide, clear

SPUTNICK, FALL COLORS

- **Tube:** Pro Tube Flexitube 40/10, clear
- **Thread:** UTC 140-denier, black
- **Butt:** In two parts, back to front: 1) Ice Wing, yellow pearl; 2) arctic fox tail, yellow
- **Split tail:** Ostrich herl, six strands on each side, topped with Krystal Flash, yellow, three strands on each side
- **Body:** Senyo's Laser Dub, transitioning from yellow to orange to red, from back to front; ribbed with large Mylar tinsel, opal; and palmered with Chinese saddle hackle, yellow, colored red at the tip so the hackle transitions opposite the dubbing color once wrapped
- **Over rib:** Small wire
- **Dubbing bump:** Senyo's Laser Dub, purple
- **Weight:** Small Pro Raw Weight
- **Under hackle:** Arctic fox tail, purple, spun in a dubbing loop
- **Wing:** Finnish raccoon, claret
- **Flash:** Angel Hair, pink copper; Krystal Flash, purple; and Krinkle Mirror Flash
- **Hackle:** In two parts, back to front: 1) ostrich herl, claret, spun in a dubbing loop; 2) marabou, wine
- **Collar:** Schlappen, purple
- **Eyes:** Jungle cock nails

Steve Perakis

Those of us who surround ourselves with other anglers know one or two people who make a point of being secretive and elusive. Very often this behavior is driven by the disturbing reality that our rivers and fish are under increasing pressure, even as their numbers are diminishing. They avoid cameras and crowds, and they work very hard to carve out some small space where they can find solitude in their fishing. Our friend Steve Perakis acknowledges that he is one of these people, though he is mellowing with age. Over the years he has been source of wisdom and inspiration, while also being a staunch advocate for keeping one's mouth shut. And let's be honest: Most people who advocate an open-mouth policy on steelhead fishing are trying to get something out of you or sell you something.

Steve is regarded by his friends and peers as a master steelheader, especially when it comes to tricking summer-run fish. We never thought he would agree to share his personal fly patterns with the world, but we lucked out, and so did you.

HOLO GNAT

- **Hook:** #10 Tiemco 7999, black
- **Tail:** Hackle fibers, black
- **Body:** Holographic Flashabou, black
- **Dubbing bump:** Hareline Custom Blend Dub, black, or alternative
- **Hackle:** Small saddle hackle, black
- **Wing:** Arctic fox tail, black

Clockwise from top: Crude Muddler, natural; Green Cree Hilton; Flood Cab; River Squid in two colors (bottom two flies); Santiam GP; Holo Gnat.

Steve takes a break from domestic responsibilities in the man cave. STEVE PERAKIS PHOTO

GREEN CREE HILTON

- **Hook:** #2-8 Tiemco 7999, black
- **Thread:** 6/0, red
- **Tail:** Wood duck flank
- **Rib:** Medium French oval tinsel, silver
- **Abdomen:** Floss, chartreuse
- **Thorax:** STS Trilobal Dub, black
- **Wings:** Creek hackle tips, flared
- **Hackle:** Soft saddle, brown

CRUDE MUDDLER, TAN

- **Hook:** #2-8 Daiichi 1850 flat-eye streamer hook
- **Thread:** 70-denier, fluorescent red
- **Tail:** Krystal Flash, golden olive
- **Body:** Diamond Braid, gold
- **Wing:** Krystal Flash, golden olive, topped with deer body hair
- **Head:** Deer body hair spun and roughly trimmed into a rectangular prism that is tilted upward in the front about 45 degrees

SANTIAM GP

- **Hook:** #3-5 Alec Jackson Steelhead Iron, black
- **Thread:** 6/0, black
- **Tail:** Bucktail, black, with two strands of Krystal Flash, peacock
- **Rib:** Small French tinsel, silver
- **Body weilings:** Two equal sections in two steps: 1) Hareline Custom Blend Dub, black, spun in a dubbing loop; 2) ring hackle of long Chinese saddle, black
- **Wing:** Two strands of Krystal Flash, peacock, topped with a golden pheasant neck or shoulder feather, dyed black

FLOOD CAB

- **Hook:** #1.5-3/0 Alec Jackson Steelhead Iron, gold
- **Thread:** 6/0, red
- **Butt:** Very small ball of Ice Dub, chartreuse
- **Tail:** Pair of slender saddle hackle tips, chartreuse
- **Body, rear half:** Medium French tinsel, silver
- **Body, front half:** Hareline Custom Blend Dub, hot pink, palmered with Chinese saddle hackle, hot pink
- **Rib:** Small wire, silver
- **Collar:** Schlappen, shell pink
- **Wing:** Micro Flashabou, pearl, topped with a small bunch of calf tail, white

RIVER SQUID, PURPLE/ORANGE

- **Tube:** Two parts: 1) Small Pro Tube Classic, purple holographic, cut to 3 cm (1³⁄₁₆″) long; 2) extra-small Pro Tube classic, clear, cut to 2.5 cm (1″) long and inserted in the other tube so that 5 mm (³⁄₁₆″) is sticking out the front
- **Weight:** Plummeting tungsten bead, gold, slid onto the extra-small front tube and lightly melted in place
- **Thread:** 6/0, orange
- **Butt:** Cactus Chenille, purple
- **Body:** Estaz, purple
- **Tentacles:** Four golden pheasant crests
- **Hackle:** In two parts, back to front: 1) long Spey hackle, purple; 2) eight strands of ostrich herl, purple
- **Flash:** Flashabou, purple
- **Collar:** Schlappen, orange
- **Cheeks:** Jungle cock nails
- **Head:** Angora goat dubbing, orange

Charlie Piette

Charlie is the manager of Tight Lines Fly Fishing Company in DePere, Wisconsin, and is widely regarded for his uncanny fishing and tying abilities. Most of his year is spent chasing smallmouth, muskies, and trout, but steelhead hold a special place in his heart. He devotes a few months a year to swinging Great Lakes rivers, and sometimes he gets out to Oregon or Washington to feed his anadromous streak. Back in 2007 or 2008—early in the development of this book—several people pointed us to Charlie as one of the best steelhead tiers in the Midwest. We're very pleased to be finally sharing his flies here.

ARCTIC FOX TEARDROP TUBE, BLACK/CHARTREUSE

- **Tube:** Eumer 15 mm x 4 mm teardrop tube, brass, with a small plastic tube inserted, 3 cm long (1³⁄₁₆″)
- **Thread:** 70- or 140-denier, black
- **Wing:** In four parts, bottom to top: 1) arctic fox body fur with guard hairs, chartreuse; 2) Krinkle Mirror Flash, chartreuse; 3) arctic fox tail with guard hairs, black; 4) Krystal Flash, pearl dyed black
- **Collar:** In two parts, back to front: 1) schlappen, black; 2) guinea hen, chatreuse
- **Cheeks:** Jungle cock nails
- **Head:** Medium or large brass conehead
- **Junction tubing:** Eumer medium tubing, clear, 1.3 cm (½″) long, fitted on protruding end of plastic tubing and glued in place, if necessary

MARABOU TUBE, BLACK/PURPLE

- **Tube:** Small HMH plastic tubing, 3.5 cm (1³⁄₈″) long
- **Thread:** 70- or 140-denier, black
- **Butt:** Hareline Dubbin, black
- **Tail:** Bucktail, black, topped with Krystal Flash, pearl dyed black
- **Body:** Ice Dub, black, palmered with schlappen, black
- **Front hackle:** In two parts, back to front: 1) marabou, purple; 2) marabou, black (wing is inserted between)
- **Wing:** Holographic Flashabou, purple haze, 20 to 25 strands tied in between the purple and black marabou
- **Collar:** Mallard or gadwall flank, long

- **Cheeks:** Jungle cock nails
- **Junction Tubing:** Standard HMH soft junction tubing, 1.3 cm (½″) long

BUNNY TAIL TUBE, BLACK/BLUE

- **Tube:** Small HMH plastic tubing, 4 cm (1½″) long
- **Thread:** 140-denier, black
- **Weight:** Medium brass dumbbell eyes, black finish
- **Tail:** Rabbit strip, black, pinned down with a few thread wraps after the rest of the fly is finished
- **Body:** Ice Dub, peacock, wrapped to 3 mm (⅛″) behind the dumbbell eyes, palmered with Polar Chenille, black
- **Wing:** Rabbit strip, black, 4.5 cm (1¾″) long
- **Flash:** Holographic Flashabou, blue, topped with standard Flashabou, blue
- **Dubbing bump:** Ice Dub, peacock, wrapped in a figure eight around the eyes
- **Hackle:** In two parts, back to front: 1) marabou, royal blue; 2) marabou, black
- **Junction tubing:** Standard HMH soft junction tubing, 1.3 cm (½″) long

STRING LEECH SCULPIN, PURPLE/BLACK

- **Shank:** Any straight-eye hook
- **Eyes:** Small or medium Ballzeyes
- **Stinger loop:** 20-pound Tuf-Line or equivalent, 6.4 cm (2½″) long
- **Tail:** Flashabou, grape
- **Body:** Polar Chenille, purple
- **Wing:** Rabbit strip, black, 6 cm (1⅜″) long; using a large sewing needle, thread stinger loop through the wing in two places and loop on hook
- **Flash:** Krystal Flash, pearl dyed black
- **Head:** Ice Dub, purple, clumped in above and below eyes and brushed back
- **Hook:** #1 or #2 Gamakatsu Wide Gap

Top row: Arctic Fox Teardrop Tube, black and chartreuse; Marabou Tube, black and purple. Second row: Bunny Tail Tube, black and blue; String Leech Sculpin, purple and black. Third row: Intruder, black; Intruder, gold and gray. Bottom: Intruder, purple.

INTRUDER, GOLD/GRAY

- **Tube:** HMH aluminum tube 5 cm (2″) long, lined with micro tubing and lightly melted on each end to hold aluminum tube in place
- **Thread:** 70- or 140-denier, black
- **Eyes:** Small Ballzeyes
- **Butt:** Ice Dub, peacock
- **Rear hackle:** In two parts, back to front: 1) schlappen, black; 2) Spey plume or ostrich herl, black, spun in a dubbing loop
- **Body:** Large flat French tinsel, gold, palmered with saddle hackle, gray
- **Under hackle:** Moose body hair, spun around the full circumference of the tube
- **Wing:** 10 to 12 strands of ostrich herl, natural gray
- **Front hackle:** Schlappen, black
- **Collar:** Mallard or gadwall flank, long
- **Head:** Ice Dub, peacock, wrapped behind and over eyes
- **Junction tubing:** Standard HMH soft junction tubing, 1.3 cm (½″) long

INTRUDER, BLACK

- **Tube:** Small HMH rigid tubing, cut to 5 cm (2″) long
- **Thread:** 70- or 140-denier, black
- **Eyes:** Medium or large painted lead, red
- **Butt:** Ice Dub, peacock
- **Rear Hackle:** Schlappen, black
- **Tail:** Ostrich herl, black, eight strands tied in on each side of the tube to create a split-tail
- **Body:** Ice Dub, peacock, palmered with Polar Chenille, black

- **Under hackle:** Moose body hair, spun around the full circumference of the tube
- **Wing:** Pair of grizzly hackle tips, tied 7.6 cm (3″) long
- **Front hackle:** Schlappen, black
- **Collar:** Mallard or gadwall flank, long
- **Head:** STS Trilobal Dub, hot pink, wrapped behind and over eyes
- **Junction tubing:** Standard HMH soft junction tubing, 1.3 cm (½″) long

INTRUDER, PURPLE

- **Tube:** Small, rigid HMH tubing cut to 5 cm (2″) long
- **Thread:** 70- or 140-denier, black
- **Eyes:** Medium or large painted lead, yellow
- **Butt:** STS Trilobal Dub, black
- **Rear hackle:** In two parts, back to front: 1) schlappen, black; 2) blue-eared pheasant shoulder, dyed purple
- **Tail:** Barred ostrich herl, purple, eight strands tied in on each side of the tube to create a split-tail
- **Body:** STS Trilobal Dub, black, palmered with Polar Chenille, purple
- **Under hackle:** Moose body hair, spun around the full circumference of the tube
- **Front hackle:** In two parts, back to front: 1) schlappen, black; 2) blue-eared pheasant shoulder, dyed purple
- **Wing:** Pair of grizzly hackle tips, tied 7.6 cm (3″) long
- **Head:** STS Trilobal Dub, black, wrapped behind and over eyes
- **Junction tubing:** Standard HMH soft junction tubing, 1.3 cm (½″) long

Dave Pinczkowski

Dave is a legendary Wisconsin fly guide and fly designer with a devoted following. Some of his background and inspiration is relayed in chapter 5, "Third Coast Swing." When it comes to steelhead flies, Dave's genius lies in creating simple, easy-to-tie forage fish imitations that are fully three-dimensional. He pops up in a number of places in this book, but for more insight into this special fly designer, be sure to check out Dave's segments in the DVD *Skagit Master Volume 4: Cracking the Code* as well has his many online tying videos.

PINCH'S SKID PLATE SKATER TUBE (ALL-NATURAL VERSION)

- **Tube:** Large Heritage Angling fluorescent tube, orange, melted and flattened with pliers to achieve a 45-degree angle. Underneath the resulting plastic head, poke a hole with a hot needle for the tippet to pass through.
- **Body:** Burnt orange dubbing containing a mix of Angora goat or seal fur and synthetics with some subtle sparkle
- **Wings:** Hen feathers
- **Head/legs:** Moose body hair
- **Hook/rigging:** Simply thread your tippet through the hole in the tube, tie on a #4 Gamakatsu B10S hook, and pull the hook up into the tube. The eye of the B10S fits perfectly in the large Heritage tube, allowing you to set the hook so it rides point down or point up, according to your preference.

PINCH'S SKID PLATE INDY SKATER

- **Tube:** Large Heritage Angling fluorescent tube, orange or green, melted and flattened with pliers to achieve a 45-degree angle. Underneath the resulting plastic head, poke a hole with a hot needle for the tippet to pass through.
- **Wing/head:** Deer body hair in preferred color. Dave's favorites are black (using a chartreuse tube), fluorescent orange (using an orange tube), and a combination of fluorescent orange and chartreuse.
- **Legs:** Krystal Flash, any color

- **Hook/rigging:** Simply thread your tippet through the hole in the tube, #4 Gamakatsu B10S hook, and pull the hook up into the tube. The eye of the B10S fits perfectly in the large Heritage tube, allowing you to set the hook so it rides point down or point up, according to your preference.

CRAFTOBER CADDIS

- **Tube:** Large Heritage Angling fluorescent tube, orange or green, melted and flattened with pliers to achieve a 45-degree angle. Underneath the resulting plastic head, poke a hole with a hot needle for the tippet to pass through.
- **Body:** Burnt orange dubbing containing a mix of Angora goat or seal fur and synthetics with some subtle sparkle
- **Wing/head:** Craft Fur, dark brown
- **Legs:** Krystal Flash, any color
- **Hook/rigging:** Simply thread your tippet through the hole in the tube, tie on a #4 Gamakatsu B10S hook, and pull the hook up into the tube. The eye of the B10S fits perfectly in the large Heritage tube, allowing you to set the hook so it rides point down or point up, according to your preference.

RECEDING HAIR LINE TUBE, SCULPIN

- **Tube:** Small Heritage Angling fluorescent tube, green
- **Layered wing:** In four parts, bottom to top: 1) Craft Fur, light brown; 2) Flashabou, copper and Kelly green; 3) Craft Fur, light olive; 4) Craft Fur, dark olive. Trim ends to create a sculpin-sized head. Barring is applied with a black Sharpie permanent marker.
- **Junction tubing:** Heritage Angling soft tubing, green
- **Hook:** #3 Gamakatsu B10S

Notes: This pattern is the model of simplicity yet provides a stunning profile with unparalleled movement.

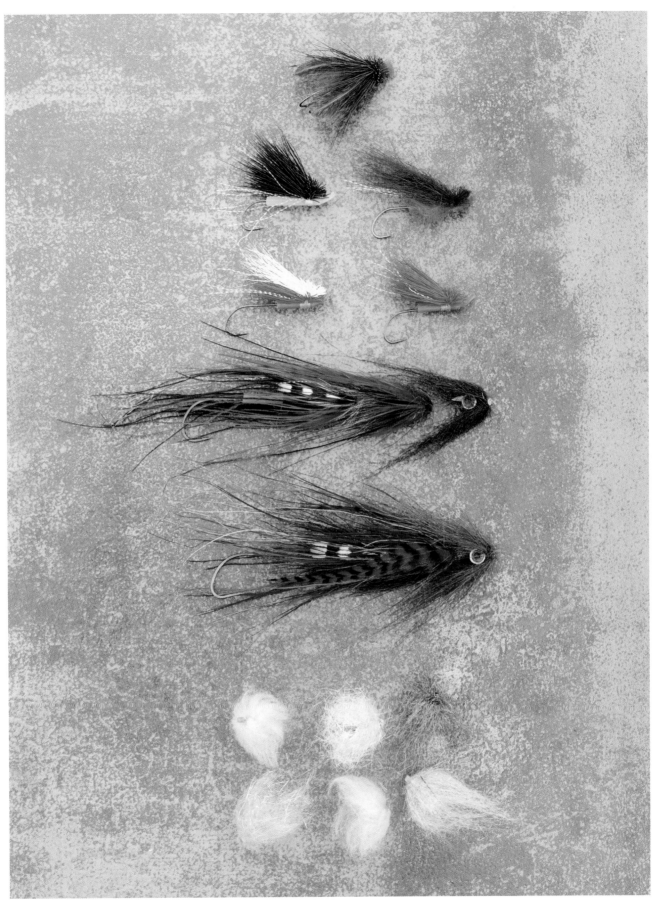

From the top: Pinch's Skid Plate Skater Tube; Pinch's Indie Skater Tube, black and green; Craftober Caddis; two-color variations of the Indie Skater Tube; Converta-truder, black and orange; Converta-truder, purple and pink; Slide-on Eggs in six colors.

From the top: Receding Hair Line Tube, Crafter Dinner Mint; Receding Hair Line Tube, sculpin; Receding Hair Line Tube, smelt; Eat a Peach Sculpin, black; Eat a Peach Leech, black; Eat a Peach Sculpin, olive.

From the top: Bad Hair Day Sculpin, Wisco Version; Bad Hair Day Converta-Tube, black and purple; three Bad Hair Day Steelhead Tube variations; Bad Hair Day Converta-Tube, Bait.

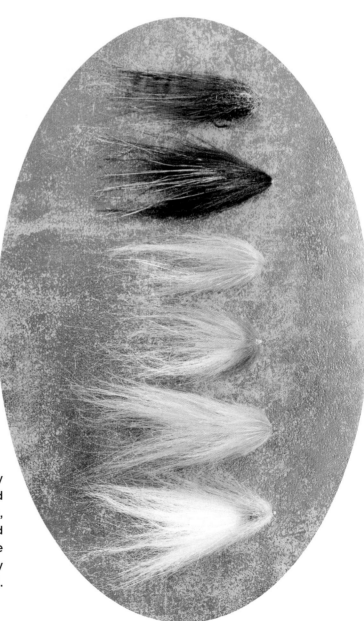

RECEDING HAIR LINE TUBE, SMELT

- **Tube:** Small Heritage Angling fluorescent tube, clear
- **Layered wing:** In four parts, bottom to top: 1) Craft Fur, white; 2) Angel Hair, green pearl; 3) Craft Fur, greenish gray; 4) Craft Fur, gray. Trim ends to create a sculpin-sized head.
- **Junction tubing:** Heritage Angling soft tubing, green
- **Hook:** #4 Gamakatsu B10S

RECEDING HAIR LINE TUBE, CRAFTER DINNER MINT

- **Tube:** Medium Heritage Angling sparkle tube, green
- **Layered Wing:** In three parts, bottom to top: 1) Craft Fur black; 2) Flashabou, grape; 3) Craft Fur black. Trim ends to create a sculpin-sized head.
- **Junction Tubing:** Heritage Angling soft tubing, green
- **Hook:** Gamakatsu B10S

BAD HAIR DAY STEELHEAD TUBE & VARIATIONS

- **Tube:** Small Heritage Angling tube, pink, green, or orange
- **Butt (optional):** Ice Dub, pearl, pink, or orange
- **Body/wing:** In four or more parts, back to front: 1) Craft Fur, white, tied in reverse around the entire circumference of the tube, sliced back using water or spit to get it out of your way; 2) Craft Fur, orange, tied in reverse; 3) Angel Hair, pink; 4) Craft Fur, pink
- **Junction tubing:** Heritage Angling soft tubing
- **Hook:** #4 Gamakatsu B10S

Notes: Dave ties his Bad Hair Day tubes in a variety of sizes and color combos, including a "double," which is built with two stations like an Intruder to achieve supreme size. Often, for longer tubes, he will repeat the middle and front reverse-clumping of Craft Fur, bringing the number of body/wing parts to five or six. Various types of flash can be integrated anywhere in the fly.

BAD HAIR DAY SCULPIN, WISCO VERSION

- **Hook:** #2 Gamakatsu B10S
- **Tail/butt:** Craft Fur, light olive and brown, simply lashed to the hook
- **Flash:** Flashabou, copper and Kelly green
- **Body/wing:** In three parts, back to front: 1) Craft Fur, dark olive, tied in reverse and slicked back; 2) Angel Hair, rusty olive; 3) Craft Fur, black, tied in reverse and slicked back
- **Head:** Ice Dub, olive, clumped and brushed back
- **Barring:** Black Sharpie permanent marker

Notes: This is Dave's original Craft Fur streamer, originally created for smallies. It quickly proved itself to be a great steelhead fly concept, prompting the tube versions that place the hook farther back. Besides the Wisconsin version described here, Dave makes his Bad Hair Days with egg heads, clumping bright Ice Dub and peach-colored Egg Yarn. This is also the fly that inspired Jason Koertge to employ reverse-clumped Craft Fur into a tube-Intruder design, resulting in the Fur Burger (page 76).

BAD HAIR DAY CONVERTA-TUBE, BAIT

- **Tube:** Large Heritage Angling fluorescent tube, orange or green
- **Tail/butt:** Craft Fur, white, simply lashed to the hook
- **Flash:** Flashabou, copper and Kelly green
- **Body/wing:** In four parts, back to front: 1) Craft Fur, white, tied in reverse and slicked back; 2) Flashabou, pearl; 3) Craft Fur, white, tied in reverse and slicked back; 4) Craft Fur, gray, tied in reverse and slicked back
- **Head:** On a separate piece of small, clear tubing (one that will fit firmly inside the large tubing used for the fly), tie on dumbbell eyes of choice then add one clump of gray Craft Fur in reverse, slick back, and center tie a couple of clumps of gray Ice dub to finish.

Notes: This style is great in any number of color combinations and weights, and it allows the angler to have a set of heads of varying weight to adjust to conditions.

EAT A PEACH SCULPIN

- **Hook:** #2 Gamakatsu B10S
- **Tail/butt:** Craft Fur, light olive and brown, simply lashed to the hook
- **Flash:** Flashabou, copper and Kelly green
- **Body/wing:** In three parts, back to front: 1) Craft Fur, light olive; 2) Flashabou, copper, Kelly green, and grape; 3) Craft Fur, dark olive, two consecutive bunches tied in reverse and slicked back
- **Head:** Ice Dub, flame, topped with Glo-Bug yarn, light roe, clumped and brushed back
- **Barring:** Black Sharpie permanent marker

EAT A PEACH LEECH

- **Tube:** Small Heritage Angling tube, pink, green or orange
- **Tail/butt:** Craft Fur, black, simply lashed to the hook
- **Flash:** Flashabou, copper and Kelly green
- **Body/wing:** In three parts, back to front: 1) Craft Fur, light olive; 2) Flashabou, copper and grape; 3) Craft Fur, black, two consecutive bunches tied in reverse and slicked back
- **Head:** Ice Dub, flame (or top with Glo-Bug yarn, light roe, clumped, and brushed back)

CONVERTA-TRUDER, RHEA

- **Tube:** Large Heritage Angling tube, pink, green, or orange
- **Butt:** Add a small bump of Ice Dub, any color, followed by a dubbing loop of deer hair and another dubbing loop of rhea fibers to create the rear "hackle."
- **Rear eyes:** Jungle cock nails
- **Body:** Ice Dub, any color, palmered with saddle hackle and ribbed with Mylar tinsel
- **Front hackle:** Spun deer hair followed by a dubbing loop of rhea fibers, and finished with a schlappen collar
- **Head:** On a separate piece of small, tubing (one that will fit firmly inside the large tubing used for the fly), tie on dumbbell eyes of choice then add one clump of Craft Fur in reverse, slick back and finish.

Notes: The removable head/weight is a fresh idea, and proof of Dave's innovative genius! This Intruder variation can be tied in any color combination; Dave likes purple/pink and orange/black the best.

Justin Pribanic

Justin is one of our Great Lakes brothers pounding it out on the public waters of Steelhead Alley and surrounding areas. Our good friend Matt Stansberry sent us in Justin's direction after seeing his flies, and we are stoked to include some here. West Coast steelheaders would do well to study Justin's contributions; compare them with those of Charlie Piette, Jerry Darkes, Kevin Feenstra, and Dave Pinczkowski; and ask themselves if there are themes here that could elevate their steelhead game. Are there woody stretches of your favorite stream that you've been ignoring because they eat flies? These guys deal with that every day and have come up with some workable options.

EMERALD SHINER

- **Tube:** Small HMH plastic tube, clear
- **Thread:** UTC 140-denier, white
- **Butt:** Ice Dub, chartreuse
- **Rear hackle:** Marabou, white
- **Body:** Diamond Braid, holographic silver
- **Front dubbing bump:** Ice Dub, chartreuse
- **Front hackle:** In three parts, back to front: 1) schlappen, white; 2) rhea, olive, and Lady Amherst pheasant center tail fibers spun in a dubbing loop; 3) marabou, white
- **Flash wing:** Krinkle Mirror Flash and holographic Flashabou, silver
- **Collar:** Guinea hen, chartreuse

Notes: Justin credits Larimer's Reverse Marabou as the structural inspiration for this Intruder-style tube fly. He took the Larimer style and developed a color scheme to imitate the most prevalent baitfish in the Great Lakes.

Top: Hackle Flash Sculpin. Second row: Polar Flash Minnow; Double Decker. Third row: Polar Flash Egg Sucking Leech; Lumber Dumper. Fifth row: Emerald Shiner. Bottom: Sculpin Somethin'.

LUMBER DUMPER

- **Tube:** Small HMH plastic tube, clear
- **Thread:** UTC 140-denier, red
- **Weight:** Medium bead chain, tied in 6 mm (¼″) behind the front end of the tube
- **Body:** Ice Dub, steelie blue, palmered with Polar Chenille, purple
- **Wing:** Grizzly barred rabbit strip, purple
- **Hackle:** Marabou, purple
- **Flash:** Krinkle Mirror Flash and holographic Flashabou, purple and blue combined
- **Collar:** Guinea hen, purple
- **Head:** Senyo's Laser Dub, hot pink

Notes: The Lumber Dumper is Justin's quick tie for chucking into wood piles. Since Great Lakes steelhead are often found congregating in log jams, it's smart to have a stock of simple bugs in the box that you don't mind losing. As Justin says, "It doesn't hurt as much as losing a full-dress Intruder."

DOUBLE DECKER

- **Shanks:** Two 20 mm Fish Skull Articulated Shanks
- **Thread:** UTC 140-denier, red
- **Stinger loop:** 30-pound Fireline, 3.2 cm (1¼″) long
- **Tag:** Small Mirage tinsel, opal
- **Dubbing bump:** Senyo's Laser Dub, hot pink
- **Hackle:** In two parts, back to front: 1) Flashabou, grape, clumped on top and bottom of shank in reverse and pulled back; 2) marabou, purple
- **Collar:** Guinea hen, pink
- **Hook:** #4 or #6 Gamakatsu Octopus, black

Notes: It's probably obvious, but in the interest of clarity, the stinger loop is tied into the first of two identical half flies. Then that first fly is inserted into the rear loop of the second shank, and the front half fly is tied.

SCULPIN SOMETHIN'

- **Shank:** #1 or #1/0 Tiemco 7999 or equivalent
- **Thread:** UTC 140-denier, black
- **Stinger loop:** 30-pound Fireline, 2.5 cm (1″) long
- **Eyes:** Small Ballzeyes
- **Tail:** Grizzly barred rabbit strip, olive
- **Butt:** Ice Dub, chartreuse
- **Body:** Flat Diamond Braid, chartreuse, palmered with UV Polar Chenille, silver
- **Under hackle:** Deer belly hair, olive, spun
- **Hackle:** In three parts from back to front, all spun in a dubbing loop: 1) Lady Amherst pheasant center tail, chartreuse; 2) ostrich herl, olive; 3) ostrich herl, black
- **Legs:** Barred silicone legs, olive with green flake/black bars, three per side
- **Collar:** Artic fox tail, black, spun in a dubbing loop
- **Hook:** #4 or #6 Gamakatsu Octopus, black

Notes: Another superb riff on the Intruder style, sized down to a crittery sculpin profile.

HACKLE FLASH SCULPIN

- **Shank:** 55 mm Fish Skull Articulated Shank, cut down to 40 mm (rear loop cut off)
- **Thread:** UTC 210-denier, black
- **Eyes:** Medium bead-chain, brass, two beads per side
- **Stinger loop:** 30-pound Fireline, 2.5 cm (1″) long
- **Tail:** Marabou, black, with two strands of Krinkle Mirror Flash down each side
- **Body:** Ice Dub, chartreuse, palmered with UV Polar Chenille, silver
- **Hackle:** Schlappen, black
- **Legs:** Barred silicone legs, olive with gold flake/black bars, three per side
- **Collar:** Extra-large guinea hen, chartreuse
- **Head:** Deer belly hair, black, spun and trimmed Muddler-style
- **Hook:** #4 or #6 Gamakatsu Octopus, black

Notes: This is Justin's interpretation of a popular Great Lakes pattern, made famous by Jerry Darkes.

POLAR FLASH EGG SUCKING LEECH

- **Shank:** 55 mm Fish Skull Articulated Shank, cut down to 40 mm (rear loop cut off)
- **Thread:** UTC 140-denier, red
- **Stinger loop:** 30-pound Fireline, 2.5 cm (1") long
- **Body:** Holographic Diamond Braid, black
- **Thorax:** Estaz, pink
- **Wing:** Finnish raccoon, black
- **Flash:** In two parts: 1) Flashabou, purple chub, over the wing; 2) Polar Flash, black rainbow, under the shank
- **Hackle:** Schlappen, black
- **Head:** Ice Dub, chartreuse, clumped and brushed back
- **Hook:** #4 or #6 Gamakatsu Octopus, black

POLAR FLASH MINNOW

- **Shank:** 55 mm Fish Skull Articulated Shank, cut down to 40 mm (rear loop cut off)
- **Thread:** UTC 140-denier, red
- **Stinger loop:** 30-pound Fireline, 2.5 cm (1") long
- **Body:** Holographic Diamond Braid, silver
- **Thorax:** Australian possum, natural (or equivalent)
- **Wing:** Ostrich herl, white
- **Flash:** In two parts: 1) Flashabou, purple chub, over the wing; 2) Polar Flash, pearl, under the shank
- **Hackle:** Schlappen, white
- **Head:** Ice Dub, chartreuse, clumped and brushed back
- **Hook:** #4 or #6 Gamakatsu Octopus, black

Matt Ramsey

Matt is one of the two dudes who own and operate Two Dudes Flyfishing in Eugene, Oregon. That puts him in the enviable position of working on some of the best steelhead waters in the universe. Summer steelhead dominate the season around Eugene, including a somewhat domesticated "Town Run" that settles into downtown Eugene throughout the summer and fall. There's great winter fishing, too—really great. But Eugene-area steelheaders are spoiled by the availability of dry-line fishing to summer fish in the Willamette, North Umpqua, and Deschutes Rivers so much of the year. It's no surprise then that Matt's contributions here lean toward sparse, buggy critters that trigger a steelhead's inner trout. That said, Matt has spent 18 years guiding for Taimen in Mongolia, which has definitely influenced his approach to steelhead but is not reflected in the flies shown here.

Matt trying to wrestle the camera from his daughter. Little did he know she was on our payroll.
HAYLEE ANN RAMSEY-CODE PHOTO

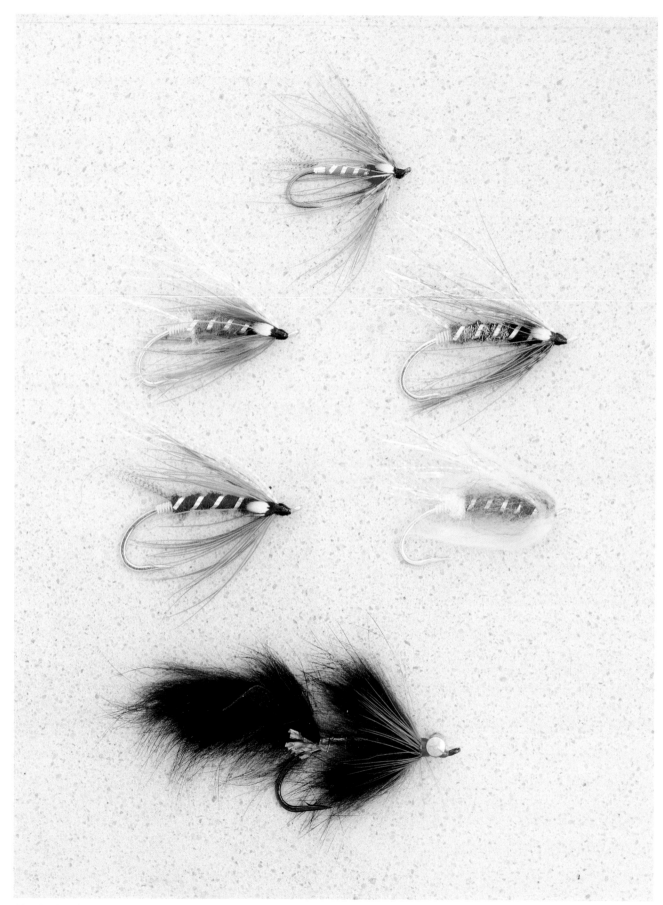

Clockwise from top: Autumn Partridge Spey; Hüsker Dü; Chromer Crack; Deep Creek Leech; Purple Spey; Blue Meanie.

AUTUMN PARTRIDGE SPEY

- **Hook:** #8 Daiichi 2441
- **Thread:** 6/0, black
- **Tag:** Flat tinsel, silver
- **Tail:** Partridge fibers
- **Body:** Floss, orange
- **Rib:** Flat tinsel, silver
- **Thorax:** STS Trilobal Dub, red
- **Hackle:** Blue-eared pheasant shoulder, light dun
- **Collar:** Long partridge neck or shoulder feather
- **Cheeks:** Jungle cock nails, tied short

Notes: This crossover from the trout world reflects the waters where Matt spends much of his time—the Upper Willamette and McKenzie Rivers surrounding Eugene, Oregon. Eugene-area guides spend most of their spring and summer days fishing for resident trout but catch a fair number of summer steelhead in the process. Consequently, there is a lot of cross-pollination between trout and steelhead patterns.

BLUE MEANIE

- **Hook:** #5 Alec Jackson's Steelhead Irons, nickel
- **Thread:** 6/0, black
- **Tag:** Twisted floss, lime green or chartreuse
- **Tail:** Krystal Flash, pearl
- **Butt:** Ice Dub, chartreuse
- **Body:** STS Trilobal Dub, kingfisher blue
- **Rib:** Flat tinsel, silver
- **Hackle:** Blue-eared pheasant shoulder, light dun
- **Collar:** Saddle hackle, kingfisher blue
- **Wing:** Krystal Flash, pearl
- **Cheeks:** Jungle cock nails, tied short

PURPLE SPEY

- **Hook:** #3 Alec Jackson's Steelhead Irons, nickel
- **Thread:** 6/0, black
- **Tag:** Twisted floss, lime green or chartreuse
- **Tail:** Partridge fibers
- **Body:** Angora goat dubbing, purple
- **Rib:** Flat tinsel, silver

- **Hackle:** Blue-eared pheasant shoulder, light dun
- **Wing:** Mirage Flashabou, opal, topped with Krystal Flash, pearl
- **Cheeks:** Jungle cock nails, tied short

HÜSKER DÜ

- **Hook:** #3 Alec Jackson's Steelhead Irons, gold
- **Thread:** 6/0, black
- **Tag:** Twisted floss, lime green or chartreuse
- **Tail:** Krystal Flash, pearl
- **Butt:** STS Trilobal Dub, hot pink
- **Rear half of body:** Ice Dub, peacock
- **Front half of body:** Angora goat dubbing, black
- **Rib:** Flat tinsel, gold
- **Hackle:** Ringneck pheasant shoulder
- **Wing:** Mirage Flashabou, opal, topped with Krystal Flash, pearl
- **Cheeks:** Jungle cock nails, tied short

DEEP CREEK LEECH

- **Hook:** #2 Daiichi 2441, black
- **Eyes:** Small or medium nickel-plated lead
- **Thread:** 210-denier, fluorescent red
- **Butt:** Wide Flashabou, pearl
- **Tail:** Rabbit strip, black
- **Body:** Large Mylar tinsel, pearl or opal
- **Rib:** Small oval tinsel, gold
- **Hackle:** Crosscut rabbit strip, black
- **Collar:** Saddle hackle, kingfisher blue

CHROMER CRACK

- **Hook:** #5 Alec Jackson's Steelhead Irons, gold
- **Thread:** 210-denier, fluorescent red
- **Tag:** Twisted floss, lime green or chartreuse
- **Tail:** Krystal Flash, pearl
- **Butt:** STS Trilobal Dub, chartreuse
- **Rear half of body:** STS Trilobal Dub, hot pink
- **Front half of body:** Angora goat dubbing, red
- **Rib:** Flat gold tinsel
- **Underwing:** Mirage Flashabou, opal, topped with Krystal Flash, pearl and a small bunch of Angora goat dubbing, red
- **Overwing:** Egg Yarn, peachy king

Wayne Richey

Wayne is one of the behind-the-scenes guys in the fly biz, connecting big-box retailers with fly-tying factories overseas. There are lots of crazy stories, none of which we can share here unless we want to join in litigation. Which we don't! Suffice it to say that Wayne dropped these flies by the office years ago, , we decided to include them for inspiration, and for the fact that they look fishy as hell. Colors are not specified in the recipes below, and these patterns can be tied in any color imaginable.

HOLLYWOOD STEELIE JOHN

- **Hook:** #2-6 Tiemco 2457
- **Bead head:** Large brass
- **Thread:** 70- or 140-denier, any color
- **Tail:** Turkey biots
- **Rib:** Medium French oval tinsel, gold
- **Abdomen:** Ice Dub
- **Horns:** Turkey biots, white
- **Wing case:** Mirage Flashabou with a bead of epoxy applied at the end
- **Thorax:** Ice Dub and grizzly barred rubber legs tied in X style
- **Dubbing collar/head:** Ice Dub in a contrasting color

Notes: The above recipe is color generic. Wayne ties the Hollywood Steelie John in a variety of bright colors, including shell pink, hot pink, purple, chartreuse, and hot orange. In every case the grizzly rubber legs match the body in color. Additional weight can be added by wrapping the shank with .020 lead wire before tying.

3-D NYMPH

- **Hook:** #408 Tiemco 2457
- **Bead head:** Medium brass
- **Thread:** 70- or 140-denier, black
- **Tail:** Turkey biots
- **Rib:** Medium wire, copper
- **Abdomen:** Hareline Dubbin with Mylar tinsel, pearl/opal, pulled over the back and ribbed over
- **Wing case:** Turkey tail fibers and two strands of Mirage Flashabou, with a bead of epoxy applied at the end
- **Thorax:** Peacock herl and round rubber legs tied in X style

Notes: The above recipe is color generic. Wayne typically ties the 3D Nymph in olive or black, and the rubber legs match the color of the body dubbing.

VITAMIN D

- **Hook:** #2-6 Tiemco 2457
- **Bead head:** Medium brass, painted orange or chartreuse
- **Thread:** 70- or 140-denier, orange or chartreuse
- **Tail:** Ringneck pheasant tail fibers
- **Rib:** Small or medium wire, copper
- **Abdomen:** Ringneck pheasant tail fibers over a tapered base of thread
- **Wing case:** Turkey tail fibers and a strand of copper wire over the top
- **Thorax:** Ice Dub, orange or chartreuse, with round rubber legs, same color as dubbing, tied in X style
- **Collar:** Dark partridge soft hackle

Top Rows: Vitamin D; middle rows: Hollywood Steelie John; bottom two rows: 3D Nymph.

Nick Rowell

Nick is one of the rising stars in the next generation of steelhead fly guides. He owns and operates Anadromous Anglers out of Portland, Oregon, and spends most of his days on the water.

FOX-WING MARABOU, SHELL PINK

- **Tube:** Pro Nanotube, clear
- **Thread:** 6/0 UNI-Thread, red
- **Butt/dubbing bump:** Ice Wing, copper, spun in a dubbing loop
- **Hackle:** Marabou, shell pink
- **Collar:** Saddle hackle, shell pink
- **Wing:** Arctic fox tail or Finnish raccoon, white
- **Junction tubing:** Pro Hookguide, clear

Notes: Nick ties these simple flies in a variety of colors, including black/blue, purple, and red.

INTRUDER, PURPLE, RED & WHITE

- **Tube:** Pro Nonotube, clear
- **Weight:** Pro Drop Weight, sized to conditions
- **Cone:** Large Pro Soft Sonic Disc, clear
- **Thread:** 6/0 UNI-Thread, purple
- **Butt/dubbing bump:** Ice Wing, copper, spun in a dubbing loop
- **Rear hackle:** In two parts, back to front: 1) arctic fox tail, claret, spun in a dubbing loop; 2) Lady Amherst pheasant tail fibers, red, spun in a dubbing loop
- **Split-tail:** Ostrich herl, natural gray, white, and claret mixed
- **Eyes:** Lady Amherst pheasant tippets, center cut and tied in on either side of the tube
- **Body:** Size 12 UNI-Mylar flat tinsel, peacock
- **Front hackle:** In four parts, back to front: 1) golden pheasant tippet, dyed purple; 2) marabou, claret; 3) ostrich herl, natural gray, white, and claret mixed; 4) Lady Amherst pheasant tail, red, spun in a dubbing loop
- **Cheeks:** Jungle cock shoulder feathers, tied in on either side of the tube Wing: Arctic fox tail or Finnish raccoon, white
- **Junction tubing:** Pro Hookguide, clear

Left column: Fox-Wing Marabou in three color combinations. Right column: three Intruders.

Charles St. Pierre

Charles St. Pierre is a professional Spey-casting instructor, evangelist for the greased-line presentation, and designer of some of the most popular steelhead patterns in use today. When it comes to fly design, Charles is a stickler for research. He has spent countless hours watching underwater video and viewing flies in swim-tanks to get an understanding of how fly design affects presentation. All that research has made him a believer in lightly dressed flies: "They impart so much more movement to the fly!"

St. Pierre is also convinced that weighted flies have become almost obsolete. "We see what happens in videos when you add weight to the fly," he said. "The flies don't move as well, and they tend to drop out of the water column." Charles is convinced that the heavy-fly mind-set is holding a lot of steelheaders back, and he does his part to spread the word.

For his stinger loops, Charles settled on Fireline years ago for its strength and relative stiffness, but he acknowledges that it can foul more than monofilament or wire. "You never want the loop to be longer than the hook you are using," he said. He also stays away from heavy hooks, which also drag a fly down and can foul more easily. See our step-by-step feature on page 111 for more background and tying instructions.

GREASED LINER

- **Hook:** #4-10 Tiemco 7989
- **Thread:** 140-denier, red
- **Tail:** Moose mane
- **Butt:** Any fine dubbing, October caddis orange
- **Body:** Senyo's Laser Dub, black
- **Collar:** Guinea hen, natural
- **Head/wing:** Moose body hair

FOX WING #1, BLACK/RED

- **Hook:** #2-10 Partridge Bartleet or substitute
- **Thread:** 140-denier, red
- **Tag:** Small French oval tinsel, gold
- **Body:** Angora goat, red for rear ⅓, black for forward ⅔
- **Rib:** Small French oval tinsel, gold
- **Collar:** Guinea hen, natural
- **Wing:** Arctic fox tail, black

FOX WING #2, BLACK/SILVER

- **Hook:** #2-10 Partridge Bartleet or substitute
- **Thread:** 140-denier, red
- **Body:** Diamond Braid tinsel, silver
- **Collar:** Chinese saddle hackle, blue over purple
- **Wing:** Arctic fox tail, black

STEELHEAD SOFT HACKLE

- **Hook:** #2-10 Partridge Bartleet or substitute
- **Thread:** 140-denier, red
- **Tag:** One wrap of medium French flat tinsel, silver
- **Body:** Floss, gold
- **Rib:** Small French oval tinsel, silver
- **Dubbing bump:** Senyo's Laser Dub, black with red
- **Collar:** In two parts, back to front: 1) guinea hen, natural; 2) blue-ear pheasant body feather, natural
- **Wing:** Arctic fox tail, red, tied short and sparse
- **Cheeks:** Jungle cock nails

STEELHEAD PUPA, BLACK/ORANGE

- **Hook:** #2-10 Partridge Bartleet or substitute
- **Thread:** 140-denier, red
- **Tag:** Small French oval tinsel, silver
- **Body:** Senyo's Laser Dub, black with red
- **Rib:** Small French oval tinsel, silver
- **Legs:** Lady Amherst pheasant tail, orange, four fibers
- **Collar:** Guinea hen, natural
- **Wing:** Jungle cock nails

POLAR CADDIS, PURPLE/YELLOW

- **Hook:** #2-10 Partridge Bartleet or substitute
- **Thread:** 140-denier, red
- **Tag:** Small French oval tinsel, gold
- **Body:** Fine yarn, yellow
- **Rib:** Small French oval tinsel, gold
- **Collar:** Guinea hen, natural
- **Wing:** Polar bear, purple
- **Cheeks:** Jungle cock nails

MODEL T

- **Hook:** Daiichi Alec Jackson Spey, #1-3/0
- **Thread:** 140-denier, red
- **Tail:** Bucktail, black (or long polar bear)
- **Body:** Three weilings made up of the same materials, each with successively longer wings: Ice Dub, steelie blue, spun in a dubbing loop, with a ring hackle of peacock neck, topped with a pair of golden pheasant neck or shoulder feathers, dyed purple
- **Cheeks:** Jungle cock nails

Notes: This is a gorgeous riff on the General Practitioner and slightly easier to tie given the lack of ribbing and pheasant tippets.

GP SPEY

- **Hook:** #1-3/0 Daiichi Alec Jackson Steelhead Iron
- **Thread:** 140-denier, red
- **Tail:** Bucktail, black, with three strands of Krystal Flash, metallic red
- **Body:** In two weilings, back to front: 1) Senyo's Laser Dub, black, topped with golden pheasant tippet, natural (with the center trimmed out) and a single golden pheasant neck or shoulder feather, natural; 2) Senyo's Laser Dub, black, palmered with extra-large guinea hen, natural, and topped with a single golden pheasant neck or shoulder feather, natural, extending to the bend of the hook
- **Rib:** Large French oval tinsel, gold
- **Collar:** Spey hackle of marabou, black
- **Wing:** Pair of golden pheasant shoulder feathers, dyed red
- **Cheeks:** Jungle cock nails

RIBBON SPEY

- **Hook:** #1-3/0 Daiichi Alec Jackson Spey
- **Thread:** 140-denier, red
- **Body:** Floss, orange, palmered with Spey hackle or schlappen, orange
- **Rib:** Medium French oval tinsel, gold
- **Collar:** Long ringneck pheasant rump
- **Wing:** Pair of golden pheasant shoulder feathers, dyed red, extending to the bend of the hook
- **Cheeks:** Jungle cock nails

BRUISED SPEY

- **Hook:** #1-3/0 Daiichi Alec Jackson Spey
- **Thread:** 140-denier, red
- **Body:** Floss, black
- **Rib:** Braided French tinsel, gold
- **Thorax:** Angora goat hair spun in a dubbing loop, palmered with long Spey hackle or marabou, black
- **Collar:** Guinea hen, kingfisher blue
- **Wing:** Pair of golden pheasant shoulder feathers, dyed red
- **Cheeks:** Jungle cock nails

FOXEE PRAWN, PINK/ORANGE

- **Shank:** 35 mm Waddington shank
- **Thread:** 140-denier, pink
- **Stinger loop:** 30-pound Fireline or equivalent, 2.3 cm (⅞") long
- **Tail:** Arctic fox tail, hot orange
- **Body:** Diamond Braid tinsel, silver, with a bump of Ice Dub, hot pink, all palmered with Chinese saddle hackle, hot pink
- **Underwing:** Arctic fox tail, hot orange, topped with fine Flashabou, pearl
- **Collar:** Guinea hen, orange
- **Overwing:** Long arctic fox tail, hot pink with black tips, topped with Angel Hair, UV white
- **Hook:** #1 or #2 Gamakatsu Octopus, black

FOXEE DOG, BLACK/BLUE

- **Shank:** 45 mm Waddington shank
- **Thread:** 140-denier, red
- **Stinger loop:** 30-pound Fireline or equivalent, 2.3 cm (⅞") long
- **Butt:** Ice Dub, steelie blue, spun in a dubbing loop
- **Rear hackle:** Extra-large guinea hen, natural
- **Tail:** Arctic xox tail, black, topped with Flashabou, metallic blue, and a pair of golden pheasant shoulder feathers, dyed black
- **Body:** Diamond Braid tinsel
- **Dubbing bump:** Ice Dub, steelie blue, spun in a dubbing loop
- **Collar:** Extra-large guinea hen, natural
- **Wing:** Arctic fox tail, black, topped with Flashabou, metallic blue, and a pair of golden pheasant shoulder
- **Hook:** #1 Gamakatsu Octopus barbless, nickel

Top row: Greased Liner; Steelhead Pupa. Second row: Steelhead Soft Hackle; Polar Caddis. Third row: Ribbon Spey; Bruised Spey. Fourth row: Fox Wing 1; Hoh Bo Spey, wine; Fox Wing 2. Fifth row: GP Spey; Model T. Row 4: Foxee Dog. Sixth row: Foxee Prawn; Foxee GP. Bottom row: Temple Tube.

FOXEE GP, ORANGE

- **Shank:** 45 mm Waddington shank
- **Thread:** 140-denier, red
- **Stinger loop:** 30-pound Fireline or equivalent, 2.3 cm (⅞") long
- **Butt:** Ice Dub, metallic red, spun in a dubbing loop
- **Rear hackle:** Extra-large guinea hen, orange
- **Tail:** Long arctic fox tail, orange with black tips, topped with holographic Flashabou, gold, a golden pheasant tippet (with center trimmed out), and a golden pheasant shoulder feather, natural
- **Body:** Small Cactus Chenille, burnt orange, palmered with grizzly saddle hackle, orange
- **Wing:** Arctic fox tail, orange with black tips
- **Collar:** Extra-large guinea hen, orange
- **Overwing:** Pair of golden pheasant shoulder feathers, natural
- **Hook:** #1 or #2 Gamakatsu Octopus, red

HOH BO SPEY, WINE

- **Shank:** 45 mm Waddington shank or equivalent
- **Thread:** 140-denier, red
- **Stinger loop:** 30-pound Fireline or equivalent, 2.3 cm (⅞") long
- **Butt:** Angora goat or Ice Dub, wine, spun in a dubbing loop

- **Body:** Angora goat or Ice Dub, black, spun in a dubbing loop, palmered with jumbo guinea hen
- **Hackle:** Marabou, black, and marabou, wine, ringed with six fibers of Lady Amherst pheasant center tail, natural
- **Flash:** Krinkle Mirror Flash, silver or pearl
- **Hook:** #1 Gamakatsu Octopus barbless, nickel

Notes: This might be the perfect all-season steelhead fly. Check out our step-by-step feature on page 112.

TEMPLE TUBE, PURPLE

- **Tube:** 25 mm plastic-lined copper tube
- **Thread:** 140-denier, red
- **Body:** Small Cactus Chenille, purple, palmered with Chinese saddle hackle, purple
- **Underwing:** Arctic fox tail, purple, clumped in reverse and folded back
- **Overwing:** Long arctic fox tail, purple with black tips
- **Flash:** Angel Hair, purple
- **Collar:** Guinea hen, purple
- **Cheeks:** Jungle cock nails
- **Junction tubing:** Medium soft tubing, 1.3 cm (½") long
- **Hook:** #1 Gamakatsu Octopus barbless, nickel

Greg Senyo

Greg is the mastermind behind Steelhead Alley Outfitters, a retailer and guide service on the south shore of Lake Erie. He's also one of the most prodigious perveyors of signature fly-tying materials in the history of the fly industry. Senyo's Articulated Shanks and Intruder Wire are great examples, and they are selling like hot cakes. But besides all the sales and marketing, Greg is also an innovative fly designer with a flair for sparkling streamers. Here we feature three of Greg's patterns in a variety of colors sure to inspire.

ARTIFICIAL INTELLIGENCE, GREEN

- **Shank:** 25 mm Senyo's Articulated Shank, green
- **Thread:** UTC 70-denier thread, olive
- **Stinger loop:** Senyo's Intruder Wire, green, 4.5 cm (1¾") long
- **Weight:** Small bead chain, two beads on each side of fly
- **Butt:** Krystal chenille, chartreuse
- **Body:** Polar Chenille, UV copper
- **Underwing:** Lady Amherst pheasant center tail, chartreuse, 12 to 15 strands
- **Overwing:** In three layers, each approximately 20 strands: 1) speckled Flashabou, copper; 2) speckled Flashabou, gold; 3) Flashabou, Kelly green
- **Hackle:** Schlappen, brown, wrapped behind and in front of the bead chain
- **Collar:** Guinea hen, chartreuse
- **Eyes:** Jungle cock nails or Real Eyes
- **Hook:** #2-4 Gamakatsu Octopus, green

Notes: Speckled Flashabou gives this pattern a great look. Fun Fur yarn (available at craft stores) can be substituted for the Polar Chenille to make an inexpensive, opaque body.

FLOW RIDER, PINK/ORANGE

- **Shank:** 40 mm Senyo's Articulated Shank, orange
- **Thread:** UTC 70-denier thread, fluorescent pink
- **Stinger loop:** Senyo's Intruder Wire, orange, 3.5 cm (1⅜") long
- **Weight:** Small bead chain, two beads on each side of fly
- **Tail:** Fuoro Fibre, hot orange
- **Rear hackle:** In two parts back to front: 1) guinea hen, orange; 2) silver pheasant body feather, hot pink
- **Rear wing:** Finnish raccoon, peach or salmon pink
- **Rear flash:** Mirage Flashabou, opal
- **Body:** Flat Diamond Braid, orange
- **Rib:** Medium French oval tinsel, silver
- **Hackle:** Guinea hen, orange, wrapped behind and in front of the bead chain
- **Front wing:** Finnish raccoon, peach or salmon pink
- **Flash:** Mirage Flashabou, opal and pink, mixed
- **Collar:** Silver pheasant body feather, hot pink
- **Eyes:** Jungle cock nails or Real Eyes
- **Hook:** #2-4 Gamakatsu Octopus, nickel

Notes: After tying a few of these, you'll want to use silver pheasant body feathers to collar more of your steelhead patterns. The peach and salmon-pink colors of Finnish raccoon are not widely available. Check out Tight Lines Fly Fishing Company in DePere, Wisconsin, for an amazing range of colors.

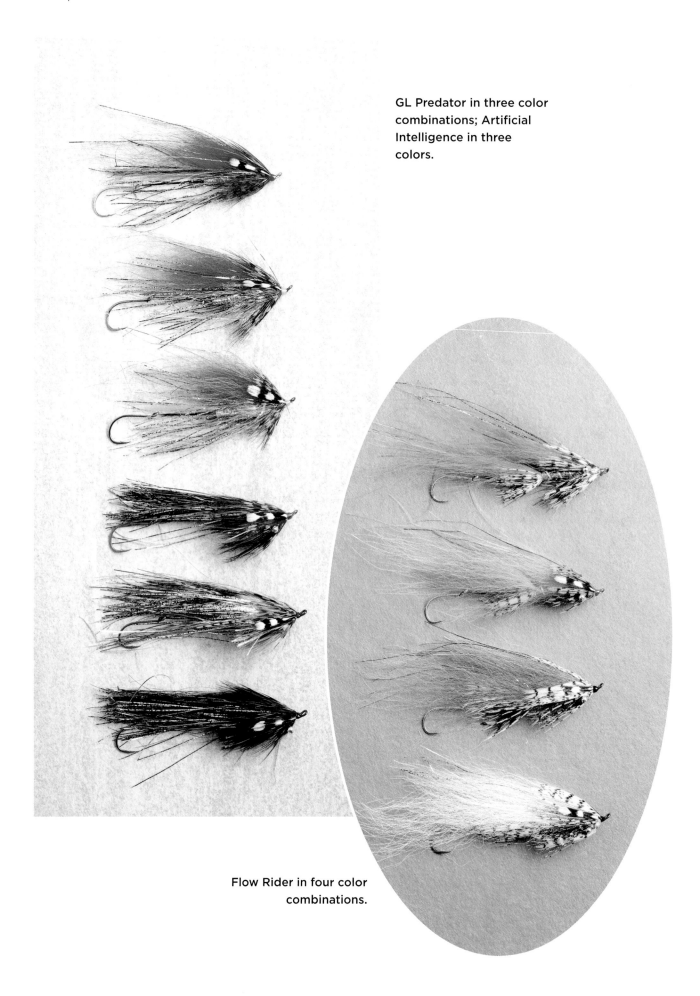

GL Predator in three color combinations; Artificial Intelligence in three colors.

Flow Rider in four color combinations.

GL PREDATOR SCANDI, PINK/PURPLE

- **Shank:** 40 mm Senyo's Articulated Shank, purple
- **Thread:** UTC 70-denier thread, cerise
- **Stinger loop:** Senyo's Intruder Wire, purple, 3.2 cm (1¼") long
- **Tag:** Medium French oval tinsel, silver
- **Tail:** Fuoro Fibre, hot pink
- **Rear body:** Flat Diamond Braid, purple
- **Rib:** Medium French oval tinsel, silver
- **Front body:** EP Streamer Brush, pink, and Senyo's Predator Wrap, UV silver, wrapped forward together
- **Wing:** Finnish raccoon, purple

- **Flash:** Krinkle Mirror Flash on sides; Flashabou, purple, over the top
- **Collar:** Guinea hen, pink
- **Eyes:** Jungle cock nails or Real Eyes
- **Hook:** #2-4 Gamakatsu Octopus, black

Notes: Senyo is the master of blending classic Atlantic salmon styles with modern synthetic materials, and this fly exemplifies his art. Greg trims off one side of the Predator Wrap to keep the fly sparse. Then, before he wraps the EP Streamer Brush and the Predator Wrap forward, he likes to color the thread base of the Predator Wrap with a Copic dye marker that matches the color of the EP brush. Finally, after the fly is finished and the head is hit with superglue, he pulls all the materials forward and paints the body with Clear Goo UV and zaps it with the light.

Marty Sheppard

Marty is half of the talent behind Little Creek Outfitters, based in Maupin, Oregon. He and his wife Mia guide steelhead trips on the John Day and Deschutes in the late summer and fall, then migrate to the west side of Mount Hood to fish the Sandy River in winter and spring. They put in a lot of days on the water chasing summer and winter fish, and they have boiled their fly-tying approach down to a few essentials. Here Marty has contributed a set of his own working flies to illustrate what matters most to him in terms of fly design.

REDNECK'S REVENGE

- **Hook:** #3 Daiichi Alec Jackson Spey
- **Thread:** 6/0 UNI-Thread, claret
- **Tag:** Floss, red
- **Tail:** Floss, red
- **Body:** STS Trilobal Dub, claret
- **Rib:** Small wire, red, wrapped over tag and body
- **Wing:** Squirrel tail, dyed red
- **Collar:** Guinea hen, claret

Marty detecting some serious metal on a perfectly gray day in early spring. MARTY SHEPPARD, LITTLE CREEK OUTFITTERS, PHOTO

Top: Redneck's Revenge. Second row: Metal Detector, blue and black, unweighted; Metal Detector, black and blue, conehead version. Bottom two flies: Metal Detector, red and orange; Metal Detector, red and pink.

METAL DETECTOR, RED/PINK/ORANGE

- **Tube:** Medium Frödin tube, fluorescent red, with a short piece of small tubing jammed into the back (which creates a solid stopper for the tippet knot)
- **Weight:** Medium cone head, copper
- **Thread:** 6/0 UNI-Thread, red
- **Body:** Polar Chenille, hot pink
- **Hackle:** Golden pheasant tippet, dyed red
- **Collar:** Marabou, red
- **Hook:** #2-4 Gamakatsu Octopus, red

Notes: Marty rigs his Metal Detectors using a 1inch no-slip mono loop. Once the knot is seated down tight, he pulls the knot into the rear section of small tubing until it stops. Since the fly is tied with the tubing connected, the pressure of the thread wraps locks the rear tubing in place and narrows the inner diameter of the junction so the knot won't pass through.

Mia Sheppard

Mia is the other half of the Little Creek Outfitters team and a remarkably accomplished outdoorswoman. Not only can she fish and tie flies, she's a champion Spey caster and an outspoken conservationist who has helped grow the ranks of women in the sport of fly fishing. Mia lives with her husband Marty and their daughter Tegan in Maupin, Oregon.

METALHEAD MUDDLER, ORANGE

- **Hook:** #8 Tiemco 700 or equivalent down-eye hook
- **Thread:** 6/0 UNI-Thread, black
- **Tail:** Ringneck pheasant tail
- **Body:** Angora goat dubbing, fluorescent orange
- **Rib:** Small wire, red
- **Wing:** Ringneck pheasant tail
- **Collar and head:** Cow elk body hair

Notes: This little Muddler is brilliant in its simplicity, and the fluorescent body makes it pop!

INTRUDLER

- **Tube:** Medium Frödin tube, fluorescent red, 5 cm (2") long
- **Tail:** Arctic fox tail, orange, topped with rhea herl, purple
- **Rear hackle:** Golden pheasant tippet, natural
- **Body:** Braidied tinsel, royal blue
- **Front hackle:** In three parts: 1) marabou, red; 2) golden pheasant tippet, natural; 3) rhea herl, purple
- **Collar and head:** Deer body hair, dyed red

BLACK DIAMOND

- **Hook:** #3 Alec Jackson Steelhead Iron, nickel
- **Thread:** 6/0 UNI-Thread, black
- **Tail:** Squirrel tail, dyed purple
- **Body:** Ice Dub, black
- **Rib:** Small wire, chartreuse
- **Collar:** Chinese saddle hackle, black
- **Wing:** Squirrel tail, dyed purple

Mia is happiest when she's waist deep in a steelhead river. Here she admires a wild hen before release.

MARTY SHEPPARD, LITTLE CREEK OUTFITTERS, PHOTO

From the top: Metalhead Muddler, shell pink; Metalhead Muddler, hot pink; Black Diamond; Intrudler, black; Intrudler, red.

Brian Silvey

From the step-by-step section on page 116: "It's probably impossible for most of us to fathom the zone that Brian Silvey inhabits. Here's a guy who swings flies for steelhead somewhere around 200 days a year and has been doing so for well over three decades. For most of that time he has been guiding on the Deschutes and Sandy Rivers and tying flies like a madman. He holds a degree in fish biology and fisheries management, is an FFF-certified casting instructor, and is among the most prolific signature tiers in the history of the fly industry."

SILVEY'S SNOW CONE, PURPLE

- **Hook:** #3 Alec Jackson Steelhead Iron, nickel
- **Thread:** 8/0 UNI-Thread, purple, and floss, fluorescent pink
- **Tag:** Floss, fluorescent pink
- **Rib:** Small wire, pink
- **Underwing:** Floss, fluorescent pink, doubled and folded
- **Body:** STS Trilobal Dub, purple
- **Hackle:** Chinese saddle hackle, purple
- **Wing:** Calf tail, white
- **Flash:** UV Polar flash, three strands

Notes: The black and green version in Brian's color plate is the most popular variation on the Snow Cone.

SILVEY'S LUCKY CHARM

- **Hook:** #3 Alec Jackson Steelhead Iron, nickel
- **Thread:** 8/0 UNI-Thread, black
- **Tail:** Golden pheasant crest
- **Body:** Floss, black
- **Rib:** Small flat tinsel, silver
- **Counter rib:** Small wire, silver
- **Hackle:** Chinese saddle, royal blue
- **Wing:** Squirrel tail, gray
- **Eyes:** Jungle cock nails

Brian, right, helps Marty with the net on a busman's holiday in British Columbia. MARTY SHEPPARD, LITTLE CREEK OUTFITTERS, PHOTO

SILVEYNATOR, BLACK/ORANGE

- **Tube:** Small tubing, clear, cut about 1½" (4 cm) long
- **Tail:** Rabbit strip, black
- **Legs:** Ostrich herl, black
- **Flash:** Angel Hair, peacock
- **Hackle:** Schlappen, black
- **Bead:** 5 to 6 mm (³⁄₁₆" to ¼") diameter brass bead, painted fluorescent orange
- **Junction tubing:** Small vinyl tubing, 13 to 20 mm (½" to ¾") long

Notes: This amazing fly is as simple as it gets, elegant in the water, and downright deadly. It can be tied in any color combination imaginable. Check out our step-by-step feature on page 117.

SILVEY'S TANDEM TUBE, BLACK/BLUE

- **Tube (main):** Small tubing, blue, cut to 1.3 cm (½") long
- **Thread:** 6/0 UNI-Thread, black
- **Tail:** Rabbit strip, black, 7 cm (2¾") long, with a short section of large diameter tubing (black) tied near end
- **Flash:** Flashabou, metallic blue, two strands on each side
- **Collar:** Schlappen, royal blue
- **Head:** Cone head, black

Notes: Rigging the Tandem Tube has perplexed neophytes since the fly first hit the market, but it's quite simple. Thread the fly onto the tippet and tie a no-slip mono loop that is longer than the distance between the two tubes. We recommend standardizing your loops to 7.6 cm (3"), since the usual distance between the tubes is 6.4 cm (2½"). With the loop completed, just push the loop through the tail tube and through the eye of the hook. Once the loop is through the eye of the hook, give it a half twist and slip it over the bend of the hook. Pull tight and swing it!

SILVEY'S TUBE SNAKE, RED

- **Tube (main):** Small tube, clear, 1.5 cm (⅝") long
- **Thread:** 6/0 UNI-Thread, fluorescent red
- **Tail:** Barred rabbit strip, red, 7 cm (2¾") long, with a short section of large-diameter tubing (orange) tied near end
- **Hackle:** In two parts, back to front: 1) marabou, red; 2) Baitfish Emulator, red
- **Collar:** Golden pheasant tippet, dyed red
- **Wings:** Grizzly saddle hackle tips
- **Topping:** Ostrich herl, red, 10 strands barred with black Sharpie permanent marker

SILVEY'S PRAWN, PEACH

- **Shank:** .040" diameter spinner wire, with 1 cm (⅜") folded over to create eye
- **Thread:** 140-denier, pink
- **Weight:** Medium brass eyes, gold finish
- **Stinger loop:** 30-pound Fireline, 2 cm (¾") long, tied in 4 cm (1½") behind the eye
- **Tail:** Angel Hair, pink pearl
- **Butt:** Medium chenille, shrimp pink
- **Horn:** Rabbit strip, peach
- **Claws:** Super Hair, peach, barred with black marker
- **Rear hackle:** In two parts: 1) golden pheasant tippet; 2) rabbit strip, peach
- **Eyes:** 6 mm holographic 3-D adhesive eyes glued to 20-pound monofilament (AquaSeal works well)
- **Body:** Large UTC Mirage Tinsel, pearl, palmered with crosscut rabbit strip, peach
- **Collar:** Golden pheasant tippet
- **Shellback:** Pair of golden pheasant shoulder feathers, natural or dyed red
- **Hook:** #2-4 Gamakatsu Octopus, red

Notes: Hats off to Brian for his ingenious reimagining of the prawn using rabbit fur! Given his long and distinguished career as an innovator, it should come as no surprise, and yet, when viewing this fly underwater, it bends the mind. We are careful to note above under "Stinger loop" the point on the shank where the fly should begin in order to achieve the desired final shank length of 4.5 cm (1¾"). Finally, be sure to prepare the glued eyes well in advance of tying the fly!

Top row, left to right: Lucky Charm, Snow Cone in two colors. Descending from second row: Tandem Tube, Tube Snake, Silvey's Prawn, Silvey's Squid. Bottom row: Silvey's Extractor, Silveynator.

SILVEY'S SQUID, ORANGE

- **Shank:** .040" diameter spinner wire, with 1 cm (⅜") folded over to create eye
- **Thread:** 140-denier, orange
- **Weight:** Medium brass eyes, gold finish
- **Stinger loop:** 30 Fireline, 2 cm (¾") long, tied in 5 cm (2") behind the eye
- **Tail:** Angel Hair, orange
- **Butt:** Medium chenille, fluorescent orange
- **Tentacles:** In two steps: 1) four saddle hackle tips, salmon, spotted with fine-tip black marker; 2) Psuedo Hair, orange, tied in clumps
- **Rear hackle:** Two turns of rabbit strip, orange
- **Eyes:** 6 mm holographic 3-D adhesive eyes glued to 20-pound monofilament (AquaSeal works well)
- **Body:** In three parts: 1) Ice Dub, orange, underlying the full length; 2) rabbit strips, orange, tied in at the front of the shank and running down both sides; 3) Crystal Skin, pearl, cut in two 6 mm (¼") wide strips, each 5.5 cm (2 3/16") long, also tied in at the front and folded back along the top and bottom of the body
- **Rib:** Medium wire, red, wrapped carefully to hold the rabbit and Crystal Skin firmly in place
- **Collar:** Two turns of rabbit strip, orange
- **Hook:** #2-4 Gamakatsu Octopus, red

Notes: This pattern displays an ingenious use of rabbit fur and hackle tips to create a living, breathing squid. Check it out in the water and be blown away! Also see notes above for Silvey's Prawn.

SILVEY'S EXTRACTOR, PURPLE/PINK

- **Shank:** .040" diameter spinner wire, with 1 cm (⅜") folded over to create eye
- **Thread:** 6/0 UNI-Thread, purple
- **Eyes:** Extra-small brass dumbbells
- **Trailing loop:** 50-pound Fireline or equivalent
- **Tail:** Ice Wing, shell pink, topped with 10 strands of ostrich herl, dyed pink
- **Butt:** Medium chenille, cerise
- **Rear hackle:** In two parts, back to front: 1) barred Spandex, cerise, 10 strands tied in evenly around the shank to create a hackle; 2) golden pheasant tippet wrapped like a wet-fly hackle
- **Body:** Flashabou, purple haze, palmered with a purple saddle hackle
- **Rib:** Copper wire
- **Front bump:** Medium or large chenille, purple
- **Front hackle:** In three parts, back to front: 1) golden pheasant tippet wrapped like a wet-fly hackle; 2) barred Spandex, purple, 10 strands tied in evenly around the shank to create a hackle; 3) two more wraps of golden pheasant tippet
- **Wing:** Angel Hair, purple, topped with 10 strands of ostrich herl, purple
- **Hook:** Gamakatsu Octopus, #4 for small versions, #2 for larger versions

Notes: This brightly colored Intruder has gained great popularity since it came out in 2012. It is typically tied in two sizes, the small version having a shank-length of 4 cm (1½") and the larger version having a shank length of 5 cm (2") or more. Popular color combinations besides the purple/pink version shown include red/red, black/chartreuse, and orange/red.

Brian Styskal

Brian is a world-class casting instructor and guide currently based in the Seattle area. He has chased steelhead since he was five years old, and he knows them better than most. He's also a great fly tier with a style all his own. We were extremely lucky to reach him when he had a little spare time to tie up the flies featured here. We know from experience that these flies represent a lot of time and effort. We greatly appreciate it, and we know you will, too.

PURPLE JESUS

- **Tube:** HMH Micro Tubing, clear, cut to 4.5 cm (1¾") long, flared (slightly melted) at both ends
- **Thread:** 70- or 140-denier, black
- **Weight:** Medium tungsten barbell eyes, tied in on the underside, butt end of the tube
- **Butt:** Seal fur, dyed gentian violet, wrapped over and around eyes and well picked out
- **Rear hackle:** In three parts, back to front: 1) long, webby grizzly saddle hackle, purple; 2) large golden pheasant tippet, dyed purple; 3) rhea, dyed royal blue, tied in at four points around circumference of tube
- **Tail:** Topping of rhea herl, dyed gentian violet, with a small bunch of Ice Wing, lavender
- **Body:** Mini flat braid, pearl, palmered with Chinese saddle hackle, purple
- **Dubbing bump:** Seal fur, dyed gentian violet
- **Front hackle:** In two parts, back to front: 1) large golden pheasant tippet, purple; 2) rhea, dyed royal blue, tied in at four points
- **Wing:** Topping of rhea herl, dyed gentian violet, with a small bunch of Ice Wing, lavender
- **Collar:** Chinese saddle hackle, purple
- **Cheeks:** Jungle cock nails
- **Junction tubing:** HMH Poly Tubing

GREEN DRAGON

- **Tube:** HMH Micro Tubing, clear, cut to 4.5 cm (1¾") long, flared (slightly melted) at both ends
- **Thread:** 70- or 140-denier, black
- **Weight:** Medium tungsten barbell eyes, tied in on the underside, butt end of the tube
- **Butt:** Seal fur, dyed Highlander green, wrapped over and around eyes and well picked out
- **Rear hackle:** In three parts, back to front: 1) long, webby grizzly saddle hackle, green; 2) rhea herl, black, tied in at four points around circumference of tube; 3) schlappen, green, or similarly long, webby hackle
- **Tail:** In three parts: 1) six peacock sword fibers on each side; 2) Polar Flash, green and gold; 3) topping of arctic fox tail, green, barred with black Sharpie permanent marker
- **Body:** Mini flat braid, lime green, palmered with schlappen, black
- **Dubbing bump:** Seal fur, dyed green
- **Front hackle:** In two parts, back to front: 1) Chinese saddle hackle, green; 2) rhea herl, black, tied in at four points
- **Wing:** In three parts: 1) six peacock sword fibers on each side; 2) Polar Flash, green and gold; 3) topping of arctic fox tail, green, barred with black Sharpie permanent marker
- **Collar:** Guinea hen, green
- **Cheeks:** Jungle cock nails
- **Junction tubing:** HMH Poly Tubing

SKAGIT SUSHI

- **Tube:** HMH Micro Tubing, fluorescent pink, cut to 4.5 cm (1¾") long, flared (slightly melted) at both ends
- **Thread:** 70- or 140-denier, white
- **Weight:** Medium tungsten barbell eyes, tied in on the underside, butt end of the tube
- **Butt:** Ice Dub, UV shrimp pink, wrapped over and around eyes and well picked out
- **Rear hackle:** In three parts, back to front: 1) schlappen, white; 2) rhea, dyed shell pink, tied in at four points around circumference of tube; 3) schlappen, shell pink
- **Tail:** Ostrich herl, white, barred with a black Sharpie permanent marker, topped with a small bunch of Ice Wing, pink

From the top: Trago Satyr; Sauk River Prawn; Green Dragon; Gwyn's Fly; Purple Jesus; Skagit Sushi.

- **Body:** In two sections, repeated: Ice Dub, UV shrimp pink, palmered with Chinese saddle hackle, light pink, and topped with Mylar tubing, pearl, as a shellback
- **Front hackle:** In two parts, back to front: 1) long, webby grizzly saddle hackle, white; 2) rhea, dyed shell pink, tied in at three points around circumference of tube
- **Wing:** Ostrich herl, white, barred with a black Sharpie permanent marker, topped with a small bunch of Ice Wing, pink
- **Collar:** Schlappen, shell pink
- **Cheeks:** Jungle cock nails
- **Junction tubing:** HMH Poly Tubing

GWYN'S FLY

- **Tube:** HMH Micro Tubing, clear, cut to 4.5 cm (1¾″) long, flared (slightly melted) at both ends
- **Thread:** 70- or 140-denier, white
- **Weight:** Medium tungsten barbell eyes, tied in on the underside, butt end of the tube
- **Butt:** Seal fur, dyed kingfisher blue, wrapped over and around eyes and well picked out
- **Rear hackle:** In three parts, back to front: 1) schlappen, Caribbean blue (custom color); 2) rhea herl, kingfisher blue, tied in at four points around circumference of tube; 3) schlappen, black
- **Tail:** In three parts: 1) two peacock sword fibers on each side; 2) Ice Wing, purple; 3) rhea herl, kingfisher blue, barred with black Sharpie permanent marker
- **Body:** Mini flat braid, lime green, palmered with Chinese saddle hackle, violet
- **Front hackle:** In two parts, back to front: 1) schlappen, Caribbean blue (custom color); 2) rhea herl, kingfisher blue, tied in at four points
- **Wing:** In three parts: 1) two peacock sword fibers on each side; 2) Ice Wing, purple; 3) topping rhea herl, kingfisher blue, barred with black permanent marker
- **Collar:** Schlappen, black
- **Cheeks:** Jungle cock nails
- **Junction tubing:** HMH Poly Tubing

SAUK RIVER PRAWN

- **Tube:** HMH Micro Tubing, clear, cut to 4.5 cm (1¾″) long, flared (slightly melted) at both ends
- **Thread:** 70- or 140-denier, orange
- **Weight:** Medium tungsten barbell eyes, tied in on the underside, butt end of the tube
- **Butt:** Seal fur, dyed orange, wrapped over and around eyes and well picked out
- **Rear hackle:** In three parts, back to front: 1) schlappen, hot orange; 2) rhea herl, orange, tied in at four points around circumference of tube; 3) schlappen, orange
- **Tail:** In three parts: 1) Ice Wing, UV pearl; 2) rhea herl, orange, barred with black Sharpie permanent marker; 3) golden pheasant shoulder feather, natural
- **Body weilings:** Two sections or equal length repeated: mini flat braid, orange, palmered with Chinese saddle hackle, orange; rhea herl, orange, tied in at three points (on top and on each side); topped with a small bunch of Ice Wing and barred with a black Sharpie permanent marker; finished with a topping of golden pheasant shoulder feather, natural
- **Junction tubing:** HMH Poly Tubing

TRAGO SATYR

- **Tube:** HMH Micro Tubing, clear, cut to 4.5 cm (1¾″) long, flared (slightly melted) at both ends
- **Thread:** 70- or 140-denier, red
- **Weight:** Medium tungsten barbell eyes, tied in on the underside, butt end of the tube
- **Butt:** Seal fur, dyed claret, wrapped over and around eyes and well picked out
- **Rear hackle:** Satyr tragopan pheasant shoulder or rump feather
- **Tail:** Rhea herl, claret, six strands tied in on each side; topped with spotted satyr tragopan breast feather
- **Body weilings:** Two repeated sections of equal length, each built in four steps: 1) mini flat braid, orange; 2) ring hackle of satyr tragopan pheasant shoulder or rump feather; 3) rhea herl, claret, four strands tied in on each side; 4) topped with a pair of spotted satyr tragopan breast feathers to create a consistent line of spots down the shellback
- **Junction tubing:** HMH Poly Tubing

April Vokey

April is one of the most recognized faces in the world of fly fishing, having worked like crazy to build her business and reputation since she started Fly Gal Ventures in 2007. After ten years of guiding full-time, April now focuses on being an FFF-certified casting instructor, an in-demand public speaker, a podcaster, and a dedicated conservationist. Oh, and she's a spectacular fly tier, which is clear from the flies featured here.

CLASSY HOOKER

- **Hook:** #1-2/0 Tiemco 7999
- **Thread:** UTC 140-denier, black
- **Tag:** Small French oval tinsel, silver
- **Butt:** Small Cactus Chenille, gray
- **Body:** Ice Dub, UV black, the front half palmered with long heron
- **Rib:** Small wire, silver
- **Collar:** In two parts, back to front: 1) schlappen, kingfisher blue; 2) schlappen, purple
- **Wing:** Gadwall flank
- **Eyes:** Jungle cock nails

April ties an Intruder for a fly-show audience.
ADRIENNE COMEAU PHOTO

NAVY DECEIVER

- **Tube:** Pro Tube Flexitube 40/10, gold
- **Thread:** UTC 140-denier, black
- **Tag:** Small Cactus Chenille, UV gray
- **Butt:** Seal dubbing, teal, spun in a dubbing loop and brushed out
- **Rear hackle:** Stacked olive rhea and olive ringneck pheasant tail
- **Body:** Silver flatbraid, palmered with dark blue Chinese hackle
- **Front hackle:** In three parts, back to front: 1) arctic fox tail, navy blue, spun in a dubbing loop, brushed and folded as wrapped forward; 2) long rhea herl, olive, stacked
- **Flash:** Flashabou, copper, three strands per side, tied long
- **Collar:** Mallard flank, dark
- **Eyes:** Jungle cock nails

Notes: This simple, sparse Intruder is possibly the most elegant and beautiful fly we received for this book, out of over 400 submissions. It exemplifies everything that the Intruder style strives for, providing a large, almost transparent profile, with maximum movement. And yet, it is so sparse that it barely exists. Total length is 13 cm (5").

SODA POP

- **Tube:** Small Pro Tube Classic, pink
- **Weight:** Small cone head, black
- **Thread:** UTC 140-denier, black
- **Butt:** Seal dubbing, fuchsia, spun in a dubbing loop and brushed out
- **Rear hackle:** Stacked rhea, hot pink
- **Body:** Flat Diamond Braid, pearl, palmered with long Chinese saddle, black (no rib)
- **Front hackle:** In two parts, back to front: 1) arctic fox tail, kingfisher blue, spun in a dubbing loop, brushed and folded as wrapped forward; 2) Ice Wing, steelie blue, spun in a dubbing loop, brushed and folded as wrapped forward; 3) long rhea herl, fuchsia, stacked
- **Shellback:** Pair of golden pheasant neck or shoulder feathers, dyed purple
- **Eyes:** Jungle cock nails

From the top: Classy Hooker; Navy Deceiver; Soda Pop; Gluttonous Leech.

GLUTTONOUS LEECH

- **Shank:** #3 Daiichi Alec Jackson Steelhead Iron, gold
- **Thread:** UTC 140-denier, black
- **Stinger loop:** 26.4-pound Surflon-coated wire, 2.5 cm (1″) long
- **Body:** Fine braided tinsel, silver
- **Hackle:** In three parts, back to front: 1) arctic fox tail, white, spun in a dubbing loop, brushed and folded as wrapped forward; 2) rhea herl, peach, spun in a dubbing loop; 3) long rhea herl, brown, spun in a dubbing loop
- **Collar:** Barred wood duck flank
- **Flash:** Krinkle Mirror Flash, four strands spread evenly around the body
- **Wings:** Long jungle cock nails, their stems stripped clean
- **Eyes:** Jungle cock nails
- **Hook:** #4 Gamakatsu Octopus, red

Notes: This shows a brilliant application of contrast and accentuated movement, with the long, paddle-shaped jungle cock nails free to swim wildly in the current. Total length is 13 cm (5⅛″).

Derek Wiley

Derek is a fisheries biologist and steelhead fanatic in Northwest Oregon. He knows steelhead like few living people. In fact he studies the movements of juvenile and adult salmonids of every species throughout the year in his home waters of Tillamook County, Oregon. That's because his professional life is spent monitoring steelhead and salmon populations as part of Oregon Department of Fish and Wildlife's Life Cycle Monitoring program. And when he's off work, what does he do?

He changes out of his work waders and into his fishing waders (both are leaky), and he gets back on the water. When the sun is down, Derek can be found cranking out bugs and filling fly boxes.

BEADSTIE BOY, BLACK

- **Shank:** Spinner wire, folded to create "hook eye"
- **Thread:** 6/0 UNI-Thread, black
- **Stinger loop:** 20-pound Maxima Chameleon, 3.2 cm (1¼″) loop
- **Body:** Diamond Braid, black
- **Tail:** Bunny strip, black, 6.2 cm (2¼″)
- **Hackle:** Marabou, black
- **Flash:** Flashabou, black
- **Collar:** In two parts, back to front: 1) five Lady Amherst pheasant tail fibers, tied in singly around the circumference of the fly; 2) guinea hen, red
- **Bead:** 6 mm, fluorescent orange
- **Hook:** #2 Gamakatsu Octopus

Notes: Leave it to a pragmatic fish biologist to boil down the most effective elements in steelhead fly design into a single, deadly pattern that is useful in all seasons. Fish this fly with confidence, but beware of the possibility that you might never again tie another pattern. Also tied in purple.

The Beadstie Boy in action. No steelhead can resist it. ROB RUSSELL PHOTO

From the top: Beadstie Boy, black; Beadstie Boy, purple; Flash Intruder, black and red; Flash Intruder, black and blue.

FLASH INTRUDER, BLACK/RED

- **Shank:** Spinner wire, folded to create "hook eye"
- **Thread:** 6/0 UNI-Thread, black
- **Eyes:** Medium brass, black
- **Stinger loop:** 20-pound Maxima Chameleon, 3.2 cm (1¼") loop
- **Butt:** Large chenille, black
- **Rear hackle/tail:** In four parts, back to front: 1) guinea hen, claret; 2) ostrich herl, black; 3) Flashabou, black; 4) schlappen, black
- **Body:** Diamond Braid, red/silver
- **Front hackle:** In four parts: 1) guinea hen, claret; 2) marabou, black; 3) Flashabou, black with one strand of metallic red on each side; 4) guinea hen, claret
- **Hook:** #2 Gamakatsu Octopus

Notes: Derek's main inspiration for this series is the employment of black Flashabou. He loves the relative subtlety of the material compared with typical flash, and he loves how it moves in the water.

Rich Zellman

Rich has made a name for himself as one of the finest steelhead guides working today. He's also a gifted fly tier and has developed some great patterns including a style of Intruder that's all his own. He fishes the rivers of Northern California and Southern Oregon, including the Trinity and the fabled North Umpqua. He's the owner and operator of Steelhead Water Guide Service.

Rich training his buddy Bo to be respectful in the presence of a wild steelhead. RICH ZELLMAN PHOTO

EXTENDED BODY SKATER

- **Hook:** #3-5 Daiichi Alec Jackson Spey, nickel
- **Thread:** Mono cord, brown
- **Tail:** Arctic fox tail, orange with black tips, with Krystal Flash, pearl, split evenly between the folded foam of extended body
- **Extended body:** 2 mm sheet foam, brown, segmented with thread
- **Legs:** Grizzly barred rubber legs, white
- **Skirt:** Guinea hen, orange
- **Thorax:** Deer body hair, dyed dark brown, spun short with tips out and trimmed to create wings
- **Ears:** Guinea hen, natural
- **Head:** 2 mm foam, brown, pulled over deer hair and secured just behind the eye of the hook

Notes: Definitely the wildest steelhead skater we have seen. Zellman surprised even himself with this one!

MINI-INTRUDER, COPPER

- **Shank:** #5 Daiichi Alec Jackson Spey, black
- **Thread:** 70-denier, gray
- **Eyes:** Small brass barbells
- **Stinger loop:** 30-pound Fireline, 1 cm (⅜") long
- **Hook:** #4 Gamakatsu Octopus, black
- **Split-tail:** Fibers from a golden pheasant shoulder feather
- **Body:** Flashabou, copper, palmered with grizzly saddle hackle, rust

- **Hackle:** Schlappen, black
- **Collar:** Guinea hen, brown
- **Wings:** Tented pair of turkey tail strips

Notes: It may seem a waste to cut the bend off an Alec Jackson Spey hook, but the arc of the hook makes for an extra-sexy body on this fly and the series that follows.

LOW WATER INTRUDER, BLACK/PURPLE

- **Shank:** #5 Daiichi Alec Jackson Spey, black
- **Thread:** 70-denier, gray
- **Eyes:** Small lead barbells, nickel plated
- **Stinger loop:** 30-pound Fireline, doubled, 2.5 cm (1") long
- **Hook:** #2 Owner SST, black
- **Butt:** STS Trilobal Dub, chartreuse, spun in a dubbing loop
- **Rear hackle:** Stripped ringneck pheasant tail, dyed black
- **Body:** Flashabou, purple, palmered with short saddle hackle, black
- **Hackle:** Turkey flat, purple
- **Flash:** Flashabou, blue
- **Collar:** Guinea hen, purple
- **Wings:** Pair of grizzly saddle hackle tips, kingfisher blue

INTRUDER, BLACK/CHARTREUSE/PINK

- **Shank:** #3 Daiichi Alec Jackson Spey, black
- **Thread:** 70-denier, gray
- **Eyes:** Medium lead barbells, nickel plated
- **Stinger loop:** 30-pound Fireline, doubled, 3.8 cm (1½") long
- **Hook:** #1 Gamakatsu Split Shot/Drop Shot, black
- **Butt:** STS Trilobal Dub, hot pink, spun in a dubbing loop
- **Body:** Flashabou, pink, palmered with stripped ringneck pheasant tail dyed black
- **Hackle:** In two parts, back to front: 1) turkey flat, chartreuse; 2) ostrich herl, chartreuse, 20 strands spun in a dubbing loop
- **Flash:** Flashabou, pearl dyed black
- **Collar:** Guinea hen, hot pink
- **Wing:** Ostrich herl, black, 12 to 15 strands tied long
- **Shellback:** Pair of grizzly saddle hackle tips, pink

DOUBLE INTRUDER, BLACK/BLUE

- **Rear shank:** Pair of #2 Daiichi 2141s, black
- **Thread:** 70-denier, black
- **Stinger loop:** Nylon-coated steel wire, black, 3 cm (1⅛") long
- **Hook:** #1/0 Owner SST, black
- **Body:** Flashabou, pink, palmered with stripped ringneck pheasant tail, dyed black
- **Hackle:** Ostrich herl, black, 15 to 20 strands spun in a dubbing loop
- **Front shank:** #3 Alec Jackson Steelhead Iron, black
- **Eyes:** Medium or large lead barbells, nickel plated
- **Connector loop/bead:** Nylon-coated steel wire threaded through the eyes of the rear fly, then threaded with a 6 mm glass bead, pink
- **Body:** In four steps: 1) tie in stripped ringneck pheasant, black, and a dubbing loop for later palmering; 2) lay down base of Flashabou, pink; 3) spin polar bear hair, kingfisher blue, in a dubbing loop and palmer over body; 4) palmer stripped ringneck pheasant tail forward
- **Hackle:** In two parts, back to front: 1) turkey flat, kingfisher blue; 2) ostrich herl, kingfisher blue, 15 to 20 strands spun in a dubbing loop
- **Flash:** Flashabou, blue
- **Collar:** Guinea hen, kingfisher blue
- **Shellback:** Pair of grizzly saddle hackle tips, kingfisher blue

Notes: Zellman sent us two of these monsters, the largest measuring 16.5 cm (6½ inches) long and sporting large barbell eyes. It stands as the largest fly we received for this book project. While it would be tempting to think that Rich tied this monstrosity only for the purposes of this book, we know that to be false. How do we know? Here's Rob: "Because I found one of these beasts stuck hard in a willow branch while fishing for spring chinook several years ago. I could barely believe my eyes. It was a year or so later when Rich's submissions for the book arrived, and I recognized the fly."

Clockwise from top left: Mini-Intruder, copper; Extended Body Skater; Low Water Intruder, black/purple; Double Intruder, purple; Intruder, black/chartreuse/pink; Double Intruder, blue; Intruder, black and orange.

APPENDIX

Business Listings

Anadromous Anglers
Proprietor: Nick Rowell
408 3rd Ave.
Oregon City, OR 97045
(949) 547-3818
anadromousanglers.com

Aqua Flies
Sebastopol, CA
aquaflies.com
Representing the signature flies of
Jason Hartwick, Paul Miller, Stuart
Foxall, Brett Jensen, and Jon Ingi
Agustsson—and growing
Notes: The best way to get ahold
of these great flies is to order them
through your local fly shop. Aqua Flies
is not a direct-to-consumer business
and relies on specialty fly shops to get
their flies in the hands of steelheaders.

Ashland Fly Shop
Proprietor: Will Johnson
399 E. Main St.
Ashland, OR 97520
(541) 488-6454
Notes: As if Ashland, Oregon, wasn't
awesome enough, it's home to a great
fly shop, which happens to be next
door to the global headquarters of
Fly Water Travel. It's also the place to
book trips with Jon Hazlett and Rich
Zellman.

**Brian Silvey's Fly Fishing Guide
Service**
Proprietor: Brian Silvey
(800) 510-1702
silveysflyfishing.com

Calypso Guide Service
Proprietor: Barrett Christiansen
(541) 484-2595
calypsoguideservice.com

**Chagrin River Fly Shop &
Outfitters**
Proprietors: Dan & Jason Pribanic
100 N. Main St. #150
Chagrin Falls, OH 44022
(440) 247-7110
chagrinriveroutfitters.com

Deschutes Angler
Proprietors: John & Amy Hazel
504 Deschutes Ave.
Maupin, OR
(541) 595-0995
deschutesangler.com

Ed Hepp
Illustrator, print designer, and creator
of the Underachiever
edhepp.com

Ethan Nickel Outfitters
Proprietor: Ethan Nickel
Eugene, OR
(541) 544-2303
Blog: flyfishoregon.wordpress.com
Notes: Ethan is the guide's guide for
Willamette, McKenzie, Deschutes,
Umpqua, and Central Oregon Coast
steelhead.

Fish the Swing Guide Service
Proprietor: Jeff Hickman (aka
Hickmanimal)
"Doomed to a life of fishing addiction."
PO Box 1565
Hood River, OR 97031
(971) 275-2269
fishtheswing.com

Fishmadman.com
Proprietors: Jesper Fohrmann & Per
Fischer
Stakhaven 8
DK-2500 Valby, Denmark
+45 22133113 or +4530111463
fishmadman.com
Notes: The coolest dry flies in the biz,
featuring a huge line of riffle-hitched
steelhead tubes.

The Fly Fisher
Proprietor: Bjorn Beech
5622 Pacific Ave. SE, #9
Lacey, WA 98503
(360) 491-0181
theflyfisher.net
Notes: Source for the Big Bore bodkin,
Bjorn's custom shank system, wire
dubbing loop tools, and specialty fly
components. Also one of the great
shops in Steelhead Country.

Fly Gal
Proprietor: April Vokey
(888) 359-4259
flygal.ca

The Fly Shop
4140 Churn Creek Rd.
Redding, CA 96002
(530) 222-3555
flyshop.com
Notes: Ground zero for the
Kamchatka Steelhead Project and a
chance to talk with Justin Miller.

Fly Water Travel
Proprietors: Ken Morrish & Brian Gies
479 Russell St. #103
Ashland, OR 97520
(541) 488-7159
flywatertravel.com

French's Fly Fishing
Proprietor: Jerry French
Bookings through Fish Head
Expeditions
(503) 539-1451
fishheadexpeditions.com

Heritage Angling Products
Wholesale only—ask for them at your
local fly shop.

Hogan Brown Fly Fishing
Proprietor: Hogan Brown
811 Heron Ln.
Chico, CA 95926
(530) 514-2453
hgbflyfishing.com
The blog: hgbflyfishing.blogspot.com

Indigo Guide Service
Proprietor: Kevin Morlock & friends
Beaver Island, MI
(231) 898-4320
indigoguideservice.com

Jeff Bright
1825 15th St. #1
San Francisco, CA 94103
(415) 317-9400
jeffbright.com

Jonny on the Spot Guide Service
Proprietor: Jon Hazlett
Bookings through Ashland Fly Shop

Kevin Feenstra Guide Service
Newaygo, MI
(231) 652-3528
feenstraguideservice.com

Little Creek Outfitters
Proprietors: Marty, Mia & Tegan
Sheppard
PO Box 343
Maupin, OR 97037
(503) 819-4035 (Marty's cell, so be
cool)
fly-fishing-guide-oregon.com
Metalheads blog: oregonsteelhead
.blogspot.com

Mr. Fox Outfitters
Proprietor: Tim Fox
Redding, CA
(530) 949-0238
mrfoxoutfitters.com
Notes: Call or e-mail to order Mr.
Fox's flies, or to book great fishing and
hunting trips in Northern California.

Northwest Speycasting
Proprietor: Charles St. Pierre
northwestspeycasting.com

**Olympic Peninsula Skagit Tactics
(OPST)**
Proprietors: Jerry French, Ed Ward, Ben
Paull & Trevor Covich
12644 Interurban Ave. S, Building 3
Tukwila, WA 98168
(206) 858-8476
opskagit.com

Ozcast Outfitters
Proprietor: Jason Osborn
Bookings through Northwest Fly
Fishing Outfitters, (503) 252-1529

Pacific Fly Fishers
Proprietor: Michael Bennett
1018 164th St. SE, Ste. A-22
Mill Creek, WA 98012
(425) 742-2402
pacificflyfishers.com

Red Spot Fly
Proprietor: Michael Decoteau
(207) 322-1144
facebook.com/redspotfly
Notes: Tier of world-class custom
steelhead, salmon, and trout flies

Scott Howell Fly Fishing
scotthowellflyfishing.com

Soul River Inc.
1926 N. Kilpatrick St., Ste. B
Portland, Oregon 97217
(503) 954-7625
soulriverrunsdeep.com

Steelhead Alley Outfitters
Proprietor: Greg Senyo
(419) 466-9382
steelheadalleyoutfitters.com

Steelhead Waters
Proprietor: Rich Zellman
(541) 890-7084

Tight Lines Fly Fishing Company
Proprietors: Tim & Sarah Landwehr
1534 Mid Valley Dr.
DePere, WI 54115
(920) 336-4106
tightlinesflyshop.com
Notes: Charlie Piette is the manager
at Tight Lines and a great resource for
steelhead fly-tying info.

Two Dudes Flyfishing
Proprietors: Matt Ramsey & Scott
Nelson
Eugene, OR
(541) 349-9519
2dudesflyfishing@gmail.com

INDEX